BASED ON A
TRUE STORY*

FACT AND FANTASY IN **100** FAVORITE MOVIES

JONATHAN VANKIN
AND JOHN WHALEN

*BUT WITH MORE CAR CRASHES

CHICAGO
REVIEW
PRESS

An A Cappella Book

Library of Congress Cataloging-in-Publication Data

Vankin, Jonathan, 1962-

Based on a true story : fact and fantasy in 100 favorite movies / Jonathan Vankin and John Whalen.— 1st ed.

p. cm.

Asterisk following title proper leads to phrase: but with more car crashes.

Includes bibliographical references.

ISBN 1-55652-559-1

1. Historical films. 2. Motion pictures—Plots, themes, etc. I. Title: Based on a true story, but with more car crashes. II. Whalen, John, 1962- III. Title.

PN1995.9.H5V36 2005

791.43'658—dc22   2004010118

Cover design: Todd Petersen
Interior design: Scott Rattray

Published by A Cappella Books
An Imprint of Chicago Review Press, Incorporated
814 North Franklin Street
Chicago, Illinois 60610
ISBN 1-55652-559-1
Printed in the United States of America
5 4 3 2 1

For G. Lawrence Vankin
1931–2004

He always worked to get to the truth of the matter,
whatever the matter happened to be.

When the legend becomes fact,
print the legend.

—John Ford

CONTENTS

Reel Three—True Crime

Reel Four—Docu-Trauma

Reel Five—Showbiz Phonies

Reel Six—Reality Strikes Out

Reel Seven—The First Casualty

Reel Eight—Kilts, Culottes, and Corsets

Reel Nine—Out of the Past

FILMS LISTED ALPHABETICALLY BY TITLE

ACKNOWLEDGMENTS

The authors wish to make grateful acknowledgment to the following individuals and institutions, all of whom made invaluable contributions to this book:

Leslie Gornstein
Deborah Vankin
Walton Shepherd
Kirsten Holly Smith
Jean F. Vankin
Jennifer Unter
Yuval Taylor
Internet Movie Database (www.imdb.com)
Los Angeles Public Libraries
Glendale/Pasadena Public Libraries
Beverly Hills Public Library

INTRODUCTION
Reality . . . What a Concept!

"Based on a true story."

That slug has appeared on hundreds of Hollywood movies over the years. But how many times have you found yourself sitting through one of these "true stories" and asking yourself (or the people around you, in an inappropriately loud whisper), "Did that really happen?" Or perhaps, "Did the virgin Queen Elizabeth really have hot sex like that?" or even, "Does the real Erin Brockovich have quite so many teeth?"

More often than not, the answer is no (as it is to all of the above). Movies are fantasy, while life is real. If the Virgin Queen did have sex, it most certainly was not hot. And Julia Roberts's teeth are not supernumerary, but merely celebrity-sized.

When movies and life come together, the marriage is often a troubled one. As you'll see in this book, there's almost as much fiction in films that are "based on" fact as there is in movies that are completely made-up. Yet those five magical words—"based on a true story"—manage to confer something special upon any movie that invokes them. There's a reason why eighteen Best Picture Academy Award winners have been based on true stories. Inspirational stories are more inspiring if they're true. Feel-good movies feel better if we know that the events they depict really happened. Films with messages of social import seem more important if they are anchored in reality. Even horror movies tend to be that much more horrifying when the opening credits inform us that the terrors we are about to witness are not completely fake, even if the special effects are.

Of course, some true stories are "truer" than others. Hollywood prefers to gauge its fidelity to reality with a flexible yardstick. Consequently, filmmakers have developed an informal lexicon designating the level of accuracy to which a given docudramatization aspires. The most rigorous designation is, of course, the aforementioned "based on a true story" claim. A more accurate way to put it might be, "based on a book or magazine article of mostly nonfiction origin." It may seem strict, but "based on a true story" nonetheless offers creative filmmakers ample wiggle room to insert important factual revisions, such as additional sex scenes, better-looking protagonists, or more car crashes.

Slightly less faithful adaptations of true stories are typically said to be "based on real events," a classification that offers generous leeway to the filmmaker who wishes to saddle his or her "real events" with completely phony characters. This designation can also be useful for another reason: sometimes, what "based on real events" really means is, "We lost a bidding war for the rights to an authoritative or famous nonfiction book, but the 'events' on which the book is based, which we're presenting here in movie form, are in the public domain, so don't even think about suing us, OK?"

But by far the loosest of the truth qualifiers is the halfhearted assertion that a film is "inspired by actual events." In fact, it's not so much an assertion as it is a disclaimer. Note the strategic deployment of the weasel words "inspired by," which vaguely hint at veracity, but in a way that cleverly evades sticky specificity. The "actual events" lending inspiration to these sorts of films are often of the proven-hoax variety. Either that, or they've been subjected to radical rewrites inspired by clueless movie executives.

Beyond the obvious allure of a true story, Hollywood has other reasons to make movies that are "torn from today's headlines" or exhumed from yesteryear's peculiar-smelling vaults, as it were:

- True stories are often easier to sell to producers, who are just as easily enthralled by real events as the rest of us.
- Money rules in Hollywood, but once a producer has become absurdly rich, the next prize to claim is prestige. True stories carry a sense of historical gravitas that allow the Spielbergs and Bruckheimers of the world to say to themselves, "I'm not just selling popcorn and bonbons to thirteen-year-olds. I am confronting important issues—while selling popcorn and bonbons to thirteen-year-olds."
- Fact-based or -related stories can afford producers a potent defense against would-be competitors. Just as alpha males in the animal kingdom establish their territories using nonverbal cues, producers who option a nonfiction book or magazine article send an unmistakably pungent signal to prospec-

tive rivals: "I've locked up the rights, so don't even think about muscling in on my run! (You self-licking cur.)"

Given that Hollywood has the hots for true stories, the key question becomes not so much "why?" as "why are the resulting movies so often so awful?" For starters, Hollywood's compulsion to hammer life's complexities into a screenplay structure with "character arcs," "turning points," and "inciting incidents" often leeches a true story of the very authenticity that made it compelling in the first place. The worst of these reality makeovers sabotage themselves with shopworn dramatic conventions designed to appeal to the lowest common denominator of moviegoer. Einstein said, "Everything should be made as simple as possible, but no simpler." Hollywood, on the other hand, loves to take things a step too far. (Fortunately, Einstein never went Hollywood, which is why the theory of relativity describes the relationship between space and time, rather than the relationship between a movie's villain and hero, who, it is inevitably revealed in the third act, are actually father and son.)

The short list of clichés often dropped in to movies "based" on real events includes concocted love interests, annoyingly obvious character "motivations," and trumped-up endings featuring more and bigger explosions.

We understand that all true stories require at least some dramatic restructuring if they are to translate successfully to the screen; real life is not so obliging as to organize itself into three discrete acts with a clear narrative through-line. As Shakespeare so eloquently put it, life's a tale told by an idiot, full of sound and fury, signifying nothing. (Or, to "punch-up" the immortal, yet wordy, Bard: "Dude, where's my plot?") The point is, as much as we try to impose narratives on our own lives, reality rarely fits into a tidy dramatic format.

Still, there *is* hope for reality on the big screen. The best reality-based films manage to find elegant, unobtrusive ways to channel their source material into an engaging dramatic narrative. Films of this breed include *Goodfellas*, *Heavenly Creatures*, *Patton*, and *Gandhi*, captivating entertainments that simultaneously offer a clear window on history.

The book you now grip in your Raisinet-stained paws represents our attempt to illuminate, explore, and, whenever necessary, rip the living crap out of Hollywood's ardent, often uncomfortable relationship with the true stories it converts into fantasy. *Based on a True Story* is not a comprehensive encyclopedia by any means. With the rate that Hollywood churns out "true" movies, comprehensiveness is a quixotic goal. This is a book, not a weekly magazine. The entries herein are grouped according to several common genres of reality-linked movies, from period epics (see the chapter titled "Kilts, Culottes, and Corsets") and films about more recent history (see "Out of the Past") to true Hollywood stories (see "Showbiz Phonies") and war movies (see "The First Casualty"), from sports spectacles (see "Reality Strikes Out") to even a few allegedly true ghost stories ("Strange . . . but True?"), and more. We've saved the biggest, most controversial reality-based movie for last: *JFK*, Oliver Stone's oft-maligned—unfairly, in our view—political/historical epic.

In the end, we've tried to offer an enthusiastic overview of more than 100 films that give some insight into Hollywood's need to couple with real life, sometimes for better, often for worse, 'til death do they part.

Jonathan Vankin & John Whalen
Los Angeles
December 2003

Keeping It Reel

A Beautiful Mind (2001)

Directed by Ron Howard
Written by Akiva Goldsman
Starring Russell Crowe and Jennifer Connelly

Russell Crowe as John Forbes Nash Jr.
© Universal Studios and DreamWorks LLC

The eminent mathematician and Nobel Laureate John Forbes Nash Jr. professes to be pleased with the film version of his life story, *A Beautiful Mind*. And why not? Nash endured three decades of debilitating mental illness and a lifetime of fractured and bizarre relationships. The moviemakers turned his ordeal into an inspirational "love conquers all" parable.

In *A Beautiful Mind*, Hollywood's distaste for "dislikable" protagonists hits a crescendo of dramaturgical dishonesty, particularly in its wildly inaccurate portrayal of paranoid schizophrenia, the psychotic disorder that crippled Nash for nearly thirty years. Director Ron Howard asserted that he didn't "set out to make a biopic"—which raises the question: "Why, then, make a movie about a real person's life?"

Howard's answer: "It is an extraordinary story . . . one of those that is so strange and ultimately very triumphant, it has to have been real or else you'd find it contrived and totally incredible." Of course, fear of the contrived and incredible never stopped Hollywood (or Howard) before. The likely truth is that the filmmakers believed that the real events of Nash's life were unacceptably unpleasant. The movie wouldn't sell.

Nash won his Nobel Prize for a great leap forward in game theory that, as the years passed, became a fundamental principle of economics. Nash's idea, soon known as "the Nash equilibrium," was the basis of the twenty-seven-page doctoral thesis he wrote in 1949 while at Princeton University. At the time, Nash was all of twenty-one years old.

In the film, Nash is already mentally ill with schizophrenic delusions by the time he arrives at Princeton—he sees an imaginary roommate. The filmmakers would have us believe that Nash, or anyone, could produce a Nobel-level work of genius while in the throes of paranoid schizophrenia. The truth is, it just doesn't—and didn't—work that way. Nash's sickness didn't set in until he was thirty (no imaginary roomie). As soon as the schizophrenia took hold, Nash's productivity came to an instantaneous halt—which comes as a surprise only to those who rely on Howard's film for their information about schizophrenia. As per Howard and screenwriter Akiva Goldsman, the symptoms of schizophrenia are limited to hallucinations that resemble an intriguing Cold War spy thriller. The actual disease, as experienced by Nash and about 1 percent of the American population at any given time, destroys any ability to think clearly, respond emotionally, or interpret information taken in through the senses.

Nash's schizophrenia was unusual in that it came on late (most cases crop up in the victim's teens or twenties) and went into remission when Nash was in his sixties. Cessation of the disease is more common than was once believed, but the film alleges that Nash essentially willed his illness away. Though Nash believes that he did just that, the fact is, no one knows why his condition subsided. It just did.

Though Nash's schizophrenia struck at the upper end of the usual timetable, it's impossible to read Sylvia Nasar's biography of him, also called *A Beautiful Mind*, without getting the impression that his mental illness was waiting to happen almost his entire life. The most charitable description of Nash's pre-schizophrenia personality would be that he was a narcissist in the extreme. A less charitable description would be that he was a complete dick. The disconnection—from reality, from other human beings—that characterizes schizophrenia was a trait of Nash's personality his whole life.

After Nash won an appointment at MIT (not a prestigious place for a mathematician in those days, but you'd never guess that from the film) he began a relationship with a Boston nurse named Eleanor Stier. And what a relationship it was. He ridiculed her inferior intellect and relative lack of education, flew into irrational rages, and criticized her every move. Worst of all, he fathered a child with her that he flatly refused to support. Granted, his actions were somewhat different than those of the standard-issue deadbeat dad. Yes, Nash played with the child and seemed to take delight in fatherhood, but it somehow never occurred to him that his obligations went beyond showing up and playing with the kid every now and then. It certainly never crossed his mind that he should marry his child's mother. He rarely introduced her to his MIT colleagues, and he never told them that he had a son.

In Howard's film, Eleanor Stier and her son by Nash, John David Stier, are erased from existence, apparently having been sacrificed on the altar of feel-goodism, although these real-life incidents reveal significant details about Nash's maladjusted personality.

Here are some other missing real-life details that would have given the movie Nash more complexity than that of a Disease-of-the-Week survivor:

- Nash was bisexual. He had relationships with at least three men. He was arrested in a Santa Monica, California, men's room for (allegedly) masturbating in front of an undercover police officer. (Nash claimed he was merely "observing human behavior.") That incident cost him his job at the RAND Corporation (called "Wheeler Institute" in the movie and relocated from the West Coast to MIT's Cambridge, Massachusetts, campus; the arrest and Nash's dismissal are never mentioned in the film).
- Nash and his wife Alicia divorced in 1962. Portrayed in the film as a loyal and loving spouse, she actually got fed up three years into Nash's schizophrenia,

at a time when Nash was off in Europe seeking political asylum as a "refugee" in Geneva. She did, however, allow him to stay in her home as a "boarder," and she did her best to support him. Their romance was rekindled after Nash's recovery; they remarried and are still together today. In the movie, Nash pays homage to his wife in a stirring acceptance speech for his Nobel Prize, as she sits misty-eyed in the audience. Her undying love for him, declares the filmic Nash, "is the reason I'm here." In actuality, Nash was excused from delivering any such speech. The brief remarks he delivered to his Princeton colleagues when he learned about the prize were mostly wisecracks about how glad he was to win it because he needed the money.

• Nash's global wanderings were also expunged to suit the film, as were many of the more bizarre aspects of his paranoid delusions. For example, he once turned down a job offer from the University of Chicago with a note explaining that he had other obligations—namely, to become the emperor of Antarctica.

Biopics must be forgiven for omitting significant portions of their subject's lives. Few of us are fortunate enough to have our life played out in three acts, with an "inciting incident," a single, well-defined conflict, and a tidy resolution—as per Hollywood screenplay requirements. In *A Beautiful Mind*, however, Howard and Goldsman have done more than streamline Nash's story. They've explored his life, not to mention his terrible disease, and discovered the marketing strategy within.

Sources and Further Reading

Murray, Rebecca and Fred Topel. "Interview with Ron Howard, Director of *A Beautiful Mind*." About.com. http://romanticmovies.about.com/library/weekly/aa121501b.htm.
Nasar, Sylvia. *A Beautiful Mind*. New York: Touchstone Books, 1998.

Catch Me If You Can (2002)

Directed by Steven Spielberg

Written by Jeff Nathanson

Starring Leonardo DiCaprio and Tom Hanks

Leonardo DiCaprio (right) as Frank Abagnale Jr. © DreamWorks LLC

Catch Me If You Can, the "true story" of a teenage con artist who passed himself off as an airline pilot and floated more than $2.5 million in bogus checks, is itself a bit of a con. The movie is based on the bestselling book of the same name, a colorful and highly embellished memoir by former juvenile grifter Frank W. Abagnale Jr. In the mid-1960s, at age sixteen, Abagnale ran away from his middle-class New York home and quickly established himself as a junior overachiever of the short con, accumulating an impressive rap sheet of audacious scams, sophisticated check forgeries, and nervy impersonations. In addition to posing as a pilot (a guise that afforded him a patina of glamour and respectability, and that lulled his marks into accepting the phony checks), Abagnale masqueraded as a doctor, a lawyer, and a college professor. By the time of his capture at age twenty-one, Abagnale was an international celebrity, at least as far as Interpol and numerous local European law enforcement agencies were concerned.

5

By the time the book *Catch Me If You Can* hit the bestseller lists in the early 1980s, Abagnale—having long since served his debt to society—had become hotly sought-after Hollywood property. After all, what producer could resist the picaresque tale of a junior overachiever who blithely and stylishly proceeded to rip off airlines, banks, and hotels to the tune of millions, in fifty states and twenty-six foreign countries, all before he reached legal drinking age?

The yarn spun in the book considerably amplifies Abagnale's real-life story in the service of narrative punch. Credit on that count evidently goes to Abagnale's ghostwriter, the late *Houston Chronicle* reporter Stan Redding. A classic newsman of the misheard-it-on-the-streets school, Redding was described in his 1987 obituary as "a rough-hewn raconteur, an indefatigable teller of tall tales." Years later, Abagnale would concur: Redding "was a great storyteller," he told a *USA Today* reporter on the eve of the film's premiere. "I always felt he embellished a lot of things, he exaggerated a lot of things, he overdramatized a lot of things."

Things like this, for example: whereas the real Abagnale impersonated a doctor for "only a few days," Redding gave his literary avatar a several-month stint running the night shift at a big-city hospital. Likewise, the real Abagnale's lawyerly posturing was a very short con, on the order of days. "In the book, it's like I'm doing this for a year," Abagnale later explained. Redding had interviewed Abagnale in four eight-hour sessions, and his typewriter took it from there.

Redding's freewheeling literary license certainly didn't hurt Abagnale, who, after serving five years in French, Swedish, and U.S. prisons, had gone straight as an antifraud consultant. Abagnale's backstory had to have been good for business. Even better, the book never lost its "heat" in Hollywood; Abagnale proceeded to option his rights half a dozen times to a succession of producers, earning himself a tidy $20,000 with each option renewal. As scams go, this one was perfectly legal. "It was the biggest racket in the world," Abagnale later told a *Newsday* reporter. "I thought, I've got to keep this up!" Ultimately, Abagnale cashed in by selling his story outright for a cool $250,000.

Eventually the project bounced over to Steven Spielberg, who, succeeding where others had failed, domesticated Redding's woolly narrative into a slick, three-act, Hollywood crowd-pleaser. Of course, in making Hollywood-brand sausage, Spielberg, screenwriter Jeff Nathanson, and star Leonardo DiCaprio felt compelled to sprinkle more additives into an already spiced-up mixture, further pulverizing the distinction between reality and artifice.

The real Frank Abagnale Jr. (center) appeared on the TV
game show *To Tell the Truth* in 1977.
Goodson-Toddman Productions, courtesy of Abagnale and Associates.

Spielberg's most piquant story seasoning was, not surprisingly, a sentimental family theme that has DiCaprio's domestically disenfranchised Abagnale
yearning for a father figure. In the film, Abagnale is clearly motivated by elementary screenwriter psychology: the mixed-up product of a broken home, he
hits the mean streets after his parents separate, and his scams against "the system" are charged by an earnest desire to right the wrongs rained upon his hapless father (Christopher Walken), a big-time dreamer and small-time schemer
forever on the wrong side of fortune. Contrast that hackneyed pathos with this
clarifying remark, found at the opening of the book: "If I wanted to lay down
a baby con, I could say I was the product of a broken home. But I'd only be
bum-rapping my parents." (As a matter of fact, in the book Abagnale offers a
somewhat less poignant motivation for his jet-setting scams: "Girls, girls, girls.")
Abagnale's parents are barely mentioned in the book. In the movie, the drama
culminates with Abagnale accepting Tom Hanks's FBI agent as a strong surrogate father figure.

The Hanks character—Special Agent Carl Hanratty—is more or less (but
mostly more), a fictional embellishment. In reality, a number of FBI agents and
cops took up the pursuit of the boy fraudster. One of them, Joe Shea, is mentioned in passing in the book, but under the fake name of "Sean O'Riley." In

the film, Tom Hanks's FBI agent—loosely based on "O'Riley"/Shea—is promoted from background figure to full-fledged costar. (Hanks came up with the "Carl Hanratty" handle by combining the names of *The Donna Reed Show* star Carl Betz and former Pittsburgh Steelers quarterback Terry Hanratty.) DiCaprio's fatherless Abagnale telephones Hanks's lonely, family-deprived Hanratty every Christmas Eve. That, according to the actual Abagnale, never happened: "Why would I do that? I didn't want the FBI to know where I was." The father-son relationship portrayed in the film is purely a "baby con" that Spielberg injects into the proceedings to feed his sentimental, displaced-family trope.

Ultimately, given the synergy of artistic enhancement running through the Abagnale/Redding/Spielberg collaboration, it's difficult to distinguish between the real and the ersatz in *Catch Me If You Can*. Screenwriter Nathanson claimed that some of the movie's deviations from the book moved the story back into closer proximity with reality. For instance, Nathanson told *USA Today* that, during chats with the real Abagnale, he learned "that there was more to the broken-home theory and more to the friendship between Abagnale and Shea than Abagnale had acknowledged."

Of course, a screenwriter enamored of a pet theme may hear exactly what he wants to hear. And a former master of the con knows how to read his mark like a book.

Sources and Further Reading

Abagnale, Frank W. *Catch Me If You Can*. With Stan Redding. New York: Grosset & Dunlap, 1980.

Seiler, Andy. "Here's the Catch: True Tail Isn't." *USA Today*, December 22, 2002.

Voboril, Mary. "Tales of an Ex–Con Man." *Newsday*, December 23, 2002.

The Hurricane (1999)

Directed by Norman Jewison

Written by Armyan Bernstein and Dan Gordon

Starring Denzel Washington, Vicellous Reon Shannon,
and Deborah Unger

Denzel Washington as Rubin
"Hurricane" Carter.
© Beacon Communications Corp.

The real Rubin "Hurricane" Carter.
Courtesy Hurricane Carter: The Other Side of
the Story, www.graphicwitness.com/carter

"The truth is a moving target, I've found," says director Norman Jewison. "When you make a film about real stories, real people, you'll never get it right, because there's always somebody who's going to disagree with you."

In the case of *The Hurricane*, the "somebody" included the families of three murder victims. Their loved ones were killed in cold blood, the family members say, by the title character of Jewison's movie, ex-prizefighter Rubin "Hurricane" Carter.

Carter may or may not be guilty of the notably horrifying triple homicide for which he spent twenty years in prison. Two juries said he was. The film makes the case for what Carter has claimed all along—that he was the innocent victim of a racist frame-up. Maybe he was, but the case presented in the movie is based on nothing but the moviemakers' imaginations.

In 1974 Carter published an autobiography, written in prison, asserting that he was persecuted for his outspoken views on the civil rights movement. In the mid-1970s his case became a cause célèbre among Hollywood's glitterati. For them, Carter was the Mumia Abu Jamal of his day, an outspoken black man imprisoned for a murder he did not commit, the victim of America's racist criminal justice system. Muhammad Ali organized a new defense for Carter. Bob Dylan read Carter's book, *The Sixteenth Round.* It inspired him to write a song, "Hurricane," whose lyrics asserted that Carter sat in prison "for something that he never done."

In 1999 director Norman Jewison, returned to the theme of his finest film, the 1967 Academy Award Best Picture winner, *In the Heat of the Night.* That film was a scalding critique of American racism, and it made its point dramatically and brilliantly. But it was fiction. Three decades later Jewison revisited the racism issue, this time with the true story of Rubin Carter.

The film that resulted was also fiction.

Around 2:30 on the morning of June 17, 1966, two armed men walked into the Lafayette Grill in Patterson, New Jersey. They immediately started blasting, shooting the bartender and three patrons (one patron survived). Then they turned and walked out. Carter was stopped by police just minutes later, but he wasn't arrested for the crime for another four months.

We can't judge the film on whether Carter was really guilty or not, though two juries nine years apart believed that he was. He was freed in 1986 on a point of constitutional law; his conviction was never overturned. The generally accepted view is that Carter was wrongly convicted. That's not a unanimous opinion by any means, however. A New Jersey newspaper reporter who covered the case was so persuaded of Carter's guilt that, even in his retirement, Joseph "Cal" Deal maintains a Web site (www.graphicwitness.com) that lays out the evidence against Carter.

We can't judge the film by the fact that it overlooks and even distorts several points of evidence (most of which appear in contemporary press accounts now accessible via Deal's Web site) that make Carter look a little less innocent than Jewison would perhaps like. The families of the murder victims, on the other hand, found the distortions offensive enough to merit a picket line at the Academy Award ceremony held in 2000 in which Washington was up for Best Actor Award (he lost to Kevin Spacey). Still, picking and choosing which facts to weave into a dramatic narrative is an artist's prerogative.

What the film can be judged by are the pure fabrications designed to make the point that Carter was the victim of racism. If indeed he was—and it is, of course, very possible, especially back in 1966—then an honest portrayal of the actual events that occurred should have been enough to get the message across. The problem is that, outside of Carter's own assertions, there has never been any evidence that racism played a role in Carter's arrest and trials.

In a case without a Mark Fuhrman to hang a racist conspiracy on, Jewison and screenwriters Armyan Bernstein and Dan Gordon went ahead and made one up. A Detective Sgt. Vincent Della Pesca, played by the beady-eyed Dan Hedaya (who always seems to play a creep), was out to get Carter since the "black punk" was eleven years old—according to the film. The Lafayette Grill murders give Della Pesca the opportunity he's been waiting for.

"Della Pesca" was apparently inspired by Vincent DeSimone, a detective who had never met Carter before the murders and was by no one's account a racist. DeSimone died several years before Carter's release (the Della Pesca character is seen in the courtroom scowling when the judge finally rules in Carter's favor). The unwarranted, if oblique, smear on their father led DeSimone's children to publish letters attempting to set the record straight.

Joey Giardello also felt smeared by the film's fictional attempt to show a racist conspiracy out to crucify Carter. Giardello was the undisputed middleweight champion in 1964. He was Carter's opponent in the only championship fight that Carter ever fought. Contrary to the Dylan lyrics, which make it appear that Carter "coulda been the champion of the world" had he not been falsely imprisoned, "the Hurricane" was not a serious contender after losing to Giardello. From that fight to the end of his career, his record was 6–8.

The fifteen-round bout between Carter and Giardello on December 14, 1964, was a decent contest, but it resulted in a clear victory for the defending champ, who scored a unanimous decision that went without protest by any of the sportswriters covering the fight or, it should be added, by Carter himself (he was quoted remarking, "I think it was mine," but otherwise, he had nothing to say).

Imagine Giardello's surprise, then, when he saw the movie and watched his screen self getting the crap beat out of him by Denzel Washington's Carter. When the judges' decision goes against Carter, and Washington shakes his head knowingly, we're supposed to believe that bigotry has denied the Hurricane of a championship belt that is rightfully his. On that point the film is so far off the mark that Giardello sued for defamation of character. The ex-boxer also set up a Web site of his own, which featured the complete video of the real fight. The lawsuit was quickly settled on undisclosed terms. Giardello's site disappeared, so it's likely that the settlement required him to take it down in order to prevent people from easily comparing the film version with the real fight.

In his commentary on the DVD version of *The Hurricane*, Jewison concedes that, "Going back over it, there's no doubt about it, Giardello won the fight." So why show it the other way around in the movie? "We did want to build some of the prejudice that existed, and it did exist whether people want to deny it or not."

No marginally aware person would deny that racism did indeed exist in the 1960s (and that it still does now), but it does no good to try to prove it with demonstrably falsified characters and events. That only makes the case weaker. There must have been actual, provable, incidents of racism in Carter's case.

Or were there?

That's the worst problem with Jewison's movie. The extreme "dramatic license" that he and his writers take makes them seem *desperate* to make a political point. We come away wondering if they have a case at all. Was Rubin Carter the innocent victim of a racist system? Based on this movie, we have no idea. If the filmmakers had to bullshit their way through the plot points, how strong can their case be?

In addition, the movie launders Carter's personality to the point of prissy sainthood, the type of person who couldn't possibly commit a violent crime, at least not without good cause. His juvenile arrest for stabbing a man during a mugging (Carter made off with the man's watch) is turned into an act of self-defense against a creepy pedophile. No mention is made of Carter's other youthful crimes, many of them violent, which by Carter's own assertion were too numerous to count. Stretching the point as far as it will go, in the movie Carter is a teetotaler, something he emphatically was not.

Using actual news footage from the 1970s, the movie shows the many celebrities who took up Carter's cause. What it doesn't show is why those celebrities vanished from the Carter case by the time of his second trial in 1976. According to Cal Deal, Carter's celebrity pals backed away after he beat up a woman who was working for his defense. Carter denied beating the woman, though her son found her "in the fetal position" on the floor of Carter's hotel room and she had to be hospitalized.

Whether Deal is correct about the connection between the celebrity disappearing act and the woman-beating allegations isn't totally clear, but it's a fact that none of the celebrities who'd rallied to Carter's side spent even a day at his retrial—the very retrial they worked to obtain.

But what about the evidence? In the movie, when Carter's supporters discover a piece of tampered evidence, it's a major third-act turning point. They find that police phone records have been changed to make it look like the murders took place at 2:45 A.M. instead of 2:30, when Carter was covered by an alibi.

That seals the deal! It proves that the Hurricane was framed.

Except for one thing. The "altered phone log" is another invention of Jewison and company. As Deal documents on his site (reproducing contemporary documents), both police reports and press accounts report the murder call coming in at 2:30.

The phone records were fine. It's Carter's alibi that was fake. At his retrial, four witnesses who had initially supported the alibi admitted committing perjury the first time around. They said they had lied under oath, under influence by Carter. It's a good thing that the makers of *The Hurricane* weren't under oath when they produced this movie.

Sources and Further Reading

Bigold, Pat. "Les Keiter in the Middle of 'Hurricane.'" *Honolulu Star-Bulletin*, February 29, 1972.

Carter, Rubin. *The Sixteenth Round: From Number 1 Contender to Number 45472*. New York: Viking Press, 1974.

Deal, Cal. "Rubin Hurricane Carter: The Other Side of the Story." http://www.graphicwitness.com/carter/index.html.

Nack, William. "True to His Words." *Sports Illustrated*, April 13, 1992.

Raab, Selwyn. "Separating Truth From Fiction in 'The Hurricane.'" *New York Times*, December 28, 1999.

Erin Brockovich (2000)

Directed by Steven Soderbergh
Written by Susannah Grant
Starring Julia Roberts and Albert Finney

Erin Brockovich—the ball-busting blonde, as opposed to the breezy block-buster she inspired—was a gift from the cinematic gods to Hollywood. Talk about a package deal. Brockovich had it all: looks, moxie, and a true story tailor-made for the big screen. A twice-divorced, working-class mother with no legal training, Brockovich had played a crucial role in the landmark legal triumph of small town America over corporate polluters.

Working as a lowly research clerk at Masry & Vititoe, a small Southern California law firm, Brockovich unearthed a cache of documents incriminating Pacific Gas & Electric Company (PG&E) in a toxic waste cover-up. For upward of two decades, PG&E had dumped more than 370 million gallons of Chromium 6, a cancer-causing chemical, into unlined ponds at its natural gas compressor station in Hinkley, California, a small town in the Mohave Desert. The chemical leeched into Hinkley's water supply, and many of the town's 3,500 residents (and their livestock) began to suffer from an array of mysterious ailments, including nosebleeds, respiratory problems, and rare cancers.

PG&E knew of the problem at least as early as 1965, yet it had consistently downplayed the dangers to the residents of Hinkley. At one point PG&E distributed fliers to the locals misleadingly suggesting that chromium was good for growing bodies: it "is an essential ingredient in the human diet, one that is often included in multiple vitamin/mineral supplements," the utility company gushed. Of course, the benign chromium found in delicious Flintstones Chewables was a compound completely different from the toxic, antirust form plaguing Hinkley.

Brockovich is credited with making the connection between Hinkley's health problems and the PG&E station. Going door-to-door, she organized and galvanized the community. In 1992 Masry & Vititoe filed a class-action lawsuit against PG&E on behalf of more than six hundred Hinkley residents. In 1996 PG&E settled the case—*Anderson v. PG&E*—for $333 million, the largest such settlement ever. Brockovich, the downtrodden divorcée who could barely make rent, earned a $2.5 million dollar bonus from her employer, bought a mansion in the upscale L.A. suburb of Agoura Hills, and lived (mostly) happily ever after.

Even better, Brockovich did it all in three-inch pumps and cleavage-squeezing bustiers. Rarely does a true story fall out of the sky fully formed to the movie industry's dream specs. But the saga of Erin Brockovich was just that: a socially uplifting David-versus-Goliath tale with tits and ass. In Hollywoodese, it was *Pretty Woman* meets *Norma Rae* (but without the prostitution).

When executive producer Carla Santos Shamberg first heard the tale from a chiropractor she shared with Brockovich (how perfectly Hollywood is that?), she instantly saw it as an ideal vehicle for the *Pretty Woman* herself, Julia Roberts. *Erin Brockovich*—the breezy blockbuster—pleased critics and crowds alike, and it earned Roberts an Oscar. Amazingly, the movie worked its box-office magic with minimal factual alterations (although some critics dispute key details, as we'll see), a testament not only to the film's top-notch talent (Roberts and director Steven Soderbergh), but also to the story's camera-ready qualities.

The real Erin Brockovich—who sold her story rights to Universal Studios for a reported $100,000—was mostly happy with the movie's accuracy, and with Roberts's sassy portrayal of her. However, Brockovich did take minor exception to the floozy factor of her onscreen character; Roberts plays Brockovich to the hilt as a trash-talking, mercurial, tough chick who parades her cleavage as a badge of honor. In interviews at the time of the film's premiere, the thirty-nine-year-old Brockovich allowed that the swearing was on the money, as were the plunging necklines, which scandalized some of her coworkers at Masry & Vititoe. But she drew the line at dangling bra straps. "I'd never let my bra strap hang out like Julia does," she told *People*. "Never."

You can't blame Brockovich for gently faulting the trailer-park trimmings in Roberts's performance. You can also see why Soderbergh and company merrily pumped up the volume: the saucier the blue-collar wench, the more savory her inevitable victory over the white-collar prudes and corporate snobs who dismiss her early on as common and tawdry. Hollywood knows full well who spreads the tub margarine on its bread.

But Brockovich and her boss, Ed Masry (played in the film by Albert Finney), apparently haven't objected to their portrayal onscreen as flawed characters occasionally succumbing to vanity and bullheadedness. Perhaps the tidy sums they both earned selling their story rights helped allay their concerns about image. The celebrity status the movie conferred on them and the firm probably doesn't hurt, either. In the end, though, it may have come down to simply this: why worry about a few human warts in a movie that depicts you as superheroes who rise to the occasion in defense of the much-oppressed common folk?

Not everyone associated with the actual case has been as satisfied with the movie, however. The heroic portrayal of Brockovich and Masry rankled more than a few Hinkley residents, who accused the law firm of mismanaging the disbursement of the settlement money.

According to Carol Smith, one of the real-life plaintiffs, "The movie is mostly lies." In an interview with the online magazine *Salon*, she accused Masry & Vititoe of cronism and nest-feathering. "If you were buddies with Ed and Erin," she said, "you got a lot of money. Otherwise, forget it."

In the movie, Brockovich personally delivers the happy news of the settlement to the original Hinkley plaintiff, Donna Jensen (played by Marg Helgenberger). Jensen weeps tears of joy when Brockovich announces the amount personally earmarked for her—five million dollars. In fact, the Jensen character was based on a real-life plaintiff named Roberta Walker, and when *Salon* tracked her down, Walker said she hadn't gotten five million dollars. "It's a big fabrication," she told *Salon*. "People look at $333 million and think, 'Wow! You got that much money?' But no."

According to *Salon*, Carol Smith was not jumping for joy as the movie plaintiffs did. "I wish the truth would come out, because a lot of us are upset," *Salon* quoted her as saying. "I understand the movie is going to make Erin and the attorneys out to be heroes. But where's the rest of our money?" After the lawyers took their cut of the award (40 percent), the 650 plaintiffs were left with $196 million, or about $300,000 per person. However, the amounts actually paid out varied, with some receiving as little as $50,000 and others reportedly getting as much as $2 million. The lawyers defended their distribution methods, saying that the sums were based on specific medical histories of each plaintiff.

But some plaintiffs disputed the amounts awarded them. Another contentious issue was the lawyer's fee collected from minors in the case. After a Bakersfield attorney began advising disgruntled Hinkley plaintiffs, the original plaintiff lawyers slapped him with a slander suit, alleging that he had defamed them when he told their former clients they had a right to sue for malpractice over the minors' fee and other issues. According to *Salon*, Masry et al subsequently dropped the slander suit and refunded some of the minors' fees, "informing the teens that 'computer errors' had generated incorrect awards."

To be fair, any complicated distribution of a massive legal settlement to hundreds of plaintiffs is bound to be fraught with glitches and perceived inequities. Let's give Masry his due. When confronted by *Salon* about these disputes, he responded with dialog that needs no cinematic punching up: "Why are you being stupid?" he said. "It was a complicated $333 million settlement. Are you an idiot?"

Still, there's a clear point to be made here about movies wrapping things up much more tidily than reality will abide.

Epilogue: In the years since the film's release, the real Erin Brockovich, being an inherently cinematic character, has had true-life adventures enough to justify a sequel. In the spring of 2001 a jury convicted a Southern California attorney, John Reiner, of trying to extort more than three hundred thousand dollars from Brockovich and Masry. According to prosecutors, Reiner—acting on behalf of Brockovich's first husband and ex-boyfriend (portrayed as a nice guy in the movie by Aaron Eckhart)—had threatened to tell the tabloids that Brockovich and Masry had sex (an unconfirmed rumor that was not dramatized in the movie). Meanwhile, Brockovich had no choice but to lay out a cool $250,000 to cover drug rehab costs for her teenage kids, whose "rags-to-riches" social upgrade had taken a toll.

OK, so maybe her continued saga wouldn't quite cut it as a theatrical sequel. But as a made-for-TV follow-up, it couldn't miss.

Sources and Further Reading

Bos, Carole D. "Erin Brockovich: The Story Behind the Movie." Lawbuzz.com. http://www.lawbuzz.com/famous_trials/erin_brockovich/erin _brockovich_ch1.htm.

Campbell, Duncan. "What Erin Brockovich Did Next." *The Guardian*, December 10, 2001.

Chan, Cecilia. "Brockovich Carries On." *Los Angeles Daily News*, March 19, 2000.

Miller, Aron. "Attorney Guilty in Brockovich Extortion." *Ventura County Star*, April 3, 2001.

Schneider, Karen S. "Gutsy Beauty." *People Weekly*, April 3, 2000.

Sharp, Kathleen. "Erin Brockovich: The Real Story." *Salon*, April 14, 2000. http://dir.salon.com/ent/feature/2000/04/14/sharp/index.html?sid=736511.

Melvin and Howard (1980)

Directed by Jonathan Demme

Written by Bo Goldman

Starring Paul Le Mat, Jason Robards, and Mary Steenburgen

Paul Le Mat as Melvin Dummar. © *Universal Studios*

The death of billionaire Howard Hughes in 1976 summoned aspiring heirs and their attorneys like sharks to chum. Because Hughes had neglected to leave behind a clearly authentic will, human nature rushed in to fill the void, resulting in no less than four hundred claimants to the three-billion-dollar estate and thirty alleged wills, in assorted flavors of plausibility.

The most famous of the heirs-not-apparent was Melvin Dummar, a part-time game show contestant and a more-time gas station owner and operator from Gabbs, Nevada. Dummar's claim on the Hughes estate derived from a mysterious document that came to be known as "the Mormon Will." Not long after the eccentric mogul's expiration, an anonymous courier deposited a three-page, handwritten note onto a desk on the twenty-fifth floor of the world headquarters of the Church of Jesus Christ of Latter-Day Saints, also known as the Mormon Church. Supposedly scrawled by Hughes himself, the document contained an unusual and surprising provision that left a one-sixteenth share of his estate (a swath of the old man's empire that was valued at a cool $156 million) to the more-than-obscure Dummar.

In short order, the gas pumper with singer/songwriter aspirations found himself thrust into the national spotlight. (Or, if you're the skeptical sort and prefer your verbs transitive, delete the word "found" and reverse the words "himself" and "thrust" in the previous sentence.) Naturally, a legal battle royale erupted over the validity of the Mormon Will pitting Hughes empire attorneys against Dummar's lawyers. Although Dummar modified his story several times after pointed contradictions arose, he cheerfully denied the claims of his opponents that he had forged the Mormon Will.

As an instant celebrity, Dummar came to represent different things to different people. To some, he was a folk hero fighting corporate fixers who would deprive him of his rightful slice of the American Dream, or at least that specific branch of the American Dream that promises instant riches and fame through a lottery-style windfall. Others saw Dummar as an entirely different sort of American icon—the shrewd opportunist playing a prime angle.

By the time Hollywood got around to dramatizing the Dummar saga for paying audiences, the courts had already ruled in favor of cynics. But you can't keep a good folk hero down; 1980's *Melvin and Howard* depicts Dummar (played by Paul Le Mat) as a naive dreamer who, through an act of good samaritanism, earns his way into Howard Hughes's will. The movie is less a forensic study of a suspect legal claim than a fable of American optimism, ambition, and, ultimately, naivete.

The film, directed by Jonathan Demme (who would later direct *The Silence of the Lambs*) and written by Bo Goldman (who won an Oscar for his screenplay), presents Dummar's story at face value. After the will surfaced, Dummar explained that, in 1967, he had picked up an eccentric old man who was hitchhiking in the Nevada desert. Per Dummar, the old man had identified himself as Howard Hughes, then asked for a ride to Las Vegas. Dummar said he had dropped the long-haired coot off in back of the Sands Hotel (where Hughes really did live), sending him on his way with a handout of pocket change. Nine years later, Dummar was surprised to learn he had been rewarded for his kindness by inclusion in Hughes's alleged will. That, at any rate, was Dummar's story.

The movie opens with Le Mat's Dummar giving Jason Robards's grizzled Hughes a lift back to Vegas. Dummar wheedles Hughes into singing along to one of his original compositions (the unfortunate "Santa's Souped-Up Sleigh"), and Hughes slowly warms to Dummar's ingenuous, working-class charm.

The film then shifts into a lengthy and episodic dramatization of Dummar's failed efforts to elevate himself out of trailer-park squalor. He coaxes his off-again, on-again exotic-dancer wife (Mary Steenburgen, in a loopy, Oscar-winning performance) into appearing on a game show, then blows her winnings on a boat. (The real Dummar made his own appearances on various TV game shows, including *Let's Make a Deal*, where he did not win big.) It's not until the final third of the film that Demme concludes the slice-of-life business and gets back to the issue at hand—the discovery of the Mormon Will and the ensuing legal controversy.

In servicing its crowd-pleasing underdog theme, *Melvin and Howard* discreetly sidesteps a host of troubling details that cast doubt on the real Dummar's tale. For starters, Dummar had initially claimed no knowledge of the Mormon Will before the Latter-Day Saints made their discovery public. But when forensic tests on the envelope in which the will had been sealed turned up a fingerprint matching Dummar's, he modified his story. This amended version is the account portrayed in the film: A mysterious agent of either Hughes or the Mormons leaves the will on Dummar's desk at his gas station. Dummar then stealthily hand-delivers it to Mormon headquarters in Salt Lake City. (The real Dummar claimed that his mysterious courier had also left a note instructing him to deliver the document to Salt Lake City; Dummar said he had burned those instructions.)

The discovery of Dummar's fingerprint on a copy of a book about a previous Hughes-related forgery cast further doubt on the Cinderella version of events. That book, *Hoax*, dealt with Clifford Irving's famously forged Howard Hughes "autobiography." Investigators found Dummar's fingerprint on a copy of the book in the library at Webster State College, where Dummar had been attending classes at the time of the Mormon Will's discovery.

Although the handwriting on the Mormon Will superficially resembled samples of Hughes's scrawl, it mirrored earlier samples of his script. In the two-year period leading up to the alleged drafting of the will, Hughes's handwriting had undergone a drastic change. Apparently, whoever wrote the will wasn't aware of Hughes's updated handwriting style.

Ultimately, after a seven-month trial, the court ruled that the will was a forgery, and Hughes died intestate. The contest for the estate would rage on for another dozen years—this time, without a stake for Dummar. In the end, twenty-one cousins would be awarded the loot, or what remained of it after the thirty million dollars in legal fees it took to attain closure had been deducted.

Melvin and Howard manages to bypass the messy details of Dummar's legal defeat and instead ends on a note of creative Hollywood uplift. Warned by his lawyer that years will likely pass before Dummar sees a nickel of Hughes's money, our folk hero nods sagely. Lessons have been learned, and character has been built. Before departing to devote quality time with his family, a less flighty and more mature Dummar allows that he'll probably not ever see a cent of the Hughes fortune. It's not until the closing credits that a legend appears onscreen informing us that Dummar's big dreams were not to pass muster in a court of law.

Sources and Further Reading

Freese, Paul L. "Howard Hughes and Melvin Dummar: Forensic Science Fact Versus Film Fiction." *Journal of Forensic Sciences,* January 1986.

Norma Rae (1979)

Directed by Martin Ritt
Written by Harriet Frank Jr. and Irving Ravetch
Starring Sally Field and Ron Liebman

Sally Field as Norma Rae. © 20th Century Fox

Twenty-five years after the movie's release, *Norma Rae* is probably best remembered as the catalyst for Sally Field's famously giddy Oscar acceptance speech ("You *like* me! You REALLY like me!"). But the 1979 docudrama left a cultural mark that was arguably more profound than the happy resolution of Ms. Field's self-esteem issues. A year after the film's release, the J. P. Stevens textile company in Roanoke Rapids, North Carolina, finally agreed to allow union representation at its mills. *Norma Rae*, which dramatized the struggle of J. P. Stevens workers to organize under the Amalgamated Clothing and Textile Workers Union (ACTWU), clearly played a role in influencing the company's concession.

Though the movie accurately concludes with a rousing victory for the mill workers, who overcame management opposition and voted in favor of union representation, reality was somewhat less triumphant. In the years following that early 1970s vote, the real J. P. Stevens had used a variety of legal tactics to thwart the implementation of the union. Field's high-profile performance as a feisty mill worker turned a spotlight on the intransigence of the real J. P. Stevens.

Following the film's release, numerous news media interviews with the "real Norma Rae"—an outspoken former J. P. Stevens mill worker named Crystal Lee—put public pressure on the company, which ultimately caved in and allowed unions at many of their mills. So here was a rare case in which Hollywood not only borrowed a page from reality, but returned the favor by helping to write a real-life happy ending. Reality to Hollywood: *You* like *me! You REALLY like me!*

Norma Rae's understated, almost documentary-esque style, along with its no-frills plotting, sets it apart from most other Hollywood odes to the working class. Credit here must go to director Martin Ritt, who not only shot the film at a real textile mill (the air is visibly thick with particles of cotton lint), but who also wisely eschewed standard Hollywood reality upgrades such as a love interest and showy speeches. But credit must also go to the decade that spawned the film: *Norma Rae* is very much a child of 1970s cinema, a time when gritty realism and unsentimental storytelling were seen as virtues, rather than causes for a mandatory rewrite.

The film is based on journalist Henry Leifermann's 1975 book, *Crystal Lee: A Woman of Inheritance*, which chronicled that second-generation mill worker's crucial role in the struggle for unionization at J. P. Stevens. The film is remarkably faithful to the real story; its deviations from the actual record are mostly minor, and are perfectly reasonable given the requirements of cinematic storytelling. The film's most noticeable dramatic embellishment is its characterization of Norma Rae as the central figure in the struggle to organize the workers. In fact, although Crystal Lee did play a major role in the battle with J. P. Stevens management, she was certainly not alone; the efforts to unionize J. P. Stevens involved at least half a dozen dedicated workers who risked their jobs to become leaders in the inchoate union. In pursuit of a strong central protagonist, however, Ritt followed the dramatic tradition of focusing on a single personality.

Like Sally Field's Norma Rae, Crystal Lee had a reputation for being a strong-willed, sexually adventurous young woman. Like Norma, Crystal had several children out of wedlock. The movie implies that Norma's unruly spirit and penchant for hell-raising were traits that eventually served her well in her battle for workers' rights. Although that analysis may or may not be accurate, it certainly *feels* right.

Like Norma Rae, Crystal Lee was a second-generation mill worker who slowly came to see the company's policies—dirt-poor wages, filthy and dangerous working conditions—as exploitative. As her character did in the film, Lee became a union advocate after attending an ACTWU meeting. Sally Field's Oscar-bait scene—in which she's fired for "insubordination" after hand-copying a divisive notice posted by management, then stands atop a desk while displaying a hand-printed sign that reads, "Union"—is an accurate portrayal of what happened to Lee.

Interestingly, *Norma Rae* might have been even more faithful to real life had it not been for Crystal Lee's efforts to assert creative control over Ritt's filmmaking. In fact, the movie most likely would have been called *Crystal Lee*. Here's what happened: after initially cooperating with Ritt's production, Lee threw a monkey wrench into the works when she began to demand a larger creative role. Ultimately, Ritt was unwilling to compromise, and Lee refused to sign a release. Consequently, the name of Sally Field's character changed from Crystal Lee to Norma Rae. And Ritt took the precaution of describing the lead character as "a fictionalized composite of several such women who became militantly involved in trying to unionize southern textile mills."

That Lee became a celebrity labor hero after the film's release may have allayed her concerns over her loss of creative control with the movie. She'd later describe the film as "as true to life as a movie can be," adding that the film "basically gives a real good view of life inside a textile plant."

But let's split one last lint-matted hair, now that we're on a roll. Although Ritt avoids the typically preposterous love story that Hollywood convention demands, he does imply a sexual attraction between Norma and the ACTWU representative, portrayed as a New York Jewish intellectual by a youngish Ron Leibman. There's even a provocative skinny-dipping scene in which the married Norma Rae coaxes an awkwardly exposed Leibman into her favorite swimming hole. (No hanky-panky ensues; the scene seems to be a sop to moviegoers who prefer their labor lessons with a dash of undress.) Of course, the skinny-dipping-for-solidarity didn't actually happen. As Lee later noted, "Isn't it a shame that we didn't have that much fun?"

Probably at least one reason it didn't happen is that the real union organizer on whom the Leibman character is based was an older man and a former coal miner, not a hip young New Yorker. According to Lee, she and the actual union organizer (Eli Zivkovich) had more of a father-daughter relationship.

So you might say she liked him, but didn't REALLY like him.

Sources and Further Reading

Leifermann, Henry P. *Crystal Lee: A Woman of Inheritance.* New York: MacMillan, 1975.

Toplin, Robert Brent. *History by Hollywood.* Chicago: University of Illinois Press, 1996.

Rosenfeld, Megan. "Through the Mill With Crystal Lee and Norma Rae." *Washington Post*, June 11, 1980.

Biker Boyz (2003)

Directed by Reggie Rock Bythewood
Written by Craig Fernandez and Reggie Rock Bythewood
Starring Laurence Fishburne, Derek Luke, and Kid Rock

(Left) The cast of *Biker Boyz*, with
Laurence Fishburne (left) as Smoke,
a character based on Manuel
Galloway, aka Pokey.
© *DreamWorks LLC*

The real Manuel Galloway, Pokey
(left), with journalist Michael Gougis,
author of the magazine article on
which the movie was based.
Photo by Kim Irwin

Sitting in a darkened cinema watching *Biker Boyz*, you can almost smell the burning rubber. Unfortunately, this sensation has less to do with film realism than with the theater parking lot emptying in record time.

In prerelease marketing, Dreamworks pitched *Biker Boyz* as a faster, furious-er *The Fast and the Furious*—but with motorcycles instead of cars, a "z" instead of an "s," and that guy from the 7-Up commercials instead of Vin Diesel. Even the lobby poster, a blur of color streaks suggesting speeds in excess of those indicated by the color streaks on *The Fast and the Furious* marketing materials, was ready to rumble: "Survival of the Fastest," it boasted. Tricked out with previously driven parts and urban shiznit aplenty, *Biker Boyz* was set to ride a sidecar to megaplex triumph.

Alas, "fast" and "furious" proved to be apt descriptors, though not of the movie's pacing or action. Rather, those adjectives perfectly described the film's rate of collapse at the box office. *Biker Boyz* couldn't even keep pace with a pup-peteer-powered marsupial; *Kangaroo Jack—in its second weekend—*left the *Biker Boyz* premiere eating box-office dust. So much for hot-rod Darwinism.

Laughably bad and tedious to boot, *Biker Boyz* is one of those big-studio wipeouts that's not even worth the effort of rubbernecking. Remarkably, the cliché-ridden melodrama was actually based on a true story.

In early 2000 journalist Michael Gougis penned a feature article for the *New Times Los Angeles*, in which he explores Southern California's little-known subculture of African American biker clubs. Titled "Biker Boyz," Gougis's piece described a "thriving" black biker scene centered on illegal street racing. The weapon of choice was a highly customized racing machine, the "street drag bike, Japanese iron that's been stretched and lowered, its engine pumped full of steroids." According to Gougis, "On back streets . . . late at night, they fire these bikes in a straight line, side by side, for a quarter mile, for money and brag-ging rights."

The story—full of sharp detail, edgy street slang, and lively characters with braggadocio to burn—was a natural for Hollywood. Too bad Hollywood—specifically, writer-director team Craig Fernandez and Reggie Rock Bythe-wood—proceeded to bleed out all that was natural about the piece and replace it with silly artifice.

Gougis's article focused on a legendary California street racer named Manuel Galloway, also known as Pokey (the nickname is meant to be ironic). By day a full-time maintenance inspector for the city of Pasadena, by night Pokey donned the "colors" of his club, the Valiant Riders, and hit the back-alley speedways of Southern California on his badass Suzuki, Big Black. Accord-ing to Gougis, tens of thousands of dollars in street bets changed hands over Pokey's grudge-match races.

Fleshing out the bigger picture, Gougis also delved into the roots of the black biker movement, which sprang up thirty years ago in reaction to racist attitudes barring African Americans from white biker clubs. According to Gougis, Biker Boyz (and Girlz) had its share of thugs, but most of its riders were blue-collar workers and professionals chasing a weekend hobby.

Unfortunately, the Dreamworks team had little interest in exploring this unique slice of L.A. subculture. Instead, the filmmakers decided to juice up some standard-issue Hollywood schlock with urban street cred. The result is a half-baked soap opera about a young Biker Boy named Kid who is haunted by his stepfather's senseless motorcycle-related death. Played by Derek Luke (who also starred in *Antoine Fisher*) sporting a freshly shaved, talcum-powdered scalp, Kid should not be confused with Vin Diesel, who, although also bald, is *not* in this movie. Nor is Kid to be confused Kid Rock, who *is* in this movie, but who plays a completely different character named Dogg. Finally, Snoop Dogg is not in this movie, either.

OK, where were we? Right: *A bald kid named Antoine Fisher haunted by his stepfather's senseless motorcycle-related death.* So haunted, in fact, that he must prove himself to be a man through a series of equally senseless motorcycle-related stunts. What's more, these efforts will ultimately lead to Hollywood's favorite implausible plot twist: Our protagonist's shocking discovery that his archrival is actually his biological father. (*Come to the dark side, Antoine Fisher!*)

Laurence Fishburne channels Darth Vader by way of the Actor's Studio in his pavement-chewing portrayal of Smoke, the reigning biker "king of Cali." Fishburne's character is loosely based on the real-life street-racing champ Pokey (who appears in the film in a brief cameo). But while the real Pokey always kept his day job, Smoke seems to maintain a high standard of living through sheer coolness alone.

As a matter of fact, no one in *Biker Boyz*, the movie, appears to have a regular job (outside of clocking in with a "DAY-UM!" every other sentence). Yet everybody has the long green to bet it all on Smoke. The implication seems to be that trash-talking street racers in Watts and Compton are the beneficiaries of vast sums of inherited wealth. Antoine Fisher's widowed mom and siblings live it up in a swanky manor straight out of a production designer's *Architectural Digest* clip file. Antoine's mom, we're told, works in some unspecified capacity "at the hospital." Judging by her obvious net worth, she must be the only world-class brain surgeon ever to marry a motorcycle mechanic.

Not only does the big picture not compute, but *Biker Boyz* also fails to get the technical details right. One example: the racers in the film ride stock Suzukis and Yamahas; actual street drag bikes are often eccentric contraptions with a bicycle-thin wheel in the front and a twelve-inch-wide tire for traction in the back. Uncool, by Hollywood standards.

Another example: At one point in the film, Darth Fishburne and his Boyz hold illegal races in broad daylight at Hollywood's most overbooked film shooting location, the Sixth Street Bridge in downtown Los Angeles (as seen in *Terminator 2, Mulholland Drive, War of the Worlds, S.W.A.T*, etc.). It takes forever for the LAPD choppers to swoop in and bust up the fun. It's almost as if Fishburne had reserved the bridge in advance through the Los Angeles Film and Video Permit Office.

One final example of reckless disregard for reality: when Kid Rock sits on a motorcycle, it doesn't immediately fall over, crushing him underneath it.

Sources and Further Reading

Alexander, Sean and Eric Bass. "Biker Boyz: The Interviews." Motorcycle.com, January 17, 2003. http://www.motorcycle.com/mo/ mcfeatures/03_Biker_Boyz_Int/index.motml.

Gougis, Michael. "Biker Boyz: They Aren't Your Father's Motorcycle Outlaws." *New Times Los Angeles*, April 13, 2000.

Fear and Loathing in Las Vegas (1998)

Directed by Terry Gilliam
Written by Terry Gilliam & Tony Grisoni and Tod Davies & Alex Cox
Starring Johnny Depp and Benicio Del Toro

Where the Buffalo Roam (1980)

Directed by Art Linson
Written by John Kaye
Starring Bill Murray and Peter Boyle

Johnny Depp as Hunter S. Thompson.
© Universal City Studios Productions, Inc.

The real Hunter S. Thompson.
Photo by Chris Buck, © Simon & Schuster.

How anyone takes as many drugs as Hunter S. Thompson and *lives* is one of the great mysteries of modern journalism. Even the estimable Norman Mailer has said that if he went on a one-day binge of Thompsonesque proportions, he'd be in the hospital, and if he did it for three days, he'd be dead. But Thompson goes on one of those monstrous benders nearly every day of his life.

Still and all, even by Thompson's own standards, the amount of consciousness-altering substances ingested by himself and his "attorney" over the course of several days in Las Vegas was superheroic in its proportions. At least, that is, according to Thompson's account of said journey in his journalism-novel-memoir hybrid *Fear and Loathing in Las Vegas.*

First published as a book in 1972 after appearing as two lengthy articles in *Rolling Stone* the previous year, *Fear and Loathing in Las Vegas* was optioned by prospective moviemakers "a shitload of times" (according to Thompson). At one point, *The Last Picture Show* author Larry McMurtry was reportedly at work on a script. But the book presents some difficulties for translation to the screen. There's no story, for one thing.

The film version finally appeared in 1998 under the helm of Terry Gilliam, former Monty Python animator and director of such oddball fare as *Brazil, The Fisher King,* and *The Adventures of Baron Munchausen.* Gilliam's wacky aesthetic seemed to make him the perfect candidate to adapt Thompson's allegedly true tale of dangerous drugs, reckless driving, and the search for meaning in the most meretricious place on Earth. Disappointingly, the film leaves out most of the book's funniest passages. While Gilliam retained some of Thompson's musings on the passing of 1960s idealism, his film is far from the "savage journey to the heart of the American dream" promised in the subtitle of Thompson's classic book. Instead, the screen version of *Fear and Loathing* amounts to a hundred and twenty minutes of two guys getting high in a hotel room.

No one really knows if everything Thompson describes in *Fear and Loathing in Las Vegas* is, strictly speaking, true. Maybe not even Thompson himself—though he still owns his tapes from the Las Vegas experience. Thompson's "gonzo journalism" method required him to affix a cassette recorder to his upper arm with adhesive tape and keep it running at all times. (The tape recorder is missing from Johnny Depp's version of Thompson, though Bill Murray wears it in the fanciful Thompson biopic *Where the Buffalo Roam.*)

Thompson's "attorney" may have a better recollection of the events that actually transpired. Then again, he doesn't seem to be in a position to talk about it. The model for "Dr. Gonzo," the "300-pound Samoan," as described by Thompson (Benicio Del Toro in Gilliam's film; Peter Boyle in the earlier *Where the Buffalo Roam*) was Oscar "Zeta" Acosta, a 250-pound Mexican American. More to the point, Acosta was a legal aid lawyer and political radical. He vanished off the face of the earth in 1974, probably murdered during a bad drug deal.

Regarding the veracity of the book, Thompson biographer Peter O. Whitmer states: "Many of the scenes in Las Vegas are less fabrications of Thompson's creativity than re-creations of actual drug-induced weirdness."

Be that as it may, what really happened, as best as one can determine, is this: Thompson was in Los Angeles on assignment for *Rolling Stone* magazine, preparing the story that would become "Strange Rumblings in Aztlan." The piece deals with police brutality against L.A.'s Hispanics, and Acosta was Thompson's main source. Thompson was already a famous writer as a result of *Hell's Angels: A Strange and Terrible Saga*, his first-person (though not exactly "gonzo") account of a year with the California biker gang. He'd met Acosta a few years earlier in Aspen, Colorado. They became friends (after a typically Thompsonesque booze-and-mayhem bonding experience), but in L.A., Thompson found it difficult to relate to Acosta, who was surrounded by a posse of hard-line Chicanos. To Acosta's friends, even talking to a gringo was a sellout. Thompson needed to get Acosta out of L.A. for at least a few days.

A *Sports Illustrated* editor called Thompson and asked if he'd cover a motorcycle race, the Mint 400, in Las Vegas. The call was fortuitous for Thompson, if not for *Sports Illustrated*. Thompson didn't have much interest in the race. He intended to approach it the same way he'd approached the Kentucky Derby in his essay "The Kentucky Derby is Decadent and Depraved." That is, he would cover an event that he had no intention of actually viewing, or gathering any information about, by getting himself into all kinds of bizarre situations, then writing about them in real time, or as close to it as he could manage. Thompson's inability to get the story, mainly due to his own superhuman drug abuse and the ensuing "bad craziness," would become the story.

Thompson also saw the assignment as a way to get Acosta out of Los Angeles. According to a biography of Thompson by Paul Perry, Thompson knew the inevitable result of a weekend in Vegas with the Falstaffian Acosta would be that "we would both go crazy and try to outdo each other." Thompson says that the pair "took enough speed to keep Hitler awake in his bunker for fifty days and enough acid to make him think he was in the Austrian Alps." No word on whether they dipped into the ether or the adrenochrome ("taken from the adrenal gland of a living human body"), which are the subjects of some of the funniest bits in the book—and the movie, for whatever that's worth.

After a weekend of debauchery in which the drug-addled duo "freaked out" the *SI* photographer assigned to work with Thompson, Acosta caught a plane back to Los Angeles, leaving his disheveled friend to cope with an unpayable hotel bill and a *Sports Illustrated* deadline. Thompson filed a 2,500-word piece for *Sports Illustrated*, which the rather conservative publication immediately rejected. He then spent, by his own account, thirty-six straight speed-fueled hours in a hotel room, scribbling down every detail of the weekend that he could recall.

Thompson then returned to Los Angeles, where he worked simultaneously on his "Aztlan" piece and his pet project, *Fear and Loathing in Las Vegas*. He had nearly finished the account of his Vegas bacchanalia when his *Rolling Stone* editor heard about another Vegas event, a convention of district attorneys. The theme of the convention: the menace of illegal narcotics. Thompson promptly rounded up Acosta and returned to Vegas for what would become the second half of the book. In both the book and the film, the twin excursions are squeezed into a single time frame.

In terms of comparing the movie to real life, that's about as far as it goes. Any further details are swimming somewhere in the basin of Thompson's dope-addled skull.

A more definitive judgment can be passed on the 1980 Bill Murray vehicle *Where the Buffalo Roam*. Murray's onscreen impersonation of Thompson is uncanny (though he neglected to emulate Thompson's male-pattern baldness). Thompson himself scripted Murray's final monologue (a chore for which he received $25,000, not bad pay in the late 1970s). Beyond that, there's almost nothing in the movie that resembles reality. *Buffalo* is a highly fictionalized account of Thompson's friendship with Acosta, which Thompson chronicled in an uncharacteristically emotional article entitled "The Banshee Screams for Buffalo Meat." (Acosta referred to himself as a "Brown Buffalo.")

In the movie, Peter Boyle plays Carl Laszlo, an Acosta-like figure who crops up in Thompson's life at the most inopportune moments, and rather inexplicably at that, repeatedly attempting to persuade Thompson to join some kind of armed revolution. The Las Vegas episodes are omitted entirely. When Acosta's son saw the movie, he commented that he didn't recognize his father at all in Boyle's character. There are several reputable biographical books on Thompson available, and Acosta himself authored an autobiography. If you have any interest in the strange legend of Hunter S. Thompson and the equally outrageous tale of his comrade-in-drugs, Oscar Acosta, skip this movie.

Sources and Further Reading

Acosta, Oscar Zeta. *The Autobiography of a Brown Buffalo*. New York: Vintage Books, 1989.

———. *Oscar "Zeta" Acosta: The Uncollected Works*. Edited by Ilan Stavans. Houston, TX: Arte Publico Press, 1996.

Carrol, E. Jean. *Hunter: The Strange and Savage Life of Hunter S. Thompson*. New York: Plume Books, 1993.

McKeen, William. *Hunter S. Thompson*. Boston: Twayne Publishers, 1991.

Perry, Paul. *Fear and Loathing: The Strange and Terrible Saga of Hunter S. Thompson*. New York: Thunder's Mouth Press, 1992.

Thompson, Hunter S. *Fear and Loathing in Las Vegas: A Strange Journey to the Heart of the American Dream*. New York: Fawcett Popular Library, 1973.

Whitmer, Peter O. *When the Going Gets Weird: The Twisted Life and Times of Hunter S. Thompson*. New York: Hyperion, 1993.

Searching for Bobby Fischer (1993)

Directed and written by Steven Zaillian
Starring Joe Mantegna, Ben Kingsley, and Max Pomeranc

Joe Mantegna (left) as Fred Waitzkin and Max Pomeranc as Josh Waitzkin. © *Paramount Pictures*

There is no search for Bobby Fischer in the movie *Searching for Bobby Fischer*. The title is more of a metaphor. The movie could be more precisely titled *Searching for the Next Bobby Fischer*. The reclusive chess legend Fischer is present as a ghostly figure, however, in this story of Fred Waitzkin, a New York sportswriter who unexpectedly finds himself the father of a six-year-old chess prodigy. Fischer appears in old TV news footage, accompanied by wistful voice-over narration by Max Pomeranc, the child actor playing the central role.

The book *Searching for Bobby Fischer*, authored by freelance magazine writer Fred Waitzkin, takes the quest for Fischer more literally. Everyone in the chess world wants to know where Fischer is, wants to get in touch with him, wonders what happened to the highly eccentric (even by chess standards) champ. But the focus of the story is Waitzkin's relationship with his son Josh as they traverse the disturbingly competitive landscape of juvenile chess.

Josh Waitzkin was better than a prodigy; he was a dominant player among the preteen set. To his fellow third-graders, he was like a little Larry Bird of the black-and-white board. Josh's youthful opponents would break out in sweat or tears at the prospect of playing him, something that the good-natured Josh found highly upsetting. In his book, Fred Waitzkin explores his own ambivalence—his guilt for "pushing" his son, which was mixed with elation over Josh's many victories—as well as the paradox of parents, himself included, who drive their kids to succeed in chess knowing full well that there's no future in it.

No future? That's an understatement. In the book, Waitzkin describes the lives of various adult chess professionals he encountered. Chess in America is not exactly a major sport. If a chess pro pulls in $10K a year, he's among the elite. Tales of poverty, drug addiction, and general social maladjustment abound. Even Josh's teacher, Bruce Pandolfini, seems like a bit of a wreck as he struggles to make ends meet by cranking out instructional chess books and teaching private lessons.

Would any parent want that for a child? Waitzkin finds one couple who refuses to send their two kids, a boy and a girl, to school. They live out of a trailer. The kids do nothing with their young lives but play chess. All day. Every day. They're disheveled and cranky. The boy and his dad sport matching shaved heads. Both kids are champions and formidable opponents for Josh. But Waitzkin, appropriately, questions the price they're paying.

The situation in the former Soviet Union (still the current Soviet Union when Waitzkin wrote his 1988 memoir) is considerably different. There, chess is the national game, and star chess players are treated like . . . stars. Not only by the public, but, more to the point, by the government. Waitzkin learned this when he took Josh on a trip to the Soviet Union, where he attempted, with limited success, to get passes to world championship matches between Anatoly Karpov and Gary Kasparov. While there, Waitzkin met with several top chess masters, including Jewish players who were shut out of government-sanctioned tournaments and prohibited from leaving the country to ply their trade elsewhere. He was under surveillance by the KGB during their stay.

The 1993 film omits the Soviet trip. It omits the shaven-domed kid who was Josh's toughest opponent and replaces him with a snotty, bow-tied little twerp under the mentorship of a smarmy, vaguely pedophilic-seeming English chess tutor. This fictional Englishman is, in the screenplay, a rival of Pandolfini's, giving Josh's teacher an additional, Hollywood-style "motivation" from the "this time it's personal" genre.

Most important, Steven Zaillian's movie, poignant as it is, wrings out the subtlety from the father-son relationship that is depicted in Waitzkin's book. In the film, the tension is reduced to repeated agonizing by Joe Mantegna as Fred Waitzkin over whether he's taking the fun out of his kid's life by pushing him too hard.

But there's always the hope, which Waitzkin and his fellow chess parents harbor, that his kid will develop into the next Bobby Fischer. Fischer was the only superstar American chess has ever produced; the only American chess player that the average guy on the street could name. Certainly he was the only one to get his picture on the cover of *Sports Illustrated*. He commanded million-dollar purses and, in 1972, defeated Soviet Boris Spassky to bring the World Chess Championship to the United States for the first—and, to date, last—time.

Fischer had some kind of a problem, though. His behavior was erratic to say the least, and at the height of his fame he quit chess and went into seclusion. The voice-over in the film recounts his mysterious disappearance, but in reality, in 1992, a year before the film was released in the United States, Fischer had indeed emerged from his two decades underground.

Sort of.

He came out of hiding to play a rematch against his old nemesis, Spassky. The one minor hitch was that the match would be played in Montenegro, which was, at the time, part of war-torn Yugoslavia—a country then under severe economic and political sanctions. By playing the match there, Fischer became a fugitive from United States justice. He'd received a letter from the U.S. Treasury Department warning him not to play the match. At a prematch press conference, his first in twenty years, he produced the letter and promptly expectorated upon it.

As it turned out, the great chess master Bobby Fischer harbored feelings of violent anti-Semitism and anti-Americanism. Still in exile today (a warrant for his arrest remains in effect), Fischer surfaced in the summer of 2004 in Japan. He declared that he would renounce his U.S. citizenship and become a Japanese citizen. He claimed that if he returned to the United States, he would be murdered. That may have been stretching it, but the U.S. certainly wouldn't have been the friendliest environment for Fischer. The Japanese government tried to deport him, but a court blocked the order and he remained incarcerated. Prior to this sudden appearance in Japan, Fischer occasionally did a radio show on a Philippine radio station, in which he played old R&B records and inveighed against Jews, whom he described as "a filthy, lying bastard people." (This despite the fact that his mother is Jewish, making Fischer himself a Jew by birth.) On September 11, 2001, Fischer used his radio broadcast to "applaud" the terrorist attacks on the United States, calling them "wonderful news." He signed off by declaring, "Death to the U.S."

Josh Waitzkin, meanwhile, remains an active chess master. He continues to play major tournaments and write books about chess.

Sources and Further Reading

Chun, Rene. "Bobby Fischer's Pathetic Endgame." *The Atlantic Monthly*, December 2002.

Waitzkin, Fred. *Searching For Bobby Fischer: The World of Chess, Observed by the Father of a Child Prodigy*. New York: Random House, 1988.

Shattered Glass (2003)

Directed and written by Billy Ray
Starring Hayden Christensen, Peter Sarsgaard, and Steve Zahn

Peter Sarsgaard as Chuck Lane.
Photo by Jonathan Wenk, © Lions Gate Films

The real Stephen Glass.
Photo by David Bartolomi, courtesy of Simon & Schuster

"When *The New Republic* was founded in 1914," says the venerable political magazine's own promotional material, "its mission was to provide its readers with an intelligent, stimulating and rigorous examination of American politics, foreign policy and culture. It has brilliantly maintained its mission for over eighty years."

Well, not *always* brilliantly. At least not in 1997 and 1998, when a twenty-five-year-old Ivy Leaguer named Stephen Glass hoaxed the magazine into printing more than two dozen pieces of "journalism" that were in fact his own fantasy. Glass faked important portions of twenty-seven feature articles. He made up at least six of them in their entirety, as if he were writing for the literary section of *The New Yorker*, or maybe *Ellery Queen's Mystery Magazine*. His stories, all of them "fluff" human-interest pieces (as opposed to the analytical policy reportage the magazine is known for) had a fantastical, too-good-to-be-true quality, and "covered" such "news" as:

- A convention of young Republicans, at which tomorrow's conservative leaders get stoned and try to rape overweight women.
- A teenage computer hacker who extorts a lucrative job as a "security consultant" from a major software firm—and shows up for a meeting with the company's executives accompanied by his agent.
- Glass himself, calling radio talk shows claiming to be a psychologist specializing in "human biting," and hilariously bullshitting his way through thirty on-air interviews.

Yes, Glass wrote a story about a hoax that was itself a hoax.

It seemed that the youthful, enthusiastic, and charmingly self-effacing Glass was always stumbling into zany situations that made for wildly entertaining feature stories rich in colorful detail and wacky characters. He got his phony stories past three *New Republic* editors-in-chief, all respected journalists in their own right (though only two are depicted in the film). It never occurred to any of them that he was completely full of crap.

And why should it have? Glass was not some freelancer e-mailing his stories from a distant corner of the United States. He was part of the "*TNR* family," a staff writer with a $45,000 salary and his own office. Heck, he was the star of the staff. When his story about the amusingly degenerate young Republicans hit the stands, offers from other magazines filled his voice mailbox. When he was exposed as a fabricator in 1998, Glass had over $100,000 in freelance deals lined up with top-rank publications including *Harper's*, *Rolling Stone*, the *New York Times Magazine,* and the John Kennedy Jr.–edited *George*.

Unlike *Quiz Show* (see page 412), a movie about fakery that itself was loaded with falsehoods, *Shattered Glass* adheres closely to the actual events of Glass's brief and disastrous journalistic career. According to Charles Lane, the *TNR* editor who uncovered Glass's perfidy (after a reporter for the *Forbes* Web site informed him that none of the details in Glass's hacker story checked out) and fired him, "In a movie that isn't a documentary but is a dramatic portrayal, the most you can hope for is that they give it a good-faith effort to represent the truth of the situation, and I think they passed the test."

Lane (played by Peter Sarsgaard in the movie) noted a few cosmetic differences between the movie and life. The filmmakers invented a girlfriend for Glass, a fellow *TNR* writer played by Chloë Sevigny, as well as a middle-aged executive who supervises the magazine's youthful staff. Lane also said that he and Glass never engaged in the lunchroom badinage scripted into the film. The film also glosses over the real reason that Lane's predecessor, Michael Kelly, was fired by *TNR* boss Martin Peretz. In the movie, it appears that Kelly gets the ax for being too loyal to his staff. He is shown standing up to his boss after Peretz, in Queeg-like fashion, has ordered his young writers to circle in red ink every comma in the magazine to teach them a lesson in comma usage. While the comma incident and Kelly's objections to it were true, it's not why he was fired. In reality, Peretz could no longer tolerate Kelly's contempt for then vice-president Al Gore, a friend of Peretz's. (As a side note, the film is dedicated to Kelly's memory. In April 2003, after *Shattered Glass* had finished shooting, Kelly—played by Hank Azaria in the movie—died in Iraq, the first American journalist killed in that war.)

Framing the firing the way he did in the movie, to highlight Kelly's unwavering support of his writers against upper management, writer-director Billy Ray was able to drive the point home that Glass exploited that very support, and the support of his costaffers, as a means to perpetrate his fraud. Hayden Christensen (best known as the teenage Darth Vader in the *Star Wars* prequels) nails the ingratiating qualities that Glass, by accounts of those who knew him, employed to endear himself to others. He's forever disparaging his own clearly stellar story ideas. Affecting a charming "boyishness," he asks anyone who questions him, "Are you mad at me?" In the opening voice-over, Ray has Christensen/Glass explain that in journalism, a field full of cocky ballbusters, a little humility goes a long way.

There are two important questions that the film leaves unanswered, however. First, why did Glass do it? The filmic Glass enters his profession as a wide-eyed idealist who never loses his sense of wonder at the magic of journalism and the wonderful stories it can tell. The real Glass, in his autobiographical novel *The Fabulist*, did not harbor any love for his chosen profession. As one reviewer put it, in Glass's book, "his thorough contempt for journalism shines through." Wreaking public relations havoc on a field you despise is at least understandable, though even in real life, Glass's motives remain puzzling. In the movie, he comes across as an inscrutable cipher.

Today, excommunicated from journalism, the onetime failed premed is a law school grad working at a New York firm.

The other question left unaddressed in the movie is why none of Glass's editors or colleagues—or for that matter, editors at the other prestigious magazines who lined up for his services—so much as raised an eyebrow at Glass's spectac-ular streak of extraordinary stories, despite their liberal use of anonymous quotes and unverifiable sources. Even strong complaints lodged by the subjects of Glass's imaginative tales (when he bothered to write about real people at all) stirred no suspicions. It took a writer at the *Forbes* Digital Tool Web site, mortified that he'd apparently missed a terrific story on his own beat, to check the facts of Glass's hacker piece and expose it as a giant lie.

After that, Lane and his staff undertook their own investigation and exposed the remainder (to their knowledge) of Glass's fabricated stories.

Most media accounts of the Glass affair explain this meltdown as the work of a deviously scheming sociopath who took incredible pains to cover his tracks, forging notes and manufacturing counterfeit supporting matter for his fictional tales. When Lane closed in on him, Glass recruited his own brother into the plot.

There's a lot of truth to that explanation, and it seems to be the one Ray subscribes to, though he doesn't push it strongly in the film. Another possible explanation, which is not touched upon in the screenplay, lies in the fact that Glass's stories invariably found great humor in the farcical and boorish habits of ordinary Americans: department store Santas, telephone psychics, salesmen, corporate managers. To the Washington insiders who fashion themselves as opinion shapers for the nation's leaders (*TNR* calls itself "the in-flight magazine of Air Force One"), Glass's tales of bumpkins and buffoons outside the beltway rang true. Glass was telling them what they wanted to hear—namely, "You and I are smart, and everyone else is stupid."

The Hollywood version of Glass is right when he says that a little humility goes a long way. A small dose might have helped his editors understand that people aren't always as laughably dumb as they appeared in the fantasy world of Stephen Glass.

Sources and Further Reading

Beckerman, Gal. "Q&A: Former *New Republic* Editor Charles Lane."
   Columbia Journalism Review, September/October 2003.
   http://www.cjr.org/issues/2003/5/qa-beckerman.asp.
Bissinger, Buzz. "Shattered Glass." *Vanity Fair*, September 1998.
Lauerman, Kerry. "'I've Had a Great Deal of Therapy.'" *Salon*, October 28,
   2003. http://archive.salon.com/ent/feature/2003/10/28/glass/.
Penenberg, Adam L. "Burden of Truth." *Reed Magazine*, November 1998.
Pogrebin, Robin. "Rechecking a Writer's Facts, a Magazine Uncovers
   Fiction." *New York Times*, June 12, 1998.

Men of Honor (2000)

Directed by George Tillman Jr.
Written by Scott Marshall Smith
Starring Cuba Gooding Jr. and Robert De Niro

The life story of Carl Brashear, the U.S. Navy's first African American deep-sea diver, is an inspirational one, to say the least. Brashear's story grew even more inspiring when, after a horrific accident onboard ship that cost him his left leg, he willed himself to become the navy's first amputee diver. Brashear's is one of those life stories that only Hollywood could come up with.

So why did Hollywood feel the need to mess with it? The 2000 drama *Men of Honor* purports to be Brashear's biopic, but, except in its broad outlines, the tale that unfolds on-screen in basically fiction.

"This isn't a connect-the-dots biography," noted screenwriter Scott Marshall Smith, with considerable understatement. "I follow Carl's life and career, but my goal was to be true to his spirit, not his shirt size."

What Brashear's shirt size has to do with the hokum that Smith threw into his script is not clear. He and director George Tillman Jr. exclude some of the more dramatic moments of Brashear's remarkable navy career and add a gaggle of high-melodrama moments that would make even Steven Spielberg cringe.

"Everyone wanted the script to resonate as much as possible, so as a dramatist, I sometimes took it up a level," Smith explained.

It's exactly that "take it up a level" attitude that drives Hollywood moviemakers to trivialize perfectly compelling true stories by loading them up with treacly bullshit. That's what Smith and Tillman have done with *Men of Honor*.

First, they've invented a fictional character whom they call "a composite of various navy men," but who resembles nothing but a worn-out cliché: the abusive drill instructor—or in this case, the abusive diving instructor. In a particularly over-the-top touch, they name this "composite" character Billy Sunday, after the fire-and-brimstone preacher. And in an even-more-over-the-top touch, they give their Billy Sunday a speech in which he compares himself to the real Billy Sunday, capped off with the line, "The only difference between him and me is that he worked for God. I *am* God!" Ouch. And in the final, most over-the-top touch of all, they cast Robert De Niro in the part and give him full license to unleash his inner Al Pacino. It's De Niro's screamingest, holleringest performance of his lengthy career—delivered, no less, in an approximation of Southern dialect.

So enamored of their phony creation are the filmmakers that they devote a good part of the film to a subplot involving Sunday's drunken rowdyism and turbulent relationship with his much younger femme fatale of a wife (played by Charlize Theron), a character who exists for no other apparent reason than to fulfill the "fabulous babe" quota in the otherwise all-male cast. (Brashear's wife, Junetta, played by Aunjanue Ellis and puzzlingly renamed Jo because "Daddy always wanted a boy" has the only other female role.)

The Billy Sunday character, along with another fabricated officer, the incorrigibly racist diving school commanding officer, Mr. Pappy (where did Smith come up with these names?), is meant to personify the bigotry that Brashear faced when he entered navy diving school in 1953. As in the film, Brashear found anonymous notes in his bunk bearing such welcoming messages as, "We're gonna drown you, nigger."

Unlike in the movie, which has Cuba Gooding Jr.'s Brashear bravely ignoring the threats, the real Brashear, deeply disheartened, decided to quit. As Hollywood often fails to recognize, even the most heroic human beings are, in the end, only human. It isn't enough, in the minds of mediocre screenwriters, that a man display extraordinary courage in extraordinary situations. He must display extraordinary courage in *every* situation.

Fortunately, the real Brashear was talked out of hanging up his air hose by another diver, who assured him that the threats were empty and that no one would actually try to hurt him.

In the movie, De Niro's sadistic Billy Sunday welcomes Brashear to the school by rousing him in the middle of the night and blasting him with a fire hose, which actually happened, though it was early in the morning and designed more to wake up the cadets than to teach Brashear a lesson in white supremacy. Later in the film, during Brashear's final diving test, Sunday, on orders from Mr. Pappy, leaves Brashear underwater for nine hours of relentless hypothermia.

Brashear recalls that his trainers attempted to sabotage his tests so that he would not graduate. But they didn't try to kill him.

In the latter part of the film, after Brashear has lost his leg and is laboring to get back on active diving duty, Sunday reappears, inexplicably redeemed from his earlier racial hatred. He volunteers to drill Brashear back into shape, prosthetic leg and all.

At this point, the character of Sunday fills in for a real person—Chief War-rant Officer Raymond Duell, whom Brashear credits with whipping him back into diving condition. There is no evidence or indication, however, that Duell was a reformed racist redneck.

"That man drove me every day, every cotton-picking day," Brashear recalls. "At the end of that year he wrote the most beautiful letter. Boy, that was some-thing. I was returned to full duty and full diving—the first time in naval his-tory for an amputee."

He won his reinstatement by showing his superiors pictures of himself per-forming various feats of physical prowess, all with an artificial leg. He never appeared before a navy physical evaluation board (he was scheduled to, on two occasions, but played hooky both times), as he does in the film's highly ridicu-lous climactic sequence. It is true that Brashear was required to take twelve steps on land under the crushing weight of a next-generation diving rig. In the movie, however, he does it right there in the hearing room, with De Niro's tough-guy drill instructor barking commands like, "Navy diver, report to this line!"

At that point, the *movie* crosses the line, from inventing things that did not happen—a necessary, if often overdone, aspect of dramatizing real events—to inventing things that would not happen, which is just annoying. But that's not enough for screenwriter Smith. He also feels the need to invent things that *could* not happen. In the movie, it takes Brashear not a year, but a quick four months to rehabilitate his amputated leg. That's what you call "taking it up a level."

The most accurate scene in the movie is, as it happens, the accident sequence. Brashear suffered the injury that cost his leg on March 25, 1966, on board the USS *Hoist*, a salvage ship that had been dispatched to recover a nuclear bomb from the ocean floor. After a midair collision, an American B-52 had embarrassingly dropped four hydrogen bombs on Spain. Fortunately for the Spaniards, the bombs were not armed. Three bombs parachuted harmlessly to the mainland, but one got lost on the ocean floor. Brashear was on deck, super-vising the bomb recovery, when a cable flew loose, sending a lead pipe swing-ing through the air. In the movie, Brashear shoves another sailor out of the way and the pipe collides with his own leg, shattering the bone.

Did Smith take that scene up a level? To the contrary, he took it down. As Brashear recalls the incident, the impact of the pipe launched him into the air, sending him into flips before he crashed on the deck. A helicopter airlifted him off the *Hoist*, dropping him roughly onto the deck of another ship. By the time he got to a hospital he was in deep shock and had no apparent pulse. He was taken to the morgue—where a doctor detected a faint heartbeat and revived him. For some reason, none of those events made it into the movie, despite their obvious high drama. Perhaps in Hollywood, the only good high drama is the kind you make up out of nowhere. If it really happened, it's not your idea, so who needs it?

Sources and Further Reading

Stillwell, Paul. *The Reminiscences of Master Chief Boatswain's Mate Carl Brashear*. Annapolis MD: United States Institute, 1998.

Topel, Fred. "Carl Brashear: The Real Action Hero." About.com. http://actionadventure.about.com/library/weekly/aa111700a.htm.

Pushing Tin (1999)

Directed by Mike Newell
Written by Glen Charles and Les Charles
Starring John Cusack and Billy Bob Thornton

John Cusack as a top-gun air traffic controller actually named Zone. *© Twentieth Century Fox Film Corporation*

A movie about men who spend the better part of their lives staring at radar displays that have all the visual sophistication of Pong, while muttering esoteric jargon into crackly radio headsets—well, it just doesn't have that cash-register ring that attracts Hollywood. For some reason, however, that didn't stop some visionary producer from purchasing the film rights to a 1996 *New York Times Magazine* article by Darcy Frey, titled "Something's Got to Give."

The lengthy article strung together anecdotal glimpses into the daily lives of air traffic controllers, the men (and they are, indeed, almost all men) who give directions to pilots of commercial airliners so that their airliners do not crash into other airliners. This is called "pushing tin," although in Frey's article the phrase is "pumping tin."

Air traffic control seems like a job for geeks, and it involves no personal physical risk, but the psychological risks are immense. Each controller is responsible, during any eight-hour shift, for thousands of human lives. The air in the control room is heavy with testosterone.

Frey's article and the movie it inspired cover the controllers at New York "Tracon" (Terminal Radar Approach Control), the busiest air traffic control center in the world. Controllers battle constantly against "going down the pipes"—that is, losing their mental grasp on the dozens of electronic dots zipping across circular radar scopes, each dot a plane carrying dozens or hundreds of human beings.

As is often the case when Hollywood "options" a magazine article, Frey's *Times Mag* piece contained nothing that would pass Robert McKee muster as *story*. So, on top of the colorful tales of macho controllers harassing Dunkin' Donuts clerks on their off-hours, screenwriters Glen and Les Charles (creators of the 1980s hit sitcom *Cheers*) overlaid a yarn about the clash between Zone, Tracon's top gun (based loosely on a character in the article called Zack), played by the always entertaining John Cusack, and a mysterious, silent, but instinctively multiskilled newcomer named Bell, played by the always annoying Billy Bob Thornton. Of course, Bell is part Native American, because in the movies, Native Americans are mysterious, silent, and instinctively good at everything. After all, they are "spiritual." White suburb-dwellers, stultified by TV and beer, are anything but.

Not surprisingly, Zone cracks up—goes down the pipes—and Bell helps him attain inner peace. Because in the movies, all Indians have inner peace and can help you attain it. But only if you're willing to do something really weird and dangerous. In the end, Zone does. Without giving it away, suffice to say, the stunt appears nowhere in Frey's article.

Anyway, the narrative is, needless to say, not the main merit of the film. What the film achieves quite well, at least judging by the article that inspired it, is capturing the psychological high-wire subculture of air traffic controllers (although it takes a few minor liberties with the details of their jobs: we often see Zone shooting off rapid-fire instructions to a series of jetliners without any pause, when the real "Zack," like all controllers, would be required to wait for the pilot to verify that he's received the instructions).

A couple of other aspects of the article that didn't make it into the movie would have presented a rather scary picture for air travelers. One is the frequency of "deals," or near-midair collisions. Deals often occur because of controller error, though they can just as easily result from a pilot's failure to properly carry out a controller's instructions. In the film, every deal is treated as, well, a big deal. As stated in the film, three deals in two-and-a-half years causes the controller responsible to be "pulled off the scopes."

But according to Frey, "at the Newark airport sector there's actually a deal a day—sometimes a deal an hour—but unless a pilot or supervisor files a complaint with the FAA within fifteen days, the incident escapes inquiry; controllers, spotting a deal on their scopes, just look around to see if they were caught."

Another major cause of deals, and a main theme of Frey's article, is equipment failure at Tracon. This is perhaps the most disturbing bit of information left out of the movie. According to Frey, writing in 1996, the radar systems, computers, and radios have "grown scandalously old and degraded. Last year, air traffic control centers—some with thirty-year-old vacuum-tube computers—suffered more blank radar scopes, dead radios, and failed power systems than in any previous year."

It is not uncommon for a controller to cruise along in full command of a sky full of airplanes, only to have his radarscope go dark like a bad TV set. The outdated technology puts more responsibility, and stress, on the controllers. And that leads to further dangerous errors.

Director Mike Newell and the Charleses elected, however, not to tell a cautionary tale of peril in the friendly skies. They went the *Cheers* route instead, making yuk-it-up banter and tangled romances among their characters the focus of their movie.

You can bet that the final scene, in which Zone croons a love ballad to his estranged wife over the pilot's headphone, would get a controller pulled off the scopes.

Sources and Further Reading

Frey, Darcy. "Something's Got to Give." *New York Times Magazine.* March 24, 1996.

Ghosts of Mississippi (1996)

Directed by Rob Reiner
Written by Lewis Colick
Starring Alec Baldwin, James Woods, and Whoopi Goldberg

James Woods as Byron De la Beckwith. *Photo by Eli Reed, © Castle Rock Entertainment*

Rob Reiner unfortunately did not make a very good movie with *Ghosts of Mississippi*. But, especially given the movie's touchy topic, he deserves credit for making a factually accurate movie—and a little credit for grasping his responsibility to do so. *Ghosts* is Reiner's film about the 1994 conviction of white supremacist Byron De la Beckwith for the assassination of civil rights leader Medgar Evers thirty-one years earlier. Where most Hollywood directors are content to shuck any obligation to historical veracity with a shrug and a "we captured the essence, that's what's important," Reiner faced the facts of factual filmmaking squarely.

"I understand that people get their history through movies," Reiner told CNN when the film came out in 1996. "I take the responsibility of being historically accurate very seriously." As if to underline his point, *Ghosts* eschews the boilerplate epigraph "based on a true story" for the more in-your-face proclamation, "This Story is True."

Reiner wasn't fudging. Much. As might be expected, he and scriptwriter Lewis Colick did take a few dramatic liberties for the sake of that screenwriter shibboleth, "conflict." Still, even the murdered activist's brother proclaimed the film "90 percent accurate,"—a damn fine accuracy percentage for any Hollywood production. Evers's widow also commended the movie's fidelity to the facts, and his son plays himself in the movie. And yet, beginning long before the movie's release, when the idea was being bandied about at the studio, controversy erupted over the film.

The hullabaloo had little to do with the factual matter on-screen. The controversy concerned the self-evident matter of skin color. Specifically, Reiner's, which, for those incapable of surmising, is of the Caucasian persuasion. Spike Lee can always be counted on to join such debates and he did, weighing in with, "The story of Medgar Evers needs to be told by an African American director. . . . No white director could ever know how to tell a story concerning the disintegration of black identity through the murder of Evers."

As with *Mississippi Burning* eight years earlier (which, like *Ghosts of Mississippi*, was produced by Fred Zollo), the core of the complaint was that Hollywood couldn't bring itself to tell a story about the civil rights struggle without a white hero. The difference was that *Mississippi Burning* operated on the absurd premise that FBI agents—*white* FBI agents—were somehow frontline warriors in the battle for racial justice. If anything, the historical record shows that the FBI could most charitably be described as "passive" in that regard. They were a lot worse than that, actually. Integration and equality were not among J. Edgar Hoover's pet causes. But *Mississippi Burning* was a fictional story. *Ghosts of Mississippi* is, as its epigraph insists, quite true. And its hero, prosecutor Bobby DeLaughter, was, and remains today, quite white.

The question, then, was whether a white director making a film with a white protagonist (DeLaughter is played by Alec Baldwin) was somehow inappropriate. The great civil rights pioneer Evers is relegated to a minor role in the story. In his only scene, he is assassinated. In Reiner's defense, producer Zollo insisted that the film was never intended to be "the Medgar Evers story," but rather "a story about the pursuit of justice of the murderer of an American hero."

The Evers assassination and the pursuant "pursuit of justice" is an incredible story. From the earliest days of the civil rights struggle, Evers was at the helm of its most inflammatory episodes. He was the first field secretary for the

NAACP in the racially torn and backward state of Mississippi. He led black voter registration drives. He investigated the murder of fourteen-year-old black child Emmett Till in 1955 (Till's killers were acquitted by an all-white jury; shortly afterward, they bragged to the press about the murder). He guided James Meredith through the ordeal of becoming the first "Negro" student at the University of Mississippi. For his troubles, he was beaten and his life was threatened so often that Evers, frankly, expected to be murdered.

Evers's name eventually turned up on a "death list" circulated by white supremacists in Mississippi. Shortly after midnight on June 12, 1963, Evers pulled into the driveway of the small home where he lived with his wife, Myrlie, and their three children. A few hours earlier that evening, President Kennedy had delivered his landmark, nationally televised address on civil rights. As Evers stepped out of his car, De la Beckwith, hiding in bushes across the street, shot Evers in the back with a high-powered rifle, killing him with a single bullet.

There was never any great mystery about who Evers's killer was. Beckwith, a fertilizer salesman and self-avowed racist (played with creepy arrogance by James Woods), dropped his rifle near the murder scene, and the scope a short distance from there. His fingerprint was on the scope. He was tried twice, both times by all-white, all-male juries. Both trials ended in hung juries. He wasn't acquitted, so the door stayed open for a third trial, but that seemed pointless. As years passed and Beckwith enjoyed his freedom (with the exception of three years spent in prison later on a weapons charge, a detail that is left out of the movie), almost all the evidence against him vanished, including his gun and the transcript of his first trial.

Evers's widow, who became a prominent activist herself, never gave up on putting Beckwith behind bars, and in 1989 the Jackson, Mississippi, district attorney's office reopened the case, much to the consternation of the community. DeLaughter devoted five years of his life to reinvestigating the murder. He tracked down all of the twenty-six-year-old leads and some new ones, as well. He found new witnesses, and, amazingly, he located the missing murder weapon—his own father-in-law had it! That weird twist is naturally written into the movie and it seems like a Hollywood embellishment, but it's not. DeLaughter's father-in-law was Russell Moore, a notoriously racist judge. There were a lot of strange goings-on in those days, and the rifle came into Moore's possession. He kept it as some kind of perverse souvenir. When DeLaughter reopened the case, his mother-in-law gave him the gun (in the movie, he barges into her home and tosses the place for it). Moore's daughter, Dixie, divorced DeLaughter during the case, an event that Reiner also includes in the movie.

Unfortunately Reiner goes a little nuts with the domestic drama angle. That's where his film takes on a cheesy, made-for-TV quality. A story that could have been a tense, true-life thriller somehow under Reiner's guidance becomes a story of one man's romantic misadventures. Or something like that. (Reiner is the guy who made *When Harry Met Sally*, after all.) His sappy attempt to make the story "personal" was not only an aesthetic blunder on Reiner's part, it was a tactical screwup, too. To tell the story through the point of view of the white prosecutor who finally put Evers's killer away— that's one thing. But did we really need to linger adoringly over the precious details of that white guy's home life?

In an effort to add some artificial suspense to the kitchen-sink drama, Reiner exaggerated threats against DeLaughter. DeLaughter did receive a bomb threat against his home, as depicted in the film, but he didn't immediately evacuate his family to a motel. The window of his car was never smashed, and a swastika was not spray-painted on its hood. DeLaughter was not in the habit of singing his daughter to sleep with "Dixie," which means that he later did not substitute "Old McDonald" for "Dixie." It seemed a gratuitous shot at the South to add that detail, as if DeLaughter rejected not only racism, but all Southern tradition.

The film concludes with a lengthy courtroom sequence that re-creates Beckwith's third trial, which ran from January 28, 1994—thirty years to the day from the start of Beckwith's first trial, in the same Jackson courtroom—until February 8, when a jury of eight blacks and four whites, with seven jurors women, convicted him. The crucial testimony in the trial came from a policeman who claimed than he saw the accused killer ninety miles away from the murder site less than an hour afterward. District Attorney Ed Peters demolished the alibi witness, and Beckwith's alibi, in persuasive and hilarious fashion. In the grand Hollywood tradition, the cross-examination scene and all of Peters's best lines go to star Alec Baldwin, who plays DeLaughter. Stolid character actor Craig T. Nelson, as Peters, gets to sit and watch.

The lamest attempt of all to "make it personal" is the film's invention of a men's room confrontation between DeLaughter and Beckwith. The scene hammers home what is already evident: that Beckwith is a racist sociopath. All things considered, however, Reiner's alterations to the true story were minor, and were almost certainly designed to make the movie warmer and more entertaining. Instead, unfortunately, they made the movie weak and cloying—and, by languishing in fuzzy scenes of DeLaughter's family life, they helped legitimize the criticism that white Hollywood cares only about white characters.

Myrlie Evers is portrayed by Whoopi Goldberg as a stock "black woman with dignity" who has very little to do in the movie besides act indignant. In reality, by the time the movie came out, only two years and ten months after Beckwith's conviction, Myrlie Evers had been elected chairwoman of the NAACP.

Byron De la Beckwith received a sentence of life behind bars, but he turned out to be a short-timer anyway. In January 2001 he died in prison at age eighty.

Sources and Further Reading

Billings, Andrew. "Achieving Authenticity in the Film *Ghosts of Mississippi*: Identity and Authorship in Historical Narratives." *Western Journal of Black Studies*, June 22, 2000.

DeLaughter, Bobby. *Never Too Late: The Prosecutor's Story of Justice in the Medgar Evers Case*. New York: Scribner, 2000.

Morris, Willie. *The Ghosts of Medgar Evers: A Tale of Race, Murder, Mississippi, and Hollywood*. New York: Random House, 1998.

A Civil Action (1998)

Written and directed by Steven Zaillian

Starring John Travolta, Kathleen Quinlan,
and Robert Duvall

John Travolta as personal-injury attorney Jan Schlichtmann.
Photo by David James, © Paramount Pictures and Touchstone Pictures. All rights reserved.

The movie poster for *A Civil Action* features a steely-eyed (and somewhat meaty) John Travolta. He stares straight ahead from out of a literally black-and-white world, assuming Hollywood's tribune-of-the-little-man promotional-materials pose.

Perhaps the best thing that can be said for the movie itself is that it lives up to the poster. In a world where corporate polluters get away with murder, Travolta's attorney character, Jan Schlichtmann, is the one man who can deliver justice. (Well, OK, the one man if you don't include the jury, the judge, and Quentin Tarantino, without whom Travolta would probably still be making talking-baby movies.) The film stock may be Kodachrome, but the world depicted by director Steven Zaillian is indeed black and white. Zaillian practically invites us to hiss at the corporate villains in the film. They may deserve it, but there's no way that Vinnie Barbarino, attorney-at-law, could ever have proved it in a courtroom. So Hollywood heroic is Travolta's character that Zaillian has him single-handedly uncovering the corporate crimes at the center of the movie: toxic dumping that leeched into the water supply of Woburn, Massachusetts, leading to a deadly leukemia "cluster."

A Civil Action is based on Jonathan Harr's bestselling nonfiction book of the same name, which recounts Schlichtmann's role as plaintiff's attorney in the 1981 class-action lawsuit against food conglomerates W.R. Grace and Beatrice Foods Company. The movie's portrayal of the ambulance-chasing Schlichtmann as the guy who blew the lid off the case nettled the bejeezus out of more than a few real-life journalists. Several who reported the story from start to finish complained that the real Schlichtmann had little involvement in the heavy investigative lifting that cleared the way for the prosecution. Instead, they insist that it was the clients, and one dauntless mother in particular, who did most of the initial yeoman's work against the Woburn polluters. The scribes also point out that Schlichtmann's real case against Grace and Beatrice had more holes in it than Woburn has smokestacks. And never, ever, did the actual, ka-ching–conscious Schlichtmann turn down a twenty-million-dollar settlement offer.

Zaillian introduces Travolta's Schlichtmann with a callous voice-over monologue cataloging the monetary value of various flavors of injury victim. Children, Travolta intones, are worth next to nothing in the world of personal injury law. This being a Hollywood production of the 1990s, there's little doubt that such heartless cynicism will magically melt away when our hero redeems himself in the cockle-warming third act.

While grooving to the sound of his own voice as a guest on a live radio phone-in show, Schlichtmann is confronted by a caller claiming to be a neglected client. The voice later materializes as a wispy and jaded Anne Anderson (Kathleen Quinlan). During a subsequent meeting with Schlichtmann, Anderson voices vague suspicions that some evildoer has caused a suspiciously high number of leukemia deaths in Woburn—including that of Anderson's own son, who died in 1981. In the film, Anderson says she has no idea whom to blame, but she wants Schlichtmann to find out and elicit an apology from the offenders.

Schlichtmann remains underwhelmed by the financial possibilities until he discovers a Beatrice truck parked near some nasty polluting action, hard by Anderson's neighborhood. Our weasel friend smells money, and off he goes to get himself some. He files a complaint against Grace and Beatrice, accusing them of dumping disease-causing waste into the community.

Schlichtmann both bankrupts himself and empties out the coffers at his law firm trying to fight the polluters. In one key scene, a Beatrice lawyer takes a twenty dollar bill out of his pocket and asks Schlichtmann how he would feel about settling the case for that bill plus six zeros, or twenty million dollars.

Schlichtmann spurns the offer, thus repudiating his first-act venality and earning his all-important cinematic redemption. Unfortunately, the jury comes back with a verdict exonerating Beatrice.

Frustrated and exhausted, Schlichtmann's colleagues kick him out of their law firm, but not before he wins a small monetary settlement from W.R. Grace. This somewhat less than triumphant ending is faithful to the real-life anti-climax of the trial, from which the corporate perps emerged relatively unscathed. But at least Woburn had found an effective tribune in Schlichtmann, without whom whistles would not have been blown . . . right?

Not according to local Woburn journalist Dan Kennedy, who insists that the real champion in the battle again the Woburn polluters was Anderson. She and the rest of the town had known since 1979 that their water was contaminated, thanks to a state investigation. They even knew for sure that the water caused leukemia—the result of a subsequent Harvard study—all before Schlichtmann graciously volunteered to tilt at Beatrice's windmill.

"Anderson's tenacity—and that of other Woburn activists—led to a new understanding of the environment, to new laws, to stricter standards of accountability for companies that handle toxic chemicals," Kennedy wrote around the time of the film's release. "Schlichtmann's story, by contrast, is one of failure."

And the real Schlichtmann did almost nothing to unearth W. R. Grace's and Beatrice's roles in the pollution scandal.

"Although Schlichtmann decided to sue . . . in part because he knew they had deep pockets, he also singled them out because that's where the government's investigation was leading," Kennedy wrote.

The movie gives the incorrect impression that Schlichtmann was a trailblazer who single-handedly exposed the Woburn polluters. Not so. In fact, the issue was well known—and was the subject of a controversial government study—long before Schlichtmann arrived on the scene.

As for that episode with the twenty dollar bill: Schlichtmann himself insists that things did not happen that way in real life, and that the defendants never would have paid twenty million dollars to settle the case. In both real life and the film, W. R. Grace ended up settling for eight million dollars. Grace never admitted any guilt, choosing instead to settle to prevent the case from dragging forward in court.

Sources and Further Reading

Harr, Jonathan. *A Civil Action*. New York: Random House, 1995.

Kennedy, Dan. "A Civil Action: The Real Story." *Boston Phoenix*, December 18, 1998.

Olson, Walter. "A Woburn FAQ: On *A Civil Action*, Skepticism Is Overdue." *Reason*, April 1999. http://reason.com/9904/co.wo.reasonable.shtml.

American Splendor (2003)

Directed and written by Shari Springer Berman
and Robert Pulcini
Starring Paul Giamatti and Hope Davis

Hope Davis as Joyce Brabner and Paul Giamatti as Harvey Pekar.
© New Line Productions, Inc.

In Harvey Pekar's *American Splendor* comic books, the "hero" dons no costume and wields no superpowers, other than the ability to get out of bed each morning and slog through another day of monotony and disappointment. Obsessive, brooding, and not always mild-mannered, he schleps the blighted streets of Cleveland, working a dead-end job as a file clerk, sleeping too much, compulsively collecting jazz records, and generally seeing half-empty glasses everywhere. Most important, he writes a comic book about himself doing all the above. In other words, he *is* Harvey Pekar. Since 1976, Pekar's starkly autobiographical *American Splendor* comics have chronicled the mundane tribulations and slight triumphs of one "Harvey Pekar," a curmudgeonly everyman illustrated in varying degrees of slouch and paunch, depending on the guest artist pushing the pencil (Pekar himself can barely draw a stick figure).

American Splendor, self-published by Pekar out-of-pocket, broke new ground in comics. In the words of comic artist Robert (as in "R.") Crumb,

Pekar's original and most famous collaborator, "There's never been anything even approaching this kind of stark realism. . . . It takes chutzpah to tell it exactly the way it happened, with no adornment, no wrap-up, no bizarre twist, nothing." In an early issue of *American Splendor*, a Crumb-drawn Pekar considers the untapped potential of comics, musing, "You c'n do as much with comics as the novel or movies or plays or anything. Comics are words an' pictures; you c'n do anything with words an' pictures!" And with that, Pekar ushered in a new genre of autobiographical comic books typified by spare realism and unsentimental introspection.

During the 1980s, as he became more well-known for both his comics and his frequent appearances on David Letterman's NBC talk show, Pekar began to chronicle his brushes with quasi-celebrity in *American Splendor*. By the early 1990s, Pekar's artistic self-replication had begotten several stage plays—and therefore, still more "Pekar" avatars, including actor Dan Castellaneta (the voice of Homer Simpson), who joined a pantheon of Pekars that already included the real one, his variously styled pen-and-ink incarnations, and the late-night TV crank who reluctantly played Letterman's foil. Finally, in 2003 came the ultimate (so far) expression of meta-Pekarism, in the form of *American Splendor*, the movie.

Based on the *American Splendor* comics and also on *Our Cancer Year*, an autobiographical graphic novel written by Pekar with his wife, Joyce Brabner, the movie managed to intermingle all previous incarnations of Harvey Pekar, plus a few new ones. Thus, Pekar's solipsistic storytelling finds its dizzy apotheosis in actor Paul Giamatti playing Pekar watching actor Donal Logue portray an actor playing Pekar in the stage production of *American Splendor*. At other points in the film, we're introduced to a child actor portraying the boyhood Pekar; several animated Pekars; video footage of the real Pekar, circa 1986, sparring with the real David Letterman; plus narration and recurring interviews with the present-day, actual Pekar.

Self-centered though they may be, Pekar's comics have always managed to steer clear of postmodernism and ironic self-reference. His personal narratives are so straightforward, sincere, and unconcerned with self-flattery that they never come across as egocentric as they ought to. On the other hand, *American Splendor*—the movie—is a different animal with a broader agenda. Yes, it intends to faithfully translate Pekar's stripped-down narratives from the comic-book page to the big screen. But the writer/director/husband/wife team of Shari Springer Berman and Robert Pulcini had something more ambitious in mind:

an exploration of the media feedback loop that oscillates between a pop artist, his audience, and his art.

According to Pulcini, he and Springer Berman decided that "what's really interesting about these comics is all of these different perspectives on this one person." As he explained in a 2004 interview with the online magazine CinemaSpeak, "We thought there must be some way to make a movie that had that same feel, which is why we have animated Harvey, Paul Giamatti Harvey, real Harvey, stock footage Harvey—we have all these different Harveys."

Their background as documentary filmmakers (prior collaborations include *The Menu: The Last Days of Chasen's* and *The Young and the Dead*, about an L.A. mortuary-turned-nightclub) clearly informed their approach to *American Splendor*. Part traditional movie narrative and part documentary, *American Splendor's* unusual blend of reality and dramatization strikes the perfect structural note for a film obsessed with the interface between truth and artifice. Thus, we watch the actual Harvey Pekar venting at David Letterman on a video monitor backstage at NBC, only to have the movie Pekar—Paul Giamatti—burst into the greenroom moments later, still fuming about the interview. It's a bit jarring, but that, after all, is the point.

Likewise, the real Pekar's croaking, Rustbelt-inflected narration is a constant reminder that the guy onscreen is just an actor (albeit one who has nailed the part perfectly—all shifty eyes, bad posture, and festering disappointment). The real McCoy's intrusions paradoxically lend an aura of authenticity to the proceedings. "Here's our man," the actual Pekar announces in the first scene (many of his comics begin with that line as well). As we see Giamatti for the first time, the real Pekar feels the need to call the film on its "Hollywood bullshit." "Yeah all right, here's me," he continues, his voice slashing mercilessly through several octaves and vocal cords, "or the guy who plays me, anyway." Later Pekar adds, "He don't look nothin' like me. But . . . whatever."

Thankfully, *American Splendor* wears these movie themes lightly, and with good humor. When Pekar attempts to persuade his long-distance phone pal, Joyce Brabner (Hope Davis), to travel to Cleveland for a blind date, she worries about what to expect. "The way Crumb draws you," she frets, "you're like a hairy ape, with all those wavy, stinky lines coming off you." Not missing a beat, Harvey fires back, "Those are motion lines! I'm an active guy!"

Most of the episodes in the film and much of the dialog are faithful recreations of Pekar's comics. Springer Berman and Pulcini gracefully weave several classic Pekar slice-of-life monologues into their larger narrative, including the hilarious "Standing Behind Old Jewish Ladies in Supermarket Lines" and "The Harvey Pekar Name Story," presented in the movie as a near-death hallucination experienced by Pekar at the height of his battle against lymphoma. The second half of the film draws heavily on *Our Cancer Year*, Pekar and Brabner's collaborative graphic novel (with illustrations by Frank Stack) about that trauma. However, Springer Berman and Pulcini have left out most of the book's sections that deal with Brabner's volunteer work as an antiwar activist.

With so many layers of Pekar, in the end it's difficult, if not impossible, to gauge the accuracy of the film. Fortunately, *American Splendor* comes with frequent built-in reality checks. When the real Joyce appears onscreen—sporting a bob dusted with gray and glasses even more owlish than the ones worn by Hope Davis—she questions her husband's narrative reliability. "Harvey tends to push the negative and the sour," she kvetches. "He just doesn't think sunshine and flowers sell."

The one scene that feels less than authentic is the reenactment of Pekar's final onscreen spat with David Letterman. That infamous exchange had been prompted by Pekar's diatribe against NBC corporate parent General Electric. Letterman blew his cool, and he banished Pekar from the talk show (although several years later he was invited back). Up until this point in the film, Pekar's Letterman appearances are shown in actual archival footage. But for this scene, Giamatti dramatizes the noisy row with the help of a Letterman stand-in, who, even though he's seen only from behind, looks, acts, and sounds nothing like Letterman. In fact, the ersatz talk-show host is so strident and humorless, the whole scene rings false. So why didn't the directors simply use the actual footage of the encounter? According to Pulcini, the actual video footage had been "immediately restricted after broadcast" and was unavailable to them.

For their part, the real Pekar and Brabner seemed pleased with the film's fidelity to their lives. In an interview published in *The Independent*, Brabner said, "I think we feel that everything is honest in spirit even when things have been changed slightly." OK, so some parts "jangle" with her, she added. For instance, "Harvey did not become a vegetarian until after he married me, nor did he have a pet cat until after I brought mine to live with him. Similarly, I'm not really such a hypochondriac."

Brabner continued the list of jangles in a *San Francisco Bay Guardian* interview: "For example, I was busting Harvey's balls about *Revenge of the Nerds* and being very ironic. And Hope [Davis] played it completely straight, so there it is, I'm immortalized as some idiot who thinks *Revenge of the Nerds* is as important as Martin Luther King's 'I have a dream' speech."

But both Brabner and Pekar are pleased with the movie's success. Its long list of accolades includes awards from the Cannes and Sundance film festivals and the National Society of Film Critics, as well as an Oscar nod for Best Adapted Screenplay. Not surprisingly, however, for Pekar, it all boils down to, "What's in it for Harvey Pekar?" As he put it during his press junket to promote the film, "It brings some hope for the future. I'm hoping I can get some work from it."

Postscript: After the film wrapped, Pekar had yet another Cancer Year. He underwent chemotherapy yet again, and by the time of the film's triumphal debut at Cannes, his lymphoma was in remission, and the next phase in meta-Pekar proliferation was already on deck. You see, at the end of *American Splendor*, we catch a glimpse of a Pekar comic book titled *Our Movie Year*. It's just a prop; a fake offered as a final, ironic comment on the endless cycle of life imitating art and vice versa. But by the time of *American Splendor's* release on DVD in February 2004, it was real—packaged with the DVD was an actual *Our Movie Year* minicomic.

Sources and Further Reading

Curry, Warren. "Filmmaking Splendor: An Interview with *American Splendor* Writers/Directors Shari Springer Berman and Robert Pulcini." CinemaSpeak.com, January 7, 2004.http://www.cinemaspeak.com/ Interviews/asdirint.html.

Garrett, Stephen. "The Conversation." *Esquire*, August 2003.

Morrow, Fiona. "Harvey Pekar and Joyce Brabner: The Party Poopers." *The Independent*, January 13, 2004.

Pekar, Harvey. *American Splendor: The Life and Times of Harvey Pekar.* Garden City, NY: Dolphin/Doubleday & Co., Inc., 1986.

Pekar, Harvey and Joyce Brabner. *Our Cancer Year.* New York: Four Walls Eight Windows, 1994.

Wolf, Miriam. "Our Movie Year." *San Francisco Bay Guardian*, September 20, 2003.

Strange but . . . True?

The Amityville Horror (1979)

Directed by Stuart Rosenberg
Written by Sandor Stern
Starring James Brolin and Margot Kidder

Margot Kidder and James Brolin as Kathy and George Lutz.
© American International Pictures

Haunted or not? That's the burning question hovering over America's most famous demonic pre-owned home.

To date, the purportedly true story of the fixer-upper from hell, by way of Amityville, New York, has spawned nearly a dozen horrifyingly crappy movies.

1979's low-rent theatrical hit, *The Amityville Horror*, bulldozed the way for a succession of even lower-rent follow-ups, including *Amityville 3-D* (pointy crucifix comin' at'cha!), a string of made-for-TV add-ons, and a series of straight-to-video knockoffs. As of late 2003, Hollywood was threatening to unleash not one, but two major theatrical remakes. No doubt about it: Amityville is the curse that keeps on giving.

The foundation of the eternal franchise is Jay Anson's 1977 nonfiction(ish) book, *The Amityville Horror: A True Story*. In 1979 schlockmeister producer Samuel Z. Arkoff (whose masterful body of work includes *Dr. Goldfoot and the Bikini Machine*, *Ghost in the Invisible Bikini*, and *C.H.O.M.P.S.*) temporarily abandoned his standard cinematic themes of supernatural beachwear and robot dogs in order to grab up the rights to Anson's spooky book. A national bestseller that had *movie adaptation* written all over it, *The Amityville Horror* recounted the terrifying ordeal of the Lutz family—George, Kathy, and their three wee Lutzes. Shortly after moving into their dream home, a six-bedroom Dutch Colonial manse skirting the waterfront of Long Island's posh Amityville, the Lutzes were besieged by a steady stream of paranormal whatnot.

The short list of infernal irritants included "demons," disembodied voice-overs ("GET OUT!"), glowing red eyes, green-slime–oozing ceilings, hell-spawned houseflies, a basement "pit to hell," and, oh yes, "Jody," the floating demon pig. (There's an implicit lesson here for prospective homeowners—never bid on a house with attic windows shaped like evil eyes.) After ten days of hellish harassment, the Lutzes, fighting off sinister urges to behave like characters out of *The Exorcist* and *The Shining*, fled in terror into the night, never to return, except for subsequent press conferences and televised séances.

As in most horror legends—real and imaginary—there was a relevant backstory attached to the Lutz haunting. In 1974, two years before the Lutz family moved in, the Amityville house had hosted a grisly tragedy: Twenty-three-year-old Ronald DeFeo Jr. had slaughtered his father, mother, two sisters, and two brothers with a high-powered rifle. Apparently, DeFeo Jr. had drugged his family at dinner, then later gone room to room, shooting them while they slept. He was tried, convicted, and sentenced to life in prison. The court found that DeFeo Jr.'s motive was his parents' two-hundred-thousand-dollar life insurance policy. The Lutzes were fully aware of the house's infamous, well, prologue when they moved in.

James Brolin and the real George Lutz (right).
Courtesy of George Lutz

The first of the Amityville movies more or less adhered to the "true story" of the Lutzes' account as laid out in Anson's book. The movie begins with a flashback to the DeFeo murders, suggesting a supernatural connection between that horror and the subsequent, albeit less terminal, evil rained upon the Lutzes.

But how "true" was the tale in first place?

The factual basis of the DeFeo murder case is beyond dispute: Ronald DeFeo Jr. really did murder his family in the Amityville house, and he remains imprisoned to this day as a result. But what of the haunted-house story told by Lutzes? Here's where factual consistency and plausibility begin to evaporate like dry ice in a carnival spook house. Through the years, the Amityville legend has spawned a network of debunkers who preside over a teeming sub-franchise of books and Web sites dedicated to exposing the legend as an outright hoax. Despite counterclaims by the Lutzes and their defenders that it's the debunkers who need debunking, the skeptics make a very convincing case for the hoax theory.

In his book *The Amityville Horror Conspiracy*, the late Stephen Kaplan exhaustively chronicled what he termed "the greatest haunted-house hoax in America." Kaplan's reputation as a paranormal researcher who believed in the existence of supernatural phenomena makes it difficult to dismiss him as a knee-jerk skeptic. What's more, the Lutzes had summoned him to Amityville soon after going public with their tale, giving Kaplan a unique inside perspective on the many discrepancies and ongoing mutations of the family's story.

Among the incongruities Kaplan cites in his book:

- At different times, the Lutzes gave conflicting accounts of how long they remained in the house. They first told local journalists and Kaplan that they had stayed for ten days. Later, they upgraded their tenure to twenty-eight days, which became the timeframe used in the book and the movie.
- George Lutz had contacted Kaplan asking the researcher to investigate the house for evidence of supernatural phenomena. Kaplan accepted, but warned Lutz that if he found evidence of a hoax, he would make it known. Lutz subsequently changed his mind, refusing to let Kaplan tour the house. However, Lutz had no qualms about bringing a parade of less skeptical investigators—faith-based demonologists, werewolf hunters, séance mediums, etc.—onto the property, usually trailed by a phalanx of TV cameramen.
- After the Lutzes sold the Amityville house, Kaplan paid its new owners a visit. They had experienced no supernatural phenomena. Kaplan and a colleague explored the house, and they found absolutely no evidence of haunting.

Kaplan accused the Lutzes of inventing a highly saleable tale after realizing that they couldn't afford their mortgage payments. Naturally, the Lutzes denied Kaplan's charges.

Over the years, more doubts would emerge. Researchers had little trouble debunking the Lutzes' famous claim of finding cloven hoofprints in the snow. Turns out, there was no snow in Amityville on that particular day.

Especially damaging to the Lutz version of events was the story told by William Weber, Ronald DeFeo Jr.'s defense attorney. Weber claimed that he had helped the Lutzes shape their story before they went public with it. Weber wanted to include the Lutzes' "experiences" in a book about the DeFeo murder case that he planned to write. Weber later told the Associated Press, "We created this horror story over many bottles of wine that George Lutz was drinking. We were creating something the public wanted to hear about." When the Lutzes beat Weber to the punch with their own book, the disgruntled attorney filed a two-million-dollar lawsuit against them, charging them with backing out of his book deal. According to Ronald DeFeo Jr.'s wife, Geraldine, who is quoted in a recent book on the DeFeo murders, Weber had planned to use the haunting hoax to secure a new trial for his client.

After the book and film turned the real Amityville house into a favorite haunt of trespassing tourists and amateur ghostbusters, its new owners sued the Lutzes as well as Anson and his publishers. According to skeptical author Joe Nickell, during the trial (the case was later settled out of court) the Lutzes "admitted that virtually everything in *The Amityville Horror* was pure fiction."

A couple of years ago author Ric Osuna asked George Lutz (who is now divorced from Kathy) about the truth in the Amityville affair. Osuna writes, "George informed me that setting the record straight was not as important as making money off fictional sequels."

Sources and Further Reading

Anson, Jay. *The Amityville Horror: A True Story.* New York: Bantam Books, 1977.

Kaplan, Stephen, and Roxanne Salch Kaplan. *The Amityville Horror Conspiracy.* Lacyville, PA: Belfrey Books, 1995.

Nickell, Joe. "Amityville: The Horror of It All." *Skeptical Inquirer,* January–February 2003.

Osuna, Ric. *The Night the DeFeos Died: Reinvestigating the Amityville Murders.* Philadelphia: Xlibris Corporation, 2002.

The Mothman Prophecies (2002)

Directed by Mark Pellington
Written by Richard Hatem
Starring Richard Gere and Laura Linney

Richard Gere as John Klein, a character loosely based on author John Keel. *Photo by Melissa Moseley, © Screen Gems, a Sony Pictures Entertainment Company*

In this eerie supernatural thriller, the title character literally phones in his performance—as a disembodied electronic voice calling Richard Gere and the rest of the cast at inconvenient hours. In the few instances that we're afforded an onscreen sighting of the creature, it's a fleeting apparition, the film equivalent of a Rorschach blotch.

In contrast, the "real" Mothman cut a much more physical presence, according to the dozens of witnesses who saw—and lost much sleep over—a seven-foot-tall, winged man-monster with glowing red eyes. Those encounters took place during the mid-1960s in and above Point Pleasant, a small West Virginia town nestled on the edge of the Ohio River.

The film *The Mothman Prophecies* is loosely based on John A. Keel's 1975 book of the same name, which chronicled the supernatural hijinks and consequent hysteria that swept Point Pleasant between 1966 and 1967. The climax of both the book and the film is the disastrous collapse of the Silver Bridge, a creaky span that plunged into the Ohio River in December 1967, taking dozens of rush-hour commuters to a watery death. The "prophecies" of the title refer to the enigmatic warnings of the Mothman and his paranormal brethren that "something awful is going to happen."

Opting for the less-is-more approach, the Hollywood adaptation of the book is not a creature feature as much as an exercise in suggestive psychological terror. Director Mark Pellington has said that he wanted to make a monster movie without a monster, a trick he mostly manages to pull off. What makes the film truly creepy is its constant implication that something unspeakable is lurking just outside our view. And that's essentially the same ingredient that makes the book such a page-turner: Keel's sober assessment that something unknown (and perhaps unknowable) spent a year wreaking metaphysical havoc on the hapless town of Point Pleasant.

Of course, Hollywood has "improved" on the book in the usual ways: onscreen, the story (and the collapse of the Silver Bridge) has been updated to present day. And the idiosyncratic Keel—a freelance reporter who played a substantial part in the real-life events of Point Pleasant—has been upgraded to aging heartthrob Gere, here portraying a fictional *Washington Post* star reporter called John Klein. While the real Keel, an astute chronicler of high strangeness, zeroed in on Point Pleasant like a curious, well, moth, to an inviting flame, Klein is driven by a motivation straight out of Screenwriting 101, which makes his stake in the story personal: After his wife glimpses the Mothman as a harbinger of her impending death, Klein becomes obsessed with Point Pleasant, where residents are seeing (and sketching, each in the accomplished style of cartoonist Ralph Steadman) the very same creature.

The film tosses in a secondary character who is also clearly inspired by Keel: a paranormal researcher called Alexander Leek ("Keel" spelled backward). Portrayed by veteran character actor Alan Bates, Leek is here to voice the theories that Keel offers in his book—that Point Pleasant's spooks might be nonhuman intelligences from another dimension. They're real, but "just not part of our consensus of what constitutes physical reality."

Thematically, the film is faithful to the spirit of the book. But as someone once said, the devil's in the details. Pellington and screenwriter Richard Hatem chose to compress the sheer sweep of the bizarre events and entities that invaded Point Pleasant into the single figure of the Mothman. In the book (and in reality), the Mothman was just one of a whole slate of unexplained phenomena and outlandish characters found loitering in West Virginia during that haunted year. Hundreds of locals—as well as outsiders, including Keel—witnessed nightly UFO sightings. Many of those who encountered the Mothman soaring overhead or lurking in the woods subsequently reported poltergeist-like hauntings in their homes. Keel and others repeatedly picked up their telephones to hear strange beeping noises or speeded-up electronic voices on the other end.

And many locals also had unsettling visits from those staple figures of UFO lore, the Men in Black (MIB)—otherworldly strangers with foreign features and often kooky mannerisms who warn saucer witnesses to keep silent, or else. In his inimitable style, Keel has described them as "those mischievous idiots who pop out of flying saucers." Whereas Keel's book is as much about the MIB as it is the Mothman, the film steers clear of the Men in Black—probably not just because Stephen Spielberg fiercely guards his copyright on the "MIB" logo. The MIB in Keel's book are often comical: their threatening notes are grammatically challenged; they abscond with ballpoint pens, laughing maniacally as they make their getaway; and one visiting MIB suddenly begins to gasp as if he's having trouble breathing Earth air, then pops a pill and recovers.

One of the key figures in Keel's book is an enigmatic MIB who called himself Indrid Cold. As Keel tells it, Cold stepped out of a UFO and introduced himself to a local appliance salesman named Woodrow Derenberger. The salesman described his new friend as a "heavily tanned" man, five feet, ten inches in height, with dark hair combed straight back and a wide grin. He wore a black topcoat over a "garment made of glistening greenish material almost metallic in appearance." Derenberger's stories of repeated visits from Cold made the salesman a local celebrity of sorts. Eventually, he claimed that Cold took him aboard a flying saucer and whisked him off for a visit to the "Planet Lanulos," in the "Ganymede Galaxy."

The film, however, takes the dramatic liberty of suggesting that the Mothman and Cold are one and the same. (At one point Klein asks Cold, via the telephone, what he looks like, and the voice replies, "It depends on who's looking.") In the film, it is the voice of Cold who warns Klein of an impending disaster "on the River Ohio." In Keel's telling, it was yet another MIB—a Mr. Apol—who began making dire predictions, only some of which proved true. In fact, Apol—whoever he was—never specifically predicted a disaster on the Ohio River; he had warned Keel of a nationwide blackout at the moment President Johnson lit the White House Christmas tree. As Keel got his candles and flashlights ready in his New York apartment, a special news bulletin interrupted the televised tree-lighting ceremony. The Silver Bridge had collapsed in Point Pleasant, killing more than forty people.

The "mischievous idiots" had done it again. "They knew this was going to happen . . . and when," wrote Keel. "And they gave me all that bilge about a power failure. They just didn't want me to be able to warn anyone."

Truth apparently is stranger than fiction—but not quite as dramatic. In the film, Klein is on the bridge as it collapses, which gives him a handy opportunity for some third-act heroism in the form of a selfless leap into the chilly waters to save his leading lady.

Sources and Further Reading

Keel, John A. *The Mothman Prophecies.* New York: Tor Books, 2002.

Sergent, Donnie and Jeff Wamsley. *Mothman: The Facts Behind the Legend.* Point Pleasant, WV: Mothman Lives Publishing, 2002.

Brotherhood of the Wolf (2001)

Directed by Christophe Gans
Written by Stéphane Cabel and Christophe Gans
Starring Samuel Le Bihan and Mark Dacascos

Between 1764 and 1767, a mysterious beast rampaged through a rural province of France, killing and, in many instances, disemboweling or decapitating 100 peasants, mostly young women. The terror wreaked throughout the country eerily presaged the terror that would be wreaked by human hands during the Great Terror three decades later.

More than two centuries after that, the "Beast of Gevaudan" legend, which had rarely been recounted outside of France, became the French cinematic thriller *Le Pacte des Loups* (*Brotherhood of the Wolf*). As obscure French legends go, perhaps none are better tailored for summer blockbusterdom. The movie was, its French producers believed, destined to "beat the Americans at their own game" of raking in boffo box office with big-budget action scenes and special effects.

Unfortunately, obscure French legends are a tough sell to U.S. audiences, no matter how much kung fu is thrown in. And though there is no historical record of chop socky being deployed against the beast, the success of *Crouching Tiger, Hidden Dragon* seemed to indicate that subtitled, historical period dramas could make good money if only they included enough martial arts. The first half of this 142-minute epic follows the facts of the case with reasonable accuracy, albeit with the insertion of several fictitious characters, before the second half flies off into a flight of chop-socky fantasy designed to up the action quotient.

It didn't work. *Brotherhood of the Wolf* earned just eleven million dollars in the United States.

Perhaps the kung fu would have worked better in real life. For close to three years, it seemed that nothing could stop the beast. The monster, whatever it was, not only claimed 100 very real lives, but, in the process of its rampage, destabilized an already unsettled region and ignited a political crisis for King Louis XV.

The basic facts: beginning in June 1764, a vicious animal rampaged through France's Gevaudan region (today known as Lozere), a rural territory south of Paris. What this creature was, exactly, remains a mystery even today.

However, the purported beast was shot and killed in 1767 by a local hunter named Jean Chastel. He was part of a massive hunting party that had been stalking the creature, with great futility, for the previous two years.

La Bête de Gevaudan attacked mostly women, a fact depicted in the film. There was probably no special reason for this gender preference other than the fact that, while the menfolk did hard labor in the crop fields, the women tended herds of cattle and flocks of sheep in open, lonely fields and pastures. The women's work made them easy targets for hungry predators.

While the movie reenacts the hunters' generally misguided attempts to track the beast, there were other efforts made that don't turn up in the movie, including a poisoning program that accomplished little more than wiping out huge quantities of livestock and sheepdogs, both of which were crucial to the livelihoods of Gevaudan's peasant farmers and shepherds.

The beast ravaged more than the throats and entrails of its victims. Its three-year rampage also devastated the Gevaudan region economically. Women became understandably reluctant to spend long days alone, tending sheep on the hillsides. Men took precious weeks away from their crops and cattle to join hunting expeditions. The work that was required to keep the economy moving simply was not getting done, and the sudden upswing in poverty exacerbated already swelling tensions among the peasantry. Three decades later, the peasants of France erupted into revolution.

But the idea of revolt was already in the air in the 1760s, causing Louis XV to pay close attention to the disturbing developments in Gevaudan. He dispatched his royal huntsman, Antoine de Bauterne, with orders to slay the Beast. In 1765 Bauterne shot a 130-pound wolf. The dread beast was vanquished, he announced. But the killings continued. It wasn't until two years later that Chastel finally killed the animal that, it appeared, had actually wreaked havoc on the region. His "Beast" was also a wolf—a deformed one.

In the film, these two incidents are conflated into one. In the movie, Bauterne's wolf was taxidermically deformed postmortem to resemble witness descriptions of the Beast, complete with spikes along the spine. As in real life, however, Bauterne's kill fails to stop the slaughter.

Brotherhood of the Wolf has a narrator, the Marquis d'Apecher, an actual historical figure who, at age nineteen, organized the hunting party that included the alleged Beast-slayer Chastel. Though he narrates, d'Apecher is a tertiary character in the story.

The two main characters of the film are the moviemaker's inventions. We have the king's own "naturalist," Grégoire de Fronsac, and his "blood brother," a Canadian Mohawk Indian named Mani, played by Mark Dacascos, the only American actor in the cast and a veteran of direct-to-video martial-arts pot-boilers. Mani, somehow, knows really good kung fu. But when Mani is slain, he transfers his Indian spirit (because Indians can do that sort of thing) to Fronsac. The once rakish Fronsac accordingly morphs into an eighteenth-century kung-fu commando, complete with scary war paint and outstanding toma-hawk-throwing skills.

This is where the movie takes all leave of the historical record.

Using his newfound tracking abilities (because all Indians are really good trackers) he uncovers the truth behind the beast. The animal itself is not a wolf, but a trained lion permanently encased in a bizarre suit of armor. It's a pitiable creature, a big kitty cat turned into a people-eater by a lifetime of heartless abuse. The abuser, and real killer, is a depraved aristocrat. Along with a rogue priest, the depraved aristocrat masterminds a conspiracy to undermine the king's rule. The Beast's killing spree and the community's attendant unrest are instru-mental to the conspiracy.

In reality, there's no evidence that the beast was anything but a wild animal on the loose. Certain witnesses, however, claimed to have seen the creature in the company of a human being, and the movie's portrayal of the beast as some type of cat "from Africa" also has a basis in the historical record. The tracks of the animal were described as catlike, with protruding claws. Based on the pat-tern of its footprints, the Beast could leap long distances—as much as thirty feet—through the air, which indicates that the animal might have been a jun-gle cat. If it was, in fact, an African cat, it would have required human care to survive in the damp French countryside.

While the "cat" theory may be mildly plausible, there were—and to this day still are—an assortment of popular explanations for just what, exactly, the beast may have been. Was it Chastel's deformed wolf? That wolf may not even have been a wolf, much less the Beast. Its carcass decomposed on the way to Paris.

Other theories held that the beast was actually:

- "punishment from God for the sins of men." Apparently that was sufficient explanation in those days.

- a demon conjured by witchcraft and sorcery. These were also widely accepted scenarios, even in the Age of Enlightenment.
- a werewolf.
- a serial killer, somehow capitalizing on unrelated wolf attacks for cover.
- a wendigo, the mythical beast of Canadian Indian lore. (Perhaps this theory inspired the inclusion of a Canadian Indian character in the fictionalized film.)
- a bear.
- a wolverine.
- a baboon.
- and so on.

The beast even bears some resemblance to the chupacabra, Puerto Rico's fearsome "goat sucker" and a favorite topic for enthusiasts of the paranormal.

We have to also consider the chance that the beast never existed at all. The killing "spree" may have been a string of random wolf and bear attacks, distorted and exaggerated for propaganda purposes. The fabricated tale may have given the king a pretext for establishing an armed presence in a region where revolt was simmering. Opponents of the king, on the other hand, could have wanted to draw that armed presence to further inflame popular sentiment against the crown.

The final possibility is that the beast fell under the heading of what's now called "cryptozoology," the study of unknown species. That branch of science is itself little known, and is usually associated with the Loch Ness Monster, Bigfoot, and other creatures of *X-Files* lore.

Writing in *Cryptozoology Review*, one researcher noted in 1996 that *La Bête de Gevaudan* fits the pattern of seven other serial mauling incidents in the nineteenth and twentieth centuries—including one that involved a "mysterious, blood-sucking, cat-like creature" that killed sixteen people in Bulgaria as recently as 1993. The animals, including the Beast, fit the description of the pine marten, a member of the Mustelid family whose best-known members are probably the otter, the ferret, and the weasel. An ordinary pine marten would be too small to match the "big as a donkey" description of *La Bête* proffered by its surviving victims, but a larger, unknown subspecies of the pine marten could fit all the criteria.

We'll never really know the truth. And even if the pine marten theory could somehow be supported by evidence, it's unlikely that it would have helped this film at the American box office. Let's face it: how many of you out there would pay good money to go see a movie called *Brotherhood of the Weasel*?

Sources and Further Reading

Jones, Alan. "Brotherhood of the Wolf: The Legend of the Beast of Gevaudin [sic]." *Shivers* 82. www.visimag.com/shivers/h82_feature.htm

Occultopedia, s.v. "Gévaudan, Beast of," www.occultopedia.com/g/gevaudan.htm.

Thompson, Richard H. *Wolf-Hunting in France in the Reign of Louis XV: The Beast of the Gevaudan*. Lewiston, NY: Edwin Mellen Press, 1992.

FairyTale: A True Story (1997)

Directed by Charles Sturridge
Written by Ernie Contreras
Starring Florence Hoath, Elizabeth Earl, Peter O'Toole,
and Harvey Keitel

Elizabeth Earl as Frances Griffiths,
with computer-generated friend.
Photo by Framestore, © Paramount Pictures

The real Frances Griffiths with
cardboard-generated friends,
photographed by Elsie Wright in
July 1917.
Courtesy of Fortean Picture Library

The oxymoronic title is a tip-off that you're in for some generous fact fudging. So it comes as little surprise that *FairyTale: A True Story* is based on actual events in much the same way that magical pixie dust is based on actual animated affidavits in the archives of Walt Disney.

The movie dramatizes the so-called "Cottingley Fairies Incident," more often referred to as the Cottingley Fairies *Hoax.* In 1917 two English schoolgirls "shocked the world," as the newspapers used to say, by photographing actual, non–computer-generated "fairies" cavorting about the West Yorkshire countryside.

No bigger than paper dolls, and bearing an uncanny resemblance to the same, the obliging sprites paused from their ethereal reveries long enough to pose alongside the girls in five now-famous photos. Sixteen-year-old Elsie Wright and her ten-year-old cousin, Frances Griffiths, had spent a productive July afternoon in the woods snapping shots of each other gazing matter-of-factly at a merry troupe of winged sylphs and high-stepping gnomes sporting belle epoch hairstyles, theatrical leggings, and an almost two-dimensional visual clarity.

Elsie's mother delivered the pictures to her local chapter of the Theosophical Society (a mover and table-shaker in the spiritualism craze of the day). One thing led to another, and the girls soon became international sensations. Ironically, perhaps, the fairies' "coming out" would not have generated quite so much global fanfare without the help of another utterly fictitious character: Sherlock Holmes. The Theosophists had passed several of the photos on to Sir Arthur Conan Doyle, the creator of the famous fictional sleuth, and Doyle published them in an article about fairies he wrote for *The Strand* magazine.

After the death of his son, Doyle had given the "elementary logic" shtick a rest in order to develop a credulous belief in the supernatural. With the celebrity author's imprimatur, Elsie and Frances's fairy pictures became the topic de riguer everywhere, at garden and tea parties alike. The newspapers stoked the controversy, many declaring the pictures an obvious hoax. Other periodicals, such as the *South Wales Argus*, saw in the photos an opportunity to defend the sanctity of childhood wonderment, as well as an editor's license to overwrite: "The day we kill our Santa Claus with our statistics we shall have plunged a glorious world into deepest darkness."

Meanwhile, Sir Arthur continued to flog the Cottingley fairies in a second *Strand* article and eventually a book, *The Coming of the Fairies*. Tourists and self-diagnosed intuitives flocked to the West Yorkshire countryside, lugging their camera gear and second sight. Despite various keyed-up reports of wee-folk appearances, the fairies stubbornly refused to sit for portraits snapped by anyone other than Elsie and Frances.

Eventually fairy fever subsided, and life in Cottingley returned to normal, with all the kidney, marrow, and suet pudding that entails. Having taken a total of five photos, the girls retired from chronicling the magical fairy kingdom on Earth.

Through the years, a parade of self-righteously objective journalists and showboat debunkers, such as illusionist James "The Amazing" Randi, would tramp through the region, hoping to let the gas out of the Cottingley Fairies legend. Of course, defrocking the "fairies" was about as relevant an endeavor as exposing the heinous Easter Bunny scam. Nevertheless, Yorkshire's favorite fairy story remained resilient, a charming staple of the local lore.

Closure eventually arrived, however. More than sixty years after the fact, the perps behind the phony fairies finally confessed to the *Times* of London. In 1983 Elsie, age eighty-two, and Frances, age seventy-six, admitted that four of the infamous photos had been hoaxed. The magical sprites had been nothing more than paper cutouts propped up with hat pins, they explained. (Hat pins once had many uses, but alas, today, none.) But Elsie and Frances insisted that the fifth picture, called "Fairies and Their Sun-Bath," was real. In 1972 photo experts at the Kodak Museum concluded that the fifth photo was a double exposure of paper cutouts in the grass. Kindly historians tend to give the old gals the benefit of the doubt, proposing that they "accidentally" double-exposed the film, thereby hoaxing themselves.

At any rate, the enchanted gate to the fairy kingdom had long since slammed itself shut when Hollywood arrived on the scene, wielding its magic crowbar. By then, the thoroughly debunked tale offered little in the way of dramatic purchase outside of a Discovery Channel documentary. But as they say in cornball fairy movies, if you believe, it will be real.

1997's *FairyTale: A True Story* is a rather schizophrenic contraption, adamant about the reality of the Cottingley Fairies, while at the same time sneakily acknowledging the hoax. In other words, the film wants to have it both ways. Computer-generated fairies flit about the screen even when there are no people nearby, indicating that the critters are objectively real. But we also get at least half a dozen clues that the girls are faking it all. The hints are just oblique enough to soar over the heads of the kiddies in the audience and annoy everyone else.

One of those clues is contained in a completely fictional subplot that plops illusionist Harry Houdini (Harvey Keitel) into the story. Keitel's Houdini serves as a sort of Greek chorus who all but winks at the audience in acknowledgment of the hoax.

At one point, Houdini tells Sir Arthur (Peter O'Toole, sober) to snoop around the girls' home for evidence of forgery. "Cover your ass," Houdini advises—rather improbably, we might add, as that particular colloquialism would not be coined for another thirty years (by American GIs). Intentionally or not, the line also sums up why screenwriter Ernie Contreras wrote Houdini into the script: Houdini's skepticism is here to affirm, in the most oblique way possible, that the pictures were hoaxed; Houdini is Contreras's own C.Y.A. insurance.

But unlike the actual Houdini, who spent the latter part of his career debunking mystical frauds, Keitel's illusionist is oddly tolerant of the girls' fairy fakery. Because they are nonprofit hoaxers, Keitel's phony Houdini gives them a pass, declaring, "I see no fraud here."

Moviegoers might not detect the fraud, either: Thanks to the miracle of computer graphics, the fairy photos we glimpse in the film are far more realistic-looking than the crude artifice on display in the originals. You can almost forgive the fictional Sir Arthur for believing his lying eyes.

Sources and Further Reading

Ebert, Roger. "Fairy Tale: Fun but Far from Factual." *Sacramento Bee,* October 26, 1997.

Opie, James. "Fairy Tale: An Untrue Story." *Oriental Rug Review,* Vol. 13, No. 2. December/January 1998.

Solitary Phoenix. "The Cottingley Fairies Incident—A Timetable." http://www.solitaryphoenix.com/TLWCottFairyTimetable.html.

The Enigma of Kaspar Hauser (1974)

Directed and written by Werner Herzog
Starring Bruno S. and Walter Ladengast

Kaspar Hauser (1993)

Directed and written by Peter Sehr
Starring André Eisermann and Jeremy Clyde

On May 26, 1828, a strange youth of about sixteen appeared in a Nuremburg town square. He could barely walk or talk, and he carried an unsigned letter stating, "I am sending you a boy who wants to serve his king." The letter went on to explain that this boy had "never been out of the house," and that, "if you can't keep him you will have to butcher him or hang him up in the chimney."

He had been locked in a dungeon, fed only bread and water, for the previous twelve years, cared for by an unknown man who occasionally drugged him to sleep, then cut his hair, washed him, and changed his bedpan. Why he was imprisoned, no one knew. Why he was released was an even bigger puzzle.

In fact, the story of Kaspar Hauser is nineteenth-century German history's equivalent of the Kennedy assassination—part myth, part mystery, complete with nefarious plots, missing evidence, and, sad to say, murder.

Under the wing of a local professor, Georg Daumer, Kaspar learned to speak very quickly. He learned to write. But his most remarkable trait was his total sense of wonder about the world he was seeing now for the first time. Kaspar had extraordinary compassion for every living thing. Even seeing a boy whack a tree with a stick brought him to tears. When he saw the starry night for the first time, he was hypnotized with amazement.

A year after he appeared in Nuremburg, someone tried to kill him. As he sat in an outhouse, a man with a veiled face struck him with a butcher knife. Kaspar survived but was never quite the same. There was then a subsequent attempt on his life, and this one was fatal. On December 14, 1832, not even five years after he was freed from his dungeon, Kaspar Hauser was stabbed to death by someone who lured him to a park at dusk by promising Kaspar information about his mother.

By one Hauserologist's count, there have been over three thousand books devoted to the topic of Kaspar Hauser. But, at least according to the Internet

Movie Database, there have been just two films based on him, both German. Werner Herzog's 1974 masterpiece *The Enigma of Kaspar Hauser* follows a basic factual outline of the story, but in its exploration of the dreamlike qualities of Kaspar's tale, it doesn't bother with most of the complicated details—and freely tampers with many minor ones. The early section of the film, which depicts Kaspar's release from captivity, his appearance in Nuremburg, and his first encounters with other human beings, is taken straight from Kaspar's own autobiography (although Herzog leaves out the "hang him up in the chimney" line from the letter). As the story moves along, however, Herzog strays further and further from the recorded facts, though much of Kaspar's dialogue is lifted from his own writings. Kaspar Hauser was never, for example, put on display in a circus sideshow. (The film's sideshow scene is one of the strangest and most indelible in the film. Signature Herzog, and completely made up.)

As with most of his films, Herzog is concerned here with the absurd beauties and horrors that only a social outsider—someone who doesn't buy into reality-by-consensus—can experience. Kaspar was certainly that. He might as well have been dropped to Earth from outer space. The film's original, German title—*Jeder für sich und Gott gegen alle*—sums up Herzog's philosophy pretty well: *Every Man for Himself and God Against All*. The director—always the consummate "independent" filmmaker (he wrote and produced as well)—displays no interest in solving the "enigma" of Kaspar's origins, or that of his untimely demise.

Peter Sehr's 1993 retelling of the legend, eponymously titled *Kaspar Hauser*, follows the known details of its enigmatic protagonist's life more or less to the letter. Then it goes further. Sehr overlays an intricate conspiracy theory onto Kaspar's astonishing tale.

The short version of the theory is that Kaspar was, in reality, the heir to the throne of Baden. He was, allegedly, born to Stephanie de Beauharnais, the adopted daughter of Napoleon and the wife of Karl, Duke of Baden. Karl and Stephanie's baby died in infancy, leaving Karl without a direct heir. Next in line for the throne was Leopold, the son of the Duchess of Hochberg, Karl's stepmother. As the story goes, the Duchess, intent on seeing her own son become king, had covertly swapped Stephanie and Karl's real baby for a diseased child that was being mothered by a servant. When that child died, it was assumed that the heir to the throne had died as well. Or so the story goes. In Sehr's version of the story, the servant girl's baby—in a scene almost impossible to watch without feeling ill—is dangled by its feet and struck brutally on the neck. The blow, which causes cerebral palsy that kills the baby, is administered by Major Johann von Hennenhoffer, who, according to the conspiracy story (and Sehr's film), murdered Kaspar Hauser twenty-one years later.

As with most plots involving royal families of Europe, the word "byzantine" doesn't even begin to describe it. Sehr lays the plotting on thick. Everyone from King Ludwig of Bavaria—mortal rival of the Badens—to every member of the usurping Hochberg dynasty seems to be manipulating poor Kaspar Hauser to one end or another.

Sehr's message—and he hammers it home—is that the powerful, with their bottomless well of decadence and venality, corrupt and destroy anything pure and innocent in humanity. The nobles and royals in Sehr's film are about as repellent and disgusting examples of humanity as you'll ever see onscreen. Purity and innocence is represented, naturally enough, by Kaspar Hauser.

While the conspiracy theory remains unconfirmed (albeit somewhat plausible), Kaspar's fall from grace is sadly true. As Sehr's film painfully portrays, it actually wasn't so much that he fell, but that he was pushed. Kaspar came under the influence of an English nobleman, Lord Stanhope, who showered him with gifts, fancy clothes, and, by Daumer's account, homosexual "caresses." Stanhope flattered Kaspar with allusions to his "noble" birth. As a result, Kaspar became condescending to the very people who gave him their time and love when he was a terrified foundling.

Stanhope promised to whisk Kaspar off to England and adopt him as a son. Instead, he dropped out of Kaspar's life. Perhaps this British aristocrat simply grew bored with his protégé. Stanhope's association with the celebrity "Child of Europe" was a status symbol. When Kaspar's fame subsided, the novelty of "fathering" the boy wore off.

Perhaps.

Given Stanhope's close ties to the House of Baden, it seems equally likely that the scenario offered in Sehr's film could be correct—namely, that Stanhope was a key player in the conspiracy to manipulate, then murder, Kaspar Hauser, whose very existence posed a dire threat to the sitting royal clan of Baden. Famed jurist Anselm von Feurbach (the man who got torture outlawed in Germany) led the investigation into Kaspar's origins and apparently had it pretty well figured out. With one slipup. He trusted Stanhope. Feurbach never connected the effete Englishman to the Baden cabal. As Feurbach was en route to report his findings, he dropped dead. Before he died, he wrote a note saying that he had been poisoned.

After promising to spirit him off to England, Stanhope deposited Kaspar in the care of Johann George Meyer, a religious fanatic. Meyer ridiculed and beat Kaspar relentlessly. When Kaspar was stabbed, Meyer accused him of faking the wound. After Kaspar died of that same wound, Meyer spread word that Kaspar's story of his twelve-year imprisonment was a hoax. Stanhope—who had ignored Kaspar entirely for almost a year—reappeared after the murder to take up that cause as well. Kaspar, he declared, was a fraud, an imposter looking for a handout who became trapped in his role once he became internationally famous.

According to Sehr, Meyer was working directly for Stanhope, taking money to keep Kaspar out of the limelight and break his spirit. That detail, like most of the conspiracy allegations, has never been proven.

Herzog himself has said that he considers the "Prince of Baden" theory "pretty much bullshit." In 1996 the German magazine *Der Spiegel* sponsored a DNA test, comparing genetic material from the bloodstain on Kaspar's shirt to the DNA of living Baden descendents. (The shirt in which he was stabbed is preserved in a museum.) The test showed no match, ruling out the conspiracy theory. Kaspar Hauser, it seemed, carried no royal blood, or royal DNA. The result "delighted" Herzog.

Not so fast! The question was thrown open again in 2002 when a TV documentary ran a second DNA test, this time using a lock of Kaspar's hair and some cells that remained on the inside of his hat. This time, the results were different. There was at least a tentative match after all.

It's hard to imagine that any determination of Kaspar's heritage could hold Herzog's interest. He finds the investigation tiresome, and it suits his artistic purpose that Kaspar's murder remains unsolved today, 170 years after the fact.

Stanhope receives only a cameo role in Herzog's *Enigma*. He attends a party at which Kaspar, stressed by the pressure to fit into polite society, flips out. The incident is based on fact, but the real Stanhope was undeterred by Kaspar's strange behavior. In Herzog's film, we never see Stanhope again. Nor does Kaspar live with Meyer. He never leaves Daumer's home, and it is there that he dies. (For unknown reasons, Herzog cast the elderly actor Walter Ladengast, who was seventy-five at the time, as Daumer; the real Daumer was just twelve years older than Kaspar—as is depicted in Sehr's film.)

Herzog's most "authentic" touch came not in his re-creation of events, but in his brilliant choice of actor for the lead role. (Herzog once made a film with an all-dwarf cast, and later, one in which all of his actors were placed under hypnosis. He made three films starring the maniacal actor Klaus Kinski, who redefined the phrase "difficult on the set." Herzog was never hesitant about eccentric casting choices.) For the part of Kaspar he selected Bruno S., whose only "acting" experience until then was in a documentary about street performers. Bruno was a diagnosed schizophrenic, the illegitimate offspring of a prostitute. He'd been severely abused and had spent most of his life in prisons and institutions—locked away like Kaspar. The young man was driving a forklift when Herzog discovered him.

Bruno captures Kaspar's marvel and melancholy flawlessly. It's one of the most astonishing performances ever filmed. However, at four feet, nine inches tall, the real Kaspar was a lot shorter than Bruno (as well as André Eisermann, who played him in Sehr's film). Though Herzog deviates from Kaspar's biography far more widely than does Sehr, he injects us directly into Kaspar Hauser's enigmatic mind. A straight recitation of the historical record never could accomplish that.

Herzog's Kaspar Hauser is an innocent in collision with a society collapsing under the weight of its own rationalism. *The Enigma of Kaspar Hauser* is about a metaphysical conflict and its psychological fallout. Even the tragic ending feels uplifting in a way, as Kaspar escapes into his dreams, where he's always felt most at home.

The battle in Sehr's *Kaspar Hauser* is not metaphysical but moral—a clash between the extremes of human cruelty and innocence. The winner? Take a guess.

Sources and Further Reading

Collison, Charlene and Michael Chase. "Kaspar Hauser, the History and the Play." http://www.mask-studio.co.uk/Article.htm (site now discontinued).

Haughton, Brian A. "Kaspar Hauser—Wild Child of Europe." Mysterious People. http://www.mysteriouspeople.com/Hauser1.htm.

Herzog, Werner. "Commentary." *The Enigma of Kaspar Hauser*. DVD. Directed by Werner Herzog. Anchor Bay Entertainment, 2002.

Masson, Jeffrey Moussaieff. *The Lost Prince: The Unsolved Mystery of Kaspar Hauser*. New York: The Free Press, 1996.

Fire in the Sky (1993)

Directed by Robert Lieberman
Written by Tracy Tormé
Starring D. B. Sweeney and Robert Patrick

D. B. Sweeney as Travis Walton.
Photo by Gregory Schwartz, © Paramount Pictures

On November 5, 1975, a twenty-two-year-old woodcutter named Travis Walton vanished in the Sitgreaves National Forest, forty-five miles outside of Snowflake, Arizona. That, at any rate, was the story his buddies brought back to town that evening in lieu of their pal. Walton and six other loggers had spent the day in the White Mountains clearing brush for the U.S. Forest Service. They claimed that on the drive back home, they'd had an altercation with a flying saucer of the eerily glowing, just-hovering-there type. Rather than battening down the door locks, the way-too-curious Walton had jumped out of the truck to investigate. Long story short, Walton had gotten himself between the space vehicle and one of those intense blue-green beams you hear so much about. The space ray "blew him back ten feet," according to Walton's boss and friend, Mike Rodgers, whose first instinct had been to stay in the truck with the other passengers while Walton and the UFO tangled. Rodgers's second instinct had been to stomp on the gas and peel the hell out of there, leaving Walton to fend for himself. Instinct number two held sway for a good forty-five miles, guiding Rodgers and his five remaining workers back to safe harbor in Snowflake.

Hearing all this and not detecting the scent of malt liquor, the local sheriff mustered a search party. Rodgers went along for the ride, showing the authorities the clearing in the woods where it all had gone down earlier that evening. Walton was nowhere to be found. As they like to say on cable TV, he had "vanished without a trace." So had the UFO, leaving behind not so much as a bent twig or otherworldly septic stain.

For nearly a week, Snowflake and the larger world beyond its borders, including the towns of Show Low and Heber, asked the burning question, "Where's Walton?" Fortunately, the answer wasn't long in coming. Five days after his sudden disappearance, Travis Walton just as suddenly reappeared, at a gas station in Heber. He wandered out of the woods hungry, shaken, and ready to relay the greatest story ever told in Northeast Arizona: his dramatic abduction by extraterrestrials who resembled five-foot-tall fetuses with mushroom-white skin.

In the wake of Walton's return, the usual media hullabaloo erupted, with UFO professors and tabloid newsmen rushing in to monopolize all the better rooms at area motels. Though many Snowflake locals took issue with the UFOlogists' faith in Walton's story, all could agree on one thing: *somebody* had been taken. Despite a few early setbacks, including a failed lie detector test, Walton and his story took off like a flying saucer. The *National Enquirer* paid Walton and the rest of Rodgers's woodcutting crew five thousand dollars for the exclusive rights to their story. Walton hit the talk-show circuit and in 1978 released *The Walton Experience*, an abductee memoir with a title that sounds more like a 1970s progressive rock band. Eighteen years after his close encounter of the publicity-generating kind, Walton scored yet again, this time by selling his book rights to Hollywood.

Fire in the Sky, released in 1993, spruced up *The Walton Experience* with a much better title and state-of-the-art special effects that managed to make

Danny DeVito–sized fetus men seem menacing. The film offers quite a few other upgrades to the original "true story." For starters, screenwriter Tracy Tormé (son of singer Mel Tormé) expunged the most damning bit of evidence against Walton's story: the failed polygraph test.

Here's what really happened: Immediately after Walton's return to Earth, a squad of *National Enquirer* newsmen arrived in Snowflake to secure the tabloid perimeter. According to Jeff Wells, one of the *Enquirer* operatives on the scene, a thousand-dollar bribe convinced Walton and his protective brother, Duane, "to shack up with us in a luxury motel on the outskirts of town." The *Enquirer* boys had arranged for John J. McCarthy, the senior polygraph specialist in Arizona, to administer the lie detector test. Walton flunked the test so spectacularly that McCarthy minced no words in his conclusion: the abduction tale was a "gross deception." According to Wells, McCarthy "said it was the plainest case of lying he'd seen in twenty years."

But the *Enquirer* home office was loath to lose its choke hold on the biggest story of the season (perhaps it had been an off year for Sasquatch). According to Wells, his higher ups "were yelling for another expert and a different result." In the end they got both, and they buried the first test.

Perhaps the fetus men returned to abduct multiple pages from Tormé's script, because *Fire in the Sky* contains no scenes depicting Walton's polygraph failure. The film also fails to document the tabloid bribes, the motel safe house, the hypnotic regression sessions that "refreshed" Walton's memory, the Walton boys' longstanding obsession with UFOs, the fact that Walton's family hadn't been terribly upset by the news of his disappearance, or the sixteen-page memo written by Wells and sent to his editors, imploring them "to kill the story," which had been "a lunatic experience from beginning to end."

Of course, Tormé does drop the occasional hint that there might be more going on here than a simple boy-meets-alien scenario. Tormé and director Robert Lieberman send clear signals to us that Walton and his pal Rodgers are in need of some fast cash—the kind that tabloids hand out for freaky UFO stories. The supermarket tabloid crew in its truck is meant to suggest premeditation. And then there are the scenes in which Rodgers (Robert Patrick) and his crew confer almost conspiratorially about sticking to their story.

But all doubt recedes in the third act as Walton's memories come flooding back and the special effects team abducts the movie from believers and skeptics alike. It's all very cool—Walton bursting out of an alien slime cocoon, dangling in a creepy zero-G solarium-type-thing, kicking some space-fetus ass, and getting stuck with lots of high-tech needles—cool, but not exactly true to the source material. In his book, the real Walton conjured a considerably less exotic UFO interior, the highlight of which was a *Star Trek*kish captain's chair complete with armrest buttons that allowed Walton to maneuver the ship.

Fire in the Sky vanished from theaters almost as abruptly as Walton had from planet Earth eighteen years earlier. Hollywood soon focused its intense greenback-seeking beam elsewhere, much to the relief of Snowflake locals. As of this writing, Walton remains the world's most celebrated long-term abductee, and he's sticking to his story. Snowflake, on the other hand, is more or less a space-fetus–free zone. Other tinhorn saucer stops may hype their Roswell Burgers, Area 51 Flavors, and Anal-Probe Floats, but Snowflake makes no mention of alien abductions or space-tripping woodcutters in its tourism circulars. You get the impression the residents would rather "The Walton Experience" had been just another pretentious rock band with two drummers.

Sources and Further Reading

Kennedy, Anson. "Fire in the Sky—The Walton Travesty." *The Georgia Skeptic*, March/April 1993.

Klass, Philip J. *UFOs: The Public Deceived*. Buffalo, NY: Prometheus Books, 1983.

Walton, Travis. *Fire in the Sky: The Walton Experience*. New York: Marlowe & Co., 1996.

Wells, Jeff. "Profitable Nightmare of a Very Unreal Kind." *The Age*, January 6, 1979.

Communion (1989)

Directed by Philippe Mora
Written by Whitley Strieber
Starring Christopher Walken and Lindsay Crouse

Christopher Walken as Whitley Strieber (left), and the real Whitley Strieber
(right). © New Line Cinema

Burdened with an innate sense of the dramatic, writers are forever wrestling
inner demons. Of course, the "demons" in question are usually the metaphorical sort—the possessive spirits of neurosis or single-malt brewing processes.

But then there's the strange case of Whitley Strieber, the high-strung sci-fi
novelist whose personal hobgoblins are apparently quite literal beasties—home-
invading, bug-eyed space midgets, to be exact. His were no mere "issues" to be
"worked out" or self-destructively indulged—Strieber's private tormenters were
real enough to wake him at all hours and administer painful rectal probes. In
his 1987 bestseller *Communion*, Strieber bared his soul to reveal that he had
been abducted, visited, harassed, and ultimately embraced as their "chosen one"
by aliens with "fierce, limitless eyes." Subtitled "A True Story," *Communion*

boldly announced itself as a searching work of autobiographical nonfiction, albeit one by an author whose previous books had been fantasy thrillers about vampires and werewolves.

The critical reviews were mixed. But the book-buying public couldn't get enough of "The Controversial *New York Times* Bestseller!" and publisher William Morrow easily recouped Strieber's "Controversial Million-Dollar Advance!" But were the events described in *Communion* really true, as Strieber insisted (and continues to insist)? Or was it all a brilliant literary stunt by a master of fantasy fiction, as Strieber's naysayers charge? Who knows? Even if the bug-eyed "visitors" are physical, material beings, rather than mere gremlins of the author's imagination, their annoying habit of appearing only to Strieber pretty much makes the distinction moot. How can you gauge the reality of a phenomenon that's invisible to everyone but Strieber (including his wife), apparently defies the laws of time and physics, and leaves behind no traces of its presence? You might as well apply Luminol on a nightmare.

Which makes it pretty pointless to reality-check the subsequent *Communion* movie. But it'll be fun, so here goes.

Apart from its laughable special effects, *Communion* the movie's most memorable feature is the self-defeating decision to cast Christopher Walken as Whitley Strieber. Not that Walken isn't brilliant here, as always. But in a story that's made or broken by the reliability of the central character, it may not have been the best idea to assign that role to Hollywood's reigning king of crazy.

Is the film faithful to the book? It ought to be: Strieber himself wrote the screenplay. And he recruited the director, Philippe Mora, who, according to *Magill's Survey of Cinema*, "also claims to have had contact with Strieber's aliens." Still, Strieber had his problems with the screen translation. "Most of the actors disbelieved my experience and had not the least interest in portraying it with any fidelity," Strieber later kvetched to *UFO Magazine*. The exception was Walken, who "didn't believe me, either, not for a moment, but he is true enough to his craft at least to try to be faithful to the subject." (Walken on Strieber, in *Movieline*: "I believe that he believes it. . . . He's eccentric, in a way that you usually find in England and Europe, where people just go about their business and nobody pays attention. But he's an American, so it's different.")

Strieber also took exception to some of director Mora's dramatic choices. "The screenplay that I wrote," he told *UFO Magazine*, "and the movie that was made were two different things. The screenplay was faithful to the book, but the movie was faithful neither to the book or the screenplay." It's probably safe to ascribe some of Strieber's dissatisfaction to authorial pride. "It was assumed," Strieber told *UFO Magazine*, "that anything Chris Walken ad-libbed would be ipso facto better than anything I had written, so he was free to ad-lib anything he pleased, and he did a lot of that."

Did Strieber mention that everyone on the set was a doubting Thomas? Here he is again, in *UFO Magazine*: "Also, since nobody believed that my experience had really happened, they felt free to change my story when it came to close encounters. Also, the budgetary problems meant that some scenes had to be changed, like it or not. The result was that the close encounter scenes are mostly so far from what happened that it isn't even possible to discuss the differences in detail. Anybody who wants to know what happened should read the books."

We'll save you the eight bucks with a quick visitation from *The Overlook Film Encyclopedia*: "The ending is different from, but no more comprehensible than, that of the book, with an encounter at the cabin replacing an equally unlikely one on the roof of Strieber's New York apartment building, in which the hero disco-dances with the aliens."

Sources and Further Reading

Casteel, Sean. "Hopkins and Strieber Movies." *UFO Magazine*, Summer 2002.

Hardy, Phil, ed. *The Overlook Film Encyclopedia: Science Fiction*. New York: The Overlook Press, 1995.

Magill's Survey of Cinema. s.v. "*Communion*."

Strieber, Whitley. *Communion: A True Story*. New York: Avon Books, 1988.

The Serpent and the Rainbow (1988)

Directed by Wes Craven
Written by Richard Maxwell and Adam Rodman
Starring Bill Pullman

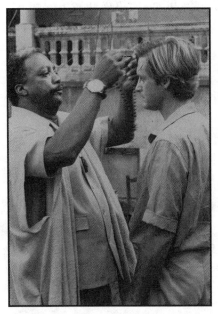

Bill Pullman (right) as Dennis Alan,
a character based on ethnobotanist
Wade Davis. © Universal City Studios, Inc.

The real Wade Davis.
© Universal City Studios, Inc.

Hollywood loves zombies. And why not? The low-budget spectacle of reani-mated corpses clawing their way back from the dead not only guarantees a mod-est box office return, it indulges a fantasy near and dear to show-business hearts: true, the Walking Undead have problems that are completely beyond the reach of Botox, but zombies remain unrivaled masters of the late-career comeback. They're like John Travolta without the Dianetics.

The modern Hollywood zombie can trace his lineage to Haitian folklore, which was exported to American shores during the early twentieth century by condescending Western ethnologists. Their overheated, often racist accounts of black voodoo magic and other less-than-noble savagery proved to be a popular template for bargain-basement Hollywood chillers. In ensuing decades, voodoo witch doctors would transmute a seemingly endless supply of B-list starlets into tranced-out, bedroom-eyed automatons, an all-too-obvious projection of Anglo-America's racial anxieties. Later, zombie movies would evolve to channel other collective fears; George Romero's flesh-eating ghouls in *Night of the Living Dead* were, on a metaphorical level, animated by the urban anxiety and social unrest of the late 1960s.

Although the Americanized zombie has become a fictional cliché—a kind of spook-house Rorschach test—the people of Haiti take their myth of the "living dead" quite seriously. To this day, a significant segment of the population believes that *Voudoun* priests have the power and skills to raise and enslave the dead. Through the years, a handful of visiting ethnographers sought to uncover the roots of that belief, but it wasn't until the early 1980s that Wade Davis, a young botanist from Harvard University, announced to the world that he had unearthed the truth about zombies—which certainly came as a shock to many folks, who had no idea that, when it came to zombies, there was any truth to be had.

Davis's 1985 bestseller *The Serpent and the Rainbow* did more than lay out a case for the existence of real Haitian zombies; it revealed the secret recipe for making a one. Perhaps more important to Hollywood was the fact that *Serpent* offered an entirely new recipe for zombie movies: *Not only are they baaa-aack, they're real!* Thus, a scant three years after the book's first printing, moviegoers were treated to the film of the same name, which assured viewers that the super-weird events depicted therein were "inspired by a true story."

Davis's zombie recipe consisted of a mysterious pharmacological powder that had long been the Holy Grail of swashbuckling ethnobotanists. (Though it may sound like it entails a lot of toad licking and rainforest vision quests, ethnobotany is actually a respected branch of the sciences that is dedicated to studying medicinal plants and the cultures that use them.) Nathan Kline, another ethnobotanist, was also known as a zombie-questing explorer. A pioneering drug researcher who had successfully developed new tranquilizers and antidepressants, Kline spent thirty years in Haiti in a fruitless search for the zombie powder that had long been rumored to exist but had never actually been found.

But in 1982 Kline uncovered a fresh lead: According to the locals, a Haitian man named Clairvius Narcisse had appeared in his sister's village—eighteen years after she had buried him in the local cemetery. Narcisse claimed to have been turned into a zombie and then sold into slavery. As director of New York's Rockland State Research Institute, Kline hired Davis to travel to Haiti, locate Narcisse, and bring back a sample of the powder.

Davis found Narcisse in Haiti, and the man confirmed that he had been exposed to a strange powder shortly before his "death." Completely paralyzed and mistaken for dead, he had remained fully conscious through the horror of being buried alive. Later that night, Narcisse told Davis, the paralysis lifted and he was exhumed, whipped, and forcibly marched cross-country to a distant province, where he was sold into slavery.

Believing that he had uncovered the reality behind the persistent myth of the "walking dead," Davis surmised that two separate drug compounds were involved in the zombification process. The first—a powder absorbed through the skin of the intended victim—was most likely a powerful neurotoxin that caused paralysis and lowered vital signs to such a point that a casual observer might not detect the shallow breathing of the victim. A second drug, administered after the paralysis subsided and the "body" was disinterred, was likely a psychotropic drug that kept victims in a "mindless" zombie state. Narcisse spoke of having no will of his own during his years as a slave, and it wasn't until much later, after he escaped his bondage, that the "trance" lifted.

As Davis tells it, he eventually gained the confidence of several *Voudoun* priests (*bokors*), who allowed him to observe as they created zombie powder from a variety of ingredients, including stinging nettles, poisonous toads, and several species of puffer fish that are native to the waters surrounding the island. Davis concluded that the most probable active ingredient was the puffer fish, which contains a potent poison called tetrodotoxin that is known to induce paralysis and death. Davis returned to the States with eight samples of zombie powder, which he had collected from various *bokors*.

Davis revisited Haiti several times between 1982 and 1984, determined to learn the how and why behind the zombie phenomenon. Eventually he located several of the secret *Voudoun* societies known to islanders as the *Bizango*, going so far as to earn entrée into several such groups and undergo initiation rites. That itself was another breakthrough, as no *blanc* had previously managed to infiltrate the mysterious *Bizango*.

It's no mystery why *The Serpent and the Rainbow* became a bestseller. On top of his scientific coups and insightful anthropological observations, Davis offered the reading public a hale first-person adventure yarn that was equal parts Indiana Jones and Margaret Mead, with a dash of Carlos Casteneda thrown in for good measure.

The inevitable movie version fell to the creative auspices of director Wes Craven, best known for his *Nightmare on Elm Street* franchise. Craven kept the book's central concepts of Haiti, zombies, and the *blanc* scientist questing for zombie powder. After all, from a storytelling perspective, the appeal is the scientific, nonsupernatural basis of the zombie phenomenon. Craven wisely held on to that element. Then he pretty much tossed the rest of Davis's book overboard.

And it's not difficult to understand why: there are certain things the public has come to expect from a rousing zombie film—black magic, evil voodoo curses, and a pretty lady in peril among them. Not one to disappoint the armrest-gripping crowds, Craven liberally mixed the horror clichés into his dramatic brew along with the zombie powder and footage of real Haitian rituals. The result is, well, a bit of a voodoo hash, Hollywood's idea of the best of both worlds. Corpses disgorge spiders and scorpions; blood gushes from walls; inanimate objects attack; spirits materialize like something out of post-production movie magic. You get the idea.

The movie ups the dramatic ante with another plot device not present in the book: a scene in which protagonist Davis (Bill Pullman) is himself powderpuffed, zombified, and buried alive. The actual Wade Davis avoided that fate; Pullman pretty much dives headlong and gung-ho into his makeshift casket. And as if the prospect of being buried alive weren't already horrifying enough, Craven has his evil *bokor* (Zakes Mokae) toss a live tarantula into the coffin for good measure. We're not complaining, mind you: this is the scene depicted on the movie poster (a Gothed-up Pullman screaming, "Don't bury me . . . I'm not dead!"), and we would have felt cheated without it.

Apart from the supernatural hoodoo and assorted Freddy Kruegerisms, the movie's most striking departure from the book lies in the motive it ascribes to zombie makers. After his immersion in Haitian *Voudoun* culture, the real Davis concluded that zombification is a form of corporal punishment administered by secret societies. Only the worst offenders of local social mores—habitual slanderers, philanderers, and greedy materialists among them—are sentenced to zombiedom, and only after a complex series of judgments has been rendered by the *Bizango*. Rejecting the ethnocentric view that the secret societies are inherently corrupt and evil, Davis believes that these particular secret societies operate as a benign local government, one that metes out justice to wrongdoers.

Craven, on the other hand, plays the zombie cultists as fascist control freaks working for the central government of "President-for-Life" Baby Doc Duvalier. By setting his version of the story several years later—1986, to be exact—Craven uses the civil unrest leading up to the expulsion of Baby Doc from Haiti as a dramatic backdrop for the story. It's actually a nifty idea, but it does invert all of Davis's careful cultural reporting. Instead of using zombification as a grassroots form of social justice, Craven's evil *bokors* are turning political dissenters into zombies. So, we've come full circle, back to the Hollywood stereotype of the bad, crazy Voodoo witch doctor gnashing his teeth and rolling his eyes.

The movie concludes by informing us that the zombie powder "is currently under intensive scientific study both in Europe and the U.S.A." Davis's samples did indeed undergo testing at various labs, but the results were somewhat less than definitive. Consequently, by the time the film hit cinemas across America, the book and its author had come under fire from a number of quarters, including some of the laboratories that had analyzed the powder. It turns out that only one of the eight samples that Davis had brought back from Haiti contained tetrodotoxin. And the amount of tetrodotoxin in that particular batch was apparently too minute to cause the paralysis described in Davis's book.

Davis was also criticized for reporting in his book that, in preliminary experiments, rats exposed to the powder had become immobilized for twenty-four hours. The pathologist who had conducted the study demurred, stating that he had not performed a formal set of tests and that Davis's disclosure was premature. Even worse for Davis, subsequent experiments failed to repeat those results. Davis was also chided for emphasizing results that supported his thesis and downplaying or omitting findings that proved contradictory.

Davis fought back in a second book, *Passage of Darkness*, this one an academic tome devoid of the derring-do, first-person narrative featured in *Serpent*. He defended his thesis by noting that different *bokors* created different formulations of the zombie powder. What's more, he reminded his critics that Haitian culture played a role in making the powder work. That is, local belief in the power of the powder gave Haitians a psychological predisposition to succumb to it. In other words, zombification is partly physical, partly psychosomatic.

Although the debate over the validity of Davis's zombie thesis continues to this day, the controversy certainly hasn't hurt his career. Davis is currently an "explorer in residence" for the National Geographic Society.

Sources and Further Reading

Davis, Wade. *The Serpent and the Rainbow*. New York: Warner Books, 1985.

Davis, Wade. *Passage of Darkness*, Chapel Hill, NC: University of North Carolina Press, 1988.

Booth, William. "Voodoo Science." *Science*, April 15, 1988.

True Crime

Heavenly Creatures (1994)

Directed by Peter Jackson
Written by Frances Walsh and Peter Jackson
Starring Kate Winslet and Melanie Lynskey

Left: Melanie Lynskey and Kate Winslet re-create the famous Parker and Hulme photograph in this publicity picture (the scene doesn't appear in the movie).

Right: The real Pauline Parker (left) and Juliet Hulme (right), photographed before they stood trial in 1954. © Miramax Films

As public spectacles of the highest order, show trials often end up revealing more about the society sitting in judgment than about the criminals being judged. Such was the case in the sensational Parker-Hulme murder trial of 1954, which led to the conviction of two schoolgirls in Christchurch, New Zealand, for that especially chilling species of murder: matricide. The evidence against sixteen-year-old Pauline Parker and fifteen-year-old Juliet Hulme was never in doubt. Far less clear were the girls' motives in luring Pauline's mother, Honora Parker, into nearby Victoria Park and bashing her head forty-five times with a stocking-covered brick.

Prosecutors, defense attorneys, the media, and locals who crowded the courthouse weren't shy about advancing theories built on speculation gleaned from the often cryptic entries in Pauline's voluminous diaries. The girls had shared an obsessive intimacy that alarmed their parents. They had also constructed elaborate fantasy worlds with role-playing and rituals that had obvious sexual overtones; Pauline's diaries contained numerous hints of erotic assignations between the two.

Consequently, the less-than-subtle subtext of the trial became "lesbianism as a corruptor of the normal social order (and a precursor to the murder of mothers)." Prosecutors vilified Pauline and Juliet as "dirty-minded little girls" who would do anything to continue their relationship, including removing obstacles to it through the commission of a "coldly, callously planned murder." Juliet's defense attorney also played the lesbian card, but toward a different end, arguing that "their homosexuality was a symptom of their disease of the mind," and therefore evidence of insanity. Meanwhile, the press teased the taboo with winking headlines such as "Wild Infatuation" and "Strange Happenings on Moonlit Lawns."

But in the absence of direct testimony from the defendants, all that fevered conjecture was probably a more accurate measure of the collective fears, ingrained prejudices, and guilty arousals of the spectators. The trial lasted only six days, with the defense failing in the end to persuade a jury that the girls, who had fully confessed to the police, were not guilty by reason of insanity. Pauline and Juliet were sent to separate prisons and forbidden from ever seeing each other again.

During the 1950s it had been easy enough for psychologists, lawyers, and newsmen to characterize Parker and Hulme as either "incurably bad" or "incurably insane" "egotists" driven by aberrant sexuality to murderous impulse. Easy enough, but not very helpful. By the 1990s a somewhat revisionist school of thought began to emerge, as scholars attempted to put the case, the girls, and their motives into a context that wasn't mired in the ideologies and prejudices of Christchurch circa 1950. In their book *Parker and Hulme: A Lesbian View*, Julie Glamuzina and Alison J. Laurie examined how contemporary attitudes about sexuality and class influenced the case and its outcome.

But the most ambitious attempt to put Parker and Hulme into a more meaningful context came from an unexpected quarter: New Zealand splatter-fest director Peter Jackson. Apart from realistic depictions of blood in the murder scene, it wasn't entirely clear what Jackson would bring to the Parker-Hulme film, which he planned to shoot on the actual locations around Christchurch where the girls had played, dreamed, and schemed. But as his writing collaborator (and the mother of his hobbits) Frances Walsh later put it, "We wanted to tell their story from a humanitarian perspective to New Zealanders who've seen the girls as monsters all this time."

The results were impressive. *Heavenly Creatures*, released in 1994, recounts the Parker-Hulme story largely from the girls' point of view. (The movie's title refers to a line in a poem written by Pauline in praise of their "genius.") Meticulously—almost obsessively—researched from court documents, news accounts, and Pauline's copious writings, *Heavenly Creatures* tracks the girls' creepily intense relationship up to and including the murder of Mrs. Parker. (The trial is not covered.) The time line of the story follows the real events with a fidelity not often seen in fact-based movies. Most of the locations are authentic—from the estate where Juliet's family lived (her father, Dr. Henry Hulme, father of the British H-bomb, was rector of Canterbury College) to the row house neighborhood where Pauline's working-class family lived to the prim public school where the girls first met.

Jackson scoured New Zealand for a Pauline Parker lookalike. He found her in fifteen-year-old Melanie Lynskey, a newcomer who delivered a startlingly accomplished performance as the brooding teenager. Because the real Juliet Hulme was English, Jackson wanted an English actress in that role, and he selected Kate Winslet (then seventeen, this was her film debut). While Lynskey's Parker is introspective and dour, Winslet's Hulme is confident and manic—which jibes with descriptions of the real Parker and Hulme.

Jackson and Walsh took the task of getting into the girls' heads quite seriously. In one of the film's bolder strokes, Jackson visually re-creates the complex fantasy worlds the girls created in their "novels," poems, and role-playing. After he learned that Pauline had sculpted figurines in plasticine, Jackson decided to depict her imaginary kingdom of Borovnia as a land populated by life-size clay kings and knights. Those scenes feature Winslet and Lynskey interacting with extras in unwieldy foam costumes that were molded to look like childish clay figurines; it's an interesting conceit that doesn't entirely work. (It's obvious that Jackson felt a certain creative connection with the girls, who had been prolific conjurers of imaginary worlds; a few years after completing *Heavenly Creatures*, Jackson would evoke one of the most elaborate fantasy worlds of all, J. R. R. Tolkien's Middle Earth in his Academy Award–winning *Lord of the Rings* trilogy.)

Although *Heavenly Creatures* succeeds at humanizing New Zealand's most infamous "monsters," it offers few new insights into what it was that possessed Pauline and Juliet to commit the most antisocial act imaginable. In the end, the film subscribes to the standard theory: Pauline and Juliet sought intimacy in each other in an effort to compensate for the lack of it at home. As the friendship developed, it began to take on a sexual aspect (tastefully depicted in the film, in accordance with Pauline's diary descriptions) that alarmed their parents. When Dr. Hulme decided to send Juliet to South Africa, the girls developed unrealistic schemes to stay together. Their plans inevitably fell apart, and Pauline grew despondent—and increasingly deranged. Deeply resenting her mother's efforts to put an end to the girls' mutual dependency, Pauline plotted the murder (writing in her journal, "So next time I write in the diary Mother will be dead. How odd, yet how pleasing") and recruited Juliet to assist in the crime.

In the end Jackson and Walsh opted to use the same old sexual-obsession-as-gateway-to-homicidal-impulse theory—the difference being, they substituted "dirty-minded little girls" with "emotionally self-medicating" little girls.

Postscript: After serving five years in separate New Zealand prisons, Pauline and Juliet were released and given new identities. Juliet rejoined her mother in England, while Pauline remained in New Zealand. Despite ongoing speculation as to their whereabouts, each lived quietly and anonymously for more than thirty years. However, shortly after the release of *Heavenly Creatures*, a New Zealand newspaper tracked Juliet down to Scotland and revealed her new identity: that of bestselling mystery novelist Ann Perry. Speaking about the case publicly for the first time, Perry, who had converted to Mormonism, objected to the film's portrayal of both her and her relationship with Pauline, calling it a gross distortion by "idiotic moviemakers." (She also admitted that she hadn't actually seen the film.) She denied that she had been a lesbian. "I find it grossly offensive," she said. "I was so innocent sexually then." She offered a few hints as to why she assisted in the murder, saying that Pauline had grown suicidal and that "I believed that if I did not do what I did she would take her own life. I'm not putting words in her mouth. All I will say is this is what I believed." She also said that she had been on medication for a chest ailment (she had tuberculosis), and that the drug may have clouded her judgment.

Three years later British newspapers located and exposed the former Pauline Parker, now living in England as Hilary Nathan. The operator of a riding school for children, she was described as "a reclusive, devout woman who attends a local Roman Catholic church every day without fail." According to a neighbor quoted in the *London Daily Mail*, "She is very eccentric and very much keeps herself to herself. She is very well spoken and appears very intelligent and well educated. But she is quite childish in a way." Nathan refused to talk to reporters, but her sister Wendy, still living in New Zealand, told the *Daily Mail*, "She has led a good life and is very remorseful for what she's done. She committed the most terrible crime and has spent forty years repaying it by keeping away from people and doing her own little thing."

Although the heavenly creatures were once again living on the same island, they had not been in touch. Asked for a comment, Perry told the *Daily Mail*, "I'd no idea where she was living. I have not seen or heard from her in all these years. But I hope things go well for Pauline. That is my hope for everyone."

Sources and Further Reading

Abrams, Adam. Fourth World—The Heavenly Creatures Web Site. http://www.geocities.com/Hollywood/Studio/2194/.

Christchurch City Libraries. "Parker-Hulme Murder Case." *Local History*. http://library.christchurch.org.nz/Heritage/ParkerHulme/.

Glamuzina, Julie and Alison J. Laurie. *Parker and Hulme: A Lesbian View*. Ann Arbor, MI: Firebrand Books, 1995.

From Hell (2001)

Directed by the Hughes Brothers
Written by Terry Hates and Rafael Yglesias
Starring Johnny Depp, Heather Graham, and Ian Holm

In the 116 years since he prowled the back alleys of Whitechapel, slicing up London's fallen women, Jack the Ripper, who was quite real at the time, has transubstantiated into a fictional character. It helps that the real Ripper was never apprehended and that, due to the loose standards of police record-keeping in Victorian Britain, there remains barely a clue to his identity. There are at least a dozen "suspects," one as likely as the next.

For those new to Ripperology (an actual subdiscipline of criminology) Jack the Ripper was a serial killer who murdered and mutilated several prostitutes in London's impoverished, crime-ridden East End during the autumn of 1888. He was never nabbed or even identified, and the very number of his victims is in dispute: while five is the generally accepted total, some Ripperologists stick by four, while others put the tally at eight—or higher.

The Hughes Brothers' careless and clumsy adaptation of the epic graphic novel *From Hell,* by writer Alan Moore and artist Eddie Campbell, adopts a conspiratorial theory of the Ripper crimes that had already been exploited by a much more entertaining film, the 1979 thriller *Murder by Decree*—namely, that the Whitechapel murders were not the handiwork of a lone psychopath. The theory contends that the perps were a cabal of Freemasons whose connections extended straight to the loftiest places in Buckingham Palace.

This "Royal Ripper" hypothesis first appeared in a 1973 BBC documentary, *The Ripper File*, which directly inspired *Murder by Decree*, a movie that had Sherlock Holmes and Dr. Watson solving the Ripper mystery. Journalist Stephen Knight, who specialized in researching the Masonic brotherhood, elaborated exhaustively on the Freemason theme in his 1976 nonfiction work *Jack the Ripper: The Final Solution.*

Graphic novelist Moore researched Ripper lore meticulously, pasting a fat section of footnotes in to his comic-book volume of Ripper fiction. Moore repeated Knight, naming royal physician Sir William Gull as the Masonic hit man. Gull, according to Knight and Moore, acted on orders from his fellow Freemasons, and perhaps Queen Victoria herself.

The Hughes Brothers also follow the "Gull did it" thesis of Moore's book. But is Gull a serious Ripper candidate? It's an appealing theory, with its overtones of dark machinations in high places. Thing is, there are very few facts to back it up. By its high scandal value alone, it remains the most fascinating (and popular) of Ripper theories. The entire scenario rests on the presumption that a direct heir to the throne, Edward, Duke of Clarence, sired a child by a Catholic prostitute, Annie Crook, whom he also married. To cover up this potentially devastating affair, the royals instructed Gull to zip the lip of anyone who knew about the baby and the marriage. The only other people who knew were other prostitutes.

Unfortunately, no documentation or eyewitness testimony that supports the occurrence of this illicit marriage has been discovered, nor has any link between the prince and Annie (who was, indeed, a real person who did have an illegitimate daughter).

The Hughes Brothers take some alarmingly broad license with another actual figure from Ripperdom: Frederick Abberline, chief investigator of the case. Diverging from Moore's book, which depicts Abberline realistically, albeit with some added detail, the Hughes Brothers' inspector (played in the movie by Johnny Depp) is a degenerate opium addict with psychic powers. If Abberline left any descendants, this portrait must have irked them greatly. Abberline was a dedicated, distinguished twenty-nine-year veteran of the Metropolitan Police.

Abberline, as far as the public record shows, did not believe that Gull was the Ripper. Abberline's chief suspect was Polish immigrant George Chapman (his real name was Severin Klosowski), a serial wife-poisoner who was hanged for three non-Ripper-attributed murders in 1903. The inspector was quoted in one London newspaper speculating on Chapman's association with the Ripper. When Chapman was arrested Abberline is reported to have remarked, "You've got Jack the Ripper there!" He named Chapman once more in a later interview that he gave after he retired from the force.

Abberline's theory that Chapman was the Ripper, though not nearly as sexy as the "royal conspiracy" theory, depends on almost as many coincidences and assumptions. Obviously, Abberline never compiled enough evidence against his preferred suspect to charge Chapman with the Ripper murders. Most likely, he possessed no evidence at all.

If an inspector on the scene couldn't nail it down, there's little hope that the Ripper enigma will ever be solved as the centuries roll by and the killer "from hell" recedes further into caliginous history.

Sources and Further Reading

Knight, Stephen. *Jack the Ripper: The Final Solution.* London: Granada Publishing Ltd., 1977.

Moore, Alan and Eddie Campbell. *From Hell: Being a Melodrama in Sixteen Parts.* Paddington, Australia: Eddie Campbell Comics, 1999.

Rumbelow, Donald. *Jack the Ripper: The Complete Casebook.* Chicago: Contemporary Books, 1988.

Ryder, Stephen P. and John A. Piper. Casebook: Jack the Ripper. http://www.casebook.org.

Monster (2003)

Directed and written by Patty Jenkins
Starring Charlize Theron and Christina Ricci

Charlize Theron as serial killer Aileen Wuornos. © *Newmarket Film Group*

If you're determined to make a movie about a sad, tragic female character driven to commit murder for the sake of love, Aileen Wuornos shouldn't be the first subject to pop into your head. Nevertheless, that seems to have been the case for Patty Jenkins, who wrote and directed the highly acclaimed, in-no-way-accurate *Monster*.

When Wuornos was caught in 1991 the press branded her "America's First Female Serial Killer." That was hyperbole. She couldn't have been the *first*. There have certainly been previous violently antisocial psychopaths who murdered repeatedly without remorse and who also happened to be women. In any event, Wuornos was one of them. She demonstrated her credentials when she ruthlessly shot to death six men, and probably a seventh whose body was never found.

Hardly a likely candidate for a heart-tugging portrayal. That, however, is how director-writer Patty Jenkins chose to present Wuornos in *Monster*, aided by a "nominate me" performance by Charlize Theron as the since-executed murderess. Theron transformed herself into Wuornos by burying her ethereal beauty under twenty extra pounds, a prosthetic overbite, and lots of freckle makeup. Somehow, Theron managed to make herself uglier than the real Wuornos.

Taken as fiction, *Monster* is an oddly touching film. Jenkins must have some skill to conjure up sympathy for a serial killer, and, with Theron's help, she pulls it off spectacularly. Sad to say, she does it by fudging.

The opening of the film delivers the requisite "based on a true story" epigraph in big, bold lettering. The question is, why? Message to Patty Jenkins: it's fine to make a movie about a desperate, abused rape victim with nothing left to lose, but don't try to tell us it's based on anything that resembles the actual facts.

There's nothing wrong at all with telling a serial killer story from the killer's point of view (as Wuornos, Theron not only appears in almost every shot, she narrates, too). But to claim that your film is based on truth when you've twisted details to make the killer a palatable, even rather likeable character goes a bit beyond dramatic license—it's dishonest. And if you happen to have any feeling for Wuornos's victims or their families, many of whom are still around, it could even be considered offensive.

The real Wuornos was obviously a psychopath (or "sociopath," to use the currently preferred term). However, as crime writer Sue Russell (who wrote a book about the case) noted, "she did not exhibit the mask of charm so often present in sociopathic personalities." According to one psychologist referenced by Russell, "where that charm is lacking, it's often replaced by a superficial but convincing way of making you feel sorry for them."

Jenkins and Theron appear to be convinced.

Aileen "Lee" Wuornos had already done prison time before she began her yearlong killing spree along the Florida highways in early December 1989. When she confessed, at the urging of her lover Tyria Moore (called Selby Wall and played by Christina Ricci in the movie), she claimed that all of her victims had attempted to rape her, and that she killed only in self-defense. The first man to die at her hands, according to Wuornos's initial confession, not only raped her but beat her, sodomized her, and tortured her by dousing her lacerated skin with rubbing alcohol.

As publicity surrounding the "first" female serial killer rolled in (first or not, Wuornos was a novelty act), she embellished her story in, seemingly, every interview she granted. And why not? Hollywood was calling, and Wuornos, uninformed about the "Son of Sam" laws that prohibit criminals from receiving money for the sale of their stories, thought she was in line to make a bundle.

All that resulted from the initial onslaught of option inquiries, however, were a crappy TV movie, which aired just a few months after Wuornos's trial, an opera (yes, an opera), and a straight-to-video movie bearing the ham-handed title *Damsel of Death*, which was nonetheless truer than *Monster* in that it showed Wuornos committing her murders naked, which she did. (She also stripped some of the bodies nude before dumping them.) While she's never been classified as a sex killer, there were obvious sexual overtones in her murders.

After a decade on death row, Wuornos recanted her "self-defense" claims. She admitted that she gunned down her victims in cold blood. She would kill again if given the chance, she said, "because I've hated humans for a long time." Jenkins buys Wuornos's rape story, for the first killing anyway, and the movie's scene leaves little to the imagination; it even includes Wuornos's inventive detail about rubbing alcohol. Although, as her fictionalized rampage continues, we see Wuornos's victims becoming increasingly "innocent," the rape scene sets us up. It is the "inciting incident" (to use the screenwriter's term) that triggers the rest of Wuornos's story, and more important, it is designed to make the audience, as Bill Clinton would say, feel her pain.

Except, by Wuornos's own admission, it never happened.

Theron plays Wuornos as a hard customer, to be sure, but one with a mushy center. All she's looking for is love. She does her best to shield her lover from the truth about her murders. She even feels remorse. As she shoots her last one, she breaks into sobs, as if her trigger finger is under the control of forces greater and crueler than herself—as her whole life has been.

According to Tyria Moore (she testified against her ex-girlfriend), the real Wuornos never tried to hide what she was doing. After committing one of her murders, she'd return in high spirits to whatever dingy hotel room or trailer they happened to be shacking up in, bragging about her crimes. Moore wouldn't let her go on with the details. She didn't want to be involved, and she fooled herself into believing that what she didn't know couldn't hurt her.

Wuornos planned her killings carefully. On most days she turned tricks on the highways, just like normal. But certain days she designated as "kill days."

On those days she packed a "kill bag," complete with a bottle of Windex to cleanse the dead men's cars of fingerprints and bloodstains. The murder victims in the film are the sketchiest of characters. None bear more than a slight resemblance to their flesh-and-blood counterparts. Some are not seen on screen at all.

Theron's version of Wuornos tones down the woman's highly obnoxious demeanor. Wuornos unadorned would not be a person to whom movie audiences could easily "relate." Nor would she offer an appealing career move for a hot young starlet, even one who was willing to submerge herself in layers of fat and ugly makeup. In addition to indulging the not-so-likeable habit of killing people, Wuornos almost always exhibited a violent temper and no control over her aggressive impulses. Quick to curse out anyone who happened to perturb her, which was everyone, she also showered profanities even on those who tried to help her.

At the end of the film, Theron's Wuornos tells the judge who sentences her to death, "I hope you rot in hell." But that's nothing compared to the relentless bile Wuornos actually spewed forth throughout her trial. Her death sentence was decided by a jury. As jurors prepared to deliberate her fate, Wuornos chose that moment to holler at them, "I hope you get raped! Scumbags of America!" After pleading no contest to the additional murders (she was tried for only one) she told the prosecutor, "I hope your wife and kids get raped in the ass."

Monster ends with Wuornos's conviction, but the eleven years between her trial and her death made for a bizarre, elongated epilogue to her unfortunate saga. Part two of the Aileen Wuornos story was the Hollywood story. Her defense lawyer somehow got involved in brokering her rights to film companies. The police detectives who caught her sold their own rights. The feeding frenzy was such that British guerilla documentarian Nick Broomfield descended on the scene. The result was his acerbic film *Aileen Wuornos: The Selling of a Serial Killer*, which portrayed almost everyone around Wuornos as tawdry and greedy.

The strangest development came courtesy of a born-again Christian woman named Arlene Pralle, who wrote a sympathetic letter to Wuornos because, she said, Jesus instructed her to. She visited Wuornos in prison many times, and she eventually legally adopted the serial killer as her daughter. She never really explained why, but when Wuornos started confessing that her self-defense stories were bogus, Pralle backed off of her maternal duties.

Those duties ended once and for all on October 9, 2002. Earlier that year, Wuornos ordered her lawyers to call off their appeals. She lobbied for her own execution by lethal injection. Florida's Governor Jeb Bush granted her wish.

Wuornos herself provided one final piece of weirdness with her last words: "I'll be back, like *Independence Day* with Jesus. June 6, like the movie, big mother ship and all. I'll be back."

There's little doubt that some Hollywood producer will be waiting for her, option check in hand.

Sources and Further Reading

Macleod, Marlee. "Aileen Wuornos: Killer Who Preyed on Truck Drivers." Court TV's Crime Library. http://www.crimelibrary.com/notorious_murders/women/wuornos/1.html.

Russell, Sue. *Lethal Intent*. New York: Pinnacle Books, 2002.

Murder in the First (1995)

Directed by Marc Rocco
Written by Dan Gordon
Starring Kevin Bacon, Christian Slater, and Gary Oldman

Kevin Bacon as Henri Young.
Photo by Anthony Friedkin, © Warner Bros. and Le Studio Canal+

Dan Gordon cowrote the screenplay for *The Hurricane*, which he uninhibitedly embellished in order to prop up its message. Four years earlier, Gordon had done the same thing, liberally fictionalizing the true story of Henri Young to drive home some point or other about the inhumane treatment of prison inmates. It's always refreshing when a studio movie actually attempts to confront a social problem, rather than churn out another piece of eye candy, but it's also rather frustrating when moviemakers use a true story to make their point, then fill their film with fiction after fiction.

It's difficult to tell what the point of *Murder in the First* is supposed to be. Young's 1941 trial for the murder of a fellow inmate led to the closing of the infamous "dungeons" of Alcatraz, where prisoners served time in solitary confinement for a variety of rule infractions, but the story presented in the film is fictionalized and sanitized past the point of recognition.

In the film, Kevin Bacon plays Young as an abused innocent, incarcerated for stealing five dollars out of a post office cash register after he'd been turned

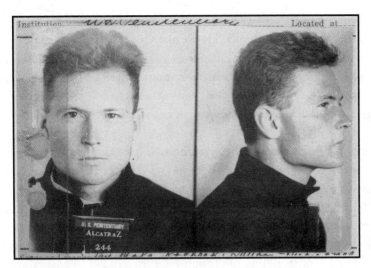

Alcatraz inmate Henri Young. *Courtesy of the National Archives and Records Administration—Pacific Region (San Francisco)*

down for a job and could not support his sister (the movie depicts the two as orphans). The fictional Young loves baseball and is still a virgin.

While in Alcatraz, Young participates in a botched escape attempt and is thrown in "the hole"—that is, solitary—for three straight years. During that time, he is periodically visited by the deputy warden (Gary Oldman), who tortures him. The chief warden is blissfully unaware of this situation because he's also in charge of two other prisons and spends very little time at any of them.

Young emerges from this ordeal, understandably, an emotional wreck. Within minutes of his release into the general population he goes berserk and stabs the prisoner who ratted him out in the neck, with a spoon. At his murder trial, his idealistic young public defender (Christian Slater) puts Alcatraz itself on trial for its cruel and unusual conditions. Despite pressure from powerful people in high places—the bad guys even beat him up—the irrepressible attorney wins Young a conviction for involuntary manslaughter rather than murder in the first degree, which would have sent Young to the gas chamber. In addition, the jury makes an impassioned plea for a full investigation of conditions at Alcatraz.

The broad outline of the screenplay is, basically, true. Young did spend a lot of time in solitary, though not three unbroken years. His cell was not a nice place by any means, but it was not a dank, pitch-black dungeon where he was stripped naked. And Young's trial did lead to an investigation of Alcatraz. But, as the writer would with Rubin "Hurricane" Carter, Gordon cleaned up Young and his past to the point that he appears in the movie to be something like a Zen monk. As if torture and persecution is only objectionable when it happens to the pure of heart and deed. The real Henri Young left home to become a teenage hobo, robbed a bank, and murdered a man in the midst of holding up a bakery.

As with *The Hurricane*, when the filmmakers need to stretch so far into fantasy to make their point, you have to wonder if they have one at all.

Young was no model prisoner. He had a lengthy record of creating disturbances, instigating inmate strikes, vandalizing his own cell, shouting at guards, and generally being a handful. He murdered Rufus McCain more than a year after he got out of solitary, and not with a spoon to the jugular in a fit of psychotic rage, but with a knife to the gut. He'd tried to kill McCain once before, as well. In short, Henri Young was a bad person. That's why it was widely believed that his claims, during his murder trial, that the Alcatraz brass got medieval on his ass were met with as much skepticism as horror.

The crusading lawyer in the movie who starts off defending the helpless Young and ends up befriending him never existed. In reality, Young had two lawyers, Sol Abrams and James M. MacInnis, who, like the Slater character, did announce to the world that they were "putting Alcatraz on trial." They succeeded in doing just that. Both Abrams and MacInnis were very young, because that's what Henri Young wanted. He requested "the most youthful attorneys I can get." In the movie he makes no such request. He can't, because he is catatonic. His lawyers also claimed, as part of Young's defense, that McCain made homosexual passes at their client.

But the liberty-taking doesn't end there. The actual warden of Alcatraz at the time, James A. Johnston, was not in charge of any other prisons and in fact, far from being an infrequent visitor to Alcatraz, lived in a house on the island. It is also untrue that, as stated in the movie, thirty-two men were transferred out of Alcatraz to mental institutions after spending time in the dungeons.

In the film and in life, Henri Young won his case. In the film, Young's courtroom victory is the culmination of his life. He returns to Alcatraz and commits suicide rather than endure continued torture there.

The real Henri Young underwent—or perhaps faked—a religious conversion, then schizophrenia. He got himself transferred out of Alcatraz and was at last released from prison in 1972, at which point he disappeared. He was sixty-one years old. It seems unlikely, but it is at least possible that he lived to see the movie that portrayed him as a martyr. If he did, he probably laughed, knowing he'd gotten away with another one.

Sources and Further Reading

Federal Bureau of Prisons. "*Murder in the First* and the U.S. Penitentiary, Alcatraz." http://www.bop.gov/ipapg/ipafirst.html.
Gazis-Sax, Joel. "Alcatraz: The Warden Johnston Years." http://www.notfrisco 2.com/alcatraz/index.html.

City by the Sea (2002)

Directed by Michael Caton-Jones
Written by Ken Hixon
Starring Robert De Niro and Frances McDormand

Whenever a film is billed "inspired by real events," you know it really means, *"considerably tidied up* from real events—with more and better redemption."

The untidy reality behind the orderly crime melodrama *City by the Sea* was explored by the late Mike McAlary in a 1997 *Esquire* magazine article about "a good cop wedged between a killer grandfather and a murderous grandson." The real-life cop was Vincent LaMarca, a retired twenty-year veteran of the Nassau County Police Department in Long Beach, New York. A faded resort town on an island near the southwestern tip of Long Island, Long Beach somewhat nostalgically hails itself the "City by the Sea." McAlary more bluntly describes it as "seedy, like bad Florida."

In stark contrast to the resort's downward mobility was Sergeant LaMarca's personal journey, which was upward by his own bootstraps from the most ignominious childhood circumstances. When LaMarca was just eleven years old, his father, Angelo LaMarca, was executed at Sing-Sing for the kidnapping and murder of an infant. Just days before going to the electric chair, Angelo confessed his guilt to his son, Vinnie. Unable to pay off his crushing debts, Angelo had been driven by desperation—and apparently his own personal demons—to snatch a child in broad daylight from its parents' home in a middle-class Nassau County neighborhood. Angelo left a note demanding two thousand dollars in ransom money, but the next day he panicked and left the child face down in the woods to die.

Vinnie and his younger sister grew up feeling the shame of their father's crimes—a kind of guilt by association. The local police treated the LaMarca children with kindness, "virtually adopt[ing]" them. After finishing high school, Vincent LaMarca entered the police academy and became a cop. It was partly an act of personal penance and partly an effort to redeem the family name. He joined the Nassau County police force, married the stepdaughter of the police chief, and over the course of a two-decade career earned a reputation as an incorruptible "hero cop."

Seven years after his retirement, LaMarca learned that his twenty-four-year-old son Joey had fled New York State after brutally murdering a tattooed ex-con named James Winston on a public beach fifteen miles north of Long Beach. The crime itself made little sense; strung out on angel dust for more than a week, Joey LaMarca apparently believed he was avenging a drug-addict-turned-Jesus freak who ran a local dive called the Bagel Club. ("I want to walk with Jesus," LaMarca had babbled incoherently to friends.) Winston and an accomplice had unsuccessfully attempted to rob the Bagel Club, a ludicrous effort that collapsed when they crashed through the ceiling tiles from the crawlspace where they were hiding. Later, Joey LaMarca and a friend jumped Winston on the beach. LaMarca repeatedly stabbed Winston in the back and in the chest before slitting his throat.

For Vincent LaMarca, who was then living in quiet retirement in Florida, it was as if a family curse had returned, despite all of his efforts at personal contrition. The Texas Rangers eventually caught up with Joey near Houston. Back in New York, Joey pled guilty to manslaughter and is now serving a sentence of fifteen to twenty-five years at an upstate prison.

As a generational tragedy of family guilt and redemption, the true story of Vincent LaMarca seems to be tailor-made for a film adaptation. Too bad director Michael Caton-Jones and screenwriter Ken Hixon felt the need to iron out the story's existential vicissitudes in favor of flat Hollywood psychology.

Whereas the actual LaMarca saga is marked by untidy, but altogether real-life ambiguities (why grandfather and grandson chose to kill remains somewhat mysterious), the film opts to frame the story as a standard tale of redemption and family crisis. In the film, Joey is a good boy gone bad (but not too bad) because he's been abandoned by his father. Meanwhile, Robert De Niro's Vincent LaMarca is not so much a man unable escape a haunted past as he is a father in denial who refuses to come to terms with past failures, including the murder committed by his father and his own failed first marriage. Instead, he turns inward and does what deadbeat dads do in big-screen melodramas: neglect their sons, thus driving junior to a life of crime.

Things were not so neatly arranged in the actual LaMarca family. In the *Esquire* story, McAlary ponders the criminal atavism that seems to plague the LaMarcas; a "murder gene," as Joey calls it, that skips from generation to generation. Both Joey and his grandfather struggled with mental illness, the grandson especially, having alternated between self-medicating and spending time in mental institutions. "There's a disease in my mind," Joey told McAlary. "My grandfather had it, too." The film avoids this angle entirely, never mentioning insanity as a possible motivator.

Vincent LaMarca, an unreconstructed cop who believes in personal accountability, strongly disagreed with his son's talk of "murder genes." "I always took the attitude," he told McAlary, "that you are responsible for your actions." In the movie, De Niro says the same, but the filmmakers undercut the honesty of the statement by tritely ascribing the LaMarca curse to a dearth of family values.

The film cleans up a half dozen other untidy elements of reality:

- Onscreen, Joey kills Winston in self-defense, rather than in a pique of crazy-bad homicidal rage.
- The cop investigating the murder just happens to be De Niro's Vincent LaMarca, satisfying the Hollywood screenwriter's rule to "make it personal."
- The filmmakers invent out of whole cloth a drug-dealing biker villain who frames Joey for a second murder, the shooting of De Niro's cop partner (now it's even *more* personal!), another invented character.
- The evil biker villain allows for a ridiculous, confusing denouement (which never really happened) in which De Niro and son mutually redeem themselves by saving each others' lives and killing the aforementioned evil biker villain.

In the end, family order is restored. Father and son are reunited through the bonding ritual of violence. In Hollywood, if not in real life, the family that slays together stays together.

Sources and Further Reading

McAlary, Mike. "Mark of a Murderer." *Esquire*, September 1997.

Blow (2001)

Directed by Ted Demme
Written by David McKenna and Nick Cassavetes
Starring Johnny Depp and Penelope Cruz

Paul Reubens as Derek Foreal.
Photo by L. Sebastian, © New Line Cinema

Anyone who ever watched an episode of *Miami Vice* knows that the cocaine explosion of the 1980s was the dastardly doing of ruthless Colombians. The Medellin Cartel even made the cover of *Time* and *Newsweek*. "Cocaine cowboys," who'd just as soon murder your mother and rape your father as look at you, assumed their place in the decade's pantheon of villainy, equaling only Mohammar Kaddafi in their ability to elicit dread. At the end of the decade, the United States actually invaded a foreign country on the pretext that its strongman leader, Panamanian dictator Manuel Noriega, was in cahoots with the cocainistas.

What we didn't hear was that the Colombian coke kingpins couldn't have gained their franchise in the States without the aid of an American drug smuggler, a Massachusetts native (complete with thick Boston accent), named George Jung.

Given the social consequences of the cocaine epidemic, one would be tempted to consider Jung a master of evil. Unless, of course, one were to judge by *Blow*, the final film from late director Ted Demme.

As played by Johnny Depp, Demme's version of Jung is a likeable, fun-loving kid from the burbs of Boston out to turn a quick buck, with no other aim than to finance the never-ending party he calls "life." Yearning to break free of his New England roots and lovable loser of a dad, Jung emigrates to the virgin turf of Manhattan Beach, California, in the late 1960s. He quickly becomes the leading marijuana connection for the surfer dudes and buxom stewardesses that populate the beach. But the real money starts rolling in when a friend from home shows up and, wildly impressed with the quality of George's stash, informs him that there's a bundle to be made peddling this primo reefer to college kids back in Massachusetts.

The screenplay is basically accurate in its presentation of Jung's early years as a pot peddler, though events are, of course, condensed. Jung's attempts at legal employment are omitted. In real life, he started a business importing Mexican sandals, and later took a job operating a pile driver. The Depp version of Jung makes an instant leap from beach bum to marijuana maven. Additionally, likely for legal reasons, Jung's real-life partner-in-crime, Richard Barile, is transformed from a bushy-bearded ex-Marine into a screamingly gay hairdresser called "Derek Foreal," who is played with androgynous abandon by Paul "Pee-Wee Herman" Reubens.

Barile owned a hair salon—that much was true. He capitalized on the then-novel fashion for men to wear long hair. He learned how to trim and style such coiffures at a time when most barbers knew only two cuts—buzz and buzzier. He kept a pool table in his front room and cut hair out of sight in the back, to maintain an atmosphere of machismo. He did not—most *definitely* did not—deal drugs out of his shop. Even in the laissez-faire climate of Manhattan Beach circa 1967, Barile maintained a healthy paranoia, storing his stash off-site and employing runners to retrieve it. In the film, Reubens's character yanks a pillow-sized pouch of the chronic from a wooden cabinet in his shop and tosses it to Depp as if it were a beach ball.

Also true is an amusing bit showing Jung's attractive stewardess gal pal ferrying parcels of pot back east. What is not true is that this fetching young thing died of brain cancer, or any kind of cancer. It's a bizarre incident to invent, but, for the film's storytellers, her "death" provided a device for getting her out of the picture.

Jung's actual arrest in Chicago for possession of sixty pounds of marijuana comes, in the movie, shortly after the fictional demise of his gal pal. The bust was the pivotal moment in George Jung's life and in the history of the American cocaine epidemic. After a brief period as a bail-jumping fugitive, Jung was incarcerated at a federal correctional facility in Danbury, Connecticut. There, he met a diminutive, intense, fastidious Colombian auto thief named Carlos Lehder.

Lehder was famous in the Danbury pen for picking the brains of his fellow inmates, who were mostly white-collar, nonviolent offenders. Lehder kept copious, detailed notes in thick manila folders fastened with string. From an embezzling bank executive, he learned the finer points of money laundering. From a Medicare-scamming doctor, he learned how to hide out on Caribbean islands. From Watergate burglar G. Gordon Liddy, he learned how to crease his pants and project an air of unquestionable authority.

From George Jung, Lehder learned how to smuggle drugs. But marijuana was not what Carlos Lehder had in mind. He was acquainted, in his hometown of Medellin, with a major Colombian criminal named Pablo Escobar, who was already making millions in the international cocaine trade. Escobar was looking to expand his U.S. business dramatically. With the newly educated Lehder and a few other top Colombian gangsters, he formed what became known as the Medellin Cartel.

George Jung became the American connection for the Medellin Cartel. More than any other U.S. citizen, he was responsible for the flood of cocaine that overran America's inner cities, suburbs, Hollywood parties, and corporate boardrooms in the late 1970s and early 1980s.

Pablo Escobar was dead by the time *Blow* was made—gunned down by Colombian police and U.S. drug enforcement agents. He is, therefore, represented in the film as his own unsettling self. He makes quite an onscreen impression in his first meeting with Jung, ordering an underling to execute an informant in front of Jung's eyes. But that was nothing—the real-life Escobar shot the informant himself.

Lehder, on the other hand, remains alive and in the federal witness protection program (albeit incarcerated under a false identity) after testifying against the above-mentioned Noriega. His character in the film is called Diego Delgado, but more than his name was changed. In keeping with the happy-go-lucky tone of Ted Demme's movie, which takes a boys-will-be-boys approach to cocaine trafficking, no mention is made of Lehder's motivations for blowing open the U.S. coke market. It was about more than money. Lehder saw himself as a latter-day Che Guevara, but he was not a Marxist. Lehder was a Hitler-worshipping fascist.

Lehder believed that Americans were too soft to resist the lure of the drug, and that if rock stars and movie stars did it, the rest of the country would follow slavishly along. Soon, Lehder predicted, the moral and political fabric of the United States would lie in tatters, ripped apart by what he called the "atomic bomb" of cocaine.

He was correct on all counts.

Though an American flag waves behind the opening titles of *Blow*, there's no mention in the movie of Lehder's politics, or of any social consequences of the cocaine trade. The word "crack" is never uttered. Demme drew up his drug-smuggling hero as a charismatic outlaw, a system-bucker in the great American tradition. The film goes so far as to invent a period of "retirement" for Jung, in which he swears off the cocaine business, making his final bust all the more poignant. The real George Jung never dropped out of the drug trade, never tried to go straight, and ultimately went the way of most criminals: he ratted out his buddies. Hardly the endearing, sympathetic figure depicted in Ted Demme's *Blow*.

The film was released in March 2001. In January 2002, Ted Demme dropped dead on a basketball court at age thirty-eight. The coroner found cocaine in his system.

Sources and Further Reading

Frontline. "Interview—George Jung." *Drug Wars.* http://www.pbs.org/wgbh/pages/frontline/shows/drugs/interviews/jung.html.

Gugliotta, Guy. *Kings of Cocaine: Inside the Medellín Cartel.* New York: Simon & Schuster, 1989.

Porter, Bruce. *Blow: How a Small-Town Boy Made $100 Million With the Medellín Cocaine Cartel and Lost It All.* New York: St. Martin's Press, 1993.

Serpico (1973)

Directed by Sidney Lumet
Written by Waldo Salt and Norman Wexler
Starring Al Pacino

Prince of the City (1981)

Directed by Sidney Lumet
Written by Jay Presson Allen and Sidney Lumet
Starring Treat Williams

Al Pacino as Frank Serpico.
© Paramount Pictures

Director Sidney Lumet stationed himself in New York instead of Tinseltown for his entire fifty-plus-year career. He got his start directing the live, meticulously scripted TV dramas of the 1950s. Maybe those are the reasons why Lumet's best films are unsentimental dramas filmed with no flashy camerawork, little (if any) musical score, and no "Oscar-worthy" actorly histrionics. Or maybe he's just a low-key guy. Lumet prefers *characters* to carry the film, as is evidenced in his adaptation of Peter Maas's book *Serpico*.

For the latter half of his twelve-year career with the NYPD, Frank Serpico—played by thirty-three-year-old Al Pacino in his "breakout" performance—was a plainclothes cop. The men of "Clothes" had the quixotic assignment of breaking up the city's gambling rackets. Serpico found that the plainclothes cops he worked with were shamelessly on the take. Their days were largely spent operating their "pad," that is, their protection racket, collecting payoffs from bookies and numbers-runners rather than busting them. Serpico refused to take money. The response from other cops: suspicion, then ostracism. Finally, he was shot in the face during a drug bust (after his transfer to the narcotics squad) as his backup officers stood back and watched.

As much as Serpico was shocked by the venality of his fellow "flunky cops," what really galled him was the stone wall that rose in his path when he tried to report the corruption to the NYPD higher-ups. His bosses, all the way into the commissioner's office, were utterly preoccupied with the departments' "image" and covering their own asses, to the point that corruption charges were the last thing they wanted to hear.

After years of beating his head against that stone wall—even when he went to the mayor—Serpico finally took his story to the *New York Times*. The paper's landmark exposé, based largely on Serpico's allegations, forced the city to investigate police corruption for the first time using an independent body, the Knapp Commission.

In terms of comparing fact to fiction, there's not much to say about Lumet's Frank Serpico, because every significant incident in the film is lifted directly from Serpico's life as recorded in Maas's biography. In some cases, events—such as when Serpico informs his corrupt colleagues that one of their nefarious "friends" is a cop killer—even come across as less dramatic in the film than in the Maas book.

In *Serpico*, only the names have been changed— if not to protect the innocent, then at least to shield the filmmakers against lawsuits. Frank Serpico's real name remains, but that's it. Nevertheless, with few exceptions each character is instantly recognizable. For example, the weasely Commissioner Delaney, who sits like a fat lump behind his desk wallowing in self-importance as he hangs Serpico out to dry, is the embodiment of Police Commissioner John F. Walsh. The

Knapp Commission found that Walsh not only ignored Serpico's charges, but that he brushed aside solid information that narcotics cops were indulging in murder, extortion, and drug dealing. Walsh retired in 1970, before the Knapp Commission had opened for business, but in the film the Delaney character is still hanging around during the hearings.

In one case, the name change unfortunately deprives a major player in the Serpico saga of his due glory. Real-life detective David Durk is depicted as Bob Blair (played by Tony Roberts, best known as a Woody Allen sidekick). The film's Blair comes off as ineffectual, self-important, and at least partly motivated by his own career ambitions to support Serpico's charges. In fairness to Lumet, that's how Durk comes off in Maas's book as well, but Durk himself was the subject of a 1996 book, *Crusader*, by James Lardner; in that book, Durk was awarded a much greater share of the credit for "hell raising" within the NYPD and for getting the Knapp Commission off the ground.

Another ineffectual character in the movie is mayoral aide Jerry Berman, who attempts to prod "hizzoner" into backing Serpico. But Berman meets only personal defeat and embarrassment due to political reasons beyond his control.

Berman was actually Jay Kriegel, whose role in the cover-up of Serpico's charges was not nearly as benign as the part played by his roman à clef alter ego. The Knapp Commission concluded that Kriegel deliberately buried Serpico's allegations. The Manhattan district attorney almost brought Kriegel up on perjury charges after his Knapp Commission testimony. According to Maas, Kriegel was spared only by the fact that the commissioners did a poor job of questioning him, leaving the DA with inadequate ammunition for a perjury case.

A name omitted from the movie altogether is that of Mayor John Lindsay. The mayor's reluctance to confront his powerful police department is a major theme of Maas's book, and while the Knapp Commission didn't say one way or the other whether Lindsay was culpable in the cover-up, it did chide "the mayor's office" for failing to investigate the Serpico story. Lumet lets Lindsay—who was in his final days as mayor of New York when the film was released—off the hook altogether by simply dropping him from the story.

Another name inexplicably dropped from the film belongs to David Burnham, the *New York Times* reporter who penned "Graft Paid to Police Here Said to Run in Millions," the original piece that covered Serpico's charges. Burnham, who supplemented Serpico's allegations with his own investigative findings, followed up with several years of hard-hitting reporting on police corruption, and he remains today one of the country's most respected investigative journalists. It's unfortunate that his courageous work gets shortchanged in the movie.

The overall impression of the New York police that oozes from the film is not only one of corruption, but of a police force that is utterly unconcerned with such trivialities as protecting public safety. Maas's book oozes even more such slime with cops whose idea of "to protect and to serve" is to bring a cot to work and sleep their shift away in an abandoned basement.

Lumet made a follow-up to *Serpico* eight years later, in which cops were shown as far more dedicated, but much more deeply corrupt. The "Special Investigations Unit" made many large drug busts, even while the elite detectives of SIU raked in thousands of dollars from shakedowns and even street sales of stolen heroin.

Again taking almost every episode of this three-hour epic straight from the factual account, this time in the form of a book by Robert Daley, *Prince of the City* was the true story of another cop who exposed corruption. But while Serpico was an honest cop who risked his life and sanity to make his allegations heard, Bob Leuci was a dirty cop who cracked under questioning by Knapp Commission investigators and turned informer. Leuci was recruited by the Knapp Commission in February 1971, coincidentally a couple of weeks after Serpico was shot, and remained a "rat" until 1974. Leuci, played by Treat Williams, is called Danny Ciello in the movie. Lumet changed everyone's name in this one—including the name of the prosecutor who guided Leuci through his harrowing testimony against his own partners, one Rudolph Giuliani.

In Daley's book, Giuliani's relationship with Leuci is quite ambiguous. Did Giuliani know or at least suspect that Leuci lied on the witness stand repeatedly when he admitted to only four illegal acts in his career? The truth, as Leuci eventually confessed to Giuliani, was that he and all of his partners committed crimes, big or small, every day. Prosecutors were divided over how to deal with Leuci. Some, including Giuliani, formed what was sarcastically dubbed the "I Love Leuci Fan Club." Others felt he was nothing but a criminal and ought to be treated like one.

In the film that split is barely touched upon and the Giuliani surrogate, D'Amato, is more a placeholder in a rumpled suit and with a plush mop of un-Giuliani-like 1970s hair.

While admirable in its factual accuracy, thematically, Lumet's film smoothes over deep moral questions in the Leuci affair. Even the central character's reasons for turning stoolie are oversimplified. Williams's Ciello breaks down and weeps with guilt over his past crimes in one of the film's early scenes. Bob Leuci's motives for turning are far murkier. At some points in the book, it almost seems as if he's doing it for thrills, striding headlong into deadly situations, hidden tape recorders strapped to his torso, even as his handlers beg him to quit. Many prosecutors worried that Leuci's extroverted, charismatic personality was the manipulative facade of a sociopath. Others thought he was looking for any friend he could get after being shunned by his police peers. The movie version, however, is much more of a straight conversion story of a bad cop turned good.

In 1997 Lumet churned out yet another New York police corruption drama, *Night Falls on Manhattan*. This one was fiction, based on a novel by *Prince of the City* author Daley. Leuci built a successful career writing crime novels.

As for Frank Serpico, he kept a low profile. The movie *Serpico* ends with him quitting the force and "living somewhere in Switzerland." He did do that, but he returned to the States to live quietly in the countryside a decade later. He resurfaced into the public eye during the New York police brutality scandals of the late 1990s, testifying at city council hearings on NYPD misconduct in 1997. Serpico declared that as far as he could see, the department was the same then as it was in his era, three decades earlier.

In 1997 the mayor of New York, the police department's most dedicated defender, was widely accused of ignoring police misconduct, much like John Lindsay had been before him. The mayor was Rudolph Giuliani.

Sources and Further Reading

Burnham, David. "Knapp Panel Says Walsh and Others Ignored Tips by U.S. on Police Crimes: Kriegel Is Scored." *New York Times*, December 28, 1972.

Cohen, Joel. "When Prosecutors Prepare Cooperators." *Cardozo Law Review*, December 2002.

Daley, Robert. *Prince of the City: The True Story of a Cop Who Knew Too Much*. Boston: Houghton Mifflin Company, 1978.

Lardner, James. *Crusader: The Hell-Raising Police Career of Detective David Durk*. New York: Random House, 1996.

Maas, Peter. *Serpico: The Cop Who Defied the System*. New York: Viking Press, 1973.

The French Connection (1971)

Directed by William Friedkin
Written by Ernest Tidyman
Starring Gene Hackman, Roy Scheider, and Fernando Rey

Gene Hackman (left) as Jimmy "Popeye" Doyle, a character based on a real cop named Eddie "Popeye" Egan, with Roy Scheider as Detective Buddy "Cloudy" Russo. © *20th Century Fox*

The French Connection is the true story of the largest heroin bust in American history. At least it was in 1962, when a team of New York City detectives and federal agents seized the drugs. The movie came out in 1971; more than thirty years later, *The French Connection* still stands as Hollywood's greatest cop movie, thanks to its down-and-dirty, hyperrealistic portrayal of police grunt work.

The movie's most famous scene, however, was an over-the-top invention.

That, of course, is the chase scene. Tough-guy detective Jimmy "Popeye" Doyle (Gene Hackman, whose performance won him an Oscar) commandeers a Chevy and tears through bustling Brooklyn streets in pursuit of a gunman who tried to kill him before hijacking an El train. The scene ends with Doyle shooting the dazed hit man in the back.

Not only did that never happen, but Eddie "Popeye" Egan—the real "Doyle," who was known as "New York's toughest cop"—drew his gun all of three times in his entire career. The chase was inserted simply because producer

Philip D'Antoni had recently made *Bullitt*, a Steve McQueen cop thriller featuring the greatest car chase ever filmed. D'Antoni demanded that *The French Connection* contain a better one.

The ill-fated gunman was modeled on French gangster Francois Scaglia, a known killer and organizer of the Marseille–New York heroin pipeline. Scaglia was not killed. He was arrested along with most of his fellow conspirators. Suave Corsican "Godfather" Jean Jehan escaped, as does his movie alter ego Alain Charnier (Fernando Rey). Unlike in the film, Jehan didn't vanish in the middle of a gunfight. Rather, he scampered back to France when news of the drug bust leaked to the press.

The case began in October 1961, when Egan and his partner Sonny "Cloudy" Grosso (*Buddy* "Cloudy" Russo in the movie, as played by Roy Scheider) spotted two-bit hood Patsy Fuca (called Sal Boca in the movie) flashing a suspiciously extravagant bankroll at the Copacabana club. That scene is staged almost verbatim in the film (though the Copa is called the Chez).

What followed was four months of grueling and decidedly unglamorous surveillance. Egan, Grosso, and dozens more cops and federal agents spent hundreds of hours sitting in parked cars and dingy basements or pounding the city's sidewalks trailing New York and French mobsters all over town. In February 1962 the countless days without showers or fresh underwear paid off. The cops uncovered 112 pounds of heroin, and they collared most of the gangsters involved in smuggling it.

Fuca was a low-level hood in New York's Lucchese crime family. Lucky for him, his uncle was powerful Lucchese capo Angelo Tumarino, who (rather foolishly) entrusted the family's drug shipments from France to his ne'er-do-well nephew. Tumarino was the reason the cops got interested in the case; they wanted to nail him. Yet there's no Tumarino character in the movie. Instead, the fictional mob Mr. Big is a crooked Jewish financier. That may seem like a curious change, but Tumarino's wife was the daughter of a Jewish gangster, and Tumarino was the Luccheses' liaison to the Jewish underworld. Subbing a Jewish mobster for Tumarino is not the stretch it would seem.

The genius of the movie is its authentically grungy depiction of police stakeouts. (Note that the film condenses the dozens of cops on the task force down to just four: Doyle, Russo, and two feds.) But as director William Friedkin has said, the problem was figuring out how to turn a "surveillance story" into a Hollywood action movie.

They solved the problem by making stuff up.

The heavy-duty fiction occurs mostly in the latter third of the movie. And most of the fictional parts are the violent parts. *The French Connection* (which transposed the story's time frame to 1971) is quite a bloodbath.

The climax of the film is a frantic shootout, with both cops and gangsters getting killed. Grosso ended Boca's heroin-wholesaling career with two shotgun blasts. The real Patsy Fuca was more fortunate. He was arrested, served eight years in prison, and lived to see himself portrayed in a major motion picture.

Elsewhere in this orgy of cinematic carnage, Doyle accidentally pumps five slugs into a federal agent who's been giving him a hard time throughout the investigation. The fed, called Bill Mulderig in the film, is based on Frank Waters, who did, in fact, exchange fisticuffs with Egan during the investigation. But no one, certainly not Egan, ever capped him. Imagine Waters's surprise when he first saw the film, only to watch himself get slain on screen. (He said he was "pissed off.")

We're sorry to report that the real "French Connection" case featured no shootouts, no killings, and no car chases. The cops made their heroin haul without undue incident. Egan pulled the first twenty-four kilos out of a ceiling in the home of Joe Fuca, Patsy's father. The remainder was stored in the basement of an apartment building. Fuca's brother Tony resided in the building, and he had been unwisely assigned to safeguard the drugs. Egan, Grosso, and the feds seized that stash and busted Tony Fuca after camping in that dark basement for twenty-one interminable days.

Egan and Grosso blasted no hoods. Or feds. Grosso showed up at the second drug seizure wearing a tuxedo. He'd just raced over from a friend's wedding.

Another major departure from fact comes when the detectives confiscate a car that, they believe, contains the heroin shipment. The scene is an exercise in auto mechanics worthy of a Daytona 500 pit crew. Police mechanic Irv Abrahams (playing himself—now that's authentic) strips the car to its frame, then reassembles it with "not a scratch" in time for its French mob owners to pick it up. In the interim, Doyle and Russo discover the entire heroin cache concealed in the vehicle.

In the actual car, mere residue of heroin was discovered. The car was not even searched until after the drugs had been seized at the locations mentioned above.

Despite the fantastical turn taken by the film, which begins with its famous chase sequence, *The French Connection* remains one of the most realistic police films among hundreds churned out by Hollywood over the years. Egan and Grosso even have roles in the film: Egan as Doyle's boss, Grosso as a federal narcotics agent.

One other detail that didn't make the film, for the excusable reason that it wasn't known until the year after the movie came out: in 1972 the 120 pounds of French-made heroin were stolen from a police evidence locker and never recovered.

Sources and Further Reading

The History Channel. "*The French Connection*: From Street to Screen." VHS.

Jones, Thomas L. "Lucchese Crime Family Epic: Descent Into Darkness, Part I." Court TV's Crime Library. http://www.crimelibrary.com/ gangsters_outlaws/family_epics/lucchese1/1.html.

Moore, Robin. *The French Connection: The World's Most Crucial Narcotics Investigation*. Boston: Little Brown and Co., 1969.

Bonnie and Clyde (1967)

Directed by Arthur Penn
Written by David Newman and Robert Benton
Starring Warren Beatty and Faye Dunaway

Sometimes a reality-based movie insinuates itself into popular culture so completely, it winds up eclipsing the actual event it chronicles. Looming large in our collective memory, the dramatic fake becomes more "real" than the reality. Arthur Penn's landmark film *Bonnie and Clyde* is one of those movies that casts a long shadow over its historical source material. Nearly four decades after the film's release, it's all but impossible to think of the famous outlaw couple without invoking the mental image of Warren Beatty's rogue charmer and Faye Dunaway's sexy spitfire hurtling blithely into a hailstorm of bullets.

At the time of the film's release in 1967, more than thirty years had passed since the execution of Clyde Barrow and Bonnie Parker in a roadside ambush near Gibsland, Louisiana. During their short criminal spree together, which spanned roughly two years (from 1932 to 1934), the fugitive couple cut a bloody path through eight states, robbing at least a dozen banks and killing fifteen people along the way. Despite those grim statistics—or maybe partly because of them—many Depression-era Americans were captivated by the saga of Bonnie and Clyde. To an increasingly dispossessed underclass, the duo represented a new breed of American desperado—charismatic, populist bank robbers who gave the comfortable fat cats that were insulated from the economic misery of the times exactly what they had coming to them.

Romanticized as folk heroes during their lifetimes, Bonnie and Clyde entered the pantheon of American folk legend after their deaths. As a result, the real Bonnie and Clyde became increasingly obscured behind a veil of dramatic embroidery—that was both flattering and defamatory. Alternately depicted as Depression-era Robin Hoods and remorseless killers, the real Bonnie and Clyde probably lay somewhere in between. (In a futile effort to exterminate their folk-hero status, FBI director J. Edgar Hoover produced four films and companion books about Bonnie and Clyde. In an introduction to one of the films Hoover appears onscreen, snarling, "I'm going to tell the truth about these rats." The secretly homosexual, cross-dressing G-man then asserts, "I'm going to tell the truth about that dirty, filthy, diseased woman.")

The film version that would become the definitive telling of the Bonnie and Clyde legend drew from the generous reservoir of fact and lore that had accumulated over the course of three decades. Although the resulting big-screen fable fell somewhat short of documentary precision, *Bonnie and Clyde* got much closer to the truth than any previous fictional treatment had. The movie's portrayal of its protagonists as charismatic antiheroes capable of sudden violence shocked critics of the day, who accused director Penn of glamorizing a "sleazy and moronic pair" (in the words of one typically overreacting review). But the historical Barrow Gang, as they were more often called, dealt in behavioral extremes. They could be charming and downright hospitable (even to the several policemen they captured and released unharmed), characteristics that enhanced their populist appeal. But they could just as easily commit murder when cornered—especially Clyde, who vowed never to be captured alive.

Despite the initial critical uproar, *Bonnie and Clyde* became a huge hit and went on to win two Academy Awards, for Best Supporting Actress (Estelle Parsons, as Clyde's hysterical sister-in-law Blanche) and Best Cinematography. In all, the film garnered ten Oscar nominations, including nods for Best Picture, Best Director, Best Screenplay, Best Actor (Warren Beatty, who also produced the film), Best Actress (Faye Dunaway), and two for Best Supporting Actor (Gene Hackman and Michael J. Pollard). More important, *Bonnie and Clyde* left a lasting mark on American cinema by almost single-handedly launching the new school of gritty, morally complex filmmaking that would flourish during the 1970s.

On the way to becoming a cinematic landmark, *Bonnie and Clyde* reinforced several popular misconceptions about the outlaw pair. Penn and his screenwriters, David Newman and Robert Benton, drew heavily from lore that exaggerates Bonnie and Clyde's reputation as Depression-era Robin Hoods. *Bonnie and Clyde* does offer several accurate examples of the duo's empathy for the common folk, however. In one such scene, Clyde pauses in the midst of a bank job to ask a farmer clutching a handful of bills, "That your money or the bank's?" "Mine," the farmer replies. "Keep it, then," says Clyde.

But Penn et al apparently needed more evidence of their protagonists' socially redemptive tendencies—so the filmmakers resorted to inventing it. In one completely fictional scene, Bonnie and Clyde encounter a displaced farmer, who's been booted from his land by cold-hearted bankers. Clyde hands his gun to the hapless sodbuster and invites him to blast away at the bank's foreclosure sign. It's an important scene meant to convey Clyde's sympathy for the economically dispossessed. When the world-weary Okie climbs into his rusty Model A pickup (what else?) and departs for greener pastures (probably L.A., where he stands a good chance of landing work as a movie extra playing world-weary Okies), Clyde proudly calls out, "We rob banks!" The implication is that Bonnie and Clyde decide to become bank robbers—or, at least, that they decide to morally justify robbing banks—as an expression of solidarity with the lumpen proletariat. It's a stirring movie moment, and it highlights the folksy connection that Depression-era Americans felt with the pair. Unfortunately, it's a huge exaggeration. In reality, Clyde's transition to bank robber was merely the result of a natural progression from petty thievery to the big leagues of felony.

Penn, Newman, and Benton burnished the title characters in other movie-friendly ways. Of course, as is always the case in fact-based films, the leads are far too Hollywood-purdy for the roles. The real Clyde Chestnut Barrow stood a mere five feet, seven inches tall (in his running-board feet) and weighed in at a spare 130 pounds. His most memorable physical feature was a set of large, pinion-like ears that gave new meaning to the word "stickup." Still, he had a reputation as a lady charmer, so Warren Beatty seems about right for the role, after all. The actual Bonnie Parker was four feet, ten inches of sinew and sass fixed to a waifish ninety-pound frame—a far aesthetic cry from the statuesque Faye Dunaway circa 1967. But contemporary accounts do refer to the actual Miss Parker as a looker—freckle-faced, with strawberry blonde curls. She was no Faye Dunaway, to be sure, but she was close enough for studio work.

The movie offers few clues about Clyde's background, opting instead to present the dashing Beatty as a familiar movie archetype—the big dreamer with more plans than luck. In fact, the actual, flesh-and-blood Clyde Barrow had a hardscrabble history that goes a long way toward explaining his later career path. The semi-illiterate son of a wholly illiterate sharecropper, Clyde came to resent the squalor of his childhood in the West Dallas slums—especially the humiliation of living in a squatter's camp. By the age of nine he was committed to a local boys school as a thief and a truant. By age eleven he was already stealing bicycles and hubcaps, and by his teens he was running with a local gang of petty thieves. More ambitious crimes followed, including car theft and small-time holdups in partnership with his brother Buck. A man of the people even then, Clyde distributed large sums of cash to his West Dallas neighbors, thus ensuring their support and silence.

As for Bonnie, what little Penn does proffer in the way of background is wrong. In the film, shortly after meeting his future partner in crime, Clyde impresses Bonnie with his powers of observation: "You came from a big old family," he says. "Yeah," she replies. (Wrong: She was actually the second of three children.) "You went to school, of course," Clyde continues, "but you didn't take to it . . . so you just up and quit one day." Bonnie nods. (Wrong again: Bonnie loved school, and she excelled at it.) Clyde seals the seduction by correctly divining that Bonnie "almost married" a "ce-ment" worker, but then thought better of it. (Strike three: When Bonnie met Clyde, she was already married, to a convicted felon serving a ninety-nine-year sentence for murder.)

Faye Dunaway's portrayal of Bonnie as the ultimate cool customer doesn't quite match up to reality, either. While on the lam with the Barrow Gang, Bonnie was often homesick and prone to hysterical crying jags. The movie version transplants this less admirable aspect of Bonnie's personality to another character—Buck Barrow's wife, Blanche.

The movie version also rewrites the early chronology of the duo, ostensibly for dramatic purposes. For instance, Beatty's Clyde first encounters Dunaway's Bonnie when he attempts to boost her mother's car. It's a "meet-cute" fiction that was wholly invented by the screenwriters. In reality, the two met under much more mundane circumstances; namely, in the greasy spoon where Bonnie worked as a waitress. In the film, Clyde immediately impresses the girl, first by revealing that he's fresh out of prison, then by showing her his revolver, which she caresses in an obviously sexual way. In the electrifying sequence that follows, sexual tension mounts as Bonnie and Clyde tempt one another into committing a crime—the holdup of a local merchant. The scene works on multiple levels: it demonstrates the sexual energy and attraction between the outlaw couple; it also says something about their codependence as criminals, one goading the other into escalating lawlessness. On yet another level, the sequence—and indeed, the entire film—is a social commentary on the use of sexuality as a means of persuasion, manipulation, and control.

That first act is powerful moviemaking, masterfully written and directed. It's also completely inaccurate. In reality, Bonnie's initiation into a (short) life of crime was far more dramatic, and it was romantically conventional. At the time of their acquaintance, Clyde had not yet been to prison. But within a month of their meeting he was arrested for multiple robberies and jailed in Waco, Texas. In a desperate and audacious act of devotion, Bonnie smuggled a

.32 revolver into the jailhouse, either by strapping it to her thigh or between her breasts. (Accounts vary on that particular point, but considering Miss Parker's gamine figure, we lean toward the former.) Clyde escaped, but was recaptured in Ohio eleven days later and extradited back to Texas, where he was tried and sentenced to hard time at the infamous Eastham Prison Farm.

Strangely, *Bonnie and Clyde* completely ignores this inherently dramatic episode. Perhaps Bonnie's motive in risking everything for Clyde—garden-variety lovesickness—proved all too conventional for a 1960s film that was more interested in a radical exploration of sexual politics.

Penn's film also glosses over Clyde's ensuing two-year term at Eastham, a brutal work farm with a reputation for delivering quite the opposite of rehabilitation. In the movie, Clyde cheerfully tells his brother Buck (Gene Hackman) that he chopped off two of his toes in an attempt to avoid the prison's punishing work details. That much is true, as is the ironic kicker to the anecdote: "Sure enough, next week I got paroled. I walked out of that godforsaken jail on crutches." But the role of Eastham in shaping Clyde's future actions may have been far more profound than the movie lets on.

To be fair to Penn, it wasn't until 1996, and the publication of John Neal Phillips's book *Running with Bonnie and Clyde*, that the full story emerged. Based on a series of interviews with former Barrow Gang members, the book revealed that while he was in Eastham, Clyde had been beaten and raped repeatedly by a vicious inmate named Big Ed Crowder. Eventually, in a desperate bid to stop the abuse, Clyde lured Crowder into a bathroom and bludgeoned him to death with a lead pipe. Only a few inmates knew of the abuse and Clyde's retaliatory murder—his first killing. Former Barrow Gang member Ralph Fults told Phillips that Eastham had hardened and embittered Clyde—who was barely twenty when he arrived at the farm—transforming him "from a schoolboy to a rattlesnake."

Leaving the armchair psychoanalysis to the cable TV criminologists, we'll just note that these recent revelations offer a bit of food for thought.

Clyde's traumatic experiences at Eastham might also explain one of the odder mysteries surrounding the Bonnie and Clyde saga: the persistent rumor that Clyde was sexually dysfunctional, bisexual, or homosexual. Hollywood's *Bonnie and Clyde* famously alludes to these rumors in several scenes that have baffled moviegoers for decades. (If you're furiously rifling through this chapter while rewinding the VHS edition of *Bonnie and Clyde*, this is the paragraph you've been looking for.) After their sexually charged first robbery together, Bonnie puts the moves on Clyde. But Clyde pulls back, announcing "I ain't much of a lover boy." Clyde fails to rise to the occasion in several subsequent attempts at boudoir action.

In an essay aptly titled, "What's It Really All About?", screenwriter David Newman later explained that he and cowriter Robert Benton had written scenes based on "rumors" that Clyde was bisexual and that the duo had engaged in ménages à trois. According to Newman, those scenes had been ix-nayed by Beatty and Penn. However, allusions to Clyde's rumored preferences remained in the movie.

As to whether the rumors are true, the record is murky. Barrow Gang member W. D. Jones claimed that he participated in threesomes with Bonnie and Clyde while they were on the run. But Bonnie and Clyde had been subject to a constant stream of false rumors, many of them promulgated by the FBI— including claims that Bonnie was a nymphomaniac and a drug addict. Ultimately it's difficult to separate the fact from the fiction. Relatives of both Bonnie and Clyde deny the accusations that Clyde was gay or impotent, however, and one of Clyde's earliest girlfriends, Eleanor B. Williams, told author Phillips that "Clyde Barrow had no problems sexually."

According to showbiz lore, which may not be any more reliable than gangster lore, Warren Beatty put the issue to rest long before shooting on *Bonnie and Clyde* commenced, when he told Arthur Penn in no uncertain terms, "I'm not playing a homosexual."

Sources and Further Reading

Cartwright, Gary. "The Whole Shootin' Match." *Texas Monthly*, February 2001.

Dallas Historical Society. "Dallas History Special Section: Bonnie and Clyde." http://www.dallashistory.org/history/dallas/bandc.htm.

Friedman, Lester D., ed. *Arthur Penn's Bonnie and Clyde*. Cambridge Film Handbooks. New York: Cambridge University Press, 2000.

Phillips, John Neal. *Running with Bonnie and Clyde*. Norman, OK: University of Oklahoma Press, 1996.

Goodfellas (1990)

Directed by Martin Scorsese

Written by Nicholas Pileggi and Martin Scorsese

Starring Ray Liotta, Robert De Niro, and Joe Pesci

Robert De Niro (left) as Jimmy Conway and Ray Liotta (right) as Henry Hill. © *Warner Bros.*

When gangsters talk, the government listens. Why shouldn't the rest of us? *Goodfellas* is based very closely on Nicholas Pileggi's 1985 bestseller *Wise Guy*, which is in turn based very closely on the nostalgic ramblings of Henry Hill, a Mafia footsoldier who, as the movie depicts, flipped on his lifelong best pals and turned federal witness to save his own ass. Hill testified in numerous mob trials, spent years in the witness protection program, and eventually emerged to become a minor celebrity on the radio call-in circuit. He also wrote three books of his own (including a cookbook of favorite mobster recipes).

Basically, Hill now makes a living off of his past as Mafia thug. Of course, Hill isn't totally beyond our sympathies as a protagonist, because he never actually killed anybody. He's just a charming ne'er do-well—a "goodfella." At least according to the movie. And the book.

During various radio call-ins, Hill has "admitted" to killing at least three people. Then he called back sometime later to retract his "confession," offering the "I was drunk" alibi. In fairness, Pileggi's book describes Hill as not "particularly vicious." In fact, "He wasn't even tough, as far as the cops could determine." Not that Hill was some kind of mob Gandhi. The movie shows him pistol-whipping a man, beating another, and helping to bury the bodies of murder victims. All of those incidents (and more like them) are true, according to Hill himself in *Wise Guy*. The bit where Ray Liotta, as Hill, retches as he and his cohorts dig up a decomposed victim—that's right out of Hill's printed account, too.

No gangster film before Martin Scorsese's adaptation of Hill's life story had quite the verisimilitude of *Goodfellas*. *The Godfather* was based on a novel by Mario Puzo, who based his book on gangster stories and myths he'd picked up around the neighborhood, as well as on library research. *Wise Guy* is a nonfiction book, and Scorsese's adaptation of it is almost amazing in its faithfulness to the source material (Pileggi cowrote the script with the director). Perhaps there can be no such thing as a nonfiction movie, but *Goodfellas* at least proves that Hollywood doesn't have to "Hollywood-ize" every true story it options. A director of Scorsese's abilities can create a masterpiece with the facts he's given, maybe adding a nip and tuck here and there, but without throwing in a car chase, a cute kid, or a climactic scene in which everyone in the courtroom gets up and sings.

Most of Scorsese's liberties with the nonfiction account fall under the relatively unimportant category of characters' names. James "Jimmy the Gent" Burke, notorious hit man and thief, becomes Jimmy Conway (Robert De Niro). Lucchese family capo (i.e., crew chief) Paul Vario is called, in the movie, Paul Cicero, and the tall, lean psychopath Tommy DeSimone is presented in the form of short, stubby psychopath Tommy DeVito, played memorably, and Oscar-winningly, by Joe Pesci. Now, Pesci brought plenty of Joe Pesci to the role, and not much of the real Tommy DeSimone other than his casual murderousness. Pesci's oft-recited-by-stoned-college-kids "Do I amuse you?" routine doesn't occur in Hill's recollections of Tommy. But Tommy's offhand murder of a hapless teenager named Spider, who has the poor judgment to tell Tommy to "go fuck yourself" (after Tommy earlier shot him in the foot for no particular reason)—that was real.

The movie omits what would have been a classic Hollywood "motivation" for Tommy. His father was a "rat," and Tommy felt that he had a bad rep to overcome. Usually, that's the type of direct-causation character motive that

Hollywood fabricates. In this case it was true, but Scorsese took it out. His version of Tommy is like a Mafia Michael Myers: a pure, motiveless killer.

Tommy and Jimmy's murder-by-beating of "made guy" Billy Batts (also an alias, but that's the name Hill uses in the book, as well) is true, too, although the killing was carried out a little differently than the movie depicts. They attempted to beat him to death with a pistol butt and, when he started banging around, still alive in the trunk of their car, they whacked him with a tire iron. The killing happened two weeks after Batts had insulted Tommy, not the same night. However, as the film portrays, that murder was the reason why Tommy later got offed himself.

The scene has Paulie's brother, Tutti, pulling the trigger after tricking Tommy into thinking he's going to a ceremony where he'll be "made," that is inducted into the secret society of La Cosa Nostra. In truth, no one really knows how Tommy died; he went off to the bogus ceremony and was never seen again. (Mob turncoat Joseph "Joe Dogs" Ianuzzi fingered Gambino-family Florida boss Tommy Agro as the triggerman.) Reportedly, Paul Vario gave the OK to hit Tommy. Vario despised DeSimone; their relationship is not explored much in the film.

The friendship between Henry and Tommy, while close, is somewhat overstated in the movie. Tommy wasn't present—in fact, he was behind bars—when Henry took his first arrest. Nor was the bootleg cigarette bust the teenage Henry's first "pinch." He'd been nabbed earlier for using a stolen credit card.

The movie itself is sort of a downscale epic, spanning Hill's career from his teenage ambition to join the mob in the mid-1950s, through his carefree days of hijacking trucks and getting the best table at the Copa in the '60s, to his jail term in the '70s and the drug bust that ended his mob career in 1980. Refreshingly, it does not bind itself to the "three-act structure" found in most Hollywood screenplays, in which a "turning point" occurs every twenty-seven minutes on the nose.

If there is a central event of the sprawling story, it is the Lufthansa heist. The six-million-dollar haul from Kennedy Airport in 1978 was, at the time, the richest robbery in American history. Who pulled it off? A bunch of Runyonesque lowlifes known as the Roberts Lounge Gang. Henry Hill was part of that crew, and Jimmy the Gent was its de facto leader. Neither of them was there that night, but Tommy DeSimone was. Burke organized the whole operation after getting the idea from a bookie named Marty Krugman (called Morrie Kessler in the movie) who had appropriated the plan from two security workers at the airport.

One of those two workers, Louis Werner, was the only individual prosecuted (and convicted) for the robbery, which remains officially unsolved twenty-five years later. As the police said, "there was never any mystery" about who did it. Police snitches gave out the names within days of the robbery. The problem was, almost everyone involved with the crime developed the nasty habit of dying, in particularly nasty ways.

The series of murders marks the closest thing to a stereotypical "turning point" in the film, though it's a really more an artful shift in tone. To that point, Henry and his pals are portrayed as something like lovable, charming rogues— a bit scary, in the case of Tommy, anyway, but undeniably attractive. After the Lufthansa heist, they're revealed as paranoid, dangerous, and constantly fearing for their lives—at each other's hands, most of all. In reality, they were like that from the start, but we can't fault the film for misrepresentation on that count. We're seeing mob life through Henry's eyes, so the movie's tenor reflects his evolving, or devolving, perceptions as he spirals rapidly downward.

We can see why. While Scorsese depicts the string of murders with a few adjustments to the facts, they are essentially presented as they happened in real life (or real death, in this case). The body of the fictional Frankie Carbone, one of the movie's few invented characters, turns up frozen solid in a meat truck. The scene seems designed for black comedy. Was this one piece of script that Scorsese made up?

Yes and no. The real story is that the corpse of one Richard Eaton, a high-stakes swindler, turned up on January 17, 1979, frozen solid in a refrigerator truck in Brooklyn. As did Frankie Carbone's in the movie, Eaton's body took two days of thawing out before the police could do anything with it. They surmised—wrongly, as it turned out— that Eaton was a money launderer for some of the Lufthansa cash, and they officially linked his murder to the robbery. Actually, Jimmy Burke killed Eaton over a $250,000 cocaine rip-off. That was the murder that finally put Jimmy the Gent away for life, courtesy of Hill's testimony. Burke died of cancer in prison in 1996.

An even more appalling murder that was indeed related to the robbery, was that of Theresa Ferrara, a twenty-six-year-old mob moll, described by Pileggi as "stunning," who made herself readily available to the Roberts Lounge boys. She does not appear in the movie, and her death goes unmentioned. Perhaps that's one event that was too horrifying to be connected with our goodfella antiheroes even in their dark and paranoid stage. There was nothing charming about the way she was disposed of. Her role in the robbery is unclear. Could be, she simply knew too much. Whatever the reason, her dismembered, decapitated torso turned up in waters off of New Jersey on May 18, 1979—the handiwork of the real "goodfellas."

Sources and Further Reading

May, Allan. "The Lufthansa Heist Revisited." Court TV's Crime Library. http://www.crimelibrary.com/gangsters_outlaws/gang/heist/1.html.

Pileggi, Nicholas. *Wise Guy: Life in a Mafia Family*. New York: Pocket Books, 1987.

Donnie Brasco (1997)

Directed by Mike Newell
Written by Paul Attanasio
Starring Johnny Depp, Al Pacino, and Anne Heche

Johnny Depp as FBI agent Joe Pistone, alias Donnie Brasco.
© Mandalay Entertainment

In the deglamorized style of *Goodfellas*, the 1997 mob flick *Donnie Brasco* gives us Mafiosi as schlubs and dimwitted thugs—who are all the dumber for permitting an FBI undercover agent to infiltrate their gang. For five years.

Joseph Pistone was the agent, using the alias Brasco. His intended three-month assignment kept him undercover from 1976 until 1981, bamboozling Bonanno family mobsters to such a degree that he came close to the "made guy" status coveted by all wise guys.

Mike Newell's interpretation of Pistone's mob memoir is faithful to the frightening-yet-pathetic portrait of mob life in the book, but it takes important liberties with the details of Pistone's experience. Newell and screenwriter Paul Attanasio are more concerned with the emotional impact that living a double life had on Pistone, rather than with the legal impact of Pistone's dual identity. Rather than making a *French Connection*–like "investigation" story, they've turned *Donnie Brasco* into a romance of sorts—between two men.

The movie centers on the relationship between Pistone/Brasco (Johnny Depp) and aging mob "soldier" Benjamin "Lefty Guns" Ruggiero, played with uncharacteristic understatement by Al Pacino. Pistone seduces Lefty, who responds like a smitten lover, showering his new object of affection with attention. Along the way, Pistone develops a genuine affection for Lefty and is heartbroken when, in the end, he must betray his new soul mate.

The actual relationship between Pistone and Ruggiero was not as emotionally charged as is depicted in the film. Pistone, at least according to his own account, saw himself as doing nothing more than performing a law-enforcement function. Depp's version of Pistone develops a loyalty to the mob that exceeds his dedication to the FBI. The movie has Pistone going AWOL from his FBI handlers for weeks, prompting senior agents to reach out to Mrs. Pistone for aid in locating their rogue operative.

The real Pistone was anything but a rogue, and he stayed in regular contact with his bosses. Also missing from the film is any mention of the backup agents who shadowed Pistone any time he wore a wire around his mob confreres.

The movie's Pistone falls so deeply into wise-guy life that his dedication to his new criminal pals usurps his devotion to wife and kids. We see Pistone sneaking away to spend fleeting moments at home in New Jersey, much to the consternation of his spouse (perpetually frowning Anne Heche), who, in the grand tradition of cop wives throughout Hollywood history, henpecks him at every opportunity.

Pistone's real family was transplanted to California for safety's sake shortly after he went undercover, an arrangement that caused the agent much conflict. As for Ruggiero's fate, Pistone was far less broken up about it than Newell's film would have us believe. Truth is, Pistone/Brasco was never all that close to Ruggiero.

Attanasio's script conflates two relationships: Pistone's friendship with Ruggiero and his friendship with Ruggiero's boss, Bonanno family capo Dominick "Sonny Black" Napolitano. Sonny Black is played by Michael Madsen as a repugnant thug—which, like most real-life mobsters, he certainly was. But Pistone, in accordance with his mission to ascend as far as he could up the Cosa Nostra hierarchy, ingratiated himself more closely with Sonny Black than with the relatively insignificant Lefty Guns. Pistone spent nights at Sonny Black's apartment, where the two men would lounge in their skivvies.

The fictional Sonny Black isn't a guy you'd want to be caught around in any kind of compromising position. He fluctuates between murderous and loutish.

He's repellant, where Pacino's Ruggiero is paternal: a concerned mentor to his protégé Brasco. The artificially sharp contrast is designed to elicit sympathy for the painful plight of an over-the-hill hit man who moans that he's "clipped twenty-six guys" with nothing to show for it—except a pet lion. (His fellow mobsters give him the purloined pet as a gift, an incident that was taken straight from real life. The real Lefty was a frequent sight around his Brooklyn haunts, taking his lion for an invigorating stroll.)

So cross-pollinated are the real Sonny and Lefty in Attanasio's script that the movie ends with Lefty receiving the comeuppance that was actually dished out to Sonny. We see Pacino, as Lefty, being "sent for"—that is, called by his Mafia bosses to a meeting, at which he will be murdered. So certain of his impending death is Pacino's Lefty that he removes all valuables and keepsakes from his person—watch, chain, rings—and places them daintily in a drawer, insuring that his Mafia executioners will not loot his corpse. This premortem denuding was, in fact, performed by Napolitano before he drove off to his own death.

As penance for getting flimflammed by Pistone, Sonny Black got whacked. Probably. A body discovered in 1982, sans severed hands, was purportedly that of Napolitano. However, in a mob trial two decades later, doubts were raised about the corpse's identification. In any case, Napolitano vanished, while Ruggiero survived to serve ten years of a fifteen-year prison sentence, having been convicted of racketeering on the strength of Pistone's testimony. While Pacino's Lefty bears no hard feelings against Donnie, his beloved surrogate son, the real Ruggiero plotted to kill Pistone after learning his secret identity (a fact that was revealed at his trial).

A few years after his release, Lefty Guns received what every gangster wants but so few ever get: death by natural causes.

The movie sensationalizes Pistone's undercover exploits. For example, Pistone never chopped up anyone's body, which he does onscreen. In keeping with the exaggeration of Pistone's/Brasco's emotional ties to his mobster life, Newell and Attanasio tack on a 1970s-style downer ending: Pistone is rewarded for his five years of sacrifice with a demeaning, perfunctory ceremony, with almost no one in attendance. He is awarded, for his pains, a check for five hundred dollars.

The FBI was rather more enthusiastic about Pistone's accomplishments than the film would have us believe, and his work did not end when the assignment did. Pistone would go on to testify against hundreds of mobsters. He received his commendation in a packed "Great Hall" in the Department of Justice headquarters in Washington, D.C., with numerous "dignitaries and government officials," applauding him, Pistone wrote.

For the onscreen version of Pistone, a man supposedly wracked by conscience for his betrayal of a close friend and father figure, however, a splashy celebration just wouldn't look right.

The real Pistone never went undercover again. Reportedly, the mob put out an "open contract" on his life. Assigned to a desk job, Pistone quit the FBI in boredom a few years later. Nevertheless, Donnie Brasco, Pistone's fictional creation, lives on—in a series of paperback novels penned by Pistone himself.

Sources and Further Reading

Pistone, Joseph and Richard Woodley. *Donnie Brasco: My Undercover Life in the Mob*. New York: Signet Books, 1997.

Dog Day Afternoon (1975)

Directed by Sidney Lumet

Written by Frank Pierson

Starring Al Pacino, John Cazale, and Charles Durning

John Cazale as Sal. © *Warner Bros.*

When *Dog Day Afternoon* hit the screens on September 21, 1975, "gay pride" was still a novel and, frankly, bizarre concept as far as most of America was concerned. New York City's Stonewall Riots had occurred only six years earlier: patrons of a Greenwich Village gay nightclub called the Stonewall had battled police during a routine raid, igniting several nights of violence and several decades of the gay rights movement. But in 1975, Hollywood, being a mirror of middle-American values, was not exactly embracing this newly assertive homosexual subculture. For that matter, Hollywood studio films with homosexual protagonists are not exactly flooding the multiplexes today, more than thirty years after Stonewall. Gay characters have proliferated to an extent, but they rarely receive better than the "goofy best friend" slot, most often in chick flicks as the confidant of a lovelorn, but unambiguously boy-crazy female lead.

Dog Day Afternoon featured not only a gay lead character, but a gay lead character portrayed by a major male star, Al Pacino. That was revolutionary in the mid-1970s, and it remains a revelation today. So why is the movie, which is undoubtedly one of the best of that cinematically fecund decade, not remembered as a landmark *gay* film?

The reason is that *Dog Day Afternoon* drastically de-emphasizes the homosexuality of Pacino's character. His sexual orientation is treated as a plot twist, and not much more. Pacino, it's been reported, felt queasy about acting gay scenes and demanded that any hint of overt sexuality be stricken from the script—even though the real guy he was playing was most emphatically, unapologetically gay.

That real guy was John Wojtowicz, a twenty-seven-year-old Vietnam veteran with no criminal history, whose bungled bank robbery riveted New Yorkers for the afternoon and evening of August 22, 1972. The robbery-turned-hostage-holding-standoff was the topic of a *LIFE* magazine article, which in turn served as the basis for *Dog Day Afternoon*. On that summer afternoon, Wojtowicz entered a small Chase Manhattan Bank branch at East Third Street and Avenue P in Brooklyn. With him were two accomplices, eighteen-year-old Salvatore Natuarale and twenty-one-year-old Robert Westenberg. It was closing time. Things quickly got weird when Westenberg, spooked by a passing police cruiser, bolted.

During a routine phone call (which the robbers, feeling foolishly self-assured, let him answer) the bank manager slyly signaled Chase's downtown office that all was not well. Quickly, an army of police and FBI agents hustled to the bank, pulling up as Wojtowicz and Natuarale were getting ready to leave with about thirty thousand dollars in hand. Rather than give up, the two novice robbers became novice hostage-takers. The ensuing drama attracted a sizable crowd, featured live radio and TV interviews with Wojtowicz via telephone, and did not conclude until 5:00 A.M. at Kennedy Airport. The bumbling but enthusiastic stickup men believed they would board a plane, which they had demanded, bound for somewhere they hadn't quite decided on yet. Instead, an FBI agent shot and killed Natuarale. Other G-men subdued Wojtowicz, who surrendered uneventfully.

Apart from the spectacle of it, with three thousand New Yorkers watching the standoff as if it were a ball game, the strangest element of the robbery was Wojtowicz's motive. He demanded that his "wife," a drag queen named Ernest Aron, be released from a mental hospital. His purpose of committing the bank job, he announced, was to acquire money for Ernie's sex-change operation.

In the film, the revelation that Sonny Worzick (the name given the Wojtowicz figure) is married to a man comes as a shock—especially because we've already been introduced to his legal wife and two children. It may have been a shock to the public that Wojtowicz was gay, but the element of surprise was blunted when he gave a telephone interview early in the standoff and announced, "I'm gay!"

The "wife," Ernie, was hauled to the bank from the hospital, where he'd been confined after a suicide attempt. But unlike the fictional Ernie—rechristened Leon and played by Chris Sarandon (then husband of actress Susan Sarandon) in his screen debut—the genuine Aron wouldn't speak to his "husband." Wojtowicz instead visited with another of his gay friends. They kissed full on the lips at the entrance to the bank. A number of Wojtowicz's gay pals showed up to witness the protracted drama. None were written into the film, and Pacino refused to play a kissing scene with Sarandon, or to play any scene with him at all, except over the phone.

Even so, Pacino, director Sidney Lumet (who earlier directed Pacino in *Serpico*), and screenwriter Frank Pierson deserve the Tinseltown equivalent of the Medal of Valor for depicting a gay character in forthright terms, even if the overt gayness of Wojtowicz is muted in the film. *Dog Day Afternoon* shows Hollywood liberalism at its most courageous. At the same time, it shows the filmmakers' leftish bent in their distortion of reality to fit their preferred political template.

In 1972 the Supreme Court had recently ruled capital punishment unconstitutional. Wojtowicz made the point, in interviews during the standoff, that abolishing the death penalty was "ridiculous." He never would have robbed the bank if the Court had not made that decision, he said. Under the Court's ruling, he could execute all of his hostages with no worries of facing death himself.

This rather unsettling proclamation was discreetly omitted from Pacino's dialog.

Wojtowicz's teenage partner in crime, Sal (played as a significantly older accomplice by then-thirty-nine-year-old John Cazale), desperately makes clear that he is "not a homosexual." Natuarale may or may not have been gay, but he hung out in gay bars, which is where Wojtowicz met him. A friend of Wojtowicz's alleged that the heist was conceived in just such a bar by a gay Chase Manhattan executive, but that claim was never verified, so the moviemakers had some justification for leaving it out of the script.

The movie's most famous scene never happened. It's another invention that redirects the movie away from a "gay pride" theme to something more acceptable to both the Hollywood Left of that era and mainstream America of any era. That's the "Attica! Attica!" scene, in which Pacino whips the crowd of onlookers into a frenzy, chanting the name of New York's most infamous prison. During the Attica uprising of 1971, New York's Governor Nelson Rockefeller—whose family name was synonymous with "the establishment"—turned the machine guns of the National Guard against rioting inmates. The massacre became an instant rallying point. Attica symbolized the power of "the system" to ruthlessly eradicate all who dared oppose it. With his invented "Attica! Attica!" chant, Pacino's character was enlarged from a symbol of gay pride into an icon of anti-establishment rage.

Yes, dear reader, back in 1975 it was still considered "cool" and "hip" to be against the government, the police, and all authority figures. From today's retrograde perspective, it's difficult to imagine a Hollywood film in which we're encouraged to cheer for a criminal who taunts police and invokes the memory of a gory prison riot as if it were the Alamo or Pearl Harbor. "Antiestablishment," the phrase itself, sounds somehow quaint to contemporary ears.

But three decades ago, Pacino's "Attica! Attica!" brought movie audiences to their proverbial feet. *Dog Day Afternoon* earned a Best Picture nomination. Could a chant of "Stonewall! Stonewall!" have accomplished the same? You don't need a test screening to figure out the answer to that one. No way—not even in the freewheeling days of 1975.

Wojtowicz earned parole in 1978 after spending six years in the slammer. He violated his parole a couple of times and did two more prison stints. He was freed for the last time in 1987. In the days before New York's Son of Sam law took effect—prohibiting criminals from making money from books and movies based on their crimes—Wojtowicz made enough cash from *Dog Day Afternoon* to bankroll Ernie's sex-change operation after all. Ernest Aron became Debbie Eden, married someone else, and died of AIDS in 1987.

Detective Sergeant Eugene Moretti, the hapless cop (played with memorable élan by veteran character actor Charles Durning) who attempts to reason with Pacino's character, was not, as it turns out, a real person.

Sources and Further Reading

Klinger, Judson. "Save Our Script." *American Film*. June 1990.

Kluge, P. F. and Thomas Moore. "The Boys in the Bank." *Life Magazine*. September 22, 1972.

Information was also drawn from numerous articles that appeared in the *New York Times* from August 22 to August 27, 1972.

Docu-Trauma

The Elephant Man (1980)

Directed by David Lynch

Written by Christopher De Vore, Eric Bergren, and David Lynch

Starring Anthony Hopkins and John Hurt

The real Joseph Carey Merrick.
*Courtesy of Jeanette Sitton/Joseph
Carey Merrick Tribute Web Site*

During his short lifetime, Joseph Carey Merrick—the so-called "Elephant Man"—provoked a response among fellow Londoners that fell somewhere between revulsion and pity. Grotesquely disfigured by an incurable genetic disorder that twisted his skeleton and flesh into masses of knotted burls and pendulous tumors, he was described by the doctor who "discovered" him in a London freak show as "the most disgusting specimen of humanity." Queen Victoria showed a little more verbal restraint when she called him "one of England's most unfortunate sons." In a letter to the *Times* newspaper, a hospital administrator captured the conflicted feelings of horror and pathos that Merrick typically aroused: "Women and nervous persons fly in terror from the sight of him . . . yet he is superior in intelligence, can read and write, is quiet, gentle, not to say even refined in his mind."

Probably not coincidentally, the prevalent sentimental view of Merrick paralleled one of the popular literary and dramatic tropes of the day: the outwardly hideous monster possessed of an infinitely "gentle soul." Not surprisingly, then, nineteenth-century Londoners were inclined to view Merrick's "teddible" plight in broad theatrical terms. As literary critics William E. Holladay and Stephen Watt would later point out, Victorian "melodrama offered audiences steeped in its conventions a ready vehicle for interpreting Merrick's experiences. His deformities, much like Quasimodo's in *The Hunchback of Notre Dame,* made him an outcast, and the true story of his fortunes and misfortunes . . . must have read like something one might see at Drury Lane or, more likely, at the Adelphi, famous in London for its melodrama." Or like something straight out of Mary Shelley's *Frankenstein*, or any number of sentimental Dickens novels about homeless waifs exploited by cruel and sadistic oppressors.

In fact, many of the misconceptions about Merrick are rooted in this tendency to romanticize and dramatize his story. Even those closest to him were guilty of confabulating tales about the Elephant Man. Sir Frederick Treves, the kindly surgeon who gave the Elephant Man a home in Whitechapel Hospital, sensationalized his patient's life in a memoir written after Merrick's death. Among Treves's inaccurate embellishments was the claim that Merrick's mother had "basely" abandoned her son when he was "so small that his earliest clear memories were of the workhouse to which he had been taken." In fact, later historians would argue quite persuasively that Mrs. Merrick treated her boy well up until her death, which occurred when he was eleven years old, and that Merrick didn't enter the Leicester workhouse until he was seventeen—and that he did so under his own volition. Reality notwithstanding, Treves's Dickensian spin on Merrick's "backstory" became the accepted version of the truth, and it would influence all subsequent dramatic interpretations of the Elephant Man saga.

(Another of the far-reaching misnomers established in Treves's memoir was his reference to the famous patient as "John Merrick," rather than Joseph Merrick, his actual name. Why Treves changed Merrick's first name remains a mystery. But the result of the error is readily evident: in the dozens of articles, biographies, and fictional accounts written since the publication of Treves's memoir, the Elephant Man is often misidentified as "John Merrick.")

Just as the Victorians had projected their own concerns and conventions onto Merrick, so did the many chroniclers and dramatists who followed them. Merrick's misshapen, amorphous physique became the literary equivalent of a Rorschach inkblot—a form whose significance and meaning varied, depending on the eye of the beholder. More than a century after his death, Merrick's story has inspired a raft of biographies, a scientific reevaluation of his medical disorder, a Tony-winning stage play (one version starred David Bowie), a TV movie based on the play, a David Lynch movie not based on the play, a novel based on the David Lynch movie, numerous parodies of both the play and movie (including, in the Jeff Goldblum comedy *The Tall Guy*, a mock Andrew Lloyd Weber–style musical titled *Elephant!*) and—strangest of all—an unsuccessful attempt by Michael Jackson to adopt the Elephant Man's bones. Naturally, the various "authors" who have written about the man have variously interpreted Merrick's story to suit their own viewpoints/philosophies/hobbyhorses. In his 1979 play *The Elephant Man*, Bernard Pomerance refashioned Merrick's life story into a polemical critique of modern imperialism. A decade later a National Institutes of Health committee, bringing modern scientific theories to bear, revised Merrick's medical diagnosis from neurofibromatosis, (also known as "Elephant Man's Disease") to something called Proteus syndrome. And as for Michael Jackson—well, we won't even hazard a guess about his Elephant Man–related motives.

The most famous of the Merrick makeovers is David Lynch's 1980 film *The Elephant Man*, starring John Hurt, forty pounds of makeup, and various Lynchian crotchets. The original script, written by Christopher De Vore and Eric Bergren, was based on two books—Sir Treves's sometimes unreliable 1922 memoir *The Elephant Man and Other Reminiscences* and anthropologist Ashley Montagu's 1971 book *The Elephant Man: A Study in Human Dignity*. (*The Elephant Man* stage play had also drawn from Montagu's book, which heavily reflected its author's humanist philosophies and theories about child rearing.) Lynch saw the material in much the same way as the Victorians and humanists like Montagu had—as a sentimental fable of "someone who was a monster on the outside but who inside was a beautiful and normal human being you fell in love with."

Shot in somber black and white at gritty locations around London, including an abandoned hospital outfitted with hissing gas lamps, Lynch's film pulsates with a vague sense of industrial menace.

According to the director, De Vore and Bergren's initial script stuck "close to the real story"—too close, it turns out. Concerned that the dramatic structure prematurely "flattened out," Lynch called for a rewrite. In a "team effort," the three set about extensively reshuffling time lines and inventing completely fictional scenes and characters in order to give the story a more cinematic (and melodramatic) shape.

As a consequence, *The Elephant Man* contains a number of major factual distortions. For instance, in the David Lynch version, Dr. Treves (Anthony Hopkins) "rescues" Merrick from a sadistic freak show manager named Bytes (Freddie Jones). Treves graciously offers the much-abused Merrick a sanctuary in Whitechapel Hospital, an arrangement that goes horribly wrong when a vengeful Bytes later returns to kidnap Merrick. This is a dramatic fabrication. In reality, not only was there no kidnapping and no wicked villain named Bytes, but Merrick would not become a resident guest of the hospital until 1886, two years after he left the freak-show business. Merrick's actual manager, Tom Norman, was a successful London freak show impresario who apparently treated his star attraction well. There's no evidence that he ever beat or kidnapped Merrick, or that he forced the Elephant Man to display himself. (In fact, Merrick profited from the association, earning two hundred pounds sterling under Norman's auspices, a considerable sum in those days.)

For dramatic oomph, Lynch has the fictional Bytes absconding to the continent with his purloined "treasure," as he terms Merrick, forcing the Elephant Man back onto the sideshow circuit. When the malnourished Merrick collapses onstage, Bytes subjects him to a savage caning and locks him in a monkey cage. Taking pity on their fellow performer, the other circus freaks release Merrick and escort him to the seaport at Ostende, Belgium.

While it's true that Merrick toured with a European freak show late in his career, no one had forced him to do so. Unfortunately, the fictional character of Bytes does somewhat resemble Merrick's manager on that continental tour, an Austrian who robbed and abandoned him in Belgium. Lynch seems to have combined the Austrian, Tom Norman, and Charles Dickens's thuggish Bill Sykes character into a single, supersized, melodramatic villain.

After his fleecing at the hands of the unscrupulous Austrian, the real Merrick managed to limp back to London. By the time he arrived at Liverpool Street Train Station in June 1886, he was suffering from bronchitis, dehydration, and malnutrition. Jeering crowds chased him through the station, an event that is dramatized in the movie's most famous scene: cornered by hordes of taunting gawkers, John Hurt's Merrick exclaims, "I am not an animal! I am a human being!" It's a great line that makes for a great movie moment, but the real Merrick never said it. Rather less eloquently, he simply collapsed. Later, he handed the police Treves's calling card, and the good doctor collected him from the police station.

It was at this point (and not two years earlier, as is inaccurately depicted in the film) that Treves offered Merrick a home at Whitechapel Hospital. Merrick would famously reside in a specially prepared apartment there for the next four years, until his death in 1890.

In addition to the dramaturgical upgrades, Lynch channeled some of his own thematic demons into his version of the Elephant Man saga. "I think everybody feels a bit like an outsider," he later explained. "Also, I think everybody hides many things inside them." The Elephant Man as a tormented keeper of inner secrets was a new twist to the tale, and it was pure Lynch. In the surreal opening scene, we witness the "birth" of the Elephant Man as a nightmare replete with the stock Lynchian effects of strobing slow motion and droning background noises. Merrick's mother, surrounded by lush vegetation, is frightened by a herd of rampaging bull elephants. She collapses to the ground, screaming silently as the distorted sound of trumpeting elephants fills the soundtrack. The shot fades to black and a puff of white smoke appears, expanding in slow motion to the sound of a baby crying. On one level, it's probably the strangest sex-to-birth scene ever committed to celluloid, complete with the unpleasant suggestions of rape and bestiality. On another level, it's a theatrical origin myth that posits the Elephant Man as a creature born almost supernaturally in a cloud of magical stage smoke.

And on a third level, surprisingly enough, the opening sequence is an accurate retelling of the origin yarn printed on the freak show leaflets used to hype the real Elephant Man. Titled "The Autobiography of Joseph Merrick," the circular began: "The deformity which I am now exhibiting was caused by my mother being frightened by an Elephant; my mother was going along the street when a procession of Animals were passing by, there was a terrible crush of people to see them, and unfortunately she was pushed under the Elephant's feet, which frightened her very much; this occurring during a time of pregnancy was the cause of my deformity."

Later in movie, we learn that the bizarre opening sequence is a part of a recurring dream that haunts Merrick. Still, Lynch reinforces the fantasy of a supernatural provenance by declining to reveal any details about Merrick's past. Anthony Hopkins's Treves is astonished to learn that Merrick can not only speak, but also read, write, and recite from the Bible by heart; but we're never told exactly how a destitute pariah became "superior in intelligence . . . not to say even refined in his mind." Lynch seems to be suggesting that the sensitive soul of an artist hails from a mysterious set of cosmic coordinates, arriving in a puff of stage smoke to recite Psalm 23 with exquisite elocution.

In fact, the real Joseph Merrick's educational history is no mystery. He attended school until he was twelve, when his father and stepmother forced him to take the first in a series of odd jobs, including the Victorian equivalent of burger flipping—cigar rolling. Later he tried his hand at street vending. When his physical handicaps and appearance interfered with sales, he sought employment in the Leicester workhouse. From there, he wrote to a freak show promoter, asking for work as a sideshow attraction, and wound up in Tom Norman's employ. By omitting these details, Lynch heightens the melodrama, clearly (and inaccurately) implying that Merrick's relationship with Bytes is not just exploitative, but tantamount to enslavement.

Lynch may be guilty of artistic mystification on an order that would make previous Merrick revisionists blush, but the director's romantic notions about Merrick's rarified spirit were in fact quite close to the Victorian view. As we've already noted, the literary concept of the gentle soul obscured by a monstrous facade was one that nineteenth-century Londoners readily applied to Merrick. Newspapers of the day marveled at Merrick's appreciation of the theater and its first lady, the actress Mrs. Madge Kendall. Much ado was made of his construction of an intricate cardboard model of a church, which he planned to present as a gift to his idol. (Alas, Mrs. Kendall sent her husband to fetch it.) It was a masterfully detailed piece of artisanship, and was supposedly modeled after the nearby St. Philip's Church. In the movie, Merrick points to the steeple of the church, which is visible from his apartment window, explaining, "I have to rely on my imagination for what you cannot see." Lynch and a century's worth of other chroniclers hail this achievement as a symbol of Merrick's ascendant creativity and refinement.

Unfortunately, as Jeanette Sitton, custodian of the Joseph Carey Merrick Tribute Web Site, points out, "I was amazed to hear [from the hospital archivist] that the church was a 'kit' product of German origin." So, it was neither a model of St. Philip's Church (which, at any rate, was not even visible from Merrick's window) nor built from scratch. "Readers may perhaps be disappointed to hear that Joseph didn't create the model from blank pieces of card," notes Sitton. But, she adds with emphasis, "*Please remember, for Joseph to build this model at all would have been an enormous task.*"

Lynch can be forgiven for replicating the misconception about the model. But he compounds the misrepresentation by having Mrs. Kendall (Anne Bancroft) pay Merrick a personal visit, perform an impromptu scene from *Romeo and Juliet* with him (complete with kiss), and dedicate a performance to him. None of this actually happened. Because of his physical deformities, the real Merrick had great difficulty speaking; most people could not understand him without Treves there to translate. The idea of him enunciating Shakespearean dialogue is fairly ridiculous. And as for the stage idol giving him the time of day—well, to put it in less-than-Victorian terms—Mrs. Kendall didn't do jack shit for Merrick.

Of course, Joseph Carey Merrick's many chroniclers have always been somewhat less interested in factual fidelity than in projecting their own metaphors, social theory, and political commentary onto a protean inkblot. In that sense, Merrick's timeless "legend," as dramatized by Lynch and dozens of others, is just another form of exploitation. Then again, so are all stories that are "based on fact." But, as manipulation goes, a sympathetic movie, book, or play sure beats a poke with a sharp cane.

Sources and Further Reading

"As of '87, He's Proteus Man (Elephant Man Found to Have Suffered from Proteus Syndrome)." *Science News*. July 25, 1987.

Holladay, William E. and Stephen Watt. "Viewing the Elephant Man." *PMLA*. October 1989.

Howell, Michael and Peter Ford. *The True History of the Elephant Man*. London: Allison & Busby, 2001.

Montagu, Ashley. *The Elephant Man: A Study in Human Dignity*. New York: Outerbridge, 1971.

Sitton, Jeanette. Joseph Carey Merrick Tribute Web Site. http://www.josephmerrick.com.

Mask (1985)

Directed by Peter Bogdanovich
Written by Anna Hamilton Phelan
Starring Eric Stoltz and Cher

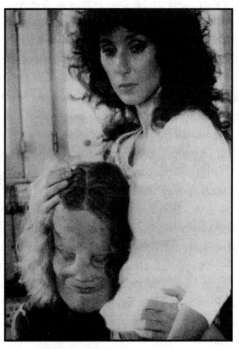

Eric Stoltz as Rocky Dennis and Cher as
Rusty Dennis. © Universal City Studios, Inc.

Most movies based on a true disease are automatically consigned to television, the medical melodrama ward of American entertainment. *Mask*, the definitive craniodiaphyseal dysplasia movie (as of this writing), was a rare exception. Big-screen director Peter Bogdanovich intercepted Anna Hamilton Phelan's script about a Los Angeles teenager grotesquely disfigured by that rare disease before the project had a chance to metastasize into a TV movie-of-the-week. Thus, Jaclyn Smith and Scott Baio's potential loss became Cher and Eric Stoltz's gain.

Mask is based on the true story of Rocky Dennis, an exceptional boy with an extraordinary affliction: an exceedingly rare genetic disorder that results in an abnormal buildup of calcium in the victim's skull. When Rocky was diagnosed at age two with craniodiaphyseal dysplasia, doctors told his mother he wasn't likely to survive past the age of seven. If he lived that long, they warned, Rocky's head would by then have enlarged to twice its normal size, pushing his eyes outward and twisting his features into a grotesque visage resembling a Halloween mask. The extreme pressures on the skull would more than likely lead to brain damage, they said.

Although he did become increasingly disfigured over the course of time, Rocky defied the grimmest of the experts' predictions by surviving well into his teens. What's more, despite his ongoing pain (he suffered from intense migraines) and the unfathomable heartbreak of being so disfigured, Rocky managed to make the best of what he had, winning friends with his upbeat personality and excelling in school as an honor student.

For the most part, *Mask* is an accurate telling of the final years of Rocky's short life—with a few Hollywood drama divagations along the way. First-time screenwriter Anna Hamilton Phelan had "discovered" Rocky in 1978, in the waiting room of UCLA's Center for Genetic Research, just six weeks before his death. Phelan later tracked down Rocky's mother, Florence "Rusty" Dennis, who sold her rights for the bargain price of fifteen thousand dollars and filled in the details of her son's story.

Produced seven years after Rocky's death, *Mask* stars Eric Stoltz in the "title" role, although you won't recognize him behind the sheer wall of foam latex lashed to his face. The prosthetic makeup effects, which earned the film its only Oscar, closely matched the real Rocky's physical features. Cher portrays Rocky's single mom, Rusty Dennis, the redheaded, feisty biker chick who's all blue-collar, Oscar-friendly sass. Because Phelan and Bogdanovich focused their story on the Dennises' stubborn refusal to indulge in self-pity, *Mask* manages to avoid some of the sentimental sinkholes in which crippling-disease movies typically wallow. As a consequence, however, the movie often feels dramatically flat—just like real life. Stoltz's Rocky is cheerfully determined to live a normal boy's life, collecting baseball cards, jamming to awful 1970s rock, dreaming of touring Europe on a Harley, and charming his fellow students into forgetting that he's wearing fifteen pounds of soon-to-be Oscar-winning foam latex makeup. In other words, an upbeat kid with a handicap remains . . . upbeat. Where's the big-screen conflict in that?

To overcome Rocky's undramatic emotional stability, Bogdanovich and Phelan resort to stagecraft. In the third act, the filmmakers give Rocky a job he never had in real life—counselor at summer camp for blind kids. This hire proves to be a boon for the filmmakers, because, lo and behold, it facilitates Rocky's serendipitous encounter with a visually impaired Laura Dern. Naturally, she "sees" the lad's pure soul and falls deeply in love with him. All is onscreen bliss until inevitable heartbreak arrives, about fifteen minutes later (movie time), in the form of Dern's superficial, emotionally "blind" parents, who intercede to break up the couple. Overcoming his heartache, Rocky learns a valuable movie-life lesson: having experienced true love—or the PG-rated, hand-holding equivalent of true love, anyway—he is now free to retire to his bedroom to die quietly.

Whether or not the real Rocky "went steady" with a blind girl (it's not clear from the scant biographical information that is available), the whole third act of *Mask* rings false—and worse, it feels completely *manipulative*. In fact, blindness did figure in the actual boy's life—but it was Rocky who had been declared legally blind, at the age of six. The movie sidesteps this unhappy side effect of his disease, most likely because that fact gets in the way of Phelan's big-hearted theme—that, apart from his cosmetic handicap, Rocky is *better* than normal on an emotional, spiritual, and intellectual level. And it is Society, with an upper-case "S," that is parked, morally, in the handicapped spot.

Phelan's Rocky is so nobler-than-thou that not even Stoltz's unaffected performance can rescue *Mask* from its gallant intent. If the filmmakers had hewed a bit closer to the small details of the real story, they might have had more success in bringing their character to life. For instance, the real Rocky was a mischievous tyke, given to scamming his neighbors by "selling [them] the newspapers he had stolen from their lawns." Now that sounds like a real kid from an actual neighborhood—much preferable to a Gandhi on training wheels.

Bogdanovich and Phelan also play the Hollywood card in their idealization of the blue-collar bikers who down many a can of beer at Cher's house. Sure they do drugs, drink too much, and roughhouse aplenty, but these are movie-style good-guy biker rednecks—the kind that always have jobs, never spout racist epithets, and run no meth labs. Their unstinting tolerance of differently challenged folk stands in stark contrast to the insensitivity of the educated classes, who greet Rocky with either condescension or barely disguised horror. To be sure, the real Rusty and Rocky welcomed bikers into their home, and Rusty led a rough-and-tumble life riding in those circles (she earned a living as a stunt biker at one point). But *Mask*'s depiction of Rocky's extended biker family verges on the bathetic—at one point there's even a scene in which the stocky, mute biker-with-a-heart-o'-gold who watches over Rocky sneaks a puppy into the lad's bedroom. Awwwww.

To its credit, *Mask* incorporates Rusty's drug addiction into the story without apology. The real Rusty had battled with drug abuse since she got hooked on speed at age nineteen. (At the time of *Mask*'s release, Rusty was clean and sober and working as a counselor at Narcotics Anonymous.) But watching the fake Rusty rifle through her secret stash (in the spice rack, natch) in a desperate effort to self-medicate her emotional pain, you almost expect Cher to belt out the plaintive refrain from her 1970s hit "Half Breed": "Things have been against me since the day I was born!" The drug angle becomes yet another of the movie's passive-aggressive emotional manipulations: creeping sentimentality with a hard-edged facade.

Mask makes it clear right up front that Rusty was clean and sober during her pregnancy until the time of Rocky's birth in 1964, thereby quashing potential audience speculation that her drug use was to blame for his condition. Whether or not that's true, it's clear that there is no known correlation between drug abuse and the onset of craniodiaphyseal dysplasia, which is an inherited genetic disorder.

One final note: The real Rocky Dennis had much better taste in music than the kid in the Hollywood version. He was a huge Bruce Springsteen fan. Unfortunately, before *Mask*'s release, the cheapskate studio cut several Bruce Springsteen songs from the film, complaining that the licensing fees were too expensive. The producers replaced those songs with several by Bob Seger, the poor man's Springsteen. And so Hollywood added insult to injury by saddling Rocky with yet another handicap: a tin ear.

Sources and Further Reading

Canning, Mary Beth. "Speaking with Anna Hamilton Phelan." *Latent Image*, Spring 1989.

Corlis, Richard. Review of *Mask*, directed by Peter Bogdonovich. *Time*, March 22, 1985.

Green, Michelle. "The Drama Behind *Mask*." *People Weekly*, March 18, 1985.

Girl, Interrupted (1999)

Directed by James Mangold

Written by Lisa Loomer, Anna Hamilton Phelan,
and James Mangold

Starring Winona Ryder, Angelina Jolie, and Whoopi Goldberg

Winona Ryder as Susanna Kaysen. *Photo
by Suzanne Tenner, © Columbia Pictures*

It was 1967. Race riots were raging across the country, weed was the drug of choice, and the Doors' single "Light My Fire" topped the charts. At one Boston-area high school, all of eighteen-year-old Susanna Kaysen's classmates had a post-graduation plan. Every one of them was going to college; they were going to be ethnobotanists and lawyers and teachers. They were going to live in big houses and have lots of children. They were going to be happy. Kaysen had a plan, too. She was going to swallow a fist full of aspirin and chase it down with a bottle of vodka. Not because young men were being shipped off to Vietnam each day and the world felt like it was coming apart, but because she had a headache.

At least that's how Winona Ryder, who plays Kaysen in the movie version of *Girl, Interrupted*, explains it. In the book, Kaysen's memoir of life inside a mental institution where she was locked up for two years after graduation, the author goes into more detail. Lots more. In fact, the book is comprised, largely, of rambling internal monologues and is more a series of episodic essays or journal entries than an integrated story. Sure, there are brief, observational sketches of fellow inmates and of day-to-day events in the hospital; but mostly, the book is a collection of introspective, adolescent ruminations on everything from the author's own tongue to feminism and the nature of authority to the fuzzy line between insanity and clarity. While this makes for an insightful take on the mid-1960s mental health establishment, the book provided little more than a blueprint, in terms of *story*, for director James Mangold to work with. "I imagined my character as a plate or shirt that had been manufactured incorrectly and was therefore useless," Kaysen wrote in her book. How do you dramatize *that*?

Nonetheless, Ryder championed the making of the film and even served as an executive producer. She had been feverishly drawn to the book, and she chose to play the character of Kaysen, even though it was a less overtly dramatic role than that of Lisa, the spirited sociopath played by Angelina Jolie.

But, fortunately for Mangold, the book wasn't entirely without potential: Kaysen's story did have certain key elements going for it. There was an intriguing premise: a depressed, alienated teen is whisked off in a taxi cab to a legendary mental hospital for a "short rest" and is locked away, against her will, for nearly two years. And there was a compelling central character: a young, articulate, middle-class suburban girl with a countercultural, acerbic edge. Still, it lacked a linear story—nothing actually *happened* in the all-female ward, where the most dramatic event of the day was chain-smoking cigarettes on the floor in front of the nurse's station. So Mangold and fellow screenwriters Lisa Loomer and Anna Hamilton Phelan had to invent one.

Some of their changes were obvious and expected, such as compressing time for the sake of narrative structure or eliminating unnecessary characters. They gathered all of the heroine's essential background information that comes in isolated snippets throughout the book—Kaysen's one-night stand with her English teacher, her suicide attempt, her habit of "wrist-banging"—and crammed it into a convenient, bite-sized backstory that unfolds in the first fifteen minutes of the movie, clarifying her motivation.

Conversely, the screenwriters credit Kaysen's "recovery" at the end of the film to the fact that she witnessed a suicide ("Seeing death, really seeing it, makes dreaming about it fucking ridiculous," Ryder says in voice-over) when in reality, no such thing happened to Kaysen. Recovery was a long, hazy, circuitous route.

Other changes were for more practical reasons. The name of the hospital was changed from McLean —an infamous, high-end "get-a-way spot" that has housed such cultural icons as Sylvia Plath, James Taylor, and Ray Charles—to Claymoore. This was done, no doubt, to protect the integrity of the real hospital, since quite a bit of invented chaos happens there in the movie.

One major departure occurs right on the surface—it involves aesthetics. "There's always a touch of fascination in revulsion," wrote Kaysen. While fascination is good for scripts, however, revulsion is more precarious, and it must be doled out in small and careful doses. Which is why, in the movie, almost all of the girls in the ward are especially beautiful mental patients. It makes crazy a whole lot easier to stomach. Face it: a bare midriff takes the sting out of shock therapy, and leather restraints can be downright sexy if Angelina Jolie is wearing them. Even the character of Polly, whose face had been horrifically disfigured in a burn accident, looks adorable when shot at the right angle. (She's a nuthouse version of Cindy Brady in pajamas, on Percocet.) And in the movie, there's no mention of the more sordid details of mental-institution life that are found in the book—an inmate who smeared herself with feces, for example.

With those technicalities out of the way, the filmmakers were free to let their imaginations roam. They beefed up a friendship between Kaysen and Lisa, giving the script a "buddy movie" feel. And they added some requisite romance to Kaysen's life by throwing in a flirtation with a male orderly and later, a visit from an old boyfriend, who swings by the hospital on his way to Canada and offers to break her out.

But the biggest inventions are the escapes. In a climactic scene in the third act, Jolie and Ryder hitchhike to Daisy Randone's, a former inmate, pad, where they end up inadvertently triggering the girl's suicide, and throughout the movie, a group of patients regularly sneak out of their rooms for midnight jaunts around the hospital. In the movie, Lisa has a set of keys to the building. In the basement there is, of all things, an abandoned bowling alley. To a jacked-up 1960s-pop soundtrack, the hottie inmates slip out for some nocturnal R&R, blissfully skipping through the halls in what ends up feeling like a choreographed tweener music video. None of this ever took place.

To the filmmakers' credit, however, most of these inventions spring from truths found in the book. The real Lisa *was* an escape artist; the filmmakers just decided to send Ryder's character along with her on one particular road trip. And Randone did commit suicide, but Kaysen wasn't around at the time to witness it. Regardless, the movie—neat, whitewashed, and three-act-structured as it is—still resonates emotionally (largely due to strong performances on Ryder's and Jolie's parts) and illuminates greater philosophical truths that are offered in the book.

In the end, the real Kaysen was diagnosed with "borderline personality disorder"—whatever that means. According to the *Diagnostic and Statistical Manual of Mental Disorders*, the disorder is characterized by, among other things, a tendency to shoplift. Suddenly, the opening lines of voice-over in the movie, delivered by Ryder as Kaysen, seem all the more appropriate: "Have you ever stolen something even though you had the cash?" she asks. Um, need we harp on the irony?! No wonder that Ryder, who was convicted of shoplifting in 2003, bonded with her character.

But there was more to Kaysen's condition than sticky fingers. In one particularly poignant scene in the movie, the girls break into a psychiatrist's office to read their medical records. "An instability of self-image, relationships, and mood. Uncertainty about goals, impulsive in activities that are self-damaging . . . a generally pessimistic attitude," Kaysen reads from her file. "Oh, that's me."

"That's everybody," Lisa retorts.

In reality, this scene never happened. Kaysen didn't see her medical records until twenty-five years later, and it took the help of a lawyer to obtain them. But the exchange rings true to the sentiment in Kaysen's book: was she really ever crazy to begin with?

And who knows how close the movie *or* the book are to what *really* happened. Memory is a flawed thing—especially if the period being conjured is marked by the regular ingestion of Thorazine, and especially if it's being reconstructed twenty-five years after the fact, which is how long Kaysen waited to write her memoir. Kaysen admits to having created composite characters in the book, combining medical histories and personality traits so patients wouldn't be as recognizable, and she purposefully kept her family out of the story to protect their privacy. The screenwriters built on Kaysen's adaptation of the truth, creating composites from composites, and in some cases inventing characters altogether. So *Girl, Interrupted* the movie is, in a way, three generations removed from reality.

"It reminds me of my life, but it isn't my life," Kaysen said after the movie was released. The one thing she overtly objected to during filming was the blatant invention of escapes. "You can't have kids sneaking out and looking at patient records. You are locked up. It is not possible and if you had the keys, you would run away—not read your patient files."

To this, Mangold responded, "It's a movie."

Sources and Further Reading

Bock Stern, Dianne. "Woman, Continuing." *The Journal News.* http://www.nyjournalnews.com/lifestyles/bookclub/books/girlinterrupted/author.html.

iVillage. "Susanna Kaysen: Starring Winona Ryder as Me." *Interviews.* http://www.ivillage.com/books/intervu/nonfict/articles/0,,167230_62470,00.html.

Kaysen, Susanna. *Girl, Interrupted.* New York: Random House, 1993.

This chapter was written by Deborah Vankin.

Veronica Guerin (2003)

Directed by Joel Schumacher
Written by Carol Doyle and Mary Agnes Donoghue
Starring Cate Blanchett and Ciarán Hinds

In the movies, journalists usually fall into one of three stereotypes:
1) obnoxious, self-centered pain-in-the-ass;
2) mindless, screaming moron;
3) unstoppable crusader for The Public's Right To Know.
The eponymous heroine of *Veronica Guerin* fits into the latter, and most flattering, category. As she did in real life.

Guerin was a crime reporter for Ireland's top newspaper, the *Sunday Independent*. She took up journalism at age thirty, after a stint as an accountant, and immediately dove into the investigative beat, digging up scandals about pedophile pastors and that sort of thing. After a few years she turned her attention to Dublin's drug scourge. She produced widely read exposés of the city's gangsters and drug lords. In her stories, the bad guys are depicted as colorful characters with flamboyant nicknames such as "the Coach," "the Monk," and "the General." She had to use false names, because Ireland's libel laws are badly biased against the press.

On June 26, 1996, one of her colorful characters shot her dead.

As shown in this Joel Schumacher-directed Jerry Bruckheimer product, Guerin was waiting at a stoplight when two men on a motorcycle pulled up beside her. One opened fire, shooting her in the heart and neck. She died on the spot.

Not the usual ending to a Bruckheimer film, which you'd think would be more likely to conclude with *her* shooting *them*. In slow motion. Bruckheimer has spent a career and made million upon millions off of movies about "winners." And winners don't get blown away at the end of a movie without a fight.

Lately, however, Bruckheimer's been bitten by the notorious Hollywood "Important Man" bug—also known as "Spielberg Syndrome"—and he's been taking on fact-based stories with weighty social themes. *Veronica Guerin* begins with Cate Blanchett, in the title role, venturing fearlessly into the Dublin slums, where teenage junkies jab rusty needles into their arms and toddlers play with syringes as if they were building blocks. It's a sordid scene and in the film, it immediately ignites her outrage.

Schumacher presents this scene as the inciting incident of the story. Problem is, the scene is false—at least, it did not occur as seen on the screen. The drug dealers Guerin targeted in her stories—the ones that evidently got her killed—were not heroin traffickers. They were in the cannabis business. Pot. Hash. This change to the real story is all the more incredible because the principles in the film are called by their real names and are still alive. The violent mobster John Gilligan, who, in the film at least, orders Guerin's murder, is now serving twenty-eight years for his cannabis-related offenses. At no time during his trial, or in any investigation, has Gilligan been linked to the smack business.

Now, a criminal's a criminal. Gilligan was a brutish thug. The scene in which he beats Guerin savagely when she shows up at his home to confront him is completely true. Same for his threat to kidnap and "ride" (sodomize) Guerin's seven-year-old son. Gilligan admitted making that threat, though he took pains to point out that just because he proposed anally penetrating a male child, that doesn't make him gay.

But let's face it—any movie in this day and age that tried to get an American audience all worked up about the evils of marijuana would be laughed out of the theater. It seems doubtful that Bruckheimer would be interested in making the 2003 version of *Reefer Madness*. More important, there's no chance that an audience would relate to the lead character. *What the hell's she getting all indignant about? A guy who sells weed?* There would be only one conclusion: that Veronica Guerin was less interested in pursuing justice than in "getting the story." Any story. In the audience's minds, she'd slide from Stereotype #3 to Stereotype #1.

Not that John Gilligan, the real one, is a character worthy of sympathy. He's not. But if he were, you'd have to feel for the guy. He was tried for Guerin's murder and acquitted, but the film leaves no doubt of his guilt. The epilogue mentions that Gilligan is doing time for drug dealing, but conspicuously omits any note of Gilligan's exoneration.

Heck, why stop there? In this movie, Gilligan is also the man behind Dublin's most famous gangland murder, the killing of Martin "the General" Cahill. The screenplay postulates that Gilligan borrowed half a million pounds from Cahill, the godfather of Dublin's underworld, to set himself up in the drug business. In the movie, rather than pay it back, he orders Cahill killed.

While Cahill's executioners were never caught, the IRA claimed that it was responsible for the murder (that's the version that's told in John Boorman's biopic on Cahill, *The General*), and no one has come up with any solid reason to doubt them. Gilligan has never been linked to the Cahill rubout.

The movie also claims that John Traynor, a mid-level sleazeball who was one of Guerin's underworld sources, organized the hit on Veronica Guerin and is now "fighting extradition" on the charge. That's simply not true.

An earlier film about Guerin, *When the Sky Falls*, had been made, but it was only released in the United Kingdom (and very briefly at that), even though an American actress, Joan Allen, played Guerin (called Sinead Hamilton in that film). That movie didn't flinch from Guerin's own personality pitfalls. Despite the obvious danger of her assignments, for example, she would sometimes cart her young son along with her.

The Bruckheimer movie touches briefly on Guerin's alleged drawbacks as a parent. In one scene that Disney, the film's studio, wanted cut out, Guerin forgets what she gave her son for his birthday. But that's as far as the movie goes in the "bad mommy" direction. The rewrites of reality in *Veronica Guerin* may not shock American moviegoers (the few who saw the movie, anyway), but in Ireland, where Guerin's murder was a national trauma, they produced considerable consternation.

It was an interesting coincidence that, in the United States, this movie was released the same month as was *Shattered Glass*, a true story about an American journalist who makes up all of his best stories to advance his own career. Guerin was often accused of careerism, but she backed up her crusade with hard reporting and, finally, with her life. On that point, *Veronica Guerin* tells the truth.

Sources and Further Reading

Hoge, William. "How a Killing Roused Irish Conscience." *New York Times Magazine*, November 23, 1996.

O'Kelly, Barry. "Guerin: Hollywood Blurs Fact and Fiction." *Sunday Business Post*, June 15, 2003.

O'Sullivan, Charlotte. "*Veronica Guerin*: A True Story?" *The Independent*, July 27, 2003.

Boys Don't Cry (1999)

Directed by Kimberly Peirce
Written by Kimberly Peirce and Andy Bienen
Starring Hilary Swank and Chloë Sevigny

Hilary Swank as Brandon Teena.
Photo by Bill Matlock, © Fox Searchlight

During her brief, harrowing life, Teena Brandon treated gender and identity as mutable qualities. For at least two years, the troubled Nebraska girl had passed herself off as a boy named Brandon, romancing a succession of unsuspecting girlfriends. When the girls eventually caught on, Brandon told shifting stories about birth defects or unfinished sex-change operations. She also freely shuffled nonsexual aspects of her identity, forging checks, stealing her girlfriends' credit cards, and fleeing from Lincoln to Humboldt and Fall City, apparently to reinvent herself.

In life, Brandon's constant shape-shifting left a trail of bewildered friends. After her shocking 1993 murder in Humboldt, Nebraska, by two ex-cons who were enraged by her transgender pose, it provoked a more academic kind of confusion. Eulogists, activists, newspersons, and assorted rubberneckers rushed in to parse and identify the meaning of Teena Brandon (or Brandon Teena) and her killing. The answers varied, depending on who was explicating. Brandon's elusive sense of self had engendered one final identity-shift, into a fuzzy concept that offered a hook for every comer with a socio-political coat to hang. She could be the victim of social injustice or redneck misogyny or childhood sex abuse. Or maybe she was a courageous trailblazer for transgender self-expression.

The 1999 docudrama *Boys Don't Cry* brought several coats to the party. The result was a powerful "message" film that advocates tolerance for alternative sexual identities, with more than a few factual distortions inserted in service of that message. In the wake of the film's release, those factual liberties became a source of controversy.

Director Kimberly Peirce first read about the case in a lengthy 1994 *Village Voice* article by Donna Minkowitz, which was published several months after the murder. According to Peirce, she immediately "fell in love with Brandon," adding in another interview that she also "felt an immediate kinship." Peirce, who describes herself as queer, rather than gay or lesbian, was attracted to Brandon's charisma, and his boldness in expressing his sexuality. "I was overwhelmed by the power of his desire to change himself into his fantasy of a boy," she told *Newsweek*. "The absolute daring and courage to go and pull it off. So I thought it was my job to bring Brandon back to life and make sense of it for everybody."

Highlighting those aspects of Brandon's personality that she admired, Peirce minimized some of his less laudable character traits. In the *Village Voice* article, Minkowitz described the darker side of Brandon as "hectoring, hounding, possessive," a person prone to jealous rages and, after a breakup, stalkerish behavior: "He would write letters and appear in person constantly, begging, wheedling, terrorizing," according to Minkowitz. The *Voice* article and other media profiles written after Brandon's death also paint a picture of a young person considerably more conflicted about his sexual identity than is the character portrayed by Hilary Swank in the film. As one of Brandon's ex-girlfriends said to Minkowitz, "The thought of being gay was much more disturbing to her than getting a sex change."

To be fair, fact-based movies often mythologize their protagonists to one degree or another, burnishing the positives and sweeping the negatives under a rug. The point is simply that the director's decision to "bring Brandon back to life" as an icon of positive sexual self-determination required downplaying other aspects of a complex person.

Brandon's mother, JoAnn Brandon, wasn't happy with *Boys Don't Cry*, calling it "a hurried, low-budget film that should never have claimed to be true." "Viewers only meet the gender-confused person, with no context of her past," she told the Associated Press. JoAnn was particularly upset that the movie failed to explain that when she was a child, Teena had been molested by a relative over the course of several years (JoAnn said she didn't know about it at the time). In JoAnn's view, Teena's cross-dressing was a self-defensive measure borne of that earlier traumatic experience. "Teena pretended she was a man so no other man could touch her," JoAnn said. JoAnn also complained that Peirce never bothered to interview her or any of Teena's relatives. Peirce did interview Lana Tisdel, Brandon's last girlfriend, and other residents of Fall City, where he had spent the last three weeks of his life. And that's the problem, insists JoAnn: "I don't understand how you can put three weeks of somebody's life up on film and win an award for it."

Others have charged that the film presents a somewhat mythologized version of Brandon. According to Jared Hohlt of *Slate* magazine, the real Brandon never used "Teena" as his last name. "He was called 'Brandon Teena' only posthumously," writes Hohlt. If so, the rechristening happened shortly after Brandon's death, because the *Voice* article refers to him as Brandon Teena.

Two other key changes raised eyebrows and ire. In the movie, Brandon and a woman friend are gunned down in the final scene. In reality, the murderers killed three people after breaking into the Humboldt farmhouse—Brandon, Lisa Lambert, and Phillip DeVine. Friends of DeVine were offended to learn that his death had been written out of the theatrical reenactment, as if he were somehow less significant than the other victims.

Also in the final scene, Peirce upped the dramatic ante by placing Brandon's girlfriend, Lana Tisdel (Chloë Sevigny), at the scene of the crime. Peirce has Lana falling asleep before the murder spree and "doing nothing about it after it has occurred," as the real Lana's lawyers put it in the real lawsuit she subsequently filed against Fox Searchlight Pictures.

But the issue of the real Lana's whereabouts during the murder is murky. Lana has always insisted that she was miles away, in her mother's trailer. On the night of the murder, the killers dropped by Lana's place, looking for Brandon. The ex-cons—John Lotter (who would receive a sentence of death for the crime) and Tom Nissen (who would get off with a life sentence)—who were upset to learn that the "boy" doin' it with Lana weren't no boy 't'all—were the same Neanderthals who had savagely beaten and raped Brandon the previous week, presumably to learn her a lesson about girl-boys gettin' real girls all excited in confusin'-like ways. (Lotter was an ex-beau of Lana's, although the movie doesn't tell us this.) John reportedly said to Lana and her sister, "I feel like killing somebody." Lana's mother told them where they could find Brandon. So Lotter and Nissen drove to Humboldt.

According to Aphrodite Jones, the author of *All She Wanted,* a true-crime book about Brandon's murder, Nissen told a police officer that Lana "was in the car" outside the crime scene, but that she had not gone into the farmhouse. Later, on the witness stand, Nissen testified that he and Lotter were the only ones in the car. So there you go. For dramatic reasons Peirce decided to move Lana into the farmhouse. Cue lawsuit.

Actually, the farmhouse scene was probably the lesser of the slights that drove Lana to litigate. The lawsuit also accused Fox Searchlight of falsely depicting her as a boozer and a druggie, and for allowing a character in the film to describe her as "lazy, white trash, and a skanky snake." Fox Searchlight eventually settled the suit. It's not known whether Lana subsequently upgraded to a double-wide.

Sources and Further Reading

Hohlt, Jared. "Double Trouble." *Slate*, October 8, 1999. http://slate.msn.com/id/36040.

Jones, Aphrodite. *All She Wanted*. New York: Pocket Books, 1996.

Miller, Francesca. "Putting Teena Brandon's Story on Film." *Gay and Lesbian Review Worldwide*, Fall 2000.

Minkowitz, Donna. "Love Hurts." *Village Voice*, April 19, 1994.

Born on the Fourth of July (1989)

Directed by Oliver Stone
Written by Oliver Stone and Ron Kovic
Starring Tom Cruise and Willem Dafoe

Tom Cruise as Ron Kovic.
Photo by Roland Neveu, © Universal City Studios, Inc.

The real Ron Kovic and director Oliver Stone. *Photo by Roland Neveu, © Universal City Studios, Inc.*

When any other Hollywood director tampers with nonfiction, it's called "taking dramatic license." When Oliver Stone does the same, the Klaxons sound, the pundits go to code red, and a state of historical revisionism is declared. Why is it that Stone so often winds up getting read the riot act when other moviemakers routinely bulldoze history with impunity? The answers are varied and complex (see *JFK*, page 428), but high on the list is the simple fact that Stone makes political movies in an age when most directors studiously avoid them. Oliver Stone films are unabashedly polemical. Consequently, they tend to piss off the oppositely minded.

As Stone films go, *Born on the Fourth of July* was relatively uncontroversial. Based on the best-selling autobiography of Vietnam veteran Ron Kovic, a U.S.

Marine whose battlefield wounds left him paralyzed from the chest down, *Born on the Fourth of July* chronicles Kovic's personal transformation from gung-ho soldier to neglected veteran to crusading antiwar activist. The film, which was cowritten by Stone and Kovic, garnered praise from critics, historians, and moviegoers alike. It earned Stone his third Oscar and star Tom Cruise his first Academy Award nomination.

And it really pissed off the political right, still smarting as late as 1989 for being cast in the collective memory as warmongering heavies. Stone carpet-bombed that theme home, pitting Kovic against a gauntlet of red-faced, bloated, jingoistic reactionaries. Not surprisingly, conservatives assailed *Born on the Fourth of July* as "a willful twisting of fact to refashion history into the dramatic and political points the moviemakers hope to make."

Was there "willful twisting" at large in the film? Certainly, but no more so than what you'd typically find in any other Hollywood "docudramatization." Did Stone's changes "refashion history?" Although that point is certainly debatable, we agree with historian Robert A. Rosenstone, who wrote, in an essay titled "Oliver Stone As Historian," that Stone's plot manipulations in *Born on the Fourth of July* were "not a complete fabrication but, rather, a cunning mixture of diverse visual elements—fact, near fact, displaced fact, invention." The movie may juggle specific details for dramatic purposes, but, as a big-picture survey of an era, it's a mostly faithful representation. As Stone himself put it, "I took creative license to make my point, and sometimes sacrificed smaller truths for larger ones."

The most obvious sacrificial offerings occur in two key scenes that dramatize police brutality against antiwar protesters. Both scenes—a 1970 student demonstration at Syracuse University and a 1972 episode at the Republican National Convention in Florida—purport to be reenactments of actual events. In the first scene, Kovic travels to Syracuse to visit a girlfriend (Kyra Sedgwick). Attending an antiwar demonstration led by yippie Abbie Hoffman (played by the real Abbie Hoffman in a cameo), the wheelchair-bound Kovic winds up stranded at the epicenter of a bloody police assault against the peaceful students. Apart from the fact that there really was a demonstration in Syracuse on that day, Stone has invented just about everything else in the scene: Kovic did not have a girlfriend; he wasn't at Syracuse University on the day of the demonstration; Abbie Hoffman did not appear at the Syracuse event; and there was no violence—police did not attack the students.

Defending his factual revisions, Stone argued that the scene compressed disparate real events into a single movie scene for dramatic purposes. (And, by giving Kovic a "lost love," Stone served the standard Hollywood purpose of milking a sentimental reaction from the audience.) Kovic may not have attended a rally that turned so violent, but police brutality against demonstrators was a common occurrence during the Vietnam era. "In a way," Stone said, "I merged Ron's story with that of other veterans, including me."

The second scene in which Stone sacrifices small facts to further an ostensibly larger truth occurs near the end of the movie. In this segment, Kovic leads a group of antiwar veterans onto the floor of the Republican National Convention. After Kovic begins to denounce the GOP to television reporters, security guards forcibly eject him. Outside the hall, a police goon squad viciously assaults the protesters. This is the scene that really got conservatives in a lather. Even if Stone was correct in his larger truth—that the Republican party contributed mightily to the prolongation of the Vietnam war and the escalation of social discord at home—the director's slaughter of the "smaller truth" was hardly fair; Republicans did not, in fact, launch a bloody suppression of legal dissent at their 1972 convention.

Having tread on conservatives, Stone found himself the target of a retaliatory nitpicking assault, and many of the film's less egregious factual enhancements were attacked in an effort to discredit the entire enterprise. Among the cluster nitpicks: Kovic didn't break his leg at the Bronx Veterans' Hospital, as shown in the film, but in his New York apartment (much later than is depicted in the film); Kovic's high school wrestling coach didn't bellow at his students like a cruel drill sergeant; and Kovic's mother wasn't the rabid anticommunist she's portrayed as in the film.

There was one other major fictional enhancement that came under attack by the film's critics. In his book, Kovic refers repeatedly to "the corporal from Georgia," a boy that Kovic worries he may have accidentally killed in a friendly fire incident during a chaotic 1967 battle. (Although Kovic's commanding officer later insisted that the matter was properly investigated and that Kovic was cleared, Kovic had his doubts about the thoroughness of the inquiry.) The movie dramatizes the battle scene and eliminates all ambiguity, leaving no doubt about Kovic's role in the accidental shooting. Stone also disposes of all doubt about the Marine Corps's response: in the film, Kovic's commanding officer unambiguously covers up the incident. This sets up the film's dramatic turning point—the moment that the movie Kovic completes his transformation from misguided soldier to enlightened antiwar activist. It happens in another completely invented scene, as Tom Cruise's Kovic travels to Venus, Georgia, to offer a humble mea culpa to the dead marine's grieving parents. In a moment of catharsis, Kovic confesses that he killed their boy. The family reluctantly, but sincerely, forgives Kovic, who is, through that act of contrition, reborn as an antiwar crusader. It's all very cinematic. And it never really happened. In reality, there is no such place as Venus, Georgia, and Kovic never apologized to, or received forgiveness from, the family of the boy he may or may not have killed.

After *Born on the Fourth of July*'s premiere, a reporter asked Kovic about that factual upgrade. The ex-marine explained that the apologia scene had been a real-life recurring nightmare for him, and that when he told the director about the dream, Stone decided to write it into the script as an actual event.

So, does Stone's rendition of the "truth" here qualify as factual atrocity or standard Hollywood operating procedure? We're inclined to go with the latter characterization. But let's give the final word to historian Rosenstone: "One way to read [Kovic's] entire autobiography is as a confession of this crime [the friendly fire incident] . . . an act of expiation, and a plea for forgiveness. To create images for this internal process, for the guilt that prompts Kovic to write . . . Stone invents an entire sequence." By dramatizing Kovic's literary act of contrition as a literal meeting in Venus, Georgia, Stone translated the whole purpose of the book (as postulated by Rosenstone) into a clear visual metaphor: the forgiveness that "by writing his book, Kovic received from the public at large."

Sources and Further Reading

Accent on Living. "Not a Pretty Picture." Interview with Ron Kovic. Spring 1990.

Rosenstone, Robert A. "Oliver Stone As Historian." In *Oliver Stone's USA: Film, History, and Controversy*, edited by Robert Brent Toplin. Lawrence, KS: University Press of Kansas, 2000.

West, Diana. "*Born on the Fourth* Lies." *Orange County Register*, March 11, 1990.

The Perfect Storm (2000)

Directed by Wolfgang Petersen
Written by William D. Wittliff
Starring George Clooney and Mark Wahlberg

George Clooney, former underwear model Mark Wahlberg,
and he-man journalist Sebastian Junger.
Photo by Claudette Barius, © Warner Bros.

He-man journalist Sebastian Junger's 1997 bestseller *The Perfect Storm* is about as gripping a tale of man against nature as any ever written—except maybe for another bestselling book that was published that same year: *Into Thin Air*, by Jon Krakauer.

Krakauer's book was a rather straightforward narrative of a 1996 disaster on Mount Everest that killed eight climbers. The story is recounted in the first person by Krakauer, who was himself a climber in one of the ill-fated expeditions, and who had been sent on assignment by the adventure-travel magazine *Outside*. The journalist, therefore, witnessed the calamity with his own rather bleary and oxygen-depleted eyes. He was lucky to escape the mountain with his life, much less a bestselling book, and part of *Into Thin Air* concerns his own moral conflict over his possible role in the tragedy. Upon its publication, it was impossible to imagine that the book would not be turned into a terrific Hollywood movie. It was a natural. But, except for a quickie made-for-the-tube thing starring a guy from *thirtysomething*, the movie never materialized.

Junger's tome, on the other hand, was a product of journalistic legwork and plenty of hours logged at the library. *The Perfect Storm* is the story of a massive storm on the high seas that sunk a Gloucester swordfish boat in 1991, drowning all six crewmen. Junger, quite obviously, was not on that boat. He was in Gloucester during the storm, though, while the doomed fishing vessel was hundreds of miles northeast, in the ocean between Nova Scotia and Newfoundland. The next day, Junger clipped out a newspaper article about a local boat, the *Andrea Gail*, that had apparently been lost at sea during the tempest. That article was the genesis of his book. Published six years later, it's brimming with arcane (albeit weirdly fascinating) technical details about the meteorology of hurricanes. Despite the dramatic subject matter, *The Perfect Storm* made a tough assignment for adaptation to the needs of Hollywood. Add to that the problem that no one, and certainly not Junger, had any real idea what took place on board the *Andrea Gail* in the last hours of its final voyage and you have even less of a recipe for an inspiring true story of the type prized by the studios. The fact that all six main characters die at the end (and rather pointless deaths at that) didn't help, either.

But Junger's book got made into a $120-million summer blockbuster. Go figure.

During the film's production there was much speculation about whether the moviemakers would opt for a new ending that allowed some or all of the fishermen onboard the *Andrea Gail* to survive in a fashion that would send audiences home in the uplifted state of escapist bliss that the studios strive for in their big-budget summer spectaculars. To the credit of director Wolfgang Petersen and screenscribe William D. Wittliff, the deceased crewmen—whose family and friends were still very much alive in Gloucester and still reeling from the tragedy nine years later—stayed dead. Their poignant death scenes were, however, entirely invented. Other than that they probably drowned, no one knows the details of their final moments. In his book, Junger pieces together accounts of other boats in crisis, as well as some biological details of death by drowning, to speculate on what the six men might have experienced as they watched their own lives draw to a close.

Even the monstrous sixty-foot wave that finally does in the *Andrea Gail* onscreen was a speculative invention, though not an implausible one. The sad reality is that the *Andrea Gail* simply vanished from radio contact in the midst of the storm and was never seen or heard from again.

The screenplay invents a through-line for the ship's captain, Billy Tyne, who in real life was one of the best and most dedicated fishermen on the east coast. As Junger tells it, every fisherman in Gloucester wanted to sail with Tyne because he always found the fish and made a boatload of cash. In the movie, Tyne (George Clooney) is on a "cold streak." He's not bringing home the fish—which is why, on this fateful mission, he risks his boat and the lives of his crew to go where the swordfish are, no matter how hazardous the weather conditions. The real Tyne was known to push his boat to the limits, but whether he deliberately led his crew on what amounted to a suicide run through the heart of the worst storm in anyone's memory will never be known. It's just a moviemaker's device to ratchet up the drama, because the drama of men fighting for their lives against gale-force winds and sixty-foot seas just wasn't dramatic enough.

In the book, there's a jaw-dropping subplot— two of them actually— involving Coast Guard and Air National Guard rescue squads. In the first, a Coast Guard rescue jumper dives into the raging ocean and swims to rescue three people trapped on a sinking boat. In the second, an Air National Guard helicopter, on its way to rescue a wayward Japanese sailboater, runs out of fuel and is ditched into the water. All the crew members but one survive, by some bizarre miracle. The movie conflates the two rescue crews into one and tells us that the ditched chopper was on its way to rescue the *Andrea Gail* when it took its plunge.

That's fiction, of course. But it's based on a real rumor. It was widely believed that the Coast Guard received a distress signal from the *Andrea Gail*— one of the mysteries of Junger's book is why the crew never sent a Mayday call—but chose not to try a rescue, believing the conditions too dangerous.

The rumor generated a great deal of resentment in Gloucester, but, as Junger noted, if conditions were too severe for even the fearless Coast Guard rescue squads, the *Andrea Gail* and its crew were already doomed. Nothing was going to change that.

Pretty depressing stuff for a summer blockbuster. The moviemakers deserve credit for sticking to the essence of the real events, especially that of the deaths of the main characters, even if they did impose some Hollywood schmaltz on top of one of the most dramatic true stories ever optioned by Hollywood.

Sources and Further Reading

Junger, Sebastian. *The Perfect Storm: A True Story of Men Against the Sea.* New York: Perennial Books, 1999.

REEL FIVE
Showbiz Phonies

Adaptation (2002)

Directed by Spike Jonze

Written by Charlie Kaufman and Donald Kaufman

Starring Nicolas Cage, Meryl Streep, and Chris Cooper

The real Susan Orlean.
Courtesy of The New Yorker/Gasper Tringale

Whatever possessed Hollywood to adapt Susan Orlean's nonfiction bestseller, *The Orchid Thief*, into a feature film? The book is a fastidiously observed, 284-page rumination on the natural history of a highly specialized genus of flora and the equally specialized breed of human fanatic who covets it. There's no denying that *The Orchid Thief* is well adapted to its native environment—that subgenre of literary nonfiction in which a sensitive author waxes writerly about a subject of microcosmic scope. But as a collection of loosely linked essays devoid of any connecting narrative, inherent suspense, or sustained central characters, the book is about as cinematic as an Ortho gardening guide.

Evidently, that didn't bother the green-light team who snatched up the rights to Orlean's book (and her 1995 *New Yorker* article, from which the book had germinated). Clearly, they envisioned a prestige project with a literary pedigree, the kind of self-consciously pensive film that inevitably involves Meryl Streep or Kevin Spacey. (Or perhaps the producers were stricken by the "orchidelerium" described in the book, a feverish state of mind that converts otherwise rational beings into orchid-obsessed pod people.)

Spacey must have been busy chasing Oscar bait elsewhere, but Meryl Streep did sign on. Thankfully, so did Charlie Kaufman and Spike Jonze, the writer/director team behind the playfully subversive *Being John Malkovich*. Given the impossible task of shaping Orlean's precocious musings into a working screenplay, it's no surprise that Kaufman quickly hit a creative brick wall. But one man's writer's block can be another's entertainment mother lode (at least, in schaden-freudian Hollywood), and Kaufman solved his dilemma with a clever conceit: He would write a movie about a screenwriter named Charlie Kaufman struggling to write a movie based on Orlean's book. In other words, he would write himself into the script, and then write himself *writing himself* into the script.

As a postmodernist stunt, the meta-narrative that Kaufman has built atop the foundation of Orlean's book is a precarious contraption, and it often risks collapsing under the weight of its self-references. Postmodernly, though, Kaufman has already built that complaint into the movie itself, circumventing the critics: At one point his onscreen likeness (Nicolas Cage, in earnest schlub mode) denounces his unfinished script as "self-indulgent, narcissistic, solipsistic," concluding the auto-flagellation with, "I'm pathetic." Maybe so, but it was probably the only treatment of Orlean's book that stood a chance of working.

According to the real-life Kaufman (who, apparently, is not "fat and bald," as Cage constantly denigrates himself in the film) the movie is accurate in its portrayal of his mounting frustration in writing the screenplay. "I was growing desperate trying to get a script done," he said. "For months I'd get up and say, 'I can't do this.'" The naval-gazing approach wasn't his first choice. "I didn't intend to write it that way. But this was what finally made the script come alive for me."

As the title suggests, *Adaptation* has thematic ambitions larger than the straightforward reportage of *The Orchid Thief*. Ultimately, the movie is about the creative process: how one form of art or literature mutates—*must* mutate—into another form in order to thrive in a new, alien environment. The themes of adaptation and mutation are present in Orlean's book, albeit on a mostly literal level: exotic and highly specialized to survive in a particular, extremely narrow tropical environment, orchids are notoriously fragile when removed from their native element. Kaufman molds Orlean's lessons in naturalism, evolution, and Darwinian natural selection into a broader metaphor that represents his own tussle to transplant her book into the alien soil of a big-screen feature film.

Much of the film's comedy stems from Kaufman's frustrated attempts to mutate *The Orchid Thief* into something that will take root in the fertilizer-rich soil of Hollywood. He wants to remain true to the simple, reflective spirit of the book, but it's a task that proves impossible. "I'd rather let the movie exist," he sermonizes to a vacant-eyed movie producer (Tilda Swinton), "rather than being artificially plot-driven." Kaufman then ticks off the list of Hollywood clichés he absolutely wants to avoid: "Characters learning profound life lessons," characters falling in love and changing in the end to become better people, etc. "Why can't there be simply a movie about flowers?" he asks. The film demonstrates exactly why there can't be a movie simply about flowers. "The book has no story!" Kaufman later sputters to his dopey agent. "It's that sprawling *New Yorker* shit!" A literal translation from book to screen would have wound up shriveled and lifeless. Still, Kaufman and Jonze manage to transfer some of the book's most lyrical sections onto film, in the form of flashbacks as Kaufman pores over the book, desperate to find creative purchase. A few beautiful short montages show us orchids—and their ingenious environmental adaptations—while Meryl Streep (as Orlean) narrates passages from the book.

Kaufman's dizzy plotting darts back and forth in time and space, from Orlean researching and writing her book to Kaufman sweating out his script (and masturbating over the picture of Streep that's on her book's dust jacket). The story (such as it is) told in *The Orchid Thief* unfolds in bits and pieces, as

Kaufman sits hunkered over his typewriter. Kaufman is mostly faithful to Orlean's reporting, which revolves around the exploits of an eccentric Florida native named John Laroche. A self-taught, self-described orchid "scholar," Laroche found himself in legal hot water in the early 1990s after he and three Seminole Indians were caught poaching two hundred rare and endangered orchid and bromeliad plants in southwestern Florida's Fakahatchee Swamp.

The real-life Orlean had followed the real-life Laroche (played in the film by Chris Cooper, in an Oscar-winning performance) as he puttered around South Florida in between court hearing dates. Laroche was the kind of outlandish character that journalists dream of finding. A charismatic schemer with a cantankerous streak at least as wide as his toothless smile, and a million plans to strike it rich, none of which ever seemed to take, he was an endlessly fascinating oddball. No doubt this is what attracted Hollywood to Orlean's book in the first place. Practically every comment out of his mouth was a diamond in the rough. "Frankly, your Honor," he confessed at his preliminary hearing, "I'm probably the smartest person I know." Kaufman lifts these dialogue gems directly from the book, and rarely resorts to writer's embellishments.

But embellishments do play a major role in the movie. And the biggest fabrication is the character of Charlie Kaufman's twin brother, Donald. Cage also plays Donald Kaufman, who in many ways is Charlie's direct opposite— as boisterous, blithe, and unreflective as Charlie is introverted, pessimistic, and trapped in his own head. The real Charlie shares a screenwriting credit for *Adaptation* with Donald Kaufman, and both were nominated for an Oscar for Best Screenplay. But in reality, Charlie Kaufman has no twin brother. After the movie's release, both Jonze and the real Charlie Kaufman were somewhat evasive on the subject of Donald. As Kaufman put it, "Crediting the script to myself and Donald is important to understanding the movie. So we don't want to say that Donald is an invention."

The invention of Donald allowed Kaufman to dramatize his own conflicted impulses as a screenwriter. The sensitive, self-doubting Charlie wants to avoid cliché and create a work of art; the high-fiving, successful Donald knows that any saleable Hollywood screenplay must adhere to certain formulaic conventions. Donald swears by real-life scriptwriting guru Robert McKee (played in the film by Brian Cox); Charlie knows that the oracular McKee is a hack, but, under the influence of his mounting frustration and writer's block, he attends one of his seminars anyway, during which McKee reduces the art of storytelling to a blustering PowerPoint presentation. "Tell you a secret," McKee says, imparting a pearl of wisdom to Charlie. "The last act makes a film. Wow them in the end and you've got a hit." But, he warns, "Don't you dare bring in a deus ex machina!" Charlie ultimately takes McKee's advice, for the most part, which launches the film into its entirely fictional third act. Charlie asks Donald for help in finishing the script, and suddenly the film changes tone dramatically, becoming a clichéd Hollywood thriller deploying every formulaic movie device in the book. In short, this is where "Donald" earns his screenwriting credit.

More than one moviegoer who hadn't read *The Orchid Thief* might have exited the theater with the mistaken impression that *New Yorker* writer Susan Orlean really did become a drug-snorting, pistol-packing moll, or that she and John Laroche really did fall madly in love. Or that "Donald" died as a result of gunshot wounds and a fatal car crash in the Everglades. Or that Laroche was actually killed in an improbable deus-ex-machina moment involving a ferocious alligator. Or that Charlie learned a profound life lesson, fell in love, and became a better person in the process.

Despite all of Donald's punching up of the third act, the movie ends on a cynical note that is all Charlie, all postmodernist bravado. It's as if the real Charlie Kaufman is throwing in the towel and conceding that any Hollywood adaptation must inevitably mutate into something awful.

Sources and Further Reading

Boxer, Sarah. "*New Yorker* Writer Turns Gun-Toting Floozy? That's Showbiz." *New York Times*, December 9, 2002.

Libby, Brian. "Writer's Block? Insert Self Into Script. Problem Solved." *Christian Science Monitor*, December 6, 2002.

Orlean, Susan. *The Orchid Thief.* Guilford, NY: Ballantine, 1998.

Ed Wood (1994)

Directed by Tim Burton
Written by Scott Alexander and Larry Karaszewski
Starring Johnny Depp and Sarah Jessica Parker

Johnny Depp (right) as Ed Wood and Martin Landau as Bela Lugosi.

Photo by Suzanne Tenner. © Touchstone Pictures. All Rights Reserved.

The real Ed Wood (left), with TV psychic Criswell and Paul "Kelton the Cop" Marco.

The 1978 death of discount film auteur Edward D. Wood Jr. went largely unnoticed by the press and public. The director of *Plan 9 from Outer Space* and other charmingly inept low-end features, Wood had toiled for years on the fringes of Hollywood, unacknowledged and unrewarded. He managed to churn out a dozen or so extremely peculiar movies, often in the sci-fi/horror genre and always to box-office indifference. His boundless enthusiasm for cinema and the unlimited energy with which he pursued his art were matched only by his infinite lack of talent at it. Though he died in alcoholic squalor, it wouldn't be strictly accurate to say that Wood suffered a late-career decline. That would imply a previous career ascension.

A few years after Wood's death, something as peculiar and unbelievable as any of his films occurred: Wood began to have a career comeback, an encore of sorts that emerged, appropriately enough, "from beyond the grave" (a standard spatial coordinate in his films). A new generation of media consumers, weaned on bad TV and drilled in late night satire, had rediscovered Wood's cheesy oeuvre of next-to-no-budget B movies. Even dead, Wood was still not ready for prime time, but late-night prowlers of the UHF band were finally ready for *him*.

For irony-obsessed baby boomers, the second coming of Ed Wood was an epiphany. During the early days of his NBC talk show, David Letterman regularly ran clips from *Plan 9*. In a book franchise based on the sarcastic appreciation of "bad cinema," film critic siblings Harry and Michael Medved (who had not yet completed his metamorphosis into a sanctimonious jackass) christened *Plan 9 from Outer Space* "the worst movie of all time." (That remains an arguable characterization, given mainstream Hollywood's huge backlist of unspeakably awful mainstream movies. At least Wood's films are compulsively watchable in a "so bad they're *good*" way, as the cliché goes.) Meanwhile, those newfangled VCR machines spread the Cult of Ed Wood beyond the insomniac hipster set.

An Edward D. Wood Jr. movie was outrageously awkward on multiple fronts, an inspired farrago of incompetence. The recipe typically began with a god-awful genre, usually misappropriated from the hot exploitation trend of the moment ("Teenage girls taking their thrills unashamed!" or "Grave robbers from outer space"); next came the script, speed-written by Wood in a single sitting, and brimming with malapropian and/or hard-boiled dialogue ("Inspector Clay's dead. Murdered. And somebody's responsible!"); Wood's stock troupe of players, a sideshow of eccentrics and show-biz has-beens, took the dialogue to the next level, emoting with acute self-consciousness. Added to that mix were the seemingly ninety-nine-cent sets that visibly wobbled when characters brushed against them, as well as Wood's slapdash approach to editing and continuity (which often resulted in shots flipping from night to day several times in the course of a single scene). The result was a toweringly incompetent opus so horrifyingly bad that it almost played like self-parody.

If his movies were "out there," Wood's personal life was stranger still. An avowed cross-dresser, Wood fetishized women's angora sweaters, on both himself and his girlfriends. Though apparently an unwavering heterosexual, he enjoyed dressing in ladies' pantsuits, and he told friends that, as a soldier during

World War II, he had worn girls' panties under his uniform. Wood's first feature film, *Glen or Glenda*, was an impassioned, if incoherent, plea for tolerance of transvestism. Wood not only wrote and directed the movie, but starred in *both* title roles, as well.

Without a doubt, there was heavy element of condescension in Ed Wood fandom. Watching one of his movies go completely wrong on every conceivable level, you couldn't help but feel superior to both the product and its maker. Likewise, snickering at Wood's incredibly strange, mixed-up personal life and his hugely miscalculated ambition conferred an implicit note of self-congratulation; after all, you were clued in to the absurdity of it all.

It fell to Wood's biographer to rescue the master manqué from easy mockery and scorn. In *Nightmare of Ecstasy*, published by Feral House in 1992, Rudolph Grey compiled the definitive oral history of Ed Wood. Grey conducted extensive interviews with dozens of the director's friends and associates, and he presented their recollections verbatim, without authorial comment. The portrait of Wood that emerged in the book was even stranger than the anecdotes that had percolated around the Cult of Wood for years. But Wood's surviving pals were obviously devoted to the man, in awe of his boundless enthusiasm, goodwill, and perseverance in the face of constant failure. Grey's book was almost reverent in tone, and irony-free. Still, the absurdity of Wood's life and art shone through more powerfully than ever. *Nightmare of Ecstasy* (the goofily lurid title would have pleased Wood) read like a tragicomedy, and it was only a matter of time before an independent filmmaker recognized its cinematic potential.

Fortunately, that filmmaker turned out to be Tim Burton, the idiosyncratic director of *Edward Scissorhands*, *Batman*, and a number of other studio-sized fantasies about misunderstood outsiders. Somehow, Burton persuaded the bemused executives at Disney to back a big-budget, professionally competent paean to the world's most incompetent director. The result was *Ed Wood*, arguably Burton's best movie to date, and a film that could have gone wrong in countless ways. That it didn't is a testament to dozens of elements coming together in the kind harmonic convergence that had always eluded the real Ed Wood.

The odd-biopic screenwriting team of Scott Alexander and Larry Karaszewski (whose work includes *The People vs. Larry Flynt* and *Man on the Moon*—see page 196) managed to pull off the seemingly impossible by wrestling a chronological story from the anecdotal chaos of Grey's book. The cast was pitch-perfect, including Johnny Depp, in a bouncy turn as the eternally unflappable Wood, and Martin Landau, giving an Oscar-winning performance as the aging, morphine-addicted Bela Lugosi. In *Ed Wood*, Tim Burton managed to channel the mutant charm of life in the margins of Hollywood, celebrating Wood's eccentricity and camp factor without condescension.

Shot in black and white (one of many built-in homages to Wood's style), *Ed Wood* covers the director's early career, from his arrival in Hollywood in the early 1950s to the 1959 release of *Plan 9*, Wood's proudest achievement. Burton wisely wraps up the story there, thus avoiding the depressing details of Wood's later life of scraping by as a writer of soft-core porn and eventually drinking himself, at age fifty-four, into an early grave.

The outré details are all here: Wood's unabashed cross-dressing ("I love women. Wearing their clothes makes me feel closer to them."); his touching friendship with a down-and-out, forgotten Bela Lugosi, who was happy to be exploited in several Wood films; the rest of the "Wood Spooks," a veritable sideshow of semi-thespians and drinking buddies, including four-hundred-pound wrestler Tor Johnson, stentorian TV psychic Criswell, and TV horror host Vampira; and, best of all, the Ed Wood creative process, which amounted to repurposing whatever happened to be at hand, so that hubcaps became flying saucers, cardboard flats became tombstones, and a chiropractor became Bela Lugosi (onscreen, with his face concealed behind the Dracula cape) after the real Lugosi died suddenly.

Moviegoers not acquainted with Ed Wood films or lore were probably baffled by Burton's *Ed Wood*. Truth may often be stranger than fiction, but to some, Wood's true-life antics, writ large onscreen and without footnotes, might seem to push the envelope of credibility to the breaking point.

Burton does take liberties with reality here and there. For instance, we see Wood directing some of his films while dressed in drag. Apparently, that only happened on the set of *Glen or Glenda*, and only then because Wood was in costume for his role. There's also a scene in which Wood meets his idol, Orson Welles, at Musso & Frank Grill, a restaurant on Hollywood Boulevard, and the two commiserate over what a pain in ass producers can be. Never happened. Perhaps the biggest dramatic invention of *Ed Wood* occurs at the climax, when Eddie and his cast attend the raucous *Plan 9* premiere in a packed theater. (As the screening begins, Depp's Wood utters the ironic line, "This is the one. I know I'll be remembered for this film.") There was indeed a *Plan 9* premiere, and it was attended by Wood and his spooks, but it certainly wasn't the exultant success depicted in the film. (*Plan 9* closed almost as soon as it opened.)

But in a larger sense, Burton's embellishments are true to the spirit of Ed Wood, who really did see himself as an artistic cousin to Orson Welles and who did proudly regard *Plan 9* as his magnum opus. Burton's closing scene has Wood and his fiancée, Kathy (Patricia Arquette), rushing out of the theater into the pouring rain. Elated by the audience reaction to his masterwork, but oblivious to the dark cloud literally dumping all over him, Wood persuades Kathy to elope with him to Vegas. He opens the door of his convertible, releasing a reservoir of water. Ever the ingenuous optimist, he's completely unfazed by the ill omens drenching him.

On a literal level, the scene is utter fiction. But as a bittersweet metaphor for Wood's infectiously blinding optimism, it's heartbreakingly true.

Sources and Further Reading

Grey, Rudolph. *Nightmare of Ecstasy*. Los Angeles: Feral House, 1994.

Confessions of a Dangerous Mind (2002)

Directed by George Clooney
Written by Charlie Kaufman
Starring Sam Rockwell and Drew Barrymore

The real Chuck Barris. *Courtesy of Miramax*

The dangerous mind in question belongs to Chuck Barris, the TV huckster behind such pop-culture milestones (or millstones, if you prefer) as *The Dating Game*, *The Newlywed Game*, and, most notoriously, *The Gong Show*. In their day, Barris's game show creations were innovative and a little bit subversive. The first two offerings simmered with an implicit, albeit highly euphemized, sexuality previously unheard of in television ("Where's the strangest place you've ever made whoopee?" went the standard *Newlywed Game* question. *Titter-titter*, went the home viewers. *Can he say that on TV?*) *The Gong Show*—a talent competition showcasing the painfully talent-free—functioned as a kind of meta-commentary on America's insatiable and pathetic quest for fame at any cost, even humiliation on national TV.

Of course, Barris's many critics also had a point when they dubbed him the "King of Schlock," the "Baron of Bad Taste," and the "Ayatollah of Trasherola." A P. T. Barnum of the idiot box, Barris always had an instinct for recognizing—and exploiting—the baser instincts of middle America. It's not without good reason that he's been referred to as the godfather of today's reality TV.

But *Confessions of a Dangerous Mind*—both Barris's 1982 memoir and the 2002 movie it inspired—is only secondarily concerned with its author's bad-boy past as a purveyor of cutting-edge junk TV. Rather, the "confessions" of the title referred to activities somewhat more subversive than saying "whoopee" in mixed company. Barris's bombshell: he claimed to have been a contract hit man for the CIA. Yes. You read that correctly. As a hardboiled freelance assassin, Barris notched upwards of thirty kills in between episodes of *The Newlywed Game*, occasionally using his glamorous TV-producer gig as a cover whilst stalking prey overseas. His targets? No, not tap-dancing Siamese twins, but, rather, cold war enemies of state who worked for the other side (remember the Soviets?). And when he wasn't wiping down his fingerprints at a crime scene, Barris was brainstorming TV's future game show sensations. Think John Le Carre bellowing, "Come on down!" and you get the idea.

That, at least, was the yarn Barris laid out in his book, which, cheekily and probably tellingly, carried the subtitle, "An Unauthorized Autobiography." You can't blame Barris if he expected boffo returns from his confession. Unfortunately, *Confessions of a Dangerous Mind* failed to ignite controversy. Although reviews were uniformly negative, a media maelstrom did not ensue. Of the 100,000 copies released, only a fraction sold. And there weren't even any international repercussions. If Barris was angling for a big comeback, this particular confession wasn't going to be his *Aloha from Hawaii* concert.

For more than a decade the book and the retired assassin-slash-producer couldn't even get arrested in America. The same TV dinner–fed public who had enjoyed the antics of bickering newlyweds and the irony of Jamie Farr judging a talent competition expressed little interest in asking the obvious question: "Come on! Isn't this whole 'hit man for the CIA' thing just another one of your innovative and subversive entertainment concepts?"

Through the years, however, Barris did "leak" a few clues. During his 1984 book tour he told reporters that he had once applied to—and been rejected by—the CIA, and that he had always speculated about how life as an agent might have been. He also "confessed" to Connie Chung that the CIA claim was a big put-on; later, however, Barris retracted the Chung confession, calling it a lie.

Meanwhile, behind the scenes Barris had been negotiating with Hollywood all along. A procession of A-listers—everyone from Johnny Depp to Russell Crowe—expressed interest in the project. Eventually, actor George Clooney latched onto the adaptation that had been penned by Charlie Kaufman, the brain behind *Adaptation* (see page 183) and *Being John Malkovich* and Hollywood's reigning master of self-referential metatext. Clooney saw the project as a launching pad for his directorial career.

The film stars Sam Rockwell, doing a dead-on impersonation of Barris, and Clooney, as his mysterious CIA spymaster. Kaufman's script takes Barris's already outré narrative and gooses it up a few levels. In it, Kaufman introduces some inventions of his own, such as the revelation that Barris's mother dressed him like a girl, and that his father was a serial killer who fried in the electric chair. Kaufman also has Barris assassinating foreigners while escorting *Dating Game* winners on junkets to West Berlin.

Rather than fussing over what's real and what's merely off-leash in the fevered imagination of Barris, the movie opts for a less-than-literal approach to the material. Kaufman and Clooney seem to be suggesting that whatever the real story might be, Barris—maligned for inventing junk TV—is a classic entertainer and storyteller who is more than willing to rewrite himself a better part, and a better ending.

Sources and Further Reading

Barris, Chuck. *Confessions of a Dangerous Mind: An Unauthorized Autobiography*. New York: St. Martin's Press, 1984.
Espinosa, Galina. "The Spy Who Gonged Me." *People*, January 13, 2003.
Stein, Joel. "Lying to Tell the Truth: Chuck Barris." *Time*, January 13, 2003.
Valby, Karen. "The Gong Goodbye." *Entertainment Weekly*, January 10, 2003.

Man on the Moon (1999)

Directed by Milos Forman
Written by Scott Alexander and Larry Karaszewski
Starring Jim Carrey and Danny DeVito

Jim Carrey as Andy Kaufman.
Photo by Francois Duhamel, © Universal Studios

The real Andy Kaufman.

During the opening scene of *Man on the Moon*, Jim Carrey, as Andy Kaufman in his "Foreign Man" persona, warns the audience about the movie they are about to see. "All of the most important things in my life are changed around and mixed up—for dramatic purposes," he stammers in that familiar Balkans-on-the-Hudson singsong. It's meant to be a quintessential Andy Kaufman moment—an absurd meta-commentary shattering the implicit agreement between a filmmaker and his audience to willingly suspend disbelief. But it's also fair warning. Milos Forman's big-budget biopic of Kaufman liberally shuffles the details, and the dates, of the short, brilliant career of the late "anticomic"/performance artist/media provocateur.

A certain amount of dramatic streamlining is inevitable in any biographical reenactment. But in this film the end result is more confounding than illuminating. Two decades after his death, the real Andy Kaufman remains a cipher. In *Man on the Moon*, all of the major episodes in Kaufman's life are more or less accounted for, and have been cleverly rearranged to fit neatly into a three-act structure. But the details never quite add up in a way that yields a satisfying insight into what made Kaufman tick. Was he nuts? A postmodern comic genius? A sociological prankster? A naive artist operating on instinct, or a savvy manipulator fully cognizant of his methods? All of the above?

To be fair, the Andy Kaufman enigma may well be insoluble. According to his last girlfriend, Lynne Marguilies (played in the movie by Courtney Love), Kaufman never let down his performance facade: "He was always on. Not once did he ever talk to me about putting on any kind of 'act.'" And the few associates who had access to the inner chambers of Kaufman's mind have little reason to reveal the true Andy Kaufman. Bob Zmuda, Kaufman's best friend, cowriter, and collaborator—and also an executive producer on *Man on the Moon*—has made a career of keeping the Andy Kaufman mythology alive. That includes donning the guise of Kaufman's most controversial character, the obnoxious lounge singer Tony Clifton. In the publicity run leading up to the movie's release, for instance, Zmuda made a number of public appearances as the abusive Clifton, at one point prompting Jim Carrey to storm out of a press conference in anger. Or was that fracas just another Kaufmanesque prank?

Zmuda's involvement is just one indicator that the filmmakers had reason to preserve the Kaufman mystique. Another reason is that, dramatically speaking, mythology usually trumps reality. Carrey, who famously refused to drop his Kaufman impersonation during the course of the shoot (to the delight of reporters and the annoyance of cast and crew), put it this way: "To explain Andy would be to negate him. He bested death because he went to the grave without ever admitting that anything was an act."

With that in mind, how accurate are the facts of Kaufman's life as presented in *Man on the Moon*? Answer: correct in all the details, yet they still make for an incomplete picture, much like Carrey's meticulous but ultimately mechanical impersonation of Kaufman. Screenwriters Scott Alexander and Larry Karaszewski—old hands at the oddball showbiz biopic, having penned scripts for both *Ed Wood* (see page 188) and director Milos Forman's previous feature, *The People vs. Larry Flynt*—cover all the Kaufman career highlights.

These include the comic's early days as stand-up comedian; his development of the Foreign Man character (who was from "Caspier," an island that sank in the Caspian Sea); his 1975 breakthrough appearance on the premiere episode of *Saturday Night Live* (doing his Mighty Mouse lip-synch routine); his reluctantly accepted role on the sitcom *Taxi* (in which his Foreign Man character became Latka Gravas, the naive mechanic); his appearances as the audience-baiting lounge lizard Clifton; his later obsession with wrestling women (he called himself the "world champion intergender wrestler"); and the famous scuffle with wrestler Jerry Lawler on *Late Night with David Letterman*.

Forman and his writers tampered with the chronologies, creating a few anachronisms that seem unintentionally appropriate. Take, for instance, the slightly jarring cameos by David Letterman, *Saturday Night Live* producer Lorne Michaels, and Kaufman's former cast members from *Taxi*. Now well into their fifties, they appear in the movie as their younger, 1970s and 1980s selves, although little was done to make them appear as young as they were back then (apart from a halfhearted hair dye job on Michaels, which disappears in a subsequent scene). Seeing famous old guys play their younger selves shatters the spell of the movie illusion, but that seems just about right in a film about a comedian dedicated to unhinging entertainment conventions.

Other anachronisms are somewhat less useful. One scene has Lorne Michaels asking *Saturday Night Live* viewers to vote in a phone poll to decide whether or not Andy Kaufman should be on the show. It's true that *SNL* viewers voted in such a poll, effectively banning Kaufman from appearing on the show again. But the poll happened in 1982—two years after Michaels had left the show. (In real life, it was producer Dick Ebersol who made the onscreen announcement.)

Less forgivable is the time line modification that relocates Kaufman's Carnegie Hall performance to the early 1980s. Kaufman's now-famous Carnegie Hall show was an over-the-top extravaganza featuring ersatz versions of the Rockettes and the Mormon Tabernacle Choir, a flying Santa sleigh, and, after the show, milk and cookies for the entire audience. In the film, Kaufman plays Carnegie Hall in 1982 or 1983, after he learns that he has inoperable cancer. Forman stages Kaufman's dream performance as part comeback, part apology to his fans for jerking them around. Which is to say: all Hollywood schmaltz. In reality, Kaufman played Carnegie hall in 1979, four years before he got sick. It isn't the time switcheroo itself that rings false, however; it's the wrongheaded

Hollywood sentiment it enables. Kaufman spent his entire career undermining smarmy show business conventions, only to have his future hagiographers employ a smarmy show business convention (the dying guy who redeems himself in the end). It's almost enough to provoke a Tony Clifton tirade: "Sap. Pap. The clap. Them's some words that rhyme with CRAP!"

But it's not so much the changing around and mixing up that's bothersome. It's what was left out of the script. Alexander and Karaszewski launch the story with a brief setup scene from Kaufman's childhood, dramatizing an anecdote the real Kaufman had told: "While all the other kids were out playing ball and stuff, I used to stay in my room and imagine that there was a camera in the wall. And I used to really believe that I was putting on a television show and that it was going out to somewhere in the world." The movie shows a prepubescent Kaufman (Bobby Boriello) performing for the wall and then for an "audience," which is comprised of his younger sister. The action then flashes forward to the adult Kaufman performing essentially the same act in a comedy club. The transition encourages us to assume that Kaufman's act was naive, childlike, and free of calculation.

But a glance at Kaufman's background suggests a more sophisticated method behind the apparent madness. As a child, the real Kaufman told jokes and performed magic tricks at children's parties—as a paid entertainer. Throughout his life he was a prolific writer of poems, short stories, and novels. He studied television and radio production at Boston's (now defunct) Grahm Junior College, and he performed his unconventional comedy act for years before being "discovered."

(Quick side note: *Man on the Moon* credits Kaufman's discovery to his business manager, George Shapiro, played by Danny DeVito. In reality it was Budd Friedman, founder of the Improv, who earned that honor. Shapiro came along later, after comedian Carl Reiner—who is Shapiro's uncle—encouraged him to add the talented newcomer to his client list.)

Man on the Moon is inconsistent on the matter of Kaufman's motives as an entertainer. At times, Forman and his writers emphasize Kaufman's alleged ingenuousness as a kind of disconnection with reality, one of many eccentric personality ticks. One example: Kaufman's insistence that he is not a comic, but, rather, an old-fashioned "song and dance man." But in other scenes, the filmmakers seem to be suggesting that Kaufman is crazy like a fox. Witness this movie line taken from an actual Kaufman quote about his performance goals:

"I'm not trying to be funny. I just want to play with their heads." It's almost as if Forman couldn't decide which Kaufman to believe, the naive performance artist or the manipulative provocateur, so he opted to represent both.

Or maybe it was just a case of Andy Kaufman striking again, this time from the great beyond. Having left his future biographers thoroughly befuddled and baffled, he effectively sabotaged their heartfelt—and thoroughly confused—homage to him.

Sources and Further Reading

The Andy Kaufman Home Page. http://andykaufman.jvlnet.com.

Zehme, Bill. *Lost in the Funhouse: The Life and Mind of Andy Kaufman.* New York: Delta, 2001.

Zmuda, Bob. *Andy Kaufman Revealed: Best Friend Tells All.* New York: Back Bay Books, 2001.

Auto Focus (2002)

Directed by Paul Schrader
Written by Michael Gerbosi
Starring Greg Kinnear and Willem Dafoe

Greg Kinnear as Bob Crane.
Photo by Frank Masi, © Sony Pictures Entertainment Inc.

The 1978 murder of quasi-celebrity Bob Crane, former star of TV's *Hogan's Heroes*, is a scandal ideally suited for reenactment on basic cable. Crane's death—like his life—was seedy, scandalous, and tragic, but in a small-screen way. An insomniac would definitely find the unsolved mystery of Crane's murder engrossing at four in the morning, shoehorned between a couple of infomercials. But translating Crane's brief show-biz career and even briefer moral and professional decline into a feature film is a dicier undertaking.

Auto Focus, director Paul Schrader's big-screen Crane biopic, more or less answers the questions foremost on the minds of insomniacs everywhere: *Who killed Bob Crane?* and *What was it with all that sex?* Along the way, the movie raises another, more distracting, question: "Who cares?" However tantalizing the unsolved mystery behind the crime, Crane's superficial character and marginal career prevent the film from rising above the dramatic level of "pop-tragedy-lite."

Schrader's take on the Crane tale is faithful to the shallow arc of the actor's true Hollywood story, as outlined in Robert Graysmith's book, *The Murder of*

Bob Crane (upon which the movie is based). The plot is *TV Guide*–simple: Crane rises from wisecracking radio DJ to wisecracking sitcom star to wise-cracking ex–sitcom star relegated to the dinner theater circuit. Along the way, he indulges his seemingly insatiable addiction to sex and autovoyeurism by seducing hundreds of young (and youngish) buxom women and videotaping himself in the varied (and often group) sex acts that typically ensued. Ulti-mately, Crane's video coitus met its interruptus when an unknown assailant slipped into his Scottsdale, Arizona, condo and bludgeoned him to death with a camera tripod while the actor slumbered. The assailant then vanished into the Arizona night, launching a minor Hollywood mystery that remains unsolved to this day.

The bulk of Graysmith's book focuses on the murder and the subsequent police investigation, with a detour along the way to explore Crane's glory days on *Hogan's Heroes*. *Auto Focus* opts for a more linear approach, following Crane's life chronologically and climaxing with his murder. (The movie's title is some-thing of an anachronism—it refers to Crane's solipsistic and often autoerotic video-sex habit; but, technically speaking, the auto-focus lens did not exist dur-ing Crane's lifetime.) Because Graysmith's main sources were the Scottsdale police detectives who first investigated the case (and apparently bungled it so spectacularly as to ensure its unsolved status), the book hews to their preferred suspect. *Auto Focus* focuses itself on the same, Crane's best bud and fellow lothario, John Henry Carpenter. A show-biz parasite who tailed Crane like a sexed-up remora feeding on the cast-offs of a much bigger fish, Carpenter organ-ized his own life around Crane's many extramarital conquests.

It was on the set of *Hogan's Heroes* that Crane met Carpenter, through fel-low cast member Richard *"Family Feud"* Dawson. At that time, Carpenter was a sales rep employed by Sony to promote its hot new videotape technology to Hollywood stars. Carpenter had already hooked up Elvis Presley, Tommy Smothers, and Dawson with cutting-edge, reel-to-reel, black-and-white video recording equipment (the "hand-held" cameras were the size and shape of a lar-gish cinderblock). Carpenter and Crane soon discovered they shared a fetish even more seductive than early-adopterism: They were both "swingers" with hi-fi smarm to burn.

Over the next decade—up until Crane's death, in fact—the two would share a creepy sexual and technofetishistic codependence—Crane, the low-watt celebrity, providing the babe magnetism, and Carpenter, his unctuous A/V pal, picking up the sloppy seconds. The two gleefully documented their conquests on blurry videotape, a home-porn ouevre featuring everything from oral sex POV shots to more elaborate group scenes. (There were also rumors that Crane dabbled in the underground bondage-and-domination scene, submitting to an L.A.-based dominatrix named Tiffany Moonlight.)

According to Crane's son, Bob Crane Jr., Carpenter and Dawson also shot "homemade videos involving women." There was no love lost between Crane and Dawson—Crane had won the coveted role of the Nazi-confounding Colonel Hogan, and Dawson reportedly resented him for it. Both men separately socialized with Carpenter for years, and immediately after Crane's death Carpenter spent a few nights chez Dawson, a retreat that apparently led the police to briefly wonder whether Dawson had a role in Crane's demise. (He didn't.)

Crane's sexual exploits had been no secret on the *Hogan's* set. Fellow cast member Werner "Colonel Klink" Klemperer told Graysmith, "I was totally aware that he collected pornographic material." (Which begs the questions, did Klemperer ever catch Crane reading such "material" on the set, and if so, did he then shout, "HoooouuuuuGAN! Stop hogging the September issue of *JUGS!*" Sadly, history offers no clarification on that point.)

Although Crane was by all accounts an undiluted heterosexual, Carpenter may have marched both ways. Per Graysmith, Bob Crane's son told police that Carpenter may have "participated in homosexual activities with another entertainer." Graysmith does not say who that other entertainer might have been.

In ascribing a possible motive to their favorite suspect, Scottsdale police zeroed in on the homosexual-crime-of-passion theory; perhaps, they suggested, Crane had rebuffed his friend's sexual advances, leading the scorned Carpenter to strike back. Although Crane was under his bedcovers at the time of his death, police found semen on his leg. And after the killer smashed Crane's skull, he had tied a length of electrical cord around the actor's neck. All of this led the police to suspect a homoerotic dimension to the killing. Had the killer masturbated over Crane after the murder? Was the cord—cut from a videotape recorder in Crane's condo—some kind of perverse reference to sexual domination? *Auto Focus* dramatizes the possibility of a homoerotic motive in several apocryphal scenes showing Crane (played by Greg Kinnear) mercilessly ribbing an increasingly agitated Carpenter (Willem Dafoe) for his queenish carriage.

The police also considered another speculative motive: Crane had apparently grown tired of Carpenter's relentless toadying (Carpenter always showed up in whichever city Crane was performing his dinner theater show, ready to swing). Crane's son told police that his dad felt Carpenter had become "a pain in the ass," and that he was ready to cut him loose. Police wondered whether Carpenter might have resented getting the bum's rush from his de facto girl procurer. To bolster this theory, police pointed out that several witnesses reported the two had a "tense" argument in a Scottsdale restaurant the day before the murder.

Auto Focus floats this theory as well, but its murder scene is deftly lensed so as not to reveal the killer's face, thereby retaining the ambiguity of the mystery.

The movie ends with Crane's death, but in real life the case dragged on for years. Botched evidence-handling undermined the investigation: right off the bat, the local coroner compromised the murder scene, going so far as to shave a patch of Crane's scalp in order to get a better look at the fatal wounds. The coroner also refused to collect a sample of the semen found on Crane's leg. Meanwhile, a parade of cops and bystanders were admitted into the condo before the crime scene had been secured, hopelessly muddling the chain of evidence.

More than a decade would pass before Carpenter was put on trial. Ultimately, he was acquitted. He died of a heart attack several years later.

Although Carpenter was the most likely suspect, the case against him was never more than circumstantial. The best evidence in the case was a series of small bloodstains on the passenger-side door of Carpenter's rental car. Although DNA testing was not yet available to the police, investigators confirmed that the dried stains matched Crane's uncommon blood type. Police speculated that Carpenter had accidentally bumped the still-bloody murder weapon against the interior door panel as he made his getaway. Proclaiming his innocence, Carpenter denied it.

The cooling case suddenly reheated fourteen years after the fact, when a previously unknown piece of photographic evidence suddenly materialized. Rifling through the aforementioned bloodstain photos, a new set of investigators discovered a photo showing what looked like a tiny fragment of human tissue imbedded in a scratch on the inside door panel. In Carpenter's subsequent trial, the jury was understandably skeptical about this miraculous new development—especially after they learned that the previous investigators had never been aware of such a picture.

Despite the artful evasion of its final scenes, *Auto Focus* does leave viewers with a clear impression that Carpenter was the killer. The Scottsdale police certainly thought so, too. But there were other suspects, including, asserts Graysmith, Crane's estranged second wife, Patti, whom Crane had met on the set of *Hogan's Heroes* (using her stage name, Sigrid Valdis, she joined the cast during the second season as Colonel Klink's buxom secretary, Hilda). The two fought frequently (he verbally, she at least once with the aid of an airborne ashtray) and were, at the time of Crane's death, involved in a nasty divorce process. According to Bob Crane Jr. (Crane's son by his first marriage), shortly before Crane's murder Patti had persuaded her husband to amend his will, leaving the bulk of his assets to her. Patti turned up on Crane's doorstep in Scottsdale just days before the murder. But she phoned him from the Seattle area on the night of the crime, which cleared her of direct involvement.

Investigators were also briefly interested in the allegedly mobbed-up husband of a woman who had shared several video-memorialized interludes with Crane.

For whatever reason or combination of reasons—police incompetence, cooling evidence trails, lack of a murder weapon—no theory ever rose above the level of reasonable doubt. Hence, Carpenter's acquittal. And with the principles now dead, the mystery is likely to linger indefinitely, just like *Hogan's Heroes* reruns.

Sources and Further Reading

Graysmith, Robert. *The Murder of Bob Crane*. New York: Crown Publishers, Inc., 1994

Rubin, Paul. "The Bob Crane Murder Case." *New Times Phoenix*, April 21, 1993; April 28, 1993; May 5, 1993.

Schrader, Paul. "Commentary." *Auto Focus*. DVD. Directed by Paul Schrader. Columbia Tristar Home Entertainment, 2004.

Sid and Nancy (1986)

Directed by Alex Cox
Written by Alex Cox and Abbe Wool
Starring Gary Oldman and Chloe Webb

Director Alex Cox established his "underground" cred in 1984 with *Repo Man*, a surreal cult movie set in the L.A. punk scene. But L.A.'s always been a derivative place, and for his next feature Cox went to the source: a movie about the original punk rockers, the Sex Pistols. Specifically, he was fascinated by the doomed romance between Sid Vicious, the Pistols' bass "player" (a term used loosely; Sid never really learned to play), and Nancy Spungeon, an American groupie.

As obnoxious, grating, and just plain over-the-top as Chloe Webb plays the role of Nancy, she and Cox barely penetrate the surface of the woman's deep depravity. A disturbed and hyperactive (though highly intelligent) child, she was diagnosed with schizophrenia as a teenager.

Before arriving in London, Spungeon was well known in the New York punk scene as a junkie hooker who traded sex for heroin as easily as most of us fork over two bucks for a Big Mac. Like many groupies, her ambition in life, if in fact she had any ambition, was fame by association, "association" being defined as having sex with musicians. She made the transatlantic trip in pursuit of Jerry Nolan, the heroin-addicted drummer of the Heartbreakers, a New York band led by the junkie's junkie of all junkie musicians, Johnny Thunders. The Heartbreakers came to England to capitalize on the London punk explosion, which had established itself as a commercial force, greatly unlike its cultish stateside counterpart. Spungeon came to England to capitalize on the Heartbreakers, but their manager, who knew her drug-addled ways all too well, kept her far away from the band.

Nolan, Thunders, and the whole Heartbreakers band are condensed in Cox's film into a single cardboard character—who sports perhaps the lamest put-on "Noo Yawk" accent ever attempted on film—by the name of Rock Head. When Rock Head appears later in the film, he's detoxified and become a fitness freak, something neither Nolan nor Thunders evidently ever did, because they both died of drug overdoses.

Nancy is seen in the film buying drugs for her New York–rocker sugar daddy, but the real Spungeon, thwarted in her attempts to hook up with Nolan, immediately drifted to England's first and foremost punk act, the Sex Pistols. Her first play targeted the band's lead singer and spiritual center, Johnny Rotten (né John Lydon) who responded with unmitigated disgust.

Undeterred, Nancy turned to Sid.

Little of this background is given more than a cursory pass in Cox's film. We know almost nothing about Sid Vicious (played quite brilliantly by Gary Oldman, in the role that made his career) except that "once I was so bored I fucked a dog." Who the hell knows whether that's true, or whether Sid (whose real name was John Ritchie) ever said any such thing. It's just as likely another of Cox's attempts to ridicule punk while simultaneously straining to establish himself as a credible exponent of the movement. Which pretty much sums up the tone of *Sid and Nancy*. It depicts the original punks as silly buffoons, but at the same time it wallows in the romanticized self-destruction that became the popular image of punk, was embodied by Sid Vicious, and later claimed a number of lives—starting with those of Sid and Nancy themselves.

Sid was a wild kid, to say the least. One of the incidents in the film has him brutally assaulting a rock critic called Dick Dent. Sid clocks Dent with his bass guitar. The episode came from an encounter that happened long before Sid became a Sex Pistol, when he was still just a punk fan extraordinaire: he attacked Nick Kent, a rather well-known English rock critic of the era, with a bicycle chain. It was that assault, on a punk club dance floor, that earned him his adopted surname, "Vicious."

As out-of-control as Sid had been in those early days, according to accounts of those who knew him, there had always been a certain innocence to him. Never terribly bright, he was nonetheless a good-natured lad always impressed with the new and different. Before the Sex Pistols, Sid fronted a band of his own, the Flowers of Romance, which, according to at least one contemporary, could have become a noteworthy punk band in its own right.

According to accounts of those same people who knew him, Sid's innocence expired as soon as he met Nancy. The London punk scene was not exactly drug free, but heroin was anathema until Nancy gave it to Sid, who became an inveterate junky almost overnight. For some reason—and we get no clue from the movie any more than from real life—he fell in love with the screeching American bottle-blonde right away.

After that, according to the film, Sid's life was a descent straight into heroin hell. That was a pretty much right-on portrayal, though in the movie, Sid is a one-dimensional character. But according to his lifelong friend Johnny Rotten—who had "washed his hands" of Sid after Nancy came along and Sid sunk into drugs and self-negation—the two had tried to start a band together in London shortly after the Sex Pistols broke up. Unfortunately, Nancy stepped in and whisked Sid away to New York.

The rest became punk history, ending with Nancy dead on the bathroom floor of the Chelsea Hotel, bled out from a knife to the stomach, and a few months later, Sid dead of a drug overdose.

No one knows what happened inside the room at the Chelsea because Sid died before going to trial. Almost immediately after the incident and to this day, dark speculation has it that Sid was set up to take the fall for the murder; that, in reality, a mysterious intruder, maybe a drug dealer, killed Nancy. Sid never gave any version of the story. He was, not unsurprisingly, in a drugged-out stupor.

Cox's version of history adheres to another theory: the pair made a suicide pact. When Sid refused to carry it out, Nancy threw one of her many inconsolable fits. In the middle of this row, and ensconced in a heroin haze, Sid stabbed the only girlfriend he'd ever had in the stomach.

While Sid's friends insisted then and now that he could never have hurt Nancy, the *Sid and Nancy* version of Nancy's murder has become legend.

What we never see in Cox's film is how the punk movement subverted, attacked, and ultimately energized British society. All we're left with is the visual metaphor for a lifestyle that destroys everyone who lives it, in the most degrading possible way.

Sources and Further Reading

Gibbs, Alvin. *Destroy: The Definitive History of Punk*. London: Britannia Press Publishing, 1996.

Lydon, John. *Rotten: No Irish, No Blacks, No Dogs*. New York: Picador Press, 1995.

Savage, Jon. *England's Dreaming: Anarchy, Sex Pistols, Punk and Beyond*. New York: St. Martin's Press, 1992.

24 Hour Party People (2002)

Directed by Michael Winterbottom
Written by Frank Cottrell Boyce
Starring Steve Coogan

On the press junket to publicize *24 Hour Party People*, reporters asked Tony Wilson what he thought of the film based on his exploits as godfather of the "Madchester" music scene of the 1980s. "It's a complete collection of lies," he pronounced. "There's an absolute disregard for truth."

And Wilson was on hand to *promote* the movie.

Of course, Tony Wilson—English TV personality-*cum*-dilettante music impresario-*cum*-coked-up nightclub promoter-*cum*-Boetheus-quoting fop—is your classic unreliable narrator. That goes for both the onscreen and real-life versions. So, not surprisingly, in his next breath at the press junket, the nonfictionalized Wilson was earnestly contradicting himself, itemizing what *24 Hour Party People* gets *right* as a specific slice of music history. "In a bizarre way it is completely true on three things: that's what punk felt like; that's what acid felt like; and that's what my part was like." Which, in a movie that seeks to capture a fleeting moment in pop zeitgeist past, pretty much covers all the territory that matters.

Most Americans are probably unfamiliar with the intertwined sagas of Tony Wilson and the Manchester musical explosion of the 1980s and early 1990s, which spanned (and cross-pollinated) the eras of post-punk, acid, and rave. Both Wilson and the bands he nurtured drew their initial inspiration from the anarchic, do-it-yourself ethos of British punk rock. Wilson, a self-proclaimed "serious journalist" by day who reported for Granada Television, by night took on the role of mother hen to a series of seminal underground bands, including, most notably, Joy Division and its later reformation as New Order. He founded the Factory Records label and later opened the famous Hacienda nightclub, where acid helped beget rave and DJ culture. Both the label and the nightclub—and along with them, Wilson's influence on the Manchester scene—eventually collapsed under the weight of his bad business sense.

24 Hour Party People follows that basic historical outline, but it also features plenty of playful digressions. Shot in a pseudodocumentary style on digital video, the film re-creates the "Madchester" phenom in a whirl of color, light, and speed. Consequently, it probably embodies the spirit—if not the letter—

of its historical source material better than any sober recitation of dates, people, and places ever could. Director Winterbottom was obviously interested in more than just reassembling cultural artifacts. At some point, the facts behind every important musical movement become tangled with the apocrypha they inevitably inspire. Thus, early in the film, when Tony Wilson discovers his wife engaged in a bathroom-stall shag with Buzzcocks front man Howard Devoto, our unreliable narrator introduces the actor portraying the washroom attendant as the actual Devoto. "This didn't really happen," the real Devoto informs the movie-watching audience. Wilson counters by paraphrasing John Ford's famous axiom, "When truth becomes legend, print the legend."

The real-life Wilson seems not to have taken those words to heart; in interviews leading up to the film's release he dismissed several scenes in the film—including the one that puts him into the back of a van with a prostitute—as lies. But even these "lies" seem in keeping with Wilson's character—in real life and onscreen—as master embellisher.

Appropriately enough, real TV personality Wilson is played in the film by real British comic Steve Coogan, best known in England for his impersonation of fake TV personality Alan Partridge. That kind of whimsical postmodernism informs much of the film. Wilson is forever citing the influences of French situationism, "signs and signifiers." At one point Coogan-as-Wilson turns to the camera to remind viewers that this film is not about Tony Wilson, but, rather, the music of Manchester. We know he's talking out of his arse—the film is certainly as much about Tony Wilson as it is about the bands on the soundtrack. But we also know that he, like the best confidence men, probably believes his own rap.

Shortly before the film had its premiere, Winterbottom admitted to one journalist that "there are a lot of things [in the film] that aren't true. [But] a lot of the things [Tony Wilson] complains about are the stories he told us in the first place. [They are] in the twilight zone between truth and fiction, and I think Tony doesn't know half the time whether it's true or not."

Sources and Further Reading

Curtis, Deborah. *Touching from a Distance: Ian Curtis and Joy Division.* London: Faber & Faber, 1995.

Parker, James. "It's a Mad, Mad, Mad, Madchester World." *American Prospect*, September 23, 2002.

Raftery, Brian M. "Life of the *Party*." *Entertainment Weekly*, September 6, 2002.

Chaplin (1992)

Directed by Richard Attenborough
Written by William Boyd, Bryan Forbes, and William Goldman
Starring Robert Downey Jr.

Robert Downey Jr. as Charlie Chaplin. © TriStar Pictures, Inc.

The real Charlie Chaplin.

"If you want to understand me, watch my movies," the fake Charlie Chaplin advises in the movie docudramatization of his life. It's a made-up line delivered by a (literally) made-up Chaplin—actor Robert Downey Jr. under several pounds of old-man latex. In the same spirit of putting words into the mouth of cinema's most beloved mute, allow us to concoct a fake Chaplin quote of our own: "And if you *really* want to understand me, for the love of God do not go near a movie docudramatization of my life."

Phony maxims aside, had the real Chaplin lived long enough to see *Chaplin*, made fifteen years after his death, he might have approved—but probably for the wrong reasons. Sir Richard Attenborough's reverent biopic strives mightily to illuminate the man behind the Little Tramp; failing that, *Chaplin* settles for pat melodrama and calculated pathos, affectations the actual Chaplin would have recognized as hallmarks of his own movies at their most indulgent. Apparently, Attenborough took his screenwriters' line about knowing Chaplin through his movies all too literally. Consequently, his docudramatized Chaplin is little more than a martyred artist haunted by the painful loss of childhood innocence and his one true love. End of story, iris out, pass the Kleenex.

In fact, if you want to understand the complicated, conflicted, comic genius that was Charlie Chaplin, his movies alone are less than instructive. In the 2003 documentary *Charlie: The Life and Art of Charles Chaplin*, film critic Richard Schickel probably got closer to the truth about the artist and the man. Chaplin, he said, was a habitual performer both onscreen and off, forever "driven by his relentless ego, by his helpless need for an audience to dominate, to lead. All the tragedies of his life stemmed from those drives and needs."

Chaplin's daughter, the actress Geraldine Chaplin (who, in an example of inspired casting, portrays her own grandmother in Attenborough's film), concurs. "It's fair to say that my father was someone who was absolutely compelled to entertain," she commented upon the release of Schickel's documentary. "He really did need an audience. But in *Chaplin*, there was this picture of a gloomy, tortured, moody man. That's just not how I remember him."

It wouldn't be fair to fault Robert Downey Jr. for failing to bring the private Chaplin to vivid life. As the old adage goes, "If it's not on the page, it's not on the stage." And in this case, it never got anywhere near the page. As a matter of fact, it's only when Downey Jr. channels the more authoritative text of Chaplin's well-known performance routines that the movie truly comes alive. In those moments, Downey Jr.'s impersonation is spot-on, marvelously capturing the trademark waddle, the elegant physicality, and the pitch-perfect comic timing that made Chaplin an international film legend.

In *Chaplin*, all the names, places, and dates are more or less unmolested by dramatic invention. In fact, only one character in the film is fictionalized: the book editor (played by Anthony Hopkins) who has been inserted into the narrative as a framing device—the skeptical "audience" to whom an aging Chaplin (Downey Jr. in his latex jowls) tells his decades-spanning story. From time to time, the Hopkins character challenges Chaplin's self-serving recollections; it's a clever way for Attenborough to acknowledge the unreliable nature of this—and, for that matter, any—biographical reenactment.

The film draws its source material from two books. The first is Chaplin's 1964 memoir (somewhat redundantly titled *My Autobiography*), which is famous for its selective recitation of the actor-director's personal and professional curricula vitae. Apparently, Chaplin gallantly excluded a number of colorful episodes from his personal life out of respect for friends, ex-wives, and countrymen still living at the time of the book's publication. But he was reluctant to reveal the secrets of his creative process for a different reason. "If people know how it's done," he said, "all the magic goes." To fill in the anecdotal lacunae in Chaplin's memoir, *Chaplin*—the movie—turns to David Robinson's hefty, 782-page biography, *Chaplin: His Life and Art*.

Attenborough manages to squeeze eight decades of that life and art into the film's 144-minute run time, beginning with Chaplin's childhood as a threadbare cockney performer up through his triumphant 1972 return to America to receive his lifetime-achievement Oscar (the prize the Academy bestows to icons on or near death's doorstep). In between those career bookends, *Chaplin* faithfully catalogs its honoree's life arc: Charlie's success as a vaudeville comedian; his tour of America and discovery by "flickers" director Mack Sennett (Dan Aykroyd); his almost accidental creation of the Little Tramp character; his subsequent rise to silent film stardom in Hollywood; his infamous jailbait fancy and the ensuing scandals; his controversial leftish politics; and, ultimately, his humiliating exile from the United States. It's a lot of ground to cover, and the sheer breadth of Chaplin's career is almost too much for any one film to frame, let alone focus on.

In an effort to impose a measure of thematic order on Chaplin's unwieldy through-line, Attenborough and his screenwriters (two other guys and script doctor William Goldman, which ought to tell you something) resort to pat movie psychology and mawkish cinema pathos. Lifting a page—and a sled— from *Citizen Kane*, Attenborough and crew saddle Charlie with a motivational Rosebud. You see, there's a reason for all that melancholia and wistful gazing into the mid-distance: Chaplin is eternally haunted by the loss of his first, and unrequited, true love. Her name was Hetty Kelly, and she was a barely pubescent dancer and doe-eyed beauty of the perched-on-a-pedestal variety. Attenborough presents the girl—played by Moira Kelly—as a sort of Rosetta stone that explains not only Downey Jr.'s incessant moping, but also Chaplin's most scandalous behavior: his serial cradle-robbing.

By means of this classic movie dodge, Attenborough seeks to rehabilitate the bobby-socks Lothario into a more audience-friendly archetype: the heavy-hearted romantic searching in vain for the lost, idealized love of his youth. In other words, one man's jailbait prowl is a nobler fellow's tragic love sonnet. When Moira Kelly reappears later in the film as Chaplin's fourth and final wife, Oona O'Neill Chaplin, the stunt casting tells us that Charlie has finally attained his ideal lady, and can therefore stop creeping us out with the teenage seduction thing. (Although Oona, the daughter of playwright Eugene O'Neill, was only seventeen at the time of her marriage to Chaplin.)

To be fair, the "ideal woman" theme has some basis in fact. In the summer of 1908 Chaplin did fall head over heels for a fifteen-year-old dancer named Hetty Kelly. The "courtship," such as it was, amounted to little more than the smitten nineteen-year-old escorting his dance-hall Venus to her subway stop on three occasions over the course of a week. Hetty clearly made a lasting impression on Chaplin, who decades later would describe her in fulsome prose as a "slim gazelle, with a shapely oval face, a bewitching full mouth, and beautiful teeth." Alas, the toothy gazelle had little interest in her earnest young suitor, and ten days into the one-way romance, Hetty treated Charlie to the belle epoch equivalent of "I have to wash my hair tonight." The sensitive lad took the rejection to heart and "never forgot," according to biographer David Robinson. "Both in his life and in his art, he seemed for many years to be trying to recapture the ecstasy he had felt in the company of Hetty Kelly." It's quite a leap from that casual aside to Attenborough's souped-up "Rosebud" trope, but fearlessly into the breach sleds the director.

Others close to Chaplin have offered slightly less romantic theories to explain his penchant for the underage. According to Lita Grey (wife number two), Charlie "was crazy about virgins." Chaplin seduced Grey in a steam room in his Beverly Hills mansion. She was fifteen; he was thirty-six. (Grey is rumored to have been the inspiration for Nabokov's novel *Lolita*.) "I have to say he was a destroyer of girls," Grey later stated. "I believe Charlie liked to see a young girl awakened."

Chaplin the movie doesn't so much avert its eyes from the infamous sex scandals as soften its focus, defusing the less sympathetic details. For instance, while the film depicts a love-struck Chaplin happily marrying a sixteen-year-old Grey, in reality it had been a shotgun wedding, prompted by an unplanned pregnancy and legal threats from Grey's lawyer uncle. According to Grey, on their wedding day (in dusty Guaymas, Mexico), her groom whispered sweet nothings such as, "On our honeymoon, I don't intend to be a husband to you, but marrying you is better than going to the penitentiary."

Nor does Attenborough dwell on Chaplin's extramarital affairs—of which he had seven during his marriage to Grey, according to the scorned woman herself. Three years before her death in 1995, Grey told *Los Angeles Magazine*, "When I was pregnant with our second child, I discovered that Charlie had paid off one of the servants and was sleeping with Marion Davies downstairs in his bedroom."

In reality, the public response to Chaplin's sex scandals and political leanings took an increasingly harsh toll on his career. Attenborough depicts the evolving public reaction to Chaplin's offscreen exploits quite accurately—he went from being adored by American audiences to being a suspected godless commie. The film does, however, take liberal dramatic license in making these points. For instance, Chaplin's dinner-party sparrings with FBI Director J. Edgar Hoover (Kevin Dunn) and a gasbag anti-Semitic Nazi never really happened. The film also offers several odd anachronisms, most notably the scene in which Charlie watches a 1950s TV broadcast of Senator Joseph McCarthy railing against the U.S. State Department, then flips to live coverage of the 1947 House Un-American Activities Committee hearings.

In the end, by declining to show us the fully dimensional Chaplin—genius, heart, warts, and all—Attenborough undercuts his well-meaning intent to celebrate the humanity of a prodigious cultural icon. Sir Richard has certainly been here before, straddling the uneasy line between biopic and "hagiopic." *Gandhi* (see page 378), his previous foray into the Great Lives genre, was also reverent to a fault. Like that film, *Chaplin* denies its rarified protagonist the documented tics, flaws, and frailties that exposed him during his lifetime as a card-carrying member of the human race.

Sources and Further Reading

Chaplin, Charles. *My Autobiography*. New York: Simon & Schuster, 1964.
Chaplin, Lita Grey and Jeffrey Vance. *Wife of the Life of the Party*. Lanham, MD: Scarecrow Press, 1998.
Chaplinmuseum.com. http://www.chaplinmuseum.com.
Davis, Ivor. "Charlie Chaplin's Scandals." *Los Angeles Magazine*, December 1992.
Doherty, Thomas. Review of *Chaplin*. *Cineaste*, Fall 1992.
Robinson, David. *Chaplin: His Life and Art*. New York: McGraw-Hill, 1985.
Wada, Linda. "Charlie Chaplin's Wives." Edna Purviance: Welcome to Paradise. http://www.ednapurviance.org/chaplininfo/chaplinwivescover.html.

Bird (1988)

Directed by Clint Eastwood
Written by Joel Oliansky
Starring Forest Whitaker and Diane Venora

Sam Wright (left) as Dizzy Gillespie and Forest Whitaker as Charlie "Bird" Parker. © *Warner Bros.*

What is it that drives jazz biographers into spasms of verbal arrhythmia? Frustrated musicianship? Ginsberg envy? Overexposure to back issues of *Downbeat* magazine? Like, dig this tortured riff from *Bird Lives!*, the definitively overwritten Charlie Parker biography:

> Seven thousand gut-busting dinners, water drinking contests, goofballs dissolved in Dixie cups, popped pills, whiskey shots with no chaser . . . two chicks balled in a single bed . . . and foaming saxophone solos crashed to a climax as shattering as the cymbal thrown at his feet across the stage of the Reno Club twenty years before.

Translation: Jazz legend Charlie "Bird" Parker, in the throes of a fatal heart attack, is watching his life riff before his eyes in the prose equivalent of a bebop sax solo! Of course, it's not clear which patient is in greater need of a defibrillator—Bird or his biographer (Ross Russell, author of the tachycardiac hipster prose).

Jazz movies are also prone to artsy bebop seizures, along with a host of related symptoms, including chronic underlighting and epidemic levels of neon signage. Clint Eastwood's solemn biopic of Charlie Parker, *Bird*, succumbs to all of the above, plus the standard jazz-movie weather outlook: partly smoky, with a 100 percent chance of rain. Eastwood, a dilettante jazzbo, had long been a Charlie Parker fan. According to the laconic actor/director, he first saw Parker play "when I was a kid in Northern California." Nicknamed "Yardbird" and later just "Bird" (supposedly because he was so fond of chicken), Parker and a coterie of jazz iconoclasts that included trumpeter Dizzy Gillespie practically invented the jazz idiom of bebop. Parker's boundless musical talent was matched only by his seemingly unlimited appetite for booze and drugs (specifically, heroin), habits that haunted him throughout his career and that led to his premature death in 1955. The official cause of death was a heart attack, complicated by pneumonia, ulcers, and cirrhosis of the liver. He was only thirty-five years old, but his chemical vices had so ravaged his body that the physician summoned to the death scene guessed he was in his fifties or sixties.

Parker's musical legacy was so profound, and his personal traumas so melodramatic, that an underlit, neon-suffused, smoky, rain-drenched Hollywood biopic was an inevitability. Whereas earlier plans failed to gel (including a 1970s project that would have starred Richard Pryor), Eastwood's enthusiasm and box-office cred finally got *Bird* off the ground. And who better to helm the definitive Charlie Parker story than a big-shot director who also happened to be a jazz fan capable of blowing a few rudimentary riffs on the cornet and trumpet?

Unfortunately, Eastwood's elementary musical chops proved to be a dangerous thing. For instance, in an effort to mimic Parker's splintered playing rhythms, Eastwood wound up employing an editing style that jumps backward and forward through time. The result is often less "jazzy" than it is baffling. In one sequence, Parker's common-law wife, Chan, has a private flashback that continues even after she physically exits the scene of her reminiscence, and a complete stranger proceeds to initiate his own personal flashback—within *her* flashback. When Mrs. Parker finally regains control of her own mental reverie, she seems completely unconcerned that a strange black man has been narrating his own backstory inside her head. All of which may lead viewers to wonder exactly who has been exposed to "goofballs dissolved in Dixie cups."

Although not credited, Ross Russell's sensationalistic 1973 Parker biography clearly exerted a strong influence over *Bird*. Taking a major cue from the aforementioned "foaming saxophone" death scene in *Bird Lives!*, Eastwood stages the last moments of Parker's life in same fevered montage of "guffaws," "popped pills," and melodramatic thunderclaps imagined by Russell. (Parker died alone and obviously took his final thoughts to the grave, so the imagery here is overheated guesswork twice removed.)

Eastwood also borrows Russell's clattering cymbal, deploying it throughout the movie as a none-too-subtle visual metaphor; we know for sure that Charlie's personal and chemical demons have cursed him yet again whenever we see slo-mo footage of a drum cymbal soaring across the screen and crashing to the floor. The image derives from an actual incident in Parker's early life: as a callow seventeen-year-old in Kansas City, Parker had flubbed the chord changes to "I Got Rhythm" during a jam session with Count Basie's drummer, Jo Jones. Jones "gonged" the kid offstage by flinging a drum cymbal onto the floor. As jazz critic Francis Davis noted in *The Atlantic Monthly*, Eastwood and his scriptwriter, Joel Oliansky, gave this incident "too much interpretive spin": "Except for overwrought conjecture by Ross Russell in a purple passage toward the end of *Bird Lives!*," Davis wrote, "there is nothing in the voluminous literature about Parker to suggest that this public humiliation haunted him for the rest of his life. On the contrary, it is usually cited as the incident that strengthened his resolve to become a virtuoso."

According to Eastwood, much of Oliansky's screenplay was based on Chan Parker's then-unpublished memoir, *My Life in E-Flat* (the book was later published by University of South Carolina Press). This may explain why the film makes no mention of the three wives Parker actually married (only two of whom he bothered to divorce) before shacking up with Chan. It may also explain the film's gloomy, fatalistic mood. Parker's relationship with Chan, a jazz fan who moved in with him and adopted his last name, spanned the last six years of his life. It was probably Parker's most painful period: those years were marked by a series of personal traumas that included the increasing deterioration of his health after more than a decade of drug and alcohol abuse; the death, from pneumonia, of his two-year-old daughter with Chan; his two failed suicide attempts (via iodine ingestion); his voluntary confinement to Bellevue mental hospital; and his bust for heroin possession, which led to the loss of his cabaret card and prevented him from performing in New York clubs.

Bird faithfully documents most of these sad events (although it mercifully omits the second suicide attempt), leaving viewers with the impression that

Parker's life was one of unrelenting pain, interrupted only by frequent heroin jags. Although Forest Whitaker's performance is competent (he learned to play the saxophone for the role, and he convincingly mimics Parker's finger flourishes in performance close-ups), it never conveys the sense of joy and playfulness that permeate the real Bird's recordings. Instead, *Bird* is so devoted to the conventional Hollywood biopic conceit of brilliant-folk-laid-low-by-their-all-too-human-frailties that it gives short shrift to Parker's outsized joie de vivre and unmitigated hedonism. As Bird's 1940s-era drummer told *Ebony* magazine, "You could say that Bird was a person who gave all of himself to just about everything that he did." Bird's first son, Leon, recalled his dad as "this kind of chubby, happy-go-lucky guy." Unfortunately, Eastwood and Whitaker portray Parker as a downbeat martyr on the road to self-destruction—which is a Bird of a different feather.

Sources and Further Reading

Davis, Francis. "Bird on Film: Charlie Parker Gets Lost in a Fan's New Movie." *The Atlantic Monthly*, November 1988.

Grove Music Online. s.v. "Parker, Charlie." (By James Patrick, ed. L. Macy), http://www.grovemusic.com.

Marshall, Marilyn. "The Real Charlie Parker: What the Movie Didn't Tell You." *Ebony*, January 1989.

Parker, Chan. *My Life in E-Flat*. Columbia, SC: University of South Carolina Press, 1993.

Peterson, Lauren. "Jazz Stuff: Biographies—Charlie Parker." *The Jazzine*. http://www.jazzine.com/jazzstuff/biographies/charlie_parker.phtml.

Russell, Ross. *Bird Lives!: The High Life and Hard Times of Charlie (Yardbird) Parker*. New York: Charterhouse, 1973.

Coal Miner's Daughter (1980)

Directed by Michael Apted
Written by Tom Rickman
Starring Sissy Spacek and Tommy Lee Jones

Sissy Spacek as Loretta Lynn. © *Universal City Studios, Inc.*

In country music, sometimes the only difference between artistic inspiration and spousal abuse is three chords and a rhyme for "heartache." That, at any rate, is the twanging subtext of *Coal Miner's Daughter*, the acclaimed 1980 biopic of Loretta Lynn, the original country diva. Sissy Spacek stars as the simple mountain gal who went from Kentucky rags to Nashville riches (with some pill-poppin' and nervous breakdownin' along the way), thanks to a whole lotta heart, a mean set of pipes, and an even meaner muse. That muse role fell to her husband and sometime manager, Oliver "Doolittle" Lynn, a World War II vet and former moonshiner who married up "Loretty" when she warn't but thirteen and he was all of twenty-one. Doolittle ('cause that's what folks say he did) was the inspiration for many of Loretta's fiery domestic anthems, including "Don't Come Home a Drinkin' (With Lovin' on Your Mind)," "Your Squaw Is on the Warpath," and "Fist City," a musical ultimatum hollered, mountain-style, at a husband-poaching hussy ("I'm here to tell ya gal to lay offa my man/If ya don't wanna go to fist city!"). Although the film's title refers to Loretta's hit ballad that pays homage to her humble beginnings, Doolittle's ("Doo" for short) dominating presence throughout the Loretta Lynn story ought to have suggested an alternative title: "One Mean Cuss's Wife."

Based on Loretta Lynn's 1976 memoir of the same name, which was cowritten with George Vecsey, *Coal Miner's Daughter* mined box-office gold and earned Spacek a well-deserved Oscar. Not only did the actress deliver a completely convincing portrait of the country star—a portrait that spanned four decades of her life, from age thirteen to her mid-forties—she also did her own singing in a pitch-perfect impression of the real "Queen of Country." Unfortunately, the Academy completely snubbed Spacek's costar, Tommy Lee Jones, whose multilayered performance as Doo is in many ways the heart and soul of the movie. Jones managed to pull off the unlikely feat of making a white-trash, drunk, philandering, bitch-slapping mo-fo (pardon our a-cussin') seem both charismatic and sympathetic. Whether or not that portrait is objectively accurate, it's certainly how Loretta saw her husband during their nearly fifty years together. (Doo died in the mid-1990s of diabetes brought on by a lifetime of a-drinkin'.)

After an almost lyrical first act that re-creates Loretta Lynn's early years in the heart of Appalachian coal-mining country, director Michael Apted and screenwriter Tom Rickman focus on the often-stormy relationship between Loretta and Doo. Loretta has always credited Doo with launching her into show business and, therefore, out of poverty. The movie pretty accurately re-creates those events, which by now are familiar to any self-respecting wearer of large belt buckles: Doo bought "Loretty" her first guitar (from Sears Roebuck—not a pawnshop, as is depicted in the movie), encouraged her to write songs, pushed her (sometimes all too literally) to perform at the local honky-tonks, arranged for her first recording, acted as her manager and promoter as the two traveled through the South, wheedling and cajoling local DJs to give her airplay, and managed her career after the hits began to happen.

Sissy Spacek's doe-eyed Loretta comes across as the passive player in a relationship obviously dominated by Tommy Lee Jones's insecure, manipulative

Doo. By all accounts that's an accurate portrayal of the pair, especially during the early days of their marriage. Apted offers an unblinking view of the relationship—including glimpses of the dirty-cheatin', no-good-wife-beatin' that Loretta alludes to in her autobiography and many of her songs. Whereas most show-biz biopics quickly drown in their own suds, *Coal Miner's Daughter* feels remarkably unsentimental in its portrayal of the pair's codepend relationship.

At the film's release, the real Loretta and Doo Lynn (his other nickname was Moonie, a reference to his days as a moonshiner) announced their approval of the film's straight-ahead, unvarnished take on their tumultuous life. According to Loretta, as the credits rolled, Doo turned to her and pronounced, "They hung close to the truth."

Of course, there may have been a note of self-delusion in that statement. Two decades after the release of *Coal Miner's Daughter*, Loretta published a second memoir, *Still Woman Enough*, in which she confessed that Hollywood had soft-pedaled certain aspects of the marriage. "Even though I made the movie people rewrite that script three times to get the 'Hollywood' out of it," she wrote, "the movie did build a sort of myth around Doo and me and our marriage. And it was one that stuck with us." Loretta implied that some viewers might have been misled by the film's implications, especially women who felt "better about their marriages when they saw me and Doo—or really, Sissy Spacek and Tommy Lee Jones—putting things back together in the movie." According to Loretta, Doo's alcoholism "affected our marriage all the way through."

But, just as *Coal Miner's Daughter* had taken pains to "noble up" some the less flattering hillbilly hijinx in Loretta's first memoir, Loretta had held back, herself. In her second book, she took pains to rectify the situation by amplifying some of Doo's less savory antics, including:

- his rather unconventional fathering techniques, which included an attempt to swap his newborn daughter with a baby boy in the hospital nursery; later tying "her to the clothesline outside"; not showing up for his third child's birth until six days after the fact; tossing the same kid into the Pacific Ocean surf at age five in a life jacket to "toughen him up," and dangling him by the ankles over a waterfall for the same reason. ("I know I like to have died," wrote Loretta.)

- the extent of Doo's womanizing, which the movie had downplayed considerably, implying that he "a-commenced to cheatin'" because he felt neglected after Loretta's career took off. In reality, Doo was chasing hillbilly heiny from the get-go, including kinfolk, like Loretta's brother's wife. After thirteen-year-old Loretta, by then four months pregnant, warned a local WAC tramp to lay off her man, Doo announced to his bride, "If I ever had any love for you, I lost it today." But like her future friend Tammy Wynette, Loretta stood by her man. "I still loved him with all the unrealistic emotion of a teenager," she later wrote.
- "Doo's drunken temper tantrums," which on one occasion led to him repeatedly pushing Loretta's head into a sink filled with water "until I began to choke."

Nor was Loretta quite the shrinking violet portrayed by Spacek in the movie. By the real Loretta's own admission, "Yes, I've been known to knock the fire out of him." Once, when Doo staggered home from a hussy clutching a bottle of whiskey, Loretta "hauled off and hit him squarely on his mouth, knocking out his two front teeth" in a cascade of blood. "I can still hear them teeth hitting the floor and bouncing," Loretta recalled, with obvious satisfaction. "Pop, pop, pop." This scene is not in the movie. However, in the final scene, Tommy Lee Jones suddenly appears to be sporting a mouthful of hillbilly crazy teeth, for no apparent reason, which, in a way, plays as a kind of homage to "Fist City."

Sources and Further Reading

Lynn, Loretta. *Coal Miner's Daughter*. With George Vecsey. Reprint, New York: Da Capo Press, 1996.

Lynn, Loretta. *Still Woman Enough*. With Patsi Bale Cox. New York: Hyperion, 2002.

Segal, David. "Ballad of Loretta Lynn." *Washington Post*, June 14, 2002.

Almost Famous (2000)

Directed and written by Cameron Crowe
Starring Billy Crudup, Kate Hudson, and Patrick Fugit

Patrick Fugit as William Miller, Cameron Crowe's cinematic
doppelgänger. *Photo by Neal Preston, © DreamWorks LLC*

Cameron Crowe describes his cinematic memoir, *Almost Famous,* as "*painfully accurate,*" and of course we'll never really know how true that is because everything in the movie happened, or supposedly happened, to him. None of it is a matter of public record or academic research projects. Even though Crowe wrote an Oscar-nominated screenplay before this (*Jerry Maguire*) no one has yet deemed him worthy of a biography, other than himself. And then only on film—this film—so there's little to compare it to.

We know that Crowe, like his alter ego "William Miller," was a teenage rock critic for the then-still-rather-hip *Rolling Stone* magazine (we're going all the way back to 1973 here— *Stone* still had two or three years of relevance remaining). We know because he has bylines in the magazine, and several of his articles are reproduced electronically on the *Almost Famous* DVD, for those who enjoy reading thirty-year-old interviews with Jimmy Page on a TV screen.

There are a few other things about what goes on in the film that we know:

The band in the movie, Stillwater, is fictional. The misadventures of William Miller as he tags along with the band on tour, and consequently the band itself, are a composite of two tours that Crowe covered for *Rolling Stone*: The Allman Brothers' 1973 tour and a Led Zeppelin tour two years later. The result of this amalgam is that Stillwater looks like a Southern rock group but sounds like a British proto-metal band.

The through-line of the loosely structured story, young Miller's repeated badgering of Stillwater guitar player Russell Hammond for an interview, is based on Crowe's frustration at trying to corner Led Zep axeman Jimmy Page. A scene in which Hammond visits Miller's home to (sort of) apologize for sabotaging the kid's big story seems inspired by an altercation Crowe experienced with Greg Allman. For some reason, Allman became convinced that the government was spying on him. (Hey, this was 1973. It wasn't so unusual.) Anyway, Allman seized all of Crowe's interview tapes, leaving the then-fifteen-year-old Crowe with nothing to write about. Allman eventually gave back the tapes and gave Crowe an apologetic phone call.

There really was a groupie who called herself Penny Lane, though Crowe says the movie character by that name is a fictionalized composite. The legendary, late rock writer Lester Bangs did indeed act as something of an informal mentor and friend to Crowe. Even a scene where Miller is "deflowered" by a bunch of groupies, Crowe has insisted, "is based on something that happened to me." We can only imagine what—but we don't really want to, thanks very much. But what we cannot know, because even Cameron Crowe doesn't really know, is how his onscreen persona compares to what he was really like, all those years ago.

Because Crowe's own memories are the only record of what really happened three decades earlier, he has the rare opportunity to create his own mythology. In the film he is the awkward ingenue who's seduced by the thrill of befriending rock stars and fulfilling his journalistic role as "the enemy."

Another longtime rock critic (one of the original rock critics, as a matter of fact), Richard Meltzer, remembers Crowe somewhat differently. "All this poppycock with little William as 'the enemy'—someone bands have reason to fear!—feels suspiciously like what in football parlance you'd call the ol' misdirection play." The youthful Crowe, says Meltzer (writing for a weekly newspaper in San Diego, Crowe's hometown) was always "inherently harmless." Meltzer relates an anecdote in which Jackson Browne explains to Meltzer (whom Browne hated) why he and other musicians liked dealing with Crowe rather than opinionated, irascible older writers like Meltzer. "We feel we get a better shake from this Cameron kid," Brown tells Meltzer. "He never challenges us . . . accepts our side of the story . . . we don't have to worry about what he'll say."

The adult Crowe remembers his younger self as the "honest and unmerciful" ideal espoused to him by Bangs. In the end of *Almost Famous*, Miller turns in a cover story about Stillwater that angers the band so greatly with its spot-on verisimilitude ("Is it that hard to make us look cool?" whines Stillwater's fictional lead singer) that they deny everything in it to *Rolling Stone*'s fact checker, thus killing the piece and, it appears for the moment, William Miller's nascent career.

Maybe Meltzer's remembering Crowe all wrong. Maybe he's just jealous of Crowe's subsequent success. But we don't have to take his word for it. We can read Crowe's actual old pieces for ourselves and see for ourselves that they are basically fluff. Which, when all is said and done, is pretty much the same thing we could say about *Almost Famous*.

Sources and Further Reading

Mariotti, Greg. "The Uncool: Cameron Crowe Online." http://www.cameroncroweonline.com.

Meltzer, Richard. "Third Spud from the Sun: Cameron Crowe Then and Now." *San Diego Reader*, 2001.

Pulver, Andrew. "Cameron Crowe: All Things Come to He Who Waits." Foreword. In *Almost Famous*, by Cameron Crowe. London: Faber & Faber, 2000.

54 (1998)

Directed and written by Mark Christopher
Starring Mike Myers, Ryan Phillippe, and Neve Campbell

Mike Myers (center) as Steve Rubell. *Photo by Kerry Hayes,*
© Miramax Films

Director Mark Christopher had an agenda for his Studio 54 movie. He wanted to do more than film a chronicle of the most famous nightclub of the 1970s. According to press accounts, Christopher's grand vision involved a bisexual love triangle, a tangled, timeless plot in which two young, bare-chested Studio 54 bartenders covet the same foxy disco chick—and each other.

Christopher emerged in defeat from his battle with the film's financiers, who desired a Middle-America-friendly retelling of the disco-era legend. He never had a chance, really. Nonetheless, such sexually nuanced arrangements would not have been unusual at 54—or as the truly hip, circa 1977, referred to it, "Studio." Gay subculture in the late 1970s was just starting to assimilate into mainstream American pop culture, and Studio 54 led the way. The trend, the music, and the lifestyle known as "disco" was a gay-only phenomenon (well, gay and European) before a few hit singles climbed the charts and Studio 54 opened.

Looking back from two decades on, as Christopher did in his Miramax-backed movie, it is amazing that one nightclub, born from an empty warehouse and erstwhile CBS TV studio at 254 West 54th Street in midtown Manhattan, could have the decisive cultural impact that Studio 54 manifestly did. Owned and operated by two Syracuse University grads from Brooklyn, Steve Rubell and Ian Schrager, Studio 54 wasted no time becoming a force when it opened on April 26, 1977. Cher, at the time a very celebrated person, made the front page of the *New York Post* as she paraded into the hyperexclusive hangout that very first night. The media cult of celebrity now seen dominating cable channels and magazine racks across America was born.

Actually, when you look back, it is equally amazing that there was an empty warehouse in midtown Manhattan. Today, that area is among the priciest real estate patches in the known universe. An unoccupied dwelling? Inconceivable.

In 1977 New York was staggering from its near-bankruptcy of two years earlier. To exacerbate matters, the Son of Sam killings were in full swing, holding the city in a grip of fear. That summer saw a record heat wave. A city-wide blackout erupted into a looting orgy. It was the perfect point in time for Americans to fall at the feet of their "beautiful people," begging for escapism, if not absolution. The founders of Studio 54 understood this urge implicitly.

Or maybe they just dug a good party. The ingredients, they knew, were simple: money, drugs, sex, and lots of each. The key, they believed, was a carefully cultivated guest list. The club grew famous for the mystique of the debauchery inside, but just as much for its capricious door policy on the street outside. Rubell—the more flamboyant of the partners and Studio 54's public face—made the brownnosing of celebrities something like a personal religion (one that quickly spread from New York to the rest of the continental United States). Yet even megastardom didn't guarantee admittance, if Rubell felt that, on any particular night, you didn't fit the mix of personas he had in mind for his nightly party. Jack Nicholson and Warren Beatty were each, on occasion, denied entry to the club. Studio 54's rep was built as much on who it turned away as who it allowed past its velvet rope.

Studio 54 was once described as "dictatorship at the door, democracy on the dance floor." Crowds clamored nightly in hopes of getting in, where they would occupy the same rarefied space as Diana Ross, Lauren Hutton, and Bianca Jagger. Perhaps they could even talk to, dance with, or, well, who knows what else with one of them. And by contemporary accounts, exactly that did happen, with some frequency.

In the movie, the ruthless door restrictions are directed primarily at shaggy-haired stoners from New Jersey. Inside the club we see, or at least hear mentioned, well-known denizens of Studio 54 milling about. Truman Capote, Liza Minnelli, Andy Warhol—1970s scenesters who look pretty kitschy from the jaded, media-inoculated perspective of the new millennium. In the 1970s, however, these sorry characters appeared to be the embodiment of a life worth aspiring to. Studio 54's role in spawning the culture of celebrity, as well as in repackaging gay nightlife for the masses, is invisible in the movie, which is more interested in—hmmm, it's difficult to tell *what* the movie is interested in.

Gay subculture? Rubell, played by Mike Myers behind a prosthetic nose and a strained Brooklyn dialect, is portrayed as unambiguously, unashamedly gay. He was that, but only to his friends. He never "came out," and he maintained a stream of "girlfriends" for public viewing, an aspect of his existence that is absent from the film. Rubell died in 1989 of AIDS-related hepatitis symptoms, but he remained in the closet the whole way. The movie does a good job of re-creating 1970s period detail, down to the giant Man in the Moon with a coke spoon that dangled insouciantly over the Studio 54 dance floor. But it conveys no feeling for the attitudes and emotions of the era. *54* is no *American Graffiti* for the '70s.

Also missing is any mention of Rubell's partner, Schrager, who was (and is) not gay and who was the business mind to Rubell's center stage showman. Doubtless, Schrager is omitted for legal reasons, but his absence is conspicuous nonetheless. You wouldn't make an Abbott and Costello movie without Abbott, or a Beavis and Butthead movie without Butthead. Schrager these days is a maven of trendy, darkly lit hotels, including New York's Paramount and L.A.'s Standard.

One aspect of 54 history *not* omitted is Rubell's habit of skimming money off the nightly take and stuffing it into garbage bags, which he hid in the club's ceiling panels. (Schrager was also in on the skim.) The movie comes to an apocalyptic climax on New Year's Eve, 1979, symbolizing the death of the decade of decadence. The calamitous evening culminates in the dance-floor death-by-drug-overdose of Disco Dottie, the eighty-year-old bewigged grandma who shook her saggy booty at 54 on a nightly basis—and with the arrest by IRS agents of Rubell on charges of tax evasion. He is led in handcuffs from his beloved club, on what was supposed to be its greatest night.

The real 54 was raided by the IRS twice; first in December 1978, then again a year later. The raids were mainly the result of Rubell's unfortunate practice of taunting the IRS in media interviews. Sure enough, investigators uncovered rampant and brazen tax fraud. The newly convicted Studio 54 founders held a final 54 bacchanal on February 3, 1980, after which they marched off to prison. They each received sentences of three-and-a-half years, but they got about two years shaved off when they "flipped," mob style, and ratted out fellow New York club owners. Rubell and Schrager hadn't been the only entrepreneurs taking full advantage of the freewheeling, all-cash nightclub business. (This was in the days when entrepreneurs, not transnational corporations, owned fashionable nightspots.) Rubell's role as stoolie, like his conflicts over his sexuality, didn't make it into the movie.

"Disco Dottie" didn't actually die on the dance floor, either. The real woman, who was known as Disco Sally, passed on at home, of a stroke, as older people, sadly, often do.

Sources and Further Reading

Colacello, Bob. "Anything Went." *Vanity Fair*, March 1996.

Gross, Michael. "Little Stevie Wonder: The Death and Life of Steve Rubell." *New York*. August 14, 1989.

Haden-Guest, Anthony. *The Last Party: Studio 54, Disco, and the Culture of the Night*. New York: William Morrow, 1997.

Lemon, Brendan. "The Real Rubell." *The Advocate*. July 21, 1998.

The Sound of Music (1965)

Directed by Robert Wise
Written by Ernest Lehman
Starring Julie Andrews and Christopher Plummer

Musicals featuring Nazis have a distinct advantage over all other musicals: the unnatural act of people suddenly bursting into song seems far less jarring when you're busy gawking at the fact that *there are Nazis in this musical!*

The Sound of Music immediately loses this advantage because it is based on a true story, which makes the crooning seem surreal all over again, Nazis notwithstanding. Because how can you possibly suspend disbelief and accept spontaneous outdoor choreography when you know that *elements of this story are true?* "Which elements?" you obsess, already lost to the magic. The part where they prance about in draperies trilling to invisible orchestral accompaniment? Or the part where Julie Andrews exposes her naked bosom to the camera? Wait—that's a different movie. But you see how musicals screw with your sense of reality? One minute it's "doe, a deer, a female deer," and the next its *Nihilism, Anarchy,* and *Nuns Flashing Their Boobs.*

Even a film critic as smart as Pauline Kael had trouble wrapping her head around the Zen koan-like concept of a "True Musical." She once wrote about *The Sound of Music,* "Wasn't there perhaps one little von Trapp who didn't want to sing his head off, or who screamed that he wouldn't act out little glockenspiel routines for Papa's party guests, or who got nervous and threw up if he had to get on a stage?"

The answer to Kael's question is easy: yes. But, as the incident in question occurred after the events depicted in the Julie Andrews movie, it wouldn't be fair to fault Rodgers and Hammerstein for failing to include a number called "You Won't Sing, So I'm Authorizing Electroshock Therapy." That particular anecdote, along with a number of others detailing the less-than-Julie Andrews–like outbursts of matron songstress Maria von Trapp, emerged long after the film had sashayed into the hearts of moviegoers worldwide.

But we've gotten ahead of the story. *Let's start at the very beginning. A very good place to start . . . When you sing you begin with do-re-mi. . . .*

(Sorry. That won't happen again.)

Here's what the 1965 movie—which was based on the 1959 Broadway play, which was based in part on Maria von Trapp's memoir and which followed two earlier German films that had also been inspired by Maria von Trapp's memoir, which was based on real events involving (remember to breathe) Nazis and musical numbers—gets right:

Captain Georg von Trapp, a former submarine commander for the Austrian navy and the widowed father of nine children, hires a young woman from a Salzburg convent, Maria Kutschera, to tutor his children. Maria teaches the children to sing folk songs and madrigals using sophisticated four-part harmonies. A year later, Captain von Trapp ditches his aristocratic fiancée and marries Maria. When the 1932 crash of the Austrian national bank costs von Trapp his fortune, Maria organizes her step-brood into a public singing sensation, the Trapp Family Singers. After Hitler seizes Austria, the Gestapo pressures von Trapp to hang a swastika from his window. He refuses. When the Nazis pressure von Trapp to join the German navy and establish a submarine base in the Adriatic Sea, the Captain and his family escape to America, leaving their past life behind.

That's all true. By the time the von Trapp saga ascended to the big screen, however, a number of story upgrades had been "value-added."

For instance, Captain von Trapp was greatly improved for the stage and screen. The actual captain had been one of those nurturing, doting fathers who would deprive dramatic storytellers of a redemptive "character arc." Movie fathers are advised to remain hard-hearted in Acts One and Two. The time for doting—don't rush it—is Act Three, when a good woman breaks through the facade and melts his icy heart. Christopher Plummer's strict, humorless patriarch created just the dramatic loophole necessary for this crucial transformation.

Among the other "fixes":

- Plummer's von Trapp forbids his little troops to make music. In reality, the von Trapp household had been awash in song long before Maria arrived with her guitar.
- The von Trapp children were renamed for the movie, given monikers that would sound more endearing and homey to American audiences. *Wiedersehen* hard-sounding Germanic names Hedwig, Werner, and Martina; hello, sweetly lilting "Louisa," "Brigitta," and "Liesl." Speaking of Liesl, no von

Trapp daughter fell in love with a junior brownshirt who later ratted out the family to the Gestapo.

- Andrews and Plummer fall haupt over heels for each other. But the real Maria didn't get all swoony when the Captain, who was twenty-five years her senior, proposed to her. "At that time, I really and truly was not in love," she confessed in her second memoir, *Maria*. "I liked him but didn't love him. However, I loved the children, and so in a way I really married the children." (Also, in real life, the betrothal of convenience did not lead to an impromptu musical duet in a gazebo.)

- More and better Nazis. In reality there was no climactic chase scene involving Nazis or vehicle-sabotaging nuns. Nor did the family flee immediately after making its public debut at a Gestapo-infested talent show; by the time they left Austria for good, they had already been performing publicly for years. Nor did the von Trapps flee into the Alps. As one of the children, little Maria, later noted, "We did not climb over the mountains with all our heavy suitcases and instruments! We left by train, pretending nothing." What's more, "the mountains we flee over in the movie would take us to Germany, right into Hitler's mouth."

Perhaps the biggest modification was to Maria von Trapp's character. Far from the perky Julie Andrews type, her stepchildren would later describe her as temperamental and prone to unpredictable, irrational mood swings and violent behavior. According to stepdaughter Maria, "She had a terrible temper. And from one moment to the next, you didn't know what hit her. We were not used to this. But we took it like a thunderstorm that would pass, because the next minute she could be very nice." Before he died of lung cancer in 1947, Captain von Trapp was often the target of Maria's rages, which manifested as screaming, furniture throwing, and door slamming.

How do you solve a problem like Maria? Well, Prozac might have helped.

After the captain's death, Maria's bipolar-ish antics began to take their toll on the family. She practically held the von Trapps hostage in a desperate effort to keep the touring performances alive. "I think my mother discouraged socializing outside the family," said the younger Maria, "because she could see that the moment one of my siblings married, there would be children and other responsibilities that would keep them out of the choir." When stepdaughter

Johanna announced her pending marriage, Maria locked her in her room, forcing the young woman to escape through the window and elope with her fiancé.

The pressure was too much for another stepdaughter, Rosmarie, who had always been afflicted with stage fright. She eventually suffered a complete nervous breakdown, then disappeared. Days later she was found wandering, disoriented, in the woods. Maria authorized electroshock therapy. Rosmarie recovered but never performed again with the group.

Ultimately, the family stopped touring. After Maria's death in 1987, the surviving von Trapps and their voluminous offspring waged a bitter legal battle over money and property. The hills were alive, with the sound of litigation.

Sources and Further Reading

Myers, Eric. "A Problem Like Maria." *Opera News*, May 2003.

O'Toole, Fintan. "The Sound of Musing: Maria von Trapp's Journey from Austria to Broadway." Knight Ridder/Tribune News Service, March 11, 1998.

von Trapp, Agathe. *Memories Before and After* The Sound of Music. Franklin, TN: Hillsboro Press, 2003.

von Trapp, Maria Augusta. *The Story of the Trapp Family Singers*. Garden City, NY: Image Books, 1957.

Reality Strikes Out

Seabiscuit (2003)

Directed and written by Gary Ross
Starring Tobey Maguire, Jeff Bridges, and Chris Cooper

Seabiscuit—the champion racehorse—was a cantankerous nag who tore up the track at his pleasure, for his pleasure. As his most constant jockey, Red Pollard, put it just after the thoroughbred's greatest and final victory, "Don't think he didn't know he was the hero."

Seabiscuit—the 2003 Hollywood blockbuster—is an altogether different kind of nag: the cinematic kind that nudges and prods to uplift and inspire. Like its self-consciously soaring musical score, it labors to evoke a sentimental response from its audience. To be fair, the heartstring-plucking in *Seabiscuit* is fairly restrained compared to the thudding bathos of many another sports film celebrating a gutsy underdog who risks it all to overachieve like crazy. But if you're looking for a nuanced portrait of the famous racing legend, his inspired but imperfect human handlers, and the troubled American era in which they toiled, triumphed, and lent hope, you won't find it here.

Where you *will* find it is in the movie's source material, Laura Hillenbrand's 2001 nonfiction bestseller, *Seabiscuit: An American Legend*. In that book, Hillenbrand tells the story of the "undersized, crooked-legged racehorse" who, during the latter part of the Depression, became a "cultural icon in America, enjoying adulation so intense and broad-based that it transcended the sport." After two years of losses in the minor leagues of racing, the misunderstood, mishandled horse with "an egg-beater gate" had been written off as an also-ran.

There the story would probably have ended for Seabiscuit, if it hadn't been for three men who saw the horse's potential and set about rehabilitating him.

Seabiscuit's rescuers couldn't have been more different. His jockey, Red Pollard, was a "tragic-faced young man" who had been abandoned as a child at a Montana racetrack. For years he had toiled as a failed jockey and a much-abused prizefighter. Seabiscuit's trainer was a "mysterious, virtually mute mustang breaker" named Tom Smith, a hobo cowboy with an uncanny knack for understanding horses. And Seabiscuit's new owner was Charles Howard, a savvy automobile mogul who, in his endless promoting of the horse, practically invented the art of sports agenting.

Working together, the three men awakened Seabiscuit's dormant talent and spirit, and guided the horse through an initially rocky, but ultimately triumphant, second career as a racing champion. Americans mired in the depths of the Depression identified with this living fable of an underdog bouncing back from the brink to succeed beyond all expectation. Seabiscuit became an American cultural phenomenon, packing the tracks beyond capacity, drawing millions to their radios to follow his epic career, and garnering more newspaper ink than even Hitler and Franklin Delano Roosevelt. As Hillenbrand put it, "There is something quintessentially American about everyone in this story. [It's about] the triumph over hardship—that's the journey toward the American dream."

That hopeful theme runs throughout the book, but Hillenbrand always anchors her story in unflinching observations of the era's sometimes unpleasant social realities. *Seabiscuit* the movie, on the other hand, is so intent on chasing the cinema-friendly themes of Hope and American Nostalgia that it occasionally loses sight of its historical context and the downbeat details therein. For instance, although the film accurately depicts the hard-knock life of jockey Red Pollard (Tobey Maguire), it often pulls up short of full disclosure—never mentioning his self-medication with alcohol, for example. Pollard drank to control chronic pain brought on by countless injuries, a habit that developed into an ongoing struggle with alcoholism.

And although the film hints at the physical abuse to which jockeys subjected themselves in order to "make weight," you never quite get the full picture. In the book, Hillenbrand describes one technique that Pollard, who was physically large for a jockey, probably employed to drop pounds: the ingestion of tapeworm eggs. After hatching, the worms would feast on its host's stomach contents, leading not only to rapid weight loss, but also malnourishment and brittle bones.

Overall, the film follows the events of Seabiscuit's career faithfully, although director Gary Ross (who also wrote the screenplay) did modify some details for dramatic purposes. For instance, although both the real Red Pollard and Seabiscuit's other main jockey, George Woolf, were both Canadian, you wouldn't know it from the film. Apparently, Canadians have no place in a movie about American idealism.

Seabiscuit's glad-handing owner, Charles Howard (Jeff Bridges), has also been upgraded in several ways. Watching the film, you might get the idea that he was a visionary who designed and built the automobiles he sold. In fact, he was merely a successful car dealer who, as they used to say, got in on the ground floor of a good thing. And although the real Howard was indeed devastated by his son's death in a car accident, the boy was fifteen when he died, not twelve as depicted in the movie. Apparently, the filmmakers decided that a father's loss of his son is more poignant when the kid is not yet a punk teenager. Meanwhile, Howard's older two sons get even less respect—they've been completely expunged from the film version.

Another victim of dramatic efficiency is Red Pollard's wife, Agnes Conlon, a nurse who had cared for him after he'd shattered his leg. She's completely absent in the film, and her real-life moment of historical glory—hanging a medal of Saint Christopher around Pollard's neck for good luck before his greatest race—has been delegated to Mrs. Howard. (Elizabeth Banks, in an otherwise thankless role that consists largely of supportive smiling.)

But those are minor nitpicks, forgivable because they don't change the overall accuracy or tone of the story.

A bit less pardonable is the film's somewhat crossed purposes. *Seabiscuit* isn't quite sure if it wants to be an understated docudrama that explores a great American myth—or the myth itself. Director Gary Ross has previously blended social realism and nostalgia, to similarly mixed results. His comic fantasy *Pleasantville* (also starring Tobey Maguire) pivoted on the *Back to the Future*-ish concept of two modern teens finding themselves trapped in an idealized 1950s TV soap opera. Ross set out to satirize misplaced nostalgia for an era that never really existed (outside of Nick at Night's lineup). But the alternative he winds up offering—black-and-white Pleasantville, literally colorized and remade into an oasis of tolerance, liberal thinking, and art appreciation—is just as much an idealized showbiz fantasy, one that never really existed outside of a Frank Capra movie.

In *Seabiscuit*, Ross has similar difficulties reconciling realism and fantasy. He wants to demonstrate that Seabiscuit lifted Depression-wracked America up from despair, giving its people something to dream about. Yet he also wants to lift his twenty-first-century audience up by those same horseshoes so that they feel the same warmth. Unfortunately, in doing so the manipulation of the fable overpowers the hard-edged sense of reality, diminishing the whole experience.

Sources and Further Reading

American Experience. "Seabiscuit—The Long Shot That Captured America's Heart." Transcript of the PBS documentary directed by Stephen Ives and written by Michelle Ferrari. http://www.pbs.org/wgbh/amex/seabiscuit/filmmore/pt.html.

Hillenbrand, Laura. *Seabiscuit: An American Legend.* New York: Random House, 2001.

Movie-O: MovieOrigins.com. "Reel Faces: Red Pollard and Seabiscuit." http://www.chasingthefrog.com/reelfaces/seabiscuit.php.

West, Gary. "Seabiscuit Movie Is an Exhilarating Ride, But Let's Be Truthful." *Dallas Morning News,* June 25, 2003.

Hoosiers (1986)

Directed by David Anspaugh
Written by Angelo Pizzo
Starring Gene Hackman, Dennis Hopper, and Barbara Hershey

Gene Hackman (right) as coach Norman Dale. *Photo by Morgan Renard, © Orion Pictures Corporation*

Hoosiers was yet another entry in an apparently unending series of 1980s "feel good" movies. The genre was actually born in the '70s, with *Rocky* and the less-remembered but equally influential *Breaking Away*. But the "triumph of the little guy" formula was mainly a creation of the post–Jimmy Carter era, when Americans still had enough of a Vietnam/Iran-hostage hangover to perceive our superpower nation as some kind of scrappy underdog.

We (American moviegoers, that is) couldn't get enough of seeing our own image inflated by Hollywood fantasies. *Hoosiers* fit the template: undermanned basketball team from tiny high school with misfit coach relies on sheer guts and ingenuity to win the Indiana State Championship. The *sacred* Indiana State Championship. But this movie transcended the genre, earned a pair of Academy Award nominations, and is widely considered the best sports film ever churned out by Hollywood. *Hoosiers* is a well-produced, well-acted piece of entertainment, but its lasting resonance is due to the fact that Hoosiers is "based on a true story." Yes, there was one scrappy underdog who *really did* win the big one.

In the movie, the Hickory Huskers, a team from a school of just 161 students, won the 1952 Indiana state title, beating much bigger South Bend Central on a last-second shot by star player Jimmy Chitwood.

In real life, the Milan Indians, a team from a school of just 161 students, won the 1954 Indiana State title, beating much bigger Muncie Central on a last-second shot by star player Bobby Plump.

A true tale, tailor-made for Hollywood. Or so it would appear.

There was one small hitch in bringing this true tale to the screen. The lives of the real Milan players and coach were, according to *Hoosiers* screenwriter Angelo Pizzo, "not dramatic enough. The guys were too nice. The team had no real conflict."

And so the Hollywoodization of a story tailor-made for Hollywood began. Marvin Wood, the quiet, religious twenty-six-year-old family man who coached Milan to the title in his second season was replaced by Norman Dale (Gene Hackman), a fiery loner in his late forties who spent a decade in the navy after punching one of his own players and subsequently being suspended, in disgrace, from coaching.

Hackman's Dale wins the title in his first season with a team that, as the sports cliché goes, comes out of nowhere. Wood was in his second year at the school, and had coached Milan to the state semifinals the season prior to winning it all. The movie also introduces an assistant coach, a hopeless alcoholic whose son just happens to be on the team—a totally made-up character, and a totally made-up subplot.

Almost every boy in the Milan school tried out for the basketball team, and Coach Wood had a full roster of ten players. In the movie, Coach Dale barely scrapes together a squad of seven. One of those players is the team's equipment manager, who is pressed into service to hit two crucial free throws in the semifinal game. The equipment manager is named Ollie, which was the real first name of Milan's equipment manager. But the real Ollie never donned a jersey, much less took a crucial free throw.

The fictional team's star, Jimmy Chitwood, refuses to play until midway through the season because he is distraught over the death of the previous coach. Chitwood's flesh-and-blood counterpart, Bobby Plump, had no such reservations and played the entire season. (Wood did indeed replace a very popular coach, but that coach did not die; he was pink-slipped for purchasing new team uniforms without the school's approval.)

With the championship on the line in the final seconds, as he sees that his coach plans to let another player take the final shot, the normally silent Chitwood speaks up. "I'll make it!" he declares. And so he does.

It was Coach Wood's plan all along to let Plump take the final shot. "I was a very shy kid," Plump said years later. "I would never have said, 'I'll make it.'"

There were some slight similarities between Coach Wood and his Hollywood doppelgänger. When Wood took over the team he endured the town's approbation by closing practices to parents and drilling the team in a new style of offense. (Unlike Norman Dale, however, Wood never had his job put to a vote during a town meeting.) More important, the film's most famous scene was taken straight from Wood's playbook. Before the championship game, Dale measures the height of the basket—his point being that the massive, fifteen-thousand-seat field house in which his kids were playing was no different than the team's own high school gym.

Wood had done exactly that before Milan's "miracle" game.

Bobby Plump has said that "there was more truth than accuracy" in the movie (which did capture, he said, the "feel" of growing up in a tiny Indiana farm town). "The final eighteen seconds were the only thing factual in the movie." Basketball aficionados, as well as film fans, will appreciate the differences between reality and Hollywood that lead up to those climactic eighteen seconds. The filmed version of the game is a fast-paced affair, with Jimmy Chitwood sinking the winning bucket with only a moment's hesitation after an in-bounds pass.

In reality, Coach Wood ordered his team to play the "slow down" style of basketball that was popular in the 1950s. Bobby Plump held the ball for a full four minutes before he took his shot—and then he missed! Plump got the ball back and held on for another full minute, running out the clock before putting up the miraculous jump shot that made Hollywood history.

Sources and Further Reading

Guffey, Greg. *The Greatest Basketball Story Ever Told: The Milan Miracle, Then and Now.* Bloomington, IN: Indiana University Press, 1993.

Marshall, Kerry D. *A Boy, a Ball, and a Dream: The Marvin Wood Story.* Indianapolis: Scott Publications, 1991.

Sports Hollywood. "The Real Hoosiers." http://www.sportshollywood.com/hoosiers.html.

Ali (2001)

Directed by Michael Mann
Written by Stephen J. Rivele, Christopher Wilkinson, Eric Roth, and Michael Mann
Starring Will Smith, Jon Voight, and Mario Van Peebles

Will Smith as Muhammad Ali.
Photo by Frank Connor, © Columbia Pictures

Muhammad Ali called himself "the Greatest," but in his time, he was greater than that. Not to say that Ali was a perfect human being—like most of us, he was a considerable distance from perfection. Nor was his greatness simply a measure of his fame, which was staggering. For years, Ali was the single most recognizable person in the entire human race. The calculated corporate "branding" that passes for fame with today's celebrities is a shallow parody of Ali's fame. He was not merely well known and commercially successful; he imposed his identity on the world.

There is, flat out, no way that a professional athlete—much less a *boxer*, for crying out loud—could have that kind of impact today. Looking back from our perch three and four decades on, it's extremely difficult to understand how Ali's personality pervaded the 1960s and early '70s, the Era of Ali.

Michael Mann's biopic of Ali doesn't help a whole heck of a lot in that regard. Mann pays fastidious attention to visual detail; *Ali* is an impeccable period piece. Mann gets his broad factual matter right, as far as it goes; he hits the important story-beats of Ali's saga. And Will Smith does a pretty good job of channeling the young Ali—even if his incarnation is weirdly somnambulant. (He does a lot of contemplative staring into space and speaks in a drowsy drawl. It's as if Will Smith is trying much harder to *not be Will Smith* than to be Muhammad Ali.)

The boxing scenes in *Ali* are the most true-to-life ever staged by Hollywood. Mann puts Smith through Ali's paces, step-by-choreographed-step, with B-level professional boxers standing in for Ali's opponents. There's no impressionistic gore, as in *Raging Bull* (see page 261), and no comic-book slugfests, as in *Rocky*. Nor does Mann have Ali seeming to win fights in which he actually took a beating, as Norman Jewison did with Rubin Carter in *The Hurricane* (see page 9). The reenactments in the film follow the real fight footage, for the most part.

Mann does not attempt to cover Ali's whole life, or even his whole career. He picks up the story shortly before the twenty-two-year-old Cassius Clay's first shot at a world championship, against fearsome former mob enforcer Sonny Liston, on February 25, 1963. The next eleven years would be the era of Muhammad Ali, culminating in his reclaiming the title belt that was stripped from him when he refused to comply with the draft and serve in the Vietnam War.

Ali's historic fight against George Foreman took place on October 30, 1974. Before the fight, boxing experts (and fans) were seriously worried that the powerful, mercurial, and merciless Foreman (who did not bear much resemblance to the roly-poly, grinning infomercial pitchman he's become today) would not merely defeat Ali, but kill him. Ali's triumph was something like a miracle, right there on *Wide World of Sports*. That's where Mann freezes the final frame of his film.

Eleven years is a small slice of Ali's life, but it was an eventful eleven years. Mann does considerable condensing and conflating of people, places, and things—the standard shorthand. But events zoom by so quickly in this movie, it's hard to figure out what Mann is trying to say with his choices. If anything.

One of the pivotal moments in Ali's early career was his break with Malcolm X, who had supported and encouraged young Cassius Clay's conversion to the Nation of Islam. Malcolm had his own rift with Nation of Islam chief Elijah Muhammad, and Ali sided with the latter. In the film, Ali's break with Malcolm is not just condensed, it's hypercondensed, squeezed into a single moment when the two meet in Africa. Malcolm (Mario Van Peebles) has just returned from his revelatory trip to Mecca, where he discovered a traditional, more racially inclusive form of Islam (as opposed to the Nation of Islam version, which made racial separatism its pillar). As Malcolm is in the process of explaining his new outlook, Ali blurts out, "You shouldn't have quarreled with the Honorable Elijah Muhammad," and walks away, never to speak to his former friend again.

It is true that Ali (then still Cassius Clay) ran into Malcolm X at a hotel in Ghana in May 1964, and the brief encounter was strained. But the breach had begun months earlier, when Malcolm spent a week visiting with Ali in Miami. Ali was the Nation of Islam's most famous member—kind of like Tom Cruise is with Scientology today. Elijah Muhammad was not unaware of Ali's value as a PR coup.

Malcolm X had already been "suspended" from the Nation, ostensibly for a disparaging comment about President Kennedy's assassination ("the chickens have come home to roost"), but really for confronting Elijah Muhammad over his very un-Islamic extramarital affairs. None of those reasons make it into the movie—the break between Ali and Malcolm is left as something of a puzzle.

The Nation of Islam was considered a serious and frightening threat in America in the early 1960s. Because the "Black Muslims" were widely feared and despised, so was Muhammad Ali. The beloved and revered Ali, the Olympic torch-lighter and president hand-shaker of today, was in those days reviled by much of white America as a dangerous revolutionary. Conversely, African Americans saw him as the ultimate symbol of pride and hope: a black man who took absolutely no shit from white people, or from anyone else. Mann barely makes an effort to illustrate the social context of Ali's conversion. He does make it clear that the government felt threatened by the Black Muslims. Mann gives us the conspiracy theory that the FBI ordered the assassination of Malcolm X.

Ali did nothing to dispel his divisive image. He kept lots of hangers-on in his entourage, but he employed no PR flacks, image consultants, or spin doctors. He was no manufactured, carefully crafted celebrity—the model displayed on magazine covers these days (Ali, incidentally, graced thirty-one covers of *Sports Illustrated*—a record even today). But Mann hides away the inflammatory Ali. We never see him stating his belief (which he put on the record in a *Playboy* interview) that black women who date white men should be killed; in fact, any interracial sex merited capital punishment as far as the young Ali was concerned.

In the same interview, Ali predicted, "America's going to be destroyed! Allah's going to divinely chastise America!" If this line would have been included in this film, which had the misfortune to hit screens only three months and a day after the 9/11 attacks, one can only wonder how that would have gone over. But Ali said it—that was what he believed during the period of his life recounted in Mann's film. Rather than get into the somewhat questionable substance of Ali's beliefs, however, Mann presents Muslimhood as an emblem of Ali's rebellion. Ali refuses to take orders from anyone. Including the U.S. government, when he refuses conscription into the army. Ali's absolute insistence on total independence comprises the theme of Mann's movie. It's not so much "Black Power" as it is "Ali Power."

But he did take orders from Elijah Muhammad. Was Ali, during those years, the headstrong, courageous individualist Mann presents—or was he a glorified cult member? From Mann's version of his bio, it's impossible to tell.

Even if it were possible, there's no time to think about it—in this two-hour, thirty-nine-minute film, events race ahead at such a kinetic pace there's barely time to figure out what just happened before we're on to the next tumultuous event. The film jumps from Ali's first defeat, his comeback loss to his arch-foil Joe Frazier in Madison Square Garden, straight to Ali's astonishing meeting with Foreman in Zaire, the "Rumble in the Jungle," more than three years later. We hear no mention of the fourteen fights that occurred in the interim. Those three-and-a-half years—from March 8, 1971, to October 30, 1974—were not insignificant. In that time period, Ali fought Frazier again and beat him. He also fought hard-punching Ken Norton and lost. Norton broke Ali's jaw, but as soon as it healed, Ali fought Norton again and won. Like Frazier, Norton was later demolished by Foreman—one of the reasons why no one thought Ali stood a chance against Foreman.

Mann also leaves out Ali's penchant for playing the race card to promote his fights. It's an uncomfortable topic, made even more awkward because Ali never played it against white opponents, who included such big-hearted but slow-footed pugs as Jerry Quarry and Chuck Wepner. (Wepner's from-nowhere story was Sylvester Stallone's inspiration for *Rocky*.) Ali directed his racial rhetoric at fellow African Americans, at Joe Frazier in particular.

Frazier was the eleventh child of a South Carolina sharecropper. The story of "Smokin' Joe" fighting his way up from poverty was almost an archetype for his generation of African Americans. Yet Ali ridiculed Frazier as an "Uncle Tom" and, most notoriously, "a gorilla." But Ali's race-baiting finds no place in Mann's film of his life.

Like the movie *Gandhi* (see page 378), *Ali* is true to the events of history without being true to the man who made that history. Unlike with Richard Attenborough's film, however, the subject of *Ali* was (and still is) alive. Muhammad Ali and his fourth wife, Lonnie, retained creative control of the project, which included approval of the script, the casting, and the choice of director. Lonnie Ali said that neither she nor her husband wanted the film to be a "whitewash," and it is not exactly that. What it turned out to be was a one-dimensional portrait, a highlight reel of Ali's complex career. Muhammad Ali was one of the most important figures of his era, which was one of the turning points of American history. Muhammad Ali, a boxer with a big mouth, changed history. Maybe the next *Ali* biopic will show us how.

Sources and Further Reading

Ali, Muhammad. *The Greatest: My Own Story*. With Richard Durham. New York: Random House, 1975.

Remnick, David. *King of the World*. New York: Random House, 1998.

Radio (2003)

Directed by Michael Tollin
Written by Mike Rich
Starring Cuba Gooding Jr. and Ed Harris

As we can see from the other biopics mentioned in this book, compressing a person's life into an hour and fifty-eight minutes of film isn't as easy as it looks. Most human lives have too much meaningful detail, or at least detail, to cram into a book, much less a screenplay with the word count of a short story.

The conventions of Hollywood storytelling make matters even trickier. Screenplay characters are supposed to have an "arc"; that is, a series of events that cause the character to "learn" and "change" in a discernible way between the opening credits and the final fade. Sad to say, most of us learn little and change even less over the course of our allotted seventy-eight-year-average time slot. Nor do our existences often contain an "inciting incident"—a single, dramatic occurrence that gets our story going.

When your screenplay's about a mentally handicapped person, the storytelling problems only get thornier. People with diminished mental ability have, sadly, even less capacity for growth and change than the rest of us. The moviemakers are therefore generally obliged to tell a story about change not in the central character, but in the rest of the cast. The supporting characters get the "arc," while the man or woman in the middle remains a constant point.

Now, Mr. Screenplay Instructor, what do you do when the other people didn't change much either, in this here true story you're adapting?

Simple. You do what Hollywood always does when true stories don't fit the screenplay manual (as if they ever do). You make it up.

Hopefully, you don't *hoke* it up. And we're pleased to report that *Radio* is a nice example of how to "Hollywood-ize" a true story without drowning it in a morass of studio saccharine.

"Radio" is the nickname of James Robert Kennedy, an Anderson, South Carolina, man with an unidentified genetic condition that causes severe mental disability. He can't read or write, couldn't speak intelligibly until he was in his twenties, and has only a rudimentary understanding of the world around him. He is a perpetual toddler in a grown man's body, with the same naive delight as a small child—and the same capacity for suffering terrible hurt.

In 1964, eighteen-year-old Radio (so named because he always carries a portable radio) was aimlessly loitering near a football field in Anderson, watching junior varsity practice. He was making all kinds of noise over there, mimicking the gyrations and hollers of the coaches and players. Harold Jones, the JV team's unpaid assistant coach, offered the young man a bottle of soda.

Jones became head coach of the varsity football team at Anderson's Hanna High School in 1985, and was also the school's athletic director, until he was fired from both jobs in 1998. Through all of those years, he was Radio's caretaker and best friend, and remains so even today. Radio lived with his mother (and for a time, a stepfather) until she died in 1994, then with his brother Walter (who does not have the genetic defect that afflicts both Radio and his other brother). But it was Coach Jones who brought Radio to school, took him for an annual doctor's checkup, and loaded the bed of a pickup with Radio's birthday gifts—a pile of them, from almost everyone at the school.

Today, almost forty years after he and Jones first met on that football field, Radio still goes to Hanna High School every day. He sits in on classes, and he "manages" the football, basketball, and track teams.

During those four decades, Radio has become one of the most beloved characters not only in Anderson, but in all of South Carolina. He was (and is) a fixture at the school. He once ran in a track race, when Jones coached the track team. He joined the ROTC, and he became a hall monitor (he wears a military uniform). He's lived a full life.

Radio was the subject of a 1996 *Sports Illustrated* article by writer Gary Smith. Filmmaker Michael Tollin, whose specialty is sports flicks, read the piece while on a ski vacation and labored for the next seven years to bring Radio's story to the screen. While he made some drastic factual adjustments, he remained respectful of the truth, never trying to make this genuinely heartwarming story any more heartwarming than it actually is.

Tollin's first problem was time frame. Radio's story has no end. He's still at Hanna High, doing the same things he's been doing for his entire adult life. In fact, the film ends with footage of the real James "Radio" Kennedy in action at the team's 2002 homecoming game. Tollin's solution was to condense the story into one year, 1976, during which he'd hit all the high points of the touching relationship between the gruff football coach and the joyful Radio.

"What we decided to do was to take a year right in the middle of this sweeping four decades," said Tollin, "and show the convergence of events that led to Radio becoming an integral part of society in this small town."

To squeeze all the relevant events in, naturally much had to be left out, and many details had to be changed. Jones is already the varsity head coach in Tollin's version, for starters. Tollin also created a "conflict" (in the storytelling sense). The local school board attempts to get Radio placed in a special facility, while the parent of a star football player wants him barred from the team because he's "a distraction."

None of those conflicts ever existed. Hanna High's principal (who, unlike in the movie, was not a black woman), has said that he recalls not a single phone call objecting to Radio's presence in school or on the sidelines.

Tollin also injects an "inciting incident." Several of the players on Jones's team bind Radio (Cuba Gooding Jr.) with tape and lock him in an equipment shed. When the Jones character, played by Ed Harris, discovers the cruel prank, he is moved to take the helpless young man under his wing, thus setting the story in motion. The scene never happened in real life. But students at the school (though not the football players) did occasionally torment Radio in his early years. A group of charming youngsters once yanked down Radio's pants and scalded his buttocks with paint thinner.

Later in the film, some players pull another nasty practical joke on Radio. They persuade him to wander into the girl's locker room, to everyone's horror—especially his own. That never happened either, though some kids once coaxed Radio into pulling a false fire alarm. Radio spent a brief but traumatic day in jail for that. In the movie, Radio also goes to jail—for leaving Christmas presents on his neighbors' doorsteps. (A cop who has "only been in town a week" refuses to believe that Radio hasn't stolen the stuff.)

One recurring cliché of Hollywood screenwriting is "motivation." All fictional characters, like all people, have motivations for their actions. But in run-of-the-mill screenplays, motivation is mechanistic. This story really begs the question of motivation, though. What everyone—in the film, in the audience, and in real life—wants to know is why Harold Jones cared for Radio the way he did.

Maybe it's a sad comment that we're baffled by the sight of a man committing an act of extraordinary kindness. No one's exactly sure why Jones did what he did, not even Jones himself. Smith's article points out that, from an early age, Jones had sympathy for people weaker than himself. But the roots of great compassion are as mysterious as the roots of great cruelty. Like Radio with his genetic condition, some people are just born that way.

That non-explanation isn't good enough for Tollin. He creates a made-up story about Coach Jones, on a paper route as a twelve-year-old, coming across a handicapped boy caged in a basement. The young Jones does nothing about it, and is haunted for the rest of his life by his own inaction. When Radio appears, it's a chance for redemption.

Only in the world of Hollywood storytelling is life that tidy and human nature so easy to understand.

Sources and Further Reading

Merron, Jeff. "How Real is the Reel Radio?" ESPN.com, November 5, 2003. http://espn.go.com/page2/s/merron/031105.html.
Smith, Gary. "Someone to Lean On." *Sports Illustrated*, December 16, 1996.

Blue Crush (2002)

Directed by John Stockwell
Written by Lizzy Weiss and John Stockwell
Starring Kate Bosworth, Michelle Rodriguez, and Sanoe Lake

Vaguely inspired by Susan Orlean's 1998 *Outside* magazine article, "Surf Girls of Maui," *Blue Crush* transplants the titular surf girls to the island of Oahu, where they are put through the paces of a *Rocky*-esque redempto-pic. Despite the resulting film's devotion to sports-movie conventions (complete with an earnest *win-one-for-the-Gipper, but-in-the-water-instead-of-on-the-gridiron* speech), director John Stockwell and writer Lizzy Weiss manage to infuse *Blue Crush* with an authentic sense of island surf culture.

Orlean spent little more than a week with her surf girls—just long enough to obsess over the girls' "awesome hair," record their gnarly slang, and, of course, inject a dozen first-person pronouns into the piece (*"I" gracefully pondered this; "I" mused eloquently about that*). As airlift journalism, Orlean's quickie article has a dilettantish feel; it barely skims the surface of a fascinating sports subculture.

Stockwell, on the other hand, is himself a surfer. He knows what it's like to crave the waves. He's ventured into the surf further than ankle deep, and it shows. Better than any surf movie before it, *Blue Crush* conveys the adrenaline-charged head rush of the sport. Stockwell dropped his camera operators into the drink; like type-A frogmen, they follow the stunt doubles (with star Kate Bosworth's face digitally superimposed) through the waves and into the collapsing pipelines. Thankfully, the entire film was shot on location, in the roiling surf, rather than in a tank on a Hollywood soundstage.

Stockwell also clearly knows a thing or two about the local surfing scene—from its universal macho posing to its various subsets of surfer cultures, from punk skateboarders to mellow hippies. In an effort to ensure verisimilitude, Stockwell hired locals as secondary actors, extras, and crew members, a move that enhances the film's feeling of authenticity. The movie relies so little on Orlean's reporting and is so superior to the article in all of its relevant details, one wonders why the filmmakers felt the need to buy the rights to the piece in the first place.

The answer to that question probably has a lot to do with name recognition, and with Hollywood's never-ending quest for literary approbation.

Orlean's bestselling book, *The Orchid Thief*, had previously been sold as the basis for the big-budget Hollywood movie *Adaptation* (see page 183); what's more, as a staff writer for *The New Yorker*, Orlean brings to any film venture the kind of literary cred that can get a project the green light. For whatever reason, Ron Howard and Brian Grazer, the guys behind Imagine Entertainment, read the *Outside* article and saw a movie in it.

Orlean's piece focused on Theresa McGregor and several other teenage surfer girls as they competed in a low-key amateur contest on Maui. "Teenage surfer girls" is the only element of the piece that carried over into the film. Realizing that Maui's gentle waves, laid-back surf community, and amateur competitors lacked the dynamism required in a wide-screen feature film, Stockwell wisely relocated his story to Oahu's Pipeline, the geographical locus of the pro surfing world. As Michelle Rodriguez's surfer girl character, Eden, warns early in the film, the walls of water at Pipeline routinely break boards and surfers alike. "Out here," she says, "you don't just get crushed; you die."

Kate Bosworth stars as Anne Marie, a teenage surfer grrl determined to compete in a male-dominated, professional surfing competition at Pipeline, but is traumatized by her near-drowning there several years earlier. As it succumbs to sports-movie conventions (*Will she or won't she find the courage to ride the Pipeline?* Duh. *Will she be true to her ideals and also find true love without compromise?* Totally. *Will the soundtrack bounce with hip-hopped remixes?* Um, *yeah*.) the film ultimately peters out, like a promising swell that never breaks. But the joy—and the crush—is up there on the screen, in the surf, and often underneath it.

Sources and Further Reading

Orlean, Susan. "Surf Girls of Maui." *Outside*, Fall 1998.
Sweedler, Dave. "Theresa McGregor: Her Life Story Portrayed on the Big Screen." *Maui Time*, September 14, 2001.

Remember the Titans (2000)

Directed by Boaz Yakin
Written by Gregory Allen Howard
Starring Denzel Washington and Will Patton

Does the auteur theory apply to anyone anymore? Back in the day, when young French geeks were getting all excited about American movies, they came up with the idea that the director is the "author" of the film. The Hollywood films that lit their fanboy fire were not unique works of art created by lone visionaries, but products, manufactured by large factories called "studios," which operated on a modified assembly-line model. For the sharp and eager scribes of *Cahiers du Cinema*, some of whom later became influential filmmakers themselves, this simply would not do.

American film just had to meet a higher aesthetic standard than hamburgers or Chevrolet station wagons. If they could prove that Hollywood films bore the personal signature of a single artist—despite the studio system—the French critics could justify their ardor. The auteur did not even have to be the director. It usually was, though the theory did not rule out the possibility that someone else may be the film's "author." Could be a star actor, could be a producer.

The auteur theory is a lot harder to apply in today's Hollywood. At least, in the era of "the system," each studio had its own distinct identity. Universal had horror; Warner Brothers was known for gritty urban dramas (because you can do "grit" on a budget); you could count on MGM for star-studded spectaculars; and RKO turned out B movies and oddball films like *King Kong* and *Citizen Kane*. The personality of each studio reflected the quirks and preferences of its autocratic boss, who kept all of his stars, directors, writers, and producers under contract.

The days of the autocratic boss are long gone, as are the days of the "contract player." Studios are now no more than subsidiaries of diversified global corporations (cash cow subsidiaries, but subsidiaries nonetheless) who compete with each other for the same pool of high-priced freelance talent. And they're all pursuing the same goal: the Big Opening Weekend. Hollywood product has grown homogeneous, leaving even less room for authorial self-expression than in the days when a handful of cigar-chomping tough-guy moguls ruled with their iron wallets.

Today's Hollywood auteurs must have the financial clout and record of box-office gross numbers to justify imposing a personal style on every flick they turn out. Steven Spielberg qualifies. But the man with the real claim to the title is Jerry Bruckheimer.

With his since-deceased (and much more flamboyant) partner Don Simpson, Bruckheimer, in the 1980s, pioneered a style of cinematic storytelling that didn't emphasize story, instead focusing on "movie moments" and, most famously, the "high concept." The Simpson-Bruckheimer style wasn't so much a storytelling formula as it was a marketing strategy. It didn't matter who the director was or who the writers were (Simpson and Bruckheimer were famous for going through writers like tissue paper, employing a dozen or so on each project, a practice Bruckheimer continues in his solo career). Simpson and Bruckheimer's movies were always recognizable for the Don and Jerry style. They bore the mark of auteurism.

The hero always wins in the end, in the World According to Don and Jerry. However, the final resolution isn't necessarily a victory of good over evil, and if it is, it's only incidental. In the Simpson-Bruckheimer universe, every victory was one of self-actualization. Our hero, never lacking for confidence in the first place, finally surmounts all obstacles and takes his rightful place among the pantheon of Übermenschen. The perfect message for the Masters of the Universe Generation.

Since his split with Simpson (and Simpson's subsequent death in 1996) Bruckheimer has branched out in his subject matter, if only slightly—but he has never abandoned the precepts that made his movies box-office smashes in the first place. He has, however, shown a new propensity for fact-based material. He produced the historical war melodramas *Pearl Harbor* (see page 273) and *Black Hawk Down* (see page 282), as well as the journalism thriller *Veronica Guerin* (see page 169). But Bruckheimer's first foray into True Storyland was the race-relations/football flick *Remember the Titans*.

But how to impose the doctrine of Bruckheimerism on a series of actual events that may or may not fit the prescription?

Bruckheimer made *Remember the Titans* from a script by Gregory Allen Howard, an L.A. escapee who'd relocated to Alexandria, Virginia. Scraping for screenplay ideas, Howard heard the story of how, in 1971, the city overcame racial strife by rallying around a high school football team, the Titans of T. C. Williams High School. The school opened in 1965 as the first fully integrated high school in Alexandria, at a time when the federal government was mandating desegregation. In 1971 the government ordered further steps to bring Alexandria's races together. Two other high schools—one mostly white, the other largely black—were folded into T. C. Williams, creating a mammoth high school and a potential racial time bomb.

The merger also created a massive, and massively powerful, high school football team—in a state (among many similarly minded Southern states) where high school football was, like the Beatles, more popular than Jesus. The Titans were an all-star team, comprised of three rosters rolled into one with the best players winning starting roles. They cruised to an undefeated season, winning all ten regular season games and three playoff games that culminated in a state championship. They not only won; they crushed everyone in their path. They outscored their opponents by a season total of 357–45. Only twice did they allow any other team to score more than ten points, and in nine games they surrendered no points at all.

Bruckheimer's erstwhile partner once stated, "Jerry and I side with the winners. We aren't interested in losers. They're boring to us."

But it's one thing to be a "a winner." It's another to be an unstoppable juggernaut. Total domination doesn't make for very interesting drama. The most glaring "Hollywood-ization" (as one former Titans player put it) of the story is found in the movie's depiction of the games themselves.

The Hollywood-ized Titans seem to be forever playing catch-up football, coming from behind to pull out thrilling last-minute victories. In the movie, the state championship is a nail-biting, low-scoring battle won, by a score of 10–7, on a last-minute fumble recovery by the Titans. Let the record show that the Titans really won that game by a score of 27–0. The opposing high school, Andrew Lewis, gained a total of *negative five* yards for the game. (The opposing team wasn't Marshall, as depicted in the movie, although the Titans actually did play and beat that team—by a score of 21 to 6, in the Titans' closest game that season—eight weeks before the championship game.)

The Titans accomplished their impressive record while coping with the integration of their own team, as well as of the school they attended. They were led by Herman Boone, a black coach who got the job over Bill Yoast, a white guy. Bruckheimer's movie correctly portrays Boone taking steps to force the racially divided team to unite by making the offensive players sit with each other on one bus while the defense took a second bus, rather than letting the kids group themselves by skin color.

Remember the Titans also posits a "movie moment" turning point, when Boone (played by Denzel Washington), whose team is practicing at Gettysburg college, wakes the players up at 3:00 A.M. and commands them to run miles through the woods until they reach the Gettysburg battlefield. There, Boone delivers a stern soliloquy on the futility of racial hatred.

That scene was a Bruckheimerism of the highest order. It's lump-in-the-throat cinema, but it never happened. The team did tour Gettysburg, but not at daybreak after a 3:00 A.M. run. Coach Boone, like his players, spent the daytime tour listening to a lecture by an octogenarian tour guide.

But the scene was in keeping with the rest of the film, which, according to former players, coaches, and T. C. Williams teachers, wildly exaggerates the racial strife that existed in Alexandria at the time. There were no picket-sign-brandishing protesters outside T. C. Williams. According to the movie, the school did not exist before 1971, which effectively wiped out a half-decade of successful, relatively smooth racial coexistence. As in the movie, the appointment of Boone over Yoast (Will Patton) caused a certain amount of resentment, though Yoast, to his credit, rose above it. There was, however, no organized conspiracy to undermine Boone (or if there was, it was unsuccessful to the point of invisibility), nor was there one to punish Yoast for supporting his new boss. The film suggests the rather absurd notion that Boone was to be fired if he lost so much as one game, because anything short of perfection would prove that blacks can't cut it.

An invented subplot involves Yoast's prospective induction into the Virginia High School Hall of Fame. His quest for this honor is thwarted when he refuses to take part in a plot to throw a game and thus get Boone fired. In reality, there was no such Hall of Fame, and while the Titans were victims of some unfair officiating, they beat everyone they played so badly that it hardly mattered if they weren't getting the calls.

One of the players is given a fictional racist girlfriend who, by the end of the movie, has learned that black people maybe aren't so bad after all. Her revelation is never explained (maybe it's because she realizes that blacks are good at football). It just stands as another eye-misting movie moment. There's also a fictional bigoted assistant coach thrown into the mix, just to drive the point home that some people just don't cotton to black folk.

There are other, more minor alterations of reality. Real-life Yoast's four daughters are condensed into one. A real-life star player who was paralyzed in an auto accident after the season here suffers that fate days before the championship game. In the film, another player is ignominiously benched midgame, though it really happened in between games. What makes all of these changes uniquely Bruckheimerian is that none are made for the purposes of convenient storytelling, the most common rationale for changing the facts—or for legal reasons, a close second. Every one of those changes is made to artificially ratchet up the "triumph of the underdog" quotient or to create more "moments." In other words, they are all made in the interest of making *Remember the Titans* not merely a conventional Hollywood movie, but a film that could have been made by only one "author"—Jerry Bruckheimer.

Sources and Further Reading

Geschwind, Melissa. "Recalling the Real Titans." *USA Today*, October 2, 2000.

Howard, Gregory Allen. "First Person: Remembering the History of *Titans*." *Los Angeles Times*, September 30, 2000.

Layden, Tim. "Does Anyone Remember the Real Titans?" *Sports Illustrated*, October 15, 2001.

Merron, Jeff. "Reel Life: *Remember the Titans*." ESPN.com. http://espn.go.com/page2/s/closer/020808.html.

The Rookie (2002)

Directed by John Lee Hancock
Written by Mike Rich
Starring Dennis Quaid and Rachel Griffiths

The real Jim Morris (left) with Dennis Quaid, who portrays
Morris in *The Rookie*.
Photo by Deana Newcomb, © Disney Enterprises, Inc. All Rights Reserved.

Maybe it says something about the times, or maybe we're just forgetting something, but, before *The Rookie* came out in 2002, had there been a great "feel good" movie since *Hoosiers*? The genre is dying out. We'll leave it to others to decide if we feel good about not feeling good. All we know is that the genre, a remnant of the "Morning in America" era, seemed somehow inappropriate in the "Monica in America" era.

A few years removed from the Starr Report, however, it was time for the "feel good" genre to rebound. *Hoosiers* found a worthy successor in *The Rookie*, another against-the-odds, "based on a true story" tale of uplift and inspiration in the sports world.

Hoosiers reformatted almost everything in its "true" story to fit your screen. The makers of *The Rookie* placed far more faith in their source material, perhaps because the events were only three years in the past, rather than three decades. The story is highly improbable, but so was the professional baseball career of Jim Morris, who, in 1999, pitched for the Tampa Bay Devil Rays—a thirty-five-year-old major league rookie, the second oldest ever. Only the great Satchel Paige, who was at least forty-one and was possibly as old as forty-eight when he first threw in the majors after a long Negro League career, was further on in years. Unless you count Dennis Quaid, who was forty-five when he played rookie Jim Morris.

What made Morris's story more unlikely—too good to be true, except it was—was the fact that he had not played baseball for a decade when he was signed to a minor league contract by Tampa Bay, and he threw the ball faster at age thirty-five than he had at age twenty-five, when he had to quit baseball after a series of surgeries to repair his aching pitching arm. Morris had played minor league ball in the Milwaukee Brewers system, but he'd never risen above the lowly Single-A level.

Like Bernard Malamud's Roy Hobbs, when Morris reappeared, his ability seemed almost supernatural. His ninety-eight-mile-per-hour fastball may not have defied the laws of physics (the subject that Morris taught at Reagan County High School in the tiny West Texas town of Big Lake when he wasn't coaching the baseball team), but it did defy the laws of physiology. Even Morris didn't believe he was throwing the ball in the high nineties. His top speed as a youngster was in the mid-eighties.

The movie gets that detail right, though it adds a fanciful scene in which Morris (who, like Dennis Quaid, is left-handed, but otherwise bears no resemblance to the actor) stops at a roadside speed detector and flings a ball past it, attempting to clock his own pitch. (Those roadside radar contraptions are set up to detect cars, which are slightly larger than baseballs.)

Beyond that scene, the movie is surprisingly understated and accurate. Jason Stark, a sportswriter who was among the first to write the Morris story in the summer of 1999, wrote after seeing the film, "It was a tale so beautiful and so perfect that only a handful of scenes in the film had to be fictionalized or even changed. Quaid, in fact, utters lines I remember Morris himself saying three years ago in Durham. And a Devil Rays scout in the movie tells Morris exactly what real-life scout Doug Gassaway told him in 1999: if he called his bosses about a thirty-five-year-old pitcher, he'd get laughed at—but if he didn't tell them about a pitcher who threw ninety-eight miles per hour, he'd get fired."

The movie wasn't without a few overextensions of the truth. A "where are they now" epigraph says that Morris pitched "two seasons" in the big leagues. He pitched *parts* of two seasons, that much is true. His entire big-league career, however, consisted of twenty-one games, with only fifteen innings pitched between September 1999 and May 2000.

A few more inventions come at the film's conclusion. The parts about Morris getting called up to the major leagues on September 19, 1999, appearing in his first game the same day, and striking out the first batter he faced—those events are all true. But this is a Disney film, after all. (It's been suggested that the film's biggest stretch is that a movie about pro baseball players qualified for a G-rating.) The mere fact that Morris got into a big-league game, finally living the boyhood dream he'd abandoned long ago, wasn't sufficiently tear-jerking. In the scene, writer Mike Rich and Director John Lee Hancock pile on heartstring-tugging moment after moment.

Morris's wife (Rachel Griffiths) and kids rush out to the bullpen before the game to tell him how much they love him and whatnot. (In reality, Morris looked into the stands for his family but couldn't find them in the crowd of forty thousand.) After the game, his whole high school team and, it seems, half the population of Big Lake shows up at the ballpark to celebrate with him. (The team was really back home in Big Lake, almost four hundred miles from the Ballpark at Arlington, watching on TV.) Then, in the mistiest-eyed moment of all, Morris hands the game ball to his father. (Sorry, Pops. "I still have the ball," the real Morris says.)

Another "moment" gets thrown in when Morris arrives at the ballpark for his first day in the big leagues. Arriving early, he wanders around the clubhouse in awe, gazing at empty jerseys bearing the names of baseball superstars such as Jose Canseco, Fred McGriff, and Wade Boggs. Actually, Morris showed up at the team hotel, where he was greeted warmly by those same superstars. The ballplayers, like everyone else, were smitten with the Morris story. Morris had already received more publicity in the minors that summer than most major league players. After he fanned that one batter, he received approximately 250 phone calls. It was Hollywood on the line.

Sources and Further Reading

Morris, Jim and Joel Engel. *The Oldest Rookie: Big League Dreams from a Small-Town Guy.* Boston: Little Brown & Co., 2001.

Merron, Jeff. "*The Rookie* in Reel Life." ESPN.com. http://espn.go.com/page2/s/closer/020410.html.

Stark, Jason. "Morris' Story Made for the Big Screen." ESPN.com, http://espn.go.com/mlb/columns/stark_jayson/1359566.html.

Raging Bull (1980)

Directed by Martin Scorsese

Written by Paul Schrader and Mardik Martin

Starring Robert De Niro, Joe Pesci, and Cathy Moriarty

Robert De Niro as Jake La Motta.
© United Artists Corporation

Jake La Motta gets prominent credit as the "consultant" to Martin Scorsese's 1980 boxing classic *Raging Bull*. He trained Robert De Niro to box. La Motta, the middleweight world champ from 1949 to 1951 and one of the top fighters of his era, sparred with De Niro for a year. "In the first six months we boxed a thousand rounds, a half hour straight every day," La Motta has said.

One assumes that La Motta limited his input to making a fighter out of the actor De Niro, whose performance as La Motta is generally considered one of the most powerful acting jobs ever put on film. (De Niro won an Oscar, though the film itself, despite its eventual status as one of the greatest ever made—it's number twenty-four on the American Film Institute Top 100 list—lost to *Ordinary People*.) If La Motta consulted on the substance of his portrayal, he's either the most honest and self-aware man ever to have a film made of his life, or the dumbest.

De Niro plays La Motta as a violent, boorish, and sexually insecure animal with no concern for anyone's feelings but his own. It's a character so repugnant and dislikeable that you don't even want to watch. Like so many movies from that era, this is one that today's Hollywood would never make. There's nothing sympathetic or redeeming about De Niro's La Motta. He punches his wife, beats up his brother, throws a fight, and is generally disagreeable and verbally abusive to anyone he comes across. He's not a "lovable rogue" or "the guy you love to hate." He's just a miserable shit.

Could La Motta have been that bad? Even the man himself was shocked by what he saw onscreen. "I was upset," he said shortly after the film came out. "Then I realized it was true. That's the way it was. I was a no-good bastard. I realize it now. It's not the way I am now, but the way I was then."

La Motta at one point said that he was "worse" than he was shown in the movie. His ex-wife Vicki, the central female character in the movie, agrees. But La Motta said he never hit any of his wives "Because if I hit 'em, they won't wake up." His brother Joey, a fighter himself before he became LaMotta's manager (Joe Pesci, in the film; the "Joey" character was a composite of the real Joey and a close friend of La Motta's) noted that La Motta never spit on the floor, as De Niro has him doing.

"Sometimes ya gotta elaborate, but the picture they portrayed is pretty accurate," La Motta said on the occasion of *Raging Bull*'s twentieth anniversary. "I would say it's about 90 percent truth."

As we can see by most of the other films mentioned in this book, "90 percent truth" is a lot more truth than you'll find in most movies "based on a true story." The film was praised for its ultrarealistic, and ultraviolent, boxing scenes when it first came out. Unlike the boxing matches portrayed in *The Hurricane*, Scorsese's reenactments of La Motta's bouts were very faithful to the actual fights. The only major liberties he took were in his version of La Motta's long-awaited title shot, which gives La Motta more credit than he deserves.

After eight years of pro boxing, mostly as a leading contender, La Motta got his first chance at the middleweight belt On June 17, 1949, against Marcel Cerdan, "the Casablanca Clouter." Unfortunately for Cerdan, he tore a muscle in the first round and ended up boxing La Motta one-armed for nine more rounds before losing on a referee's stoppage. Even more unfortunately for Cerdan, he died in a plane crash before his scheduled rematch with La Motta. He probably would have won the title back. La Motta wasn't as good as Cerdan. Instead, it took La Motta another two years and three title defenses to lose his championship.

When he did, he lost it to his greatest rival, Sugar Ray Robinson, who many boxing experts name as, "pound for pound," the greatest fighter of all time. La Motta and Robinson fought six, count 'em six, bouts against each other, once fighting twice in three weeks. (The fight game was a lot different back then. Fighters actually fought for a living.)

LaMotta took tremendous pride in handing Robinson the first loss of his career after forty straight victories. That came in their second match. La Motta landed a punch that sent Robinson sprawling through the ropes. But in the sixth fight, the title match, Robinson (who won five of the fights) outlasted La Motta and pummeled the tired champ in the thirteenth round. La Motta, letting pride get the better of him, held on to the ropes and let Robinson pulverize him rather than drop to the canvas.

Scorsese re-creates all of those details meticulously. He throws in one bit of dramatic flair, however. After the referee, at last, stops Robinson's pounding and ends the fight, La Motta, his face looking like bad hamburger, staggers over to Robinson's corner and grumbles, "I never went down, Ray. You never got me down."

This mucho macho moment has become part of boxing lore, but La Motta says it never happened.

"I never said it," La Motta recalled. "That is probably what I would have said if I did say something, but I never did. I don't even remember if I was talking at that time. I had too much respect for Ray."

We might as well believe La Motta. He certainly isn't shy about hiding anything else about the dark days of his fight fame. The absurdly obvious way he tanks a fight in Madison Square Garden against Billy Fox, an opponent who shouldn't even have been in the same ring as La Motta, looks like a comedy bit in Scorsese's film. But it's no joke.

"I was supposed to be throwing a fight to this guy, and it looked like I was going to end up holding him on his feet," La Motta recalled. "If there was anybody in the Garden who didn't know what was happening, he must have been dead drunk."

The movie ends with a chubbied-up La Motta fading into oblivion as a bad nightclub comic. (De Niro packed on fifty-five pounds for this part of the picture, becoming one of the first Hollywood actors to deliberately gain weight for a role, a now frequent practice.) La Motta had rescinded into obscurity by 1980, but the movie changed all that. He developed a somewhat successful career doing personal appearances as a comic and raconteur. He also marketed his own line of spaghetti sauce. At this writing, he's still alive at eighty-two, and his life may be more relaxed than in his younger years, but it's no less tragic. In 1998 he lost both of his sons in one year: one to cancer, at age fifty, one in a plane crash, at age forty-nine.

Sources and Further Reading

Dominguez, Robert. "Raging Bull No Longer." *New York Daily News*, August 4, 2000.

LaMotta, Jake. *Raging Bull: My Story*. With Joseph Carter and Peter Savage. New York, Da Capo Press, 1997.

Merron, Jeff. "Reel Life: *Raging Bull*." ESPN.com, http://espn.go.com/page2/s/closer/020703.html.

Eight Men Out (1988)

Directed and written by John Sayles
Starring John Cusack, D. B. Sweeney, and David Strathairn

John Cusack as George "Buck" Weaver. © Orion Pictures Corporation

The real George "Buck" Weaver.

Thanks to the 1989 eye-moistening Kevin Costner fantasy *Field of Dreams*, Rag-time Era baseball great "Shoeless" Joe Jackson enjoyed a brief moment as a mythic icon, American-style, albeit four decades posthumously. Shoeless Joe was sort of the original "Natural." An illiterate country bumpkin from South Carolina (hence the appellation "Shoeless"), the boy could hit a baseball. Catch and throw one darn well, too. Jackson ended his career with the second-highest batting average of all time (still is). He was possibly the best all-around player of his time, with the exception of Ty Cobb. But unlike Cobb, Jackson loved the game for the sake of the game, not as an outlet for inner demons and sociopathic aggression. By all accounts, Shoeless Joe Jackson had a sweet, simple personality.

The legend of Shoeless Joe took its first turn, a sad turn, into mythos when he was banned from professional baseball for life as a result of taking part in the "Black Sox" scandal of 1919, when several Chicago White Sox players conspired with gamblers to throw the World Series.

According to an account in the *New York Times*, Jackson left the courtroom after confessing his role in the fix to a grand jury to find a bunch of little kids waiting for him outside. One boy tugged at his sleeve and pleaded, "It isn't true, is it, Joe?" To which Jackson is reported to have replied, "Yes, boys, I'm afraid it is." As the anecdote spread through newspapers across the country, the youngster's question became the more mellifluous, "Say it ain't so, Joe!"

The mythical version of that incident appears in John Sayles's otherwise demythologized film about the White Sox scandal, *Eight Men Out*. Sayles employs some storytelling techniques to make the complex saga of the scandal that nearly destroyed baseball easier to follow, but for the most part, all historical dramas should be this faithful to the facts—without skimping on the dramatics.

Sayles uses several composite characters. The sportswriter Hugh Fullerton, who first exposed the fix and was vilified for it even when the players' confessions vindicated his reporting, is assembled from several different reporters, including the real Fullerton, who broke different aspects of the story (he's played in the movie by quintessential Chicagoan Studs Terkel). The little boy who delivers the scandal's most famous line can't even be called a composite. He's more like an archetype. Sayles gets the major players in the story mostly right, however, re-creating their machinations based on information found in Eliot Asinof's definitive 1963 book on the "Black Sox." There's the eight players who took part in (or at least had first-hand knowledge of) the plot; the underworld characters, lowlifes, and big shots who organized and bankrolled the fix; and Charles Comiskey, the penurious owner of the White Sox, who kept his players the lowest-paid in the game, even in an era when ballplayers didn't make all that much. The scene in which Comiskey pays his players their promised "bonuses" for winning the pennant in cheap champagne rather than cash is absolutely true, except that it happened when the White Sox won the pennant in 1917, not 1919. (In 1917 the Sox won the World Series, fair and square.)

As in most of his films, Sayles has a social concern to convey. To him, the ballplayers were as much vics as perps, driven to carry out their on-field fraud by the cruel greed of management. They were laborers fighting for a piece of what was rightfully theirs. It is an odd choice on Sayles's part, then, to omit what is generally believed about Comiskey—namely, that the owner himself knew about the fix and may even have profited from it. Sayles chooses instead to present Comiskey as a buffoon who, despite his Scrooge-like treatment of his players, ends up a hapless, whining victim.

Sayles finds a more genuinely sympathetic character in third baseman George "Buck" Weaver, played with appropriate earnestness by John Cusack. Weaver's story is more tragic, or perhaps pathetic, than Jackson's. At least Shoeless Joe actually took money. Weaver's only crime was sitting in on some of the secret meetings in which the conspiracy was hatched. He never took a dime and, like Jackson, played outstanding ball in the 1919 World Series. The "Eight Men Out" were tried as a group; although Weaver demanded a separate trial, he was denied. He then demanded to take the witness stand in his own defense, but he was denied that opportunity as well. He protested his innocence throughout the proceedings but was banished from baseball for life along with the others anyway.

With his nearly stenographic dedication to Asinof's book, it is curious that Sayles couldn't resist falling for the myth of Shoeless Joe—though his film came out a year before *Field of Dreams*. Sayles's version of Jackson is a childlike innocent who goes along with the fix without enthusiasm. He does it only because everyone else is doing it. He allows one teammate to place an envelope containing five thousand dollars on his dresser. What he does with the money, if anything, is unclear.

While there are some indications (which aren't mentioned in Sayles's movie) that Jackson may have intended to take the money to Comiskey in order to blow the whistle on the fix, when Jackson talked to the grand jury he admitted that he'd been promised twenty thousand dollars and complained loudly to his teammates when he didn't get the balance of his payment after the series.

Sayles also has the gamblers instigating the conspiracy, when it was probably the idea of one of the ballplayers, first baseman Chick Gandil. Gandil approached the Boston mobster Sports Sullivan, who in turn went for financing to the country's crime kingpin, Arnold Rothstein. None of the gamblers who fixed the series were ever brought to trial. Only the players suffered that fate. Their true crime, of course, was robbing little boys like the one in the courthouse of their wide-eyed innocence.

The movie ends with another nod to myth. Weaver watches from the stands at a semi–pro ball game in New Jersey. There's a familiar-looking player on the team. It is Joe Jackson. A fan thinks he has recognized Jackson, but when he asks Weaver, who goes unrecognized, the dispirited ex-ballplayer shakes his head. "It's not him," he says.

It *was* Jackson, though, and, in actual fact, he was recognized when he appeared on the New York semi-pro circuit. A local promoter built a barnstorming team around Jackson, who made some money off the deal. Jackson later played on a Louisiana team with his "Black Sox" teammates Eddie Cicotte and Charles "Swede" Risberg, who, according to Jackson, had threatened to kill him if he talked to the grand jury. Finally, in 1924, Jackson got a lawyer and sued Comiskey for eighteen thousand dollars in unpaid wages. A jury awarded him almost the full amount, but a judge inexplicably tossed out the jury's verdict, claiming that Jackson had committed perjury by denying involvement in the fix to which he'd admitted in his grand jury testimony.

Buck Weaver also sued and settled out of court. As the movie states, he spent the rest of his life trying to clear his name. He applied for reinstatement into baseball every year, but was always denied. Joe Jackson died in 1951 at age sixty-two. Buck Weaver died five years later. He was sixty-six.

Sources and Further Reading

Asinof, Eliot. *Eight Men Out: The Black Sox and the 1919 World Series.* New York: Holt, Rinehart and Winston, 1963.

Frommer, Harvey. *Shoeless Joe and Ragtime Baseball.* Dallas, TX: Taylor Publishing Company, 1992.

The First Casualty

Patton (1970)

Directed by Franklin J. Schaffner
Written by Francis Ford Coppola and Edmund H. North
Starring George C. Scott and Karl Malden

What would happen today, now, in the twenty-first century, if a United States Army general visited a hospital near the front lines and started slapping soldiers? Would the public rise up in righteous indignation, or would anyone even give a crap?

General George S. Patton did it during the invasion of Sicily in 1943—twice (in reality; the film condenses both incidents into one). Home-front reaction was not terribly favorable. In fact, so not-psyched was the American public that those little slaps may have altered the course of World War II—for the worse.

General Dwight D. Eisenhower never felt he could really trust Patton after those, and a few other, bad PR incidents. Eisenhower's wariness was one of the factors in his decision to put the brakes on Patton as he stormed across Europe toward Berlin, where Patton's Third Army could have ended the war in the autumn of 1944 rather than in May of 1945, several months and thousands, maybe millions of lives later.

The Oscar-winning film version of Patton's WWII career is arguably the best war flick ever produced by Hollywood, yet Eisenhower is not a character in the film. The Supreme Commander of Allied Forces in Europe, and Patton's friend of thirty years, appears only as an offscreen presence, a name spoken in dialogue by other characters. As a result, a rather large element of Patton's character is excised from what is, after all, more a "character study" than a "war movie."

The two men were friends for thirty years and the rapid deterioration of their relationship was a key to understanding not only Patton himself, but also the progress (or lack thereof) of the Allied campaign in Europe. Patton eventually became so disillusioned with what he saw as Eisenhower's favoritism toward the British, and toward Field Marshal Bernard Montgomery in particular, that he took to railing against Eisenhower in private, deriding him as "the best general the British have got." In Patton's eyes, that was but a step short of "the best general the Communists have got." According to one of Patton's top commanding generals, Patton's "real feelings about Eisenhower, as often expressed to me, couldn't be printed."

Patton felt somewhat more warm toward his subordinate-turned-superior General Omar Bradley, but even Bradley did not have Patton's full respect as a soldier. In his posthumously published diary, Patton rather ungenerously deemed his "loyal friend" to be "a man of great mediocrity," going on to damn Bradley with faint praise. "Bradley has many of the attributes which are considered desirable in a general. He wears glasses, has a strong jaw and says little."

None of Patton's condescension toward Bradley is elucidated in the movie, and that is likely no coincidence. The screenplay is based in part on Bradley's own book, *A Soldier's Story*, and Bradley himself served as a paid advisor to the production.

Eisenhower's own son, John, was mystified by the omission of his father from the movie. The surviving members of Patton's family, on the other hand, were perfectly happy to be left out of Francis Ford Coppola's Academy Award–winning script. Had it been up to them, there would have been no *Patton* movie. They first heard of the idea in 1954, when Warner Brothers was planning a Patton biopic. The immediate reaction of Patton's daughter, Ruth, was anger. "The movies cheapen everything they touch," she said. Apart from opposing the project on general principle, which she and the rest of Patton's family always did, Ruth was worried that any potential movie would focus on the popular image of Patton as being crude, profane, and boorish. While they understood that their patriarch presented that public image of himself deliberately, the real George S. Patton was, Ruth said, "a well-bred and considerable gentleman . . . who was adored by small children, dogs and old ladies."

The success of George C. Scott's deservedly feted performance was that he captured both sides of Patton, despite being a rather incorrect physical type for the part. Scott's gravel-voiced, barrel-chested Patton remains imbedded on the popular psyche not only because many more people have seen the Hollywood Patton than have ever glimpsed the real one, but because Scott's portrait seems to fit the preconceived notions of "Old Blood 'n' Guts" (Patton's popular nickname, of which he was less than fond).

Two decades after Scott's memorable portrayal, a real-life version of the Patton stereotype appeared in the form of Gulf War commander "Stormin'" Norman Schwarzkopf. The historical Patton, however, was no Schwarzkopf—or George C. Scott. He was a tall, slender man with a high-pitched voice not infrequently described as "squeaky." While Scott accurately portrayed Patton's gentility, his enjoyment of flattery, and his Francophilia (Patton was a "gentleman soldier" from a wealthy family), he also captured Patton's crudity and earthiness. If anything, the film bowdlerizes Patton's preferred mode of expression, perhaps to ensure the PG rating that would allow the big-budget war flick to recoup its costs by reaching as wide an audience as possible. (*Patton* cost twelve million dollars, a formidable amount in 1970; two years later, *The Godfather* would cost half as much.)

Patton believed that to inspire his troops, he had to speak their language, and that was a language peppered with words like "cocksucker" and phrases such as "son-of-a-fucking-bitch." Patton had an ideological commitment to profanity.

"When I want my men to remember something important, to really make it stick, I give it to them double-dirty," he said. "You can't run an army without profanity. An army without profanity couldn't fight its way out of a piss-soaked paper bag."

Nowhere was the film's squeamishness about Patton's language more evident than in the iconic pre-credit sequence of the film. Scott, as Patton, steps out onto a large stage in front of the biggest American flag anyone has ever seen and gives his troops a pep talk about how all real Americans love war and "love the sting of battle." The strongest language he uses, however, are the words "bastard" and "sons of bitches." Even Patton's actual (and crowd-pleasing) pronouncement that reporters who cover the war "don't know any more about real fighting than they know about fucking," is tempered down. In the scene, "fucking" is replaced by the schoolmarm-ish "fornicating."

Several other incidents in *Patton* have real-life counterparts, but the film-makers embellished them for dramatic effect.

Near the beginning of the film, Patton complains to a British aerial commander about the lack of air support for his troops. As if to underscore his point, at that very moment, German fighters strafe Patton's headquarters. The feisty general leaps out of his window, directly into the path of the bullets, and fires on the planes with his pistol. A similarly fortuitous coincidence did happen, but the planes strafed a few blocks down the street, and Patton, his "blood 'n' guts" reputation notwithstanding, did not chase after them on foot armed only with a .45.

Patton's forces race Montgomery's to liberate Messina. Of course Patton wins. When Montgomery arrives, Patton is waiting for him, appearing quite smug. Montgomery greets him by saying, "Don't smirk, Patton. I shan't kiss you!" That was a real line, but Monty never said it. Field Marshall Harold Alexander was the British commander who declined to plant one on Patton. But the rivalry between Patton and Montgomery was a central through-line for the film, so Monty got the quip.

In the central, character-defining moment of the film, Patton comes across a battlefield strewn with the corpses of his own soldiers as well as those of Germans. Looking around, he declares, "I love it! God help me, I love it so!" More even than the soldier-slapping scene, that moment makes Patton appear to be some kind of an unhinged psychopath. But not only did the incident never happen, but Patton did not "love" the devastation of war. He chose to be a soldier when he could have chosen any profession, and he undoubtedly loved battle and, more than anything, victory. The sight of dead troops, especially his own, however, never caused Patton any emotions but sorrow and revulsion.

Sources and Further Reading

Farago, Ladislas. *Patton: Ordeal and Triumph*. New York: Astor-Honor, Inc., 1964.

Hirshson, Stanley. *General Patton: A Soldier's Life*. New York: HarperCollins, 2002.

Province, Charles M. *The Unknown Patton*. San Diego, CA: CMP Publications, 2002.

Pearl Harbor (2001)

Directed by Michael Bay
Written by Randall Wallace
Starring Ben Affleck and Josh Hartnett

Computer-generated infamy from Jerry Bruckheimer's
extremely loud *Pearl Harbor*.
© *Touchstone Pictures and Jerry Bruckheimer, Inc. All Rights Reserved.*

Michael Bay had directed nothing but commercials and music videos (which are also commercials) before he made *Bad Boys* for Don Simpson and Jerry Bruckheimer in 1995. Since then, Bay has directed four straight Bruckheimer movies, and nothing else. He made a sequel to *Bad Boys*, a movie about two guys who break all the rules. He made *The Rock*, a movie about two guys who save San Francisco from terrorists. And he made *Armageddon*, a movie about five guys who save the world from an asteroid.

One has to wonder, then, what qualified Bay to make a movie about perhaps the most traumatic event in United States history, 9/11 notwithstanding—the December 7, 1941, attack on Pearl Harbor ("A date which will live in infamy," said President Franklin Roosevelt, in his historic radio address). Bay's only apparent qualification is that the producer of 2001's *Pearl Harbor* was Jerry Bruckheimer. How surprising was it, then, that this epic, released in the year of the Pearl Harbor attack's sixtieth anniversary, turned this monumental American military defeat and human tragedy into a $135-million Hollywood action and romance spectacular?

"There are historians who are going to say we got this wrong, that wrong," said Bay, in an interview with *National Geographic*. "But it's not about that. It's the essence. Did we get the *essence* of what happened? That's what it's all about."

Bay could have been speaking about almost any history-based Hollywood film. It is certainly arguable whether the "essence" of the events of Pearl Harbor amounted to an action movie with a love story thrown in. The film is over-loaded with fictional characters, fictionalized real ones, and heavy-handed melodrama—all fast-cut to the pace of, well, a commercial or a music video. On the other hand, the broad outlines of major events are followed closely enough to at least be considered credible, if not faithful.

On the "give 'em credit" side of the ledger, Bay and writer Randall Wallace—known for the hero-worshipping Mel Gibson vehicles *Braveheart* (see page 307) and *We Were Soldiers* (see page 286)—take pains to show the Japanese rationale for the "sneak attack": the Americans were cutting off Japan's oil supply. What the movie does not explore is Japan's policy of extreme aggression leading up to the U.S. oil embargo.

When the heavily made-up John Voight as FDR refers in his famous speech to "the Empire of Japan," moviegoers have no idea why Japan is, indeed, an "empire." The once-fanatically isolationist nation started colonizing its neighbors at the point of a bayonet in 1894 when it started a war with China over Korea—and won. In 1904 the Japanese started a war with Russia over Manchuria—and won. In 1931 Japan launched an all-out invasion of Manchuria. By the mid-1930s, Japan was a military dictatorship that posed a serious threat to the entire East.

The Japanese rationale all along was economics. Japan was, and is, a small island with few natural resources. When economic depression swept the world in 1929, Japan took a beating. The Japanese believed that to survive, they needed to conquer.

Twenty-first century standards of political correctness mandate that the racism of the past be renounced in any major Hollywood production. In Wallace's *We Were Soldiers*, which he wrote and directed, the Vietnamese were portrayed sympathetically and the racial epithet "gook" was never uttered, even though there probably wasn't a GI in Vietnam who didn't use the word dozens of times a day. It would be the height of PC revisionism if we never heard the

Actual image of the attack on Pearl
Harbor.

word "Jap" in *Pearl Harbor*, and we do hear it, though the occasional references to "those Jap suckers" seem rather limp.

In *Pearl Harbor*, the Japanese are, if not good guys, then at least not bad guys. There are no bad guys in this flick. Everyone's a hero. Even the real-life commander of the Pearl Harbor base, Admiral Husband Kimmel, is drawn as a decisive tough guy doing his best to keep his troops ready for war. You'd never know that in reality he lost his job, having been blamed for ignoring warnings of an impending attack and failing to keep the base on high alert when a Japanese strike appeared imminent.

In terms of military history, the movie focuses on three major episodes, all of which are more or less accurate, at least in the most general details. It's in the particulars that the film makes concessions to mythologizing.

First, we see the "Eagle Squadrons," American pilots who flew for the British Royal Air Force before America's entrance into the war. The squadron, or more precisely, squadrons (Americans flew in three separate RAF units), consisted of

244 American volunteer pilots. Unlike Ben Affleck's character in the movie, they were all civilians. Thousands of Americans tried to sign up, but the British took only a select few. About half of the Americans who flew for Britain died in its skies.

The movie's determination to follow two fictional boyhood buddies, played by Affleck and Josh Hartnett, from fade in to fade out leads to the fictional elements of the plot. Not only were no American military pilots involved in the Eagle Squadrons, but no Eagle Squadron pilots later ended up getting their planes in the air at Pearl Harbor. Several American pilots got off the ground that day; on that point the film is correct. The two most memorable were Kenneth Taylor and George Welsh. Like Affleck and Hartnett's characters, they barreled through enemy bombs and bullets to reach their planes. But they weren't boyhood friends who'd become entangled in a love triangle. The only reason they weren't caught sleeping at the time of the attack is that they'd been up all night playing cards. Between them, they brought down six Japanese planes, and they earned Distinguished Service medals for their heroism.

Other pilots who made it into the air got shot down by "friendly" antiaircraft guns, something that Bay and Wallace elected not to show us.

Finally, the movie follows our two fighter ace heroes into the "Doolittle Raid." Four months after Pearl Harbor, Major James Doolittle led sixteen bombers on a mission to strike the heart of Tokyo. At the time, it was supposed to be impossible to hit the Japanese mainland from the air. There was no way aircraft carriers could get close enough to Japan to launch bombers—and in any case, carrier runways designed for nimble fighter planes were far too short to launch bulky bombers.

The movie does an excellent job of illustrating those problems and how they were overcome. The improbable scene in which Doolittle himself flies the first bomber off the deck of the aircraft carrier *Hornet* seems to have been made for Hollywood—but it really happened. If anything, getting the bombers in the air was even tougher than the film depicts. Because—as is shown in the movie—the *Hornet* is spotted by Japanese patrol boats, the planes had to be launched two hundred miles from the planned takeoff point. Unlike in the movie, they took off into a raging storm, with waves rocking the *Hornet* from side to side to side as the bombers struggled to get airborne. All sixteen B-25s got into the air successfully and hit their targets in Japan. However, there's no report of the bombers taking antiaircraft fire over Japan, as is shown in the movie. The Japanese were caught by surprise.

Because of the early launch, the planes didn't have enough fuel to reach their landing points in Chinese Manchuria. Only one of them landed intact. There were seventy-nine men on the mission. Four died when their planes crash-landed; three were caught and executed by the Japanese. Five others were captured and remained POWs for the duration of the war.

Most criticism of the movie has to be reserved not for its occasional fictionalizing of historical events, but for its sappy plot, almost painfully typical of Hollywood, which requires that every conflict be somehow personalized. In real life the Japanese tried to conquer Asia, but in a Michael Bay movie, love conquers all.

How "Hollywood" is *Pearl Harbor*? After the attack, the Japanese commander of the raid, Admiral Isoruku Yamamoto (played by veteran Japanese American, one-named actor Mako) utters his famous quote, "I fear all we have done is to awaken a sleeping giant." But Yamamoto never actually said that. The source of the line is *Tora Tora Tora*—a Hollywood movie about Pearl Harbor released in 1970.

Historical postscript: Yamamoto was demonstrably downbeat about the war against the States. As befitted his negative attitude, he never got a chance to see his pessimism fulfilled. On April 18, 1943, the Americans caught up to the man who planned Pearl Harbor as he flew into the South Pacific on what was supposed to be a morale-boosting troop inspection. The U.S. gunners shot him out of the sky.

Sources and Further Reading

Beyond the Movie: Pearl Harbor. VHS. Directed by Kevin Bachar. National Geographic Society, 2001.

Toland, John. *Infamy: Pearl Harbor and Its Aftermath*. New York: Doubleday, 1982.

Enemy at the Gates (2001)

Directed by Jean-Jacques Annaud
Written by Jean-Jacques Annaud and Alain Godard
Starring Jude Law and Ed Harris

Jude Law as Vassili Zaitsev.
Photo by Alex Bailey, © Paramount Pictures

The fog of war obscures many things, the truth most famously, and few episodes in the history of modern warfare were foggier than the Battle of Stalingrad.

Enemy at the Gates claims to be "based" on a true story, though in the United Kingdom this claim was changed to the fuzzier "inspired by." The British are splitting hairs, when you consider that there is considerable doubt about whether the story is true at all or is a pure invention. Or something in between. Even if the tale at the center of this European-produced war epic is pure fiction, the moviemakers get at least a partial pass. They're not the ones who fabricated the events in the movie (not all of them, anyway). They may simply be repeating decades-old Soviet propaganda.

Stalingrad makes a somewhat unlikely subject for a Hollywood flick. Even in the post–Cold War world, Communists don't make the most attractive heroes to American moviegoers. In its U.S. release, *Enemy* fell well short of earning back its seventy-million-dollar budget (shared among U.S. and European studios), which was, it appears, no lesson to the makers of *K-19: The Widowmaker* (see page 300), a $100-million "true" thriller set entirely inside a Soviet submarine, released the very next year, which cost its filmmakers even more money. Had the battle not offered the Soviet Red Army as its good guys against the invading Nazis, Stalingrad still would have proven difficult for Hollywood to handle. The six-month conflagration was both the decisive battle of World War II and its most grueling. And gruesome. Before starting the war, Hitler signed a nonaggression pact with the Soviet leader, Stalin. But Hitler's ambitions to conquer all of Europe doomed that deal. He launched the Nazi invasion in June 1941. On August 23, 1942, the Nazis launched a massive air strike in the city of Stalingrad, followed soon after by a ground invasion. Situated on the banks of the powerful Volga River, Stalingrad was the cornerstone of Soviet defenses. By defending the city they defended the river, which prevented the Germans from crossing into the southern oil fields.

To both Hitler and Stalin, the city's strategic value soon fell into second place behind its symbolic importance. Because the city was christened after Stalin himself, the Soviet leader refused to let it fall and, with equal fanaticism, Hitler lusted to conquer the place. The battle dragged into a gory stalemate. German and Soviet soldiers fought hand-to-hand, or with knives and bayonets. Corpses in the street were as common as rats. When it was over, fewer than two thousand civilians remained in the city that had half a million just six months earlier. The Germans lost 400,000 troops, the Soviets 700,000. But the Nazis were cut off and beaten.

Amid the carnage were hundreds of incredible stories. The most famous was the great sniper "duel." Snipers played a major part in the Soviet way of fighting. Vassili Zaitsev was considered the best sniper of them all. He didn't have the highest kill rate, but he had reportedly slain forty Germans in just ten days. The Soviet press discovered him and made the young deer hunter from the Ural Mountains into a national celebrity and a living symbol of Soviet fighting spirit.

Hitler took note of the Zaitsev phenomenon. Kill Zaitsev, he surmised, and he would deal a terrible blow to Soviet morale. He sent his own top sniper, Major König, to Stalingrad with the sole purpose of hunting down Zaitsev and killing him.

The winner of the duel, predictably, was Zaitsev—and the Soviet propaganda machine. The Soviet hero slew König with a single bullet after decoying the German into giving up his position for the briefest moment. That was all it took to get off the fatal shot.

Zaitsev, who was indeed a real person and a successful sniper, was immortalized as an official hero of the Soviet Union. Even before getting to the sniper duel, however, the film fictionalizes his story. He was not herded into battle on a cattle car, an ignorant peasant from the Urals sent to the slaughter. That's the first big scene of the movie, which outdoes the D-Day scene in *Saving Private Ryan* for brutal, shaky-camera verisimilitude.

The real-life Zaitsev had an elementary school education and had served as a bookkeeper in the Army before an officer discovered his skills with a rifle.

But could the stirring story of a sniper showdown be true? It forms the plot of *Enemy at the Gates*, with Jude Law as Zaitsev and Ed Harris as König —and Joseph *"Shakespeare in Love"* Fiennes as Danilov, the Soviet "political officer" who discovers Zaitsev and builds him into an icon.

According to Anthony Beevor, author of a best-selling history of the Stalingrad battle, there was no Danilov and there was no König. There was, it follows Socratically, no sniper "duel," either.

"Daily reports were sent from Stalingrad to the chief of Red Army Agitation and Propaganda," said Beevor, "many of them dealing with the so-called sniperist movement within the 62nd Army [the chief unit defending Stalingrad], yet there is not one mention of the famous duel."

The commander of the Sixty-second Army later wrote his own memoir of Stalingrad and included the sniper duel as if it were true. (König is called Heinz Thorwald in his version.) The sniper story made compelling reading and was repeated in several subsequent tomes on the battle. Historian Beevor is not swayed. He calls the tale, and the mythical Major König (or Thorwald), "entirely invented by Soviet propaganda specialists."

What? You mean Hollywood moviemakers aren't the only ones who invent stories out of thin air and call them "true?" Soviet propaganda specialists did it, too?

Interesting.

But the myth was not enough for French director Jean-Jacques Annaud, who also cowrote the script. In the movie, he includes a female sniper named Tania Chernova, who claimed to be Zaitsev's girlfriend. In one scene in the undeniably atmospheric and rather effective film, Zaitsev and Chernova (Rachel Weisz) make love against a backdrop of squalor and tragedy, somehow signifying, in true Hollywood fashion, that romance, or at least sexual attraction, transcends even the worst of human brutality. Give Annaud some credit here—he invented the incident, but it is based on the real-life history of a friend of his who was conceived when his parents were surrounded by wartime destruction.

Chernova was another real person; she is interviewed in the book *Enemy at the Gates* by William Craig. But Beevor states definitively that in his research, which included interviews with other Stalingrad snipers, it was evident that there were no female snipers in the epic battle. Beevor adds that the movie's emphasis on the wartime romance, while not unrealistic (though in this case not true), "obstructs any serious examination of the basically psychotic character required in an outstanding sniper."

We never see that aspect in Law's performance. Watching him, it is easy to forget that he's playing a man whose job is to shoot defenseless, unsuspecting people to death from a hiding place hundreds of yards away. "Basically psychotic," indeed.

To emphasize that Zaitsev is a "good" sniper and König an evil one, Annaud concocts another character—a kid. It's a time-tested formula: if you want to get audiences bawling in their seats, kill a kid. That's exactly what Annaud has his König do. The nasty Nazi doesn't even shoot the kid—he hangs him. And leaves him dangling in public. Now that's *eee*-vil—but it's very un-sniper-like behavior.

Speaking of un-sniper-like, in the legend, Zaitsev shoots König from a distance after tricking him into poking his head out from his cover. Annaud ditches that uninspiring conclusion and stages a showdown in the street. Beevor confronted Annaud over this scene, which not only did not happen, but *would* not have happened. Snipers do not roam the streets looking for a fight. They hide, shoot, and run away.

Annaud answered as a true filmmaker. The scene, the climax of a story set amid the grimmest battle of the world's worst war, was Annaud's tribute to Sergio Leone and his spaghetti Westerns.

Sources and Further Reading

Beevor, Anthony. *Stalingrad*. New York: Viking Press, 1998.

Beevor, Anthony. "Why the Camera Always Lies." *Sunday Telegraph*, March 4, 2001.

Notes of a Sniper. http://www.notesofasniper.com.

Black Hawk Down (2001)

Directed by Ridley Scott

Written by Ken Nolan

Starring Josh Hartnett, Eric Bana, and Ewan McGregor

Hollywood's careful reconstruction of Mogadishu mayhem.
© Columbia Pictures

The U.S. military mission to Somalia in the early 1990s is mostly forgotten now. Not many people paid attention while it was going on. But most Americans remember the pictures of two dead U.S. soldiers, their bodies dragged naked through the streets by an angry Somali mob.

The operation, which began in 1992 as a famine-relief project, culminated with a vicious firefight on October 3, 1993. One hundred sixty U.S. Special Forces—Army Rangers and Delta Force—battled hundreds, perhaps thousands, of Somali militia loyal to clan warlord Mohamed Farrah Adid in the streets of Mogadishu. When the fighting ended, eighteen Americans were dead, as were between five hundred and one thousand Somalis.

Eight years later, director Ridley Scott's *Black Hawk Down* re-created the bloody battle, Hollywood style. The film is gruesomely realistic and remarkably accurate in its depictions of the battle's most dramatic events. It is filled with vivid images. Yet the one image that everyone remembers, the bodies in the streets, is nowhere to be seen.

Journalist Mark Bowden, who wrote the book *Black Hawk Down* (as well as the screenplay's first draft) told an interviewer: "The photos conveyed a false story—defeat and humiliation. The real story is substantially different."

Scott and screenwriter Ken Nolan prudently refrain from hammering a Hollywood happy ending onto the battle. On the other hand, sending the audience home with images of defiled American corpses dancing in their heads—well, it just wouldn't do. The need to offer some sense of uplift—or even some sense of *sense*—in what's really a pretty depressing spectacle may account for other omissions and alterations to the true story as well.

We'll enumerate those shortly. First, it should be pointed out that, though the film reenacts most of the minidramas Bowden describes in his moment-by-moment account, in smoothing out the chaotic narrative and supplying top-billed actors with plenty of face time, the movie ascribes various acts of heroism to the wrong people.

One example: the movie's most excruciating scene shows the film's central character, Sergeant Matt Eversmann, and a young medic struggling vainly to save the life of wounded Private Jamie Smith. Smith has been shot in the leg. His femoral artery is severed and coiled up into his pelvis. The medic must reach into the wound with his hands while Eversmann holds the wound wide open.

Sad to say, that really happened, and Private Smith indeed died under those terrible circumstances (in the film, Smith is wounded saving the life of a fellow soldier; Smith was actually shot in the act of trying to shoot a Somali who was shooting at him). God knows, Eversmann was as courageous as anyone, but, in actuality, he'd made it back to base camp when Lieutenant Larry Perino and thirty-one-year-old Delta Force medic Kurt Schmid were desperately working to save Smith's life. Ah, but Eversmann is played by Josh Hartnett, the film's star, the only member of its ensemble to get his name over the credits and his picture on the poster.

Delta Force commando Norm "Hoot" Hooten gets just a few passing mentions in the book. The movie version of Hooten, acted by rising Australian star Eric Bana, has been transformed into a Rambo-like supersoldier. When he's not dispensing folksy, Texas-style, man's-gotta-do-what-a-man's-gotta-do sermonettes, the fictional Hoot coolly mows down rows of hostile Somali militiamen from the machine gun turret of a Humvee, blasts an enemy commander to kingdom come with the poor sap's own rocket launcher, and generally walks around being invincible as he performs feat after fictional feat of derring-do.

The flesh-and-blood Hooten (who reportedly was one of the Delta "operators" dispatched to Afghanistan after 9/11), surely possesses considerable valor, but his onscreen incarnation must make him extraordinarily proud, or extraordinarily embarrassed.

Another Delta commando in the movie forms an avuncular bond with a novice Ranger named Grimes, who has bumbled his way out of a desk job and into his first combat mission. "Grimes" is based on a Ranger named John Stebbins, but the Pentagon asked the filmmakers to change the character's name because the real Stebbins is inconveniently serving a thirty-year sentence in military prison, having been convicted of sexually abusing his own preteen daughter.

This character surgery simplifies the confusing story somewhat. But it's the film's omission of the Somali side of the fight, covered nicely in Bowden's book, that strips the film of any complexity. "Somalis bad, Americans good," is the message we take from *Black Hawk Down*.

Bowden includes a lengthy account of the captivity of American pilot Michael Durant. Shot down in the second Black Hawk helicopter to crash, Durant was taken prisoner. He drops out of the film at that point.

In reality, Adid's men treated Durant humanely for eleven more days, taking the opportunity, they believed, to prove that they were not savages after all.

You'd never guess from the film that they're anything but. Adid is never portrayed. The catalyst of the entire tragedy becomes nothing but a depersonalized icon of evil. We are told in a prologue that Adid is responsible for the famine that had killed three hundred thousand Somalis (which is basically true), that Adid's men were behind the massacre and public disembowelment of twenty-seven Pakistani peacekeepers on June 5 (also true), and that Adid "declared war" on the UN peacekeepers.

No mention is made of the July 12 U.S. helicopter attack on a Mogadishu home at which Adid's top advisers had gathered. The raid caused dozens of Somali deaths and injuries. The gratitude that the Somalis had felt toward the United States turned to hatred.

Black Hawk Down is so eager to portray Adid as the incarnation of everything awful that it opens with an incident, one day before the battle, in which

Adid's men machine-gun civilians as they collect food from the Red Cross. No such slaughter took place the day before the battle.

Some mention of those incidents—and the editing-out of the phony food massacre scene—would have gone a long way toward explaining why Somalis fought against the Americans that day with such ferocity. Instead, we're left with a small band of heroic, almost exclusively white soldiers fending off a relentless attack by hordes of faceless African tribesmen. The scene invokes nothing so much as a modern-day remake of *Zulu*.

Sources and Further Reading

Bowden, Mark. *Black Hawk Down: A Story of Modern War*. New York: Penguin Books, 2000.

Bowden, Mark. Online interview with Jesse Kornbluth. America Online.

Loeb, Vernon. "After Action Report." *Washington Post Magazine*. February 27, 2000.

We Were Soldiers (2002)

Directed and written by Randall Wallace
Starring Mel Gibson, Sam Elliott, and Greg Kinnear

Mel Gibson as Hal Moore.
Photo by Stephen Vaughan, © Paramount Pictures

Every war movie, on some level, has the same theme: "Why We Fight."

Why *do* we fight? The answer depends on when you happen to be alive. Each war defines its era, and each era defines its war movies.

The popular answer nowadays seems to be "You fight for the guy beside you." War, according to Hollywood circa 1998–2003, is not fought so that good may triumph over evil. Nor even so that America may triumph over everyone else. We fight wars to affirm the buddyhood of man.

Like *Black Hawk Down*, another movie about a lost-cause American conflict that finds meaning in the camaraderie of men in combat, *We Were Soldiers* tells us almost nothing about the war in which it is set—in *Soldiers'* case, Vietnam. The sum total of what we learn about the Vietnam conflict from this film is that it was the setting for a fierce battle of noble Americans against a "tough, determined" and equally noble enemy.

We Were Soldiers re-creates the Battle of Landing Zone X-ray, November 14–16, 1965, and events leading up to it. "X-ray" was a clearing amid the forest and the elephant grass of the Ia Drang Valley in South Vietnam's strategically crucial Central Highlands. ("Ia" means "river.") The U.S. Army's First Battalion, Seventh Cavalry, commanded by tough-but-fair military lifer Lieutenant Colonel Harold G. Moore, was ordered to helicopter in to the valley in search of a North Vietnamese regiment that had attacked an American camp days earlier. This was not to be a battle for territory. Moore's mission was to locate the enemy and kill as many of them as possible.

When the X-ray battle was over, 79 American soldiers were dead, and 121 more were wounded. Almost two thousand North Vietnamese soldiers of the People's Army of Vietnam (PAVN) were killed.

The film presents the battle so free of context that it doesn't even mention a second, even bloodier battle following LZ X-ray. After Moore and his troops departed the battlefield, their reinforcements from the Second Battalion marched two miles to "Landing Zone Albany." On the way, they were stopped cold by the regrouped PAVN forces. More than twice as many Americans—151, to be exact—died at LZ Albany than at X-ray. The Americans escaped only when it was deemed safe to bring in an air strike without worrying about "friendly fire" deaths because so many Americans were dead already. LZ Albany takes up the second half of Moore's book, though he wasn't there. But it didn't make the movie. Not even as a postscript.

The way *We Were Soldiers* tells it, it's difficult to even know whom the Americans were fighting. The word "Communist" is only uttered once in the entire film, and then by Lyndon Johnson, the real one, in archive footage. Instead, the North Vietnamese are defined simply as "the enemy," a force to be respected, even feared. Then killed.

New York Times correspondent Neil Sheehan recounted that when he choppered into the battlefield on the second day of the Ia Drang battle, he found Moore shouting, "By God, they sent us over here to kill Communists and that's what we're doing!" Moore was a soldier, but he wasn't fighting only for the "men beside him." He knew that Vietnam was a political struggle.

In the film, on the other hand, Moore apparently has no idea who he's fighting, except that they're "the enemy." If director/writer (and producer) Randall Wallace had included the Sheehan incident (or any scene in which Moore ranted about his desire to "kill Communists"), the character portrayed by Mel Gibson would have come across, from today's perspective, as a dangerous fanatic who was hell-bent on sending young men to their deaths as martyrs to the Cold War.

In Wallace's vision, Moore was an honorable soldier doing the honorable job of soldiering, not Joe McCarthy with an M-16.

Another word never uttered in this movie is "gook." This derogatory racial term turned up with casual regularity in contemporary accounts of the battle. A *Saturday Evening Post* article by Private First Class Jack P. Smith, his first-person account of the LZ Albany debacle, is filled with references to "gooks." Smith, who miraculously survived the battle after playing dead as a Vietnamese gunner lay right on top of his "corpse," is not some redneck. He's the son of broadcasting legend Howard K. Smith, now a distinguished TV newsman in his own right. If he felt no qualms about printing "gook" over and over in the *Saturday Evening Freaking Post*, you can bet that the soldiers on the battlefield dropped the epithet left and right.

Now, try to imagine if the movie had showed its heroes dropping the word "gooks" (not to mention "slopeheads") left and right. It seems understandable that Wallace didn't want that. Looking back from the relatively enlightened perspective of 2002, a bunch of racist, anticommunist fanatics would not make the most sympathetic protagonists.

Nor does Wallace want to undercut himself by hinting at the existence, much less the outcome, of the subsequent battle (perhaps he's saving that for the sequel), and he certainly doesn't touch on the disastrous end of the war that finally came about a decade after the events portrayed in *We Were Soldiers*.

None of those minor details matter when military honor derives not from fighting (i.e., killing and dying and getting maimed) for your country or for an ideal, but from "watching the back of the guy next to you." That is the definition of heroism in this latest (if not greatest) generation of Hollywood war flicks.

In *We Were Soldiers*, Mel Gibson, as Lieutenant Colonel Hal Moore, addresses his troops right before they're set to leave for Vietnam, telling them, "They say we're leaving home. We're going to what home was always supposed to be." Which seems a curious assertion unless you think of "home" as a place where you kill dozens of people and will, very likely, yourself die a sudden and gruesome death. But the fictional Moore's point is that the most important thing about the battlefield is not whom you kill, why you kill them, or why you will die. It's that you stick together as a family.

The real Moore never compared a battlefield to "home," at least not in his book *We Were Soldiers Once . . . And Young*, the basis for this movie. Moore did make (and keep) an inspirational promise to his troops: he would be the first on the battlefield and the last to leave. From that single homily, Wallace extrapolated a stirring sermon on the nature of brotherhood and inserted it into Gibson's mouth.

Wallace names the speech as his favorite moment in his film, which is not surprising: Wallace has made a career in Hollywood out of melodramatizing war and the military. He wrote the screenplays for Gibson's Oscar-winning vehicle *Braveheart* (see page 307) as well as for the execrable *Pearl Harbor* (see page 273).

We Were Soldiers gives Wallace his most inherently dramatic material yet. As a thrilling battlefield drama, his film works masterfully. But how faithful is Wallace to the true events?

The Vietnam War started long before American soldiers landed, dating to the time when the Southeast Asian country was a colony of France. Wallace pays a nod to history by opening with a prologue set in June 1954, in the Central Highlands, where he portrays the destruction of the French Mobile Group 100 (GM 100), an elite French force that crumbled under a Viet Minh ambush.

The film depicts the ambush without comment, except for a bit of narration informing us that this is where "the story begins." The ambush, which wiped out more than half of GM 100 (though judging by the filmed version, you'd never know there were any survivors at all), took place a few months after the Viet Minh victory in the epic battle of Dien Bien Phu. The French-Indochina war effectively ended at Dien Bien Phu, but the communist Viet Minh army refused to stem the bloodshed until the last French soldier left their country. They were making a point—namely, "Leave and don't come back." The French got the message. The price in lives was too high to stay in a country they didn't really care about.

Wallace crams it all into one battle that ends in a ruthless massacre of wounded, with the Viet Minh commander ordering, "Kill all they send and they'll stop coming." It's an effective dramatic device, but Wallace takes one major liberty. In his version, the Viet Minh commander is the same man—Lieutenant Colonel Nguyen Huu An—who later commands the PAVN troops against Moore's battalion in Ia Drang. Just minutes later (during the credit sequence, as a matter of fact) Wallace shows Moore studying a book on the French-Indochina conflict. He flips open to a page with a picture of the "massacre" and a photograph of Lieutenant Colonel An.

Trouble is, the Viet Minh were highly secretive; no one knows who their officers were. But in a Hollywood movie, every fight must be "personal," so the anonymity of the Viet Minh gives way to Wallace's version of *Patton v. Rommel*, with Moore facing down an army commanded by the man whose tactics he has obsessively studied before ever coming to Vietnam.

The whole "French" sequence typifies Wallace's own tactics: follow the true story, but "punch it up," as a development exec might say.

One minor "punch-up" occurs in the film's—and the book's—saddest subplot, the death of Lieutenant Jack Geoghegan. An idealistic former missionary with a newborn baby back home, Geoghegan commanded one of Moore's platoons. He died attempting to rescue one of his wounded men.

In the film, he reaches his fallen friend, hoists him on his shoulders, and makes it halfway to safety—when he is cut down by two bullets through the chest.

According to eyewitness accounts, Geoghegan was, depressingly, gunned down before he managed to take a single step toward the wounded soldier. He was shot in the back and the head.

A major punch-up comes at the climax of the film, the final charge of Moore's troops that ends the battle in a semblance of victory, however Pyrrhic, for the American forces. Wallace really punches this one up, ending it like a Vietnam version of a third-rate Western, with the cavalry coming to the rescue. Just as Moore and his troops assault a PAVN machine-gun bunker, facing certain death in a hail of bullets, helicopter gunships appear out of nowhere, their own machine guns spitting fiery death. The PAVN are mowed down, and thus endeth the battle.

Earlier in the film, Wallace correctly depicts the critical role that air support played in allowing Moore's forces to "win" the battle. He didn't need to make the point again, falsely. His big, crowd-pleasing ending seemed more than a little out of place in a film that, in most other respects, goes out of its way to underline the hollowness of the Ia Drang battlefield victory.

The battle was decided by a number of factors. Most battles are. Key to this one were the reinforcements that came in during the final night, unknown to the PAVN. The North Vietnamese attacked at dawn, assuming they would easily overrun a torn-up company on the American's left flank. Instead, they ran into fresh troops with fresh supplies. They redirected their attacks toward other platoons and were cut down. When they tried one more, all-out attack at 6:55 A.M., the Vietnamese were decimated by American artillery blasts. At 9:55 A.M., Moore's troops began their sweep outward, as is depicted in the film. When they ran into Vietnamese fire, they called in an air strike. Not helicopters, but jet fighter-bombers. After that, Moore wrote, "it was no contest at all. We crushed all resistance."

Awe-inspiring American air power and the terrible price American troops paid for victory come together in the movie's most horrifying scene—and in this scene, Wallace had no need to embellish. A U.S. bomber accidentally blasts Moore's own troops with napalm. UPI reporter Joe Galloway (who coauthored the book with Moore in 1992) attempts to aid a horribly burned soldier. Following instructions from a medic, Galloway grabs the man's legs, only to have the soldier's boots melt away in his hands, along with the soldier's skin. Galloway is left holding the man's exposed bones.

The scene is straight from life. When Galloway saw the finished film, almost four decades later, he had to cover his eyes. "That incident was my personal nightmare for thirty-six-and-a-half years," he said. "It still is."

To give Wallace further credit for veracity, he *was* faithful to actual events even when said faithfulness produced high-cringe-factor moments. *We Were Soldiers* took a certain amount of critical ribbing for its corny battlefield dialogue. One dying soldier's final words are, "I'm glad I could die for my country." More than a few expire with, "Tell my wife I love her" on their lips. Both lines sound like, well, bad war movie dialogue. But they were, indeed, real words spoken by real dying men, as reported by fellow soldiers who watched them die. (For example, Lieutenant Henry Herrick, who led an ill-considered charge headlong into a Vietnamese ambush, said, "If I have to die, I'm glad to give my life for my country," according to Sergeant Ernie Savage, who was lying beside him.)

Still, Wallace's inaccuracies are irritating. Just as the omission of "Communists" and "gooks" can be interpreted as a concession to today's sensibilities, the film's attitude toward the media also reflects a 2002 perspective. As the film and the battle winds down, a helicopter delivers a group of reporters to the now-quiet battlefield. (In the film, Galloway—played by Barry Pepper—is the only reporter on the scene during the battle, but in reality others were there, including Peter Arnett, who became famous twenty-five years later as the only correspondent in Baghdad during the Gulf War, reporting for CNN.)

When the offensively fresh-faced media throng attempts to interview Gibson's Colonel Moore, he turns his back, speechless. His incredulous expression says, "You shallow fools couldn't possibly understand."

Actually, the exact opposite happened. Moore, in his book, speaks to the reporters at length. He tells them, "Brave American soldiers and the M-16 rifle won a victory here." Not only that, but Moore explains in detail why he believes in "openness" with the press.

Present-day Hollywood movies habitually portray reporters as shallow, unethical, or both—reflecting the feelings of Hollywood celebrities, perhaps? But even more important, when the film's Moore gives reporters the cold shoulder, he's affirming that only soldiers can understand what transpired here.

Fair enough, but *We Were Soldiers'* "band of brothers" logic amounts to a glorification of professional soldiering. Only soldiers can understand; only soldiers are qualified to hold opinions on war and battle. Galloway is the one sympathetic reporter in the movie, and he is pressed into combat duty (also true-to-life; Galloway wielded a rifle during the battle and on other occasions in Vietnam). His credentials as a battle-hardened tough guy are beyond question.

"Hate the war, love the warrior." Hal Moore drummed that motto into Gibson's head as he studied for the role. It's hard to argue with that sentiment. Plain humanity demands empathy and respect for ordinary men thrown into extraordinary conditions of extreme violence and horror. Despite its Hollywood punch-ups and conspicuous omissions, *We Were Soldiers* is a powerful, affecting film, for exactly that reason.

At the same time, the film lifts the Ia Drang battle, and the Vietnam War, out of the context of broader humanity. You wouldn't know it from this movie, but it is possible to live a worthwhile, even heroic life without ever being a soldier (or the worshipful, smiling wife of one). You don't have to kill people or be killed to discover the meaning in your everyday existence. You can even hold the legitimate belief that the Vietnam War was a terrible thing without actually having fought in it.

And what about a warrior like Hal Moore, who asks only to be loved? When a man chooses to spend his life killing other men simply because he's ordered to, and for reasons he barely understands—how lovable is that?

Sources and Further Reading

Koltnow, Barry. "Mel Gibson's Back in Action in Vietnam Movie." *Orange County Register*, February 26, 2002.

Luedeke, Kirk A. "Death on the Highway: The Destruction of Groupement Mobile 100." *Armor Magazine*, January/February 2001.

Moore, Lt. Gen. Harold G. and Joseph L. Galloway. *We Were Soldiers Once . . . And Young*. New York: Harper Perennial, 1993.

Sheehan, Neil. *A Bright Shining Lie*. New York: Random House, 1988.

Smith, PFC Jack P. "Death in the Ia Drang Valley." *Saturday Evening Post*, January 28, 1967.

Swager, Brent. "Rescue at LZ Albany." *Vietnam Magazine*, October 1999.

Young, Marilyn B. *The Vietnam Wars 1945–1990*. New York: Harper Perennial, 1991.

Casualties of War (1989)

Directed by Brian De Palma
Written by David Rabe
Starring Michael J. Fox and Sean Penn

Hamburger Hill (1987)

Directed by John Irvin
Written by James Carabatsos
Starring Dylan McDermott and Steven Weber

Michael J. Fox, as Eriksson, and Sean Penn, as Meserve, are "Casualties of War."
© Columbia Pictures Industries, Inc.

In contrast to the saintly portrayal of Vietnam-era army grunts in *We Were Soldiers*, Brain De Palma's *Casualties of War* offers a darker view—of infantrymen who rape and murder a teenage girl for no reason other than to "have some fun."

De Palma's film came out in 1989, before the Gulf War or even the Panama invasion. Before Somalia, and long before Kosovo and Afghanistan. Despite the liberal use of the U.S. military during the Reagan and Bush 1980s, in 1989 that odd affliction known as "Vietnam syndrome" still plagued public morale.

"Vietnam syndrome" meant different things to different people, but it never meant anything good. It's hard to imagine a Vietnam film with the tone of *Casualties of War* coming out of Hollywood today, even one that more or less faithfully re-creates a true, albeit horrific incident, as De Palma's film does. De Palma's source material was a *New Yorker* article, twenty years old by the time the film came out, by Daniel Lang, who started his career with the magazine covering World War II from North Africa and Italy.

"Casualties of War," published in the October 18, 1969, *New Yorker*, was written rather late in Lang's career (he died in 1981) and consisted mainly of an interview with a former Private First Class whom Lang called Sven Eriksson (Lang changed the man's name, as he did for all the soldiers in the article). Eriksson described an incident that occurred in November 1966 when he took part in a five-man, five-day reconnaissance patrol in Vietnam's Central Highlands (the same region where, one year earlier, the battle depicted in *We Were Soldiers* had taken place). Before the patrol embarked, its commanding sergeant, twenty-year-old "Tony Meserve," gave his routine briefing to the four men under his command, but included one detail that struck Eriksson as anything but routine.

"For the morale of the squad," Meserve explained, the five of them would, at the outset of the mission, find a suitable Vietnamese girl to take with them, "for the purpose of boom-boom, or sexual intercourse, and at the end of five days we would kill her." (That quote from Lang's article was taken from the testimony of another man in the patrol, at his own court-martial.)

Back in the "civilized" United States, only serial killers dream up those kinds of plans, much less carry them out. De Palma's film asks whether the morality of "civilization" applied in Vietnam. Or whether ordinary men, like Meserve, who committed acts of monstrous evil over there were themselves "a kind of war casualty."

In Lang's piece, Meserve—who had just a few weeks left on his tour of duty at the time of the incident—is described as a "considerate, agreeable man," and a skilled, courageous soldier who undergoes a change, developing "a mean streak toward the Vietnamese." The movie illustrates these points in the usual, oversimplified way. We see Meserve bravely rescuing Eriksson from a Viet Cong trap at the start of the film (which never happened). We see Meserve's best friend killed in a Viet Cong ambush (another invented incident; sometime earlier, Eriksson's platoon had been ambushed, but Meserve and Eriksson did not fight together before the ill-fated patrol).

Actor grunts on Hamburger Hill. © *Paramount Pictures*

In any case, showing Meserve lose his buddy to "Charlie" provides just the type of mechanistic "motivation" that turns up time and time again in Hollywood storytelling. And as usual, the "he does this because someone else did that" logic cuts the feet out from under any real exploration of human psychology. The truth is, no one knows why Meserve did what he did. No one knows why the other men acted the way they did, less like a platoon of soldiers than a homicidal cult.

The film relies heavily on Lang's article in re-creating the atrocity. The troops, led by Meserve and his gung-ho-to-the-point-of-psychosis corporal, the fictitiously named Ralph Clark, abducted a young girl named Mao (called Oahn in the screenplay; for whatever reason, De Palma changed her name, though Lang did not). After marching her through the highlands most of the day, they found an abandoned "hootch," or hut, to use as their command post. They forced the girl to clean the place up for them, then promptly gang-raped her.

Eriksson, sickened, refused to take part. Meserve and Clark threatened him, telling him he'd become a "friendly casualty" unless he took his turn. Eriksson still refused. The next morning (in the movie, it's all the same day) Meserve has lost interest in the girl, who by now is very sick and coughing heavily. He ordered Eriksson to kill her, again threatening Eriksson's life. The private again refused.

Not long afterward, Meserve comes across some Viet Cong. During the ensuing firefight, Eriksson is left at the hootch to guard the doomed girl. In Lang's article, Eriksson does nothing but sit with her and think—*how could he save her?* He decides that there's not a damn thing he can do. A "thinking" scene apparently didn't work for De Palma and screenwriter David Rabe. Their Eriksson (played by Michael J. Fox) attempts to escape with her into the forest, until the menacing Clark returns unexpectedly. One of the most moving elements of Lang's article is that the real Eriksson remained haunted by the fact that he did nothing, and that's missing from the film.

Later, when Meserve spies a squadron of American helicopters coming their way, everyone gets "jumpy" about having their victim around, so Meserve gives Clark the go-ahead to stab her to death with his hunting knife.

For De Palma and Rabe, the girl's death presents another opportunity to ramp up the melodrama. As in Lang's article, the girl somehow survives Clark's knife attack. Instead of crawling away into a bush, she walks along a bridge in the middle of a firefight. Meserve orders his men to shoot her and they do, all except Eriksson. She plummets cinematically off the bridge.

Her death, as it was described in the *New Yorker* piece, was less "visual," but more gut-wrenching. As she crawls away, the soldiers fire at her, including Eriksson, though he deliberately fires away from her. But no one hits her, so Clark walks over to her and fires point blank, blowing away her skull.

The film gives a highly condensed, but basically accurate, account of Eriksson's attempts to report the atrocity after the platoon returns to base, only to meet with indifference from superior officers—until finally finding a sympathetic chaplain. Many of the details of Eriksson's ordeal are fictionalized in minor ways, but De Palma adds only one glaring fabrication. It's true that Eriksson was thought to be in danger from his fellow soldiers, but in the film, Clark attempts to murder Eriksson with a grenade. Eriksson escapes and clubs Clark on the head with a shovel.

De Palma also invents a whole new character in the five-man patrol: Hatcher (played by John C. Reilly), an amiable idiot who goes along with the rape and kidnapping. No such character appears in the article.

At the end of the movie, each of the four men are found guilty and their sentences are read. De Palma hints that "they're not going to do any real time," but doesn't back that point up by stating how severely their sentences were, in fact, reduced. Even Clark, who was originally sentenced to life "at hard labor," got his time knocked down to eight years. Meserve's original ten-year term was reduced to eight as well.

Casualties of War was an out-of-place product for Hollywood even by 1989. In the '80s, the ruling version of Vietnam was *Rambo*, in which one super-soldier returns to Vietnam years later to single-handedly win a war that the entire U.S. military could not win in nine years of combat. We know *that* one wasn't based on a true story. But *Rambo* had competition in *Platoon*, Oliver Stone's fictional (though vaguely autobiographical) grunt's-eye view of Vietnam's horrors.

Somewhere in the middle was *Hamburger Hill*, a fictionalized, though well-researched, account of a savage 1969 battle that cost fifty-five American lives and 629 North Vietnamese lives, all to capture a hill that had, according to the Major General Melvin Zais, who commanded the operation, "no tactical significance." Peace negotiations were already underway in Paris, and the war was supposed to be ending—which made the all-out effort to capture a meaningless hill even more absurd.

Senator Edward Kennedy was outraged by the raid on "Hill 937" (rechristened "Hamburger Hill" by some anonymous soldier, or maybe reporter, with a good sense of gallows humor), in which troops of the 101st Airborne assaulted the hill no less than eleven times before finally prevailing. Kennedy called the attack "senseless and irresponsible."

Zais brushed aside Kennedy's criticisms, saying, "I know for sure he wasn't here."

The film was written (and produced) by James Carabatsos, himself a Vietnam veteran of the First Air Cavalry. His earlier credits included *Heartbreak Ridge*, a Clint Eastwood vehicle that was the first and, to date, only war film about the U.S. invasion of Grenada.

Released in 1987, *Hamburger Hill*'s mission was the same as that of *We Were Soldiers* fifteen years later—to rehabilitate the image of the American fighting man in Vietnam and to establish that only the fighting man can understand battle: no one else—certainly not the media or politicians—have any business holding an opinion. *Hamburger Hill*, if this is possible, is even less subtle than *We Were Soldiers*. In a key scene, the soldiers meet a TV newsman at the bottom of the hill after one in their series of bloody, futile attacks. The somewhat implausibly obnoxious reporter provokes the troops by reciting Kennedy's comments (which actually were not uttered until *after* the battle). A platoon sergeant (played by not-yet-famous Dylan McDermott) growls at the reporter, "You haven't earned the right to be on this hill!"

The path from *Hamburger Hill* to *We Were Soldiers* is pretty clear. But as those two films try to refashion our memories of Vietnam by aggressively wiping away any vestiges of the war's political and, more important, moral dimensions, as if the dignity of the soldier—sacrosanct though it may be—is an end in itself. *Casualties of War* stands on the other end of the spectrum, a film about how the moral rot of the war infected everyone, leaving even a good man like Eriksson haunted. There has not been a Vietnam film like it since.

Sources and Further Reading

Hoffman, Daniel. "Hamburger Hill: The Army's Rationale." Reprinted in *Reporting Vietnam: Part One, American Journalism 1959–1969*. New York: The Library of America, 1998.

Lang, Daniel. "Casualties of War." Reprinted in *Reporting Vietnam: Part One, American Journalism 1959–1969*. New York: The Library of America, 1998.

MacPherson, Myra. *Long Time Passing: Vietnam and the Haunted Generation*. Garden City, NY: Doubleday and Company, 1984.

K-19: The Widowmaker (2002)

Directed by Kathryn Bigelow
Written by Christopher Kyle
Starring Harrison Ford and Liam Neeson

Harrison Ford as Soviet submarine captain Alexei Vostrikov.
Photo by George Kraychyk, © Paramount Pictures

Captain First Rank Nikolai Zateyev, former commander of Soviet submarine K-19.
Courtesy of Mrs. Antonina Zateyev, Kathryn Bigelow, and Peter A. Huchthausen

When Hollywood studio bosses shell out nine-figure budgets, they expect to see something spectacular: flying superheroes, exploding asteroids, the sinking of the *Titanic*, or at least a few Hobbits.

What they do not have in mind, one imagines, is 138 minutes inside a submarine. A Soviet submarine. Filled with Communists. Now *there's* a formula for boffo box-office.

Submarines are cramped, dingy, and slow. Communists are, well, Communists. Somehow, however, *K-19: The Widowmaker*—a 1960s period piece about a Soviet nuclear submarine—got made. Predictably, it provided little bang for its makers' hundred-million bucks. The film reportedly earned about one-third of its budget at the box office—a flop of nuclear proportions, much like the near-meltdown that occurred onboard the sub.

It seems fitting that no one went to see this movie, because the 1961 nuclear disaster aboard K-19—the first Soviet nuke-powered, ballistic-missile sub—remained unreported for twenty-eight years. The disaster claimed the lives of twenty-two crewmen. Eight perished days after they'd marched straight into a radiation storm to repair an overheating atomic reactor. That's a Hollywood-worthy act of self-sacrifice, except that radiation poisoning doesn't make for much of a Hollywood ending. Another fourteen men suffered radioactive exposure that killed them within two years. The remainder of the submarine's 177 crew members suffered symptoms of radiation sickness for the rest of their lives.

The Soviets hushed up the nuclear accident, as they did all of their nuclear accidents, until the Worker's Paradise collapsed under the weight of its own idiocy in 1991. The survivors of K-19 were listed in official Soviet military records as suffering from mental disorders and stress. Any doctor who wrote down a diagnosis of "radiation sickness" could earn an early retirement in the Gulag.

Director Kathryn Bigelow wrote of her personal determination to tell the story of K-19 in an essay titled "Uncharted Waters: The Genesis of *K-19*." She traveled to the former Soviet Union and visited Mrs. Nikolai Zateyev, widow of the submarine's captain. She met surviving K-19 crewmembers. All greeted her with skepticism but left imploring her to "tell this story." It seems, therefore, an odd decision by Bigelow and her screenwriters (including an uncredited Tom Stoppard) to film a story that is almost entirely fiction.

Only the broadest outlines of the actual incident remain (although we're tempted to say that the most unrealistic part of this movie is Harrison Ford muttering his lines in a Russian accent). Production designers did, however, re-create the K-19's interior in obsessive-compulsive detail. But in this "human story of courage, duty and impossible decisions" (per the film's own PR material), most of the characters are inventions—including a heroic rookie officer who single-handedly stops the nuclear nightmare.

Names of those characters who are actually "based on" actual people are changed: Nikolai Zateyev becomes Alexei Vostrikov and the amiable Executive Officer Vladimir Yenin is rechristened Mikhail Polenin. The movie concocts a hokey subplot in which Polenin (played by Liam Neeson) is demoted from captaincy of the K-19 and is replaced by the strict disciplinarian Vostrikov (played by Ford). Polenin is forced to serve under his rigid and seemingly irrational command. But Vostrikov is no Captain Queeg. He's an underwater General Patton. Nonetheless, his tough-guy posturing leads to a mutiny as the nuclear crisis reaches its peak.

Accounts of the K-19's disastrous voyage surfaced decades after the fact, during the *glasnost* era. They show that the personalities of K-19's two top officers are more or less correct in the movie. Yenin was the nice-guy father figure, Zateyev the stern disciplinarian. The movie's subplot, however, was pure fancy. Yenin was never demoted, Zateyev was respected, and there was no mutiny. Zateyev made sure of that by jettisoning all sidearms that were onboard except his own and those of his most trusted officers.

Bigelow & Co. crunch a lengthy time line of events into one highly eventful voyage of the K-19. K-19 was an ill-fated ship. The Soviets rushed their nuclear fleet into the water. The film touches on their appalling contempt for safety, but leaves out Zateyev's vociferous complaints that his boat was anything but seaworthy. K-19—like every sub in the Soviet armada—suffered some malfunction every time it floated from port. On one training mission, K-19 dove to its "crush depth" of three hundred meters and promptly sprung a leak, tipped hard to port, and surfaced flat on its side.

Bigelow compresses all of K-19's training voyages into a single mission, in which K-19 travels to the Arctic Circle and fires a ballistic missile as a test. The fictional K-19 endures rigorous drills, makes it to the Arctic, fires the test missile, then receives a new assignment from Moscow: patrol the eastern seaboard of the United States between Washington, D.C., and New York. Presumably, the submarine is prepared to unleash nuclear Armageddon on those cities as soon as Moscow gives the word.

That would be a lot for any submarine to handle. The real K-19, whose mishap-laden trial runs took place prior to its ill-fated test-missile mission, never sailed far enough to fire its payload. The sub's reactor overheated halfway into its month-long maiden voyage.

You'd think a nuclear accident would be a sure sign that it's time to put a ship into dry dock, but K-19 was back in the water less than three years later. In February 1972 K-19 had another accident that, though nonnuclear, was in some ways more horrifying. A fire swept through several compartments, killing twenty-eight men. The sub surfaced into a hurricane, which meant that a rescue ship couldn't get everyone off the boat. For three weeks, K-19 bobbed and rolled in the rocky waters, with twelve men trapped in total darkness inside the sub's torpedo compartment. They survived on canned food and droplets of water from condensation on the walls. (It was during the 1972 disaster that the crippled K-19 was photographed by American aircraft, *not* during the 1961 nuclear accident, as in the movie.)

Once again, K-19 went right back to sea. It was not decommissioned until 1991, after two more major fires onboard. Today, the submarine rusts in the waters of the Arctic Ocean, along with dozens of other Cold War Soviet subs, at a top-secret Russian naval base. A smaller ex-Soviet sub, part of an educational exhibit in Florida, doubled for the star-crossed K-19 in Hollywood's hundred-million dollar bomb.

Sources and Further Reading

Huchthausen, Peter. *K-19 The Widowmaker: The Secret Story of the Soviet Nuclear Submarine*. Washington, D.C.: National Geographic Society, 2002.

National Geographic. "K-19 and Other Subs in Peril." http://www.nationalgeographic.com/k19/.

Gallipoli (1981)

Directed by Peter Weir
Written by David Williamson
Starring Mel Gibson and Mark Lee

Mel Gibson and Mark Lee as two fictional sprinters on the front lines of Gallipoli. © Paramount Pictures Corporation

Gallipoli is an antiwar film from the classic mold. Set in World War I, arguably the most insane and wasteful war ever fought, it has no problem making its point about the insanity and wastefulness of war. Unfortunately, this Australian production is also an anti-British film, and to make that point, it had to invent and distort several facts.

Directed by Peter Weir, who later graduated from Australia to Hollywood with such films as *Dead Poets Society* and *The Truman Show, Gallipoli* is a mostly fictitious story of two friends, both talented sprinters, who join the Australian army in World War I. One joins out of youthful and, as is made tragically clear, misguided idealism. The other, a cynical drifter (played by a very youthful Mel Gibson), joins because there's not much else for him to do, and besides, girls like the uniform.

Their brief military careers take them to the shores of Turkey, at Gallipoli, where the British, with the Australian forces under their command, attempt to break through the Turkish lines. The plan is to press onward to Constantinople, thus "knocking Turkey out of the war" and depriving the Germans of a valuable ally. Like many battles in "the Great War," the Battle of Gallipoli was a pointless exercise in trench warfare, leaving hundreds slaughtered with nothing to show for it on either side. Needless to say, the adventure of these two young men ends in senseless tragedy. The storming of the Nek was a botched raid on a Turkish machine-gun position in which hundreds of Australian soldiers charged from their trenches only to be mowed down within seconds by the enemy's guns.

In fact, though Weir doesn't give credit to his source (only to a "story" by himself), Gallipoli appears to be based on the 1922 novel *Tell England*, a huge bestseller at the time by Ernest Raymond, which was first filmed in 1931. In the earlier film, our ill-fated hero reaches the Turkish position and takes it out before dropping dead. Weir's movie is much bleaker, ending on a freeze-frame of its naive, seventeen-year-old protagonist taking two fatal bullets just a few yards out of his trench. His death accomplishes less than nothing.

Weir gets some basic details right. One of the main causes of the catastrophe at the Nek was the inexplicable failure of officers to synchronize their watches. The Australian soldiers of the glamorous Light Horse Brigade (*sans* horses) were supposed to commence their charge immediately after a solid half-hour of mortar fire that would pound the Turks out of their trenches. But because of the watch snafu, the shelling stopped seven minutes too soon. The Turks had plenty of time to regroup, and once the attack began, the Australians were sitting ducks.

Weir got the mistake right, but the deliberately malicious intent of the British commanders he got wrong. In Weir's telling, orders for the suicidal attack come from a British commander who insists that his Australian troops must continue their charge in order to distract from a British landing at a beach up the coast. And that's not what happened. The attack was designed to protect a division of New Zealand soldiers who were attacking from another direction. Nor did a British officer issue the inflexible orders for the assault, deliberately sending more than six hundred Australian men to their deaths. The attack was planned by the British General William Birdwood, but it was led by Australian officers. It's not as if the British were not culpable, but, though the Nek was an Australian charge in which 372 Australians lost their lives in a matter of minutes, over 300 of them falling, according to one historian, "in an area the size of a tennis court," the British lost more young men in the Battle of Gallipoli than did any other nation. But Weir has British soldiers frolicking on the beach while their Australian comrades are busy getting slaughtered a short jaunt to the south.

Nothing absolves the British command of responsibility for the lunacy at Gallipoli, but to pit "the evil British" against "the valiant Australians" is simply incorrect. Weir subverted his own antiwar message by morphing his film into an unjustified diatribe against the British, basically pandering to Australian patriotism by restating the long-standing Australian mythology of the Battle of Gallipoli. His film ends up telling us not that World War I—and, by extension, all war—is madness, but only that the British are mad. Thanks to Weir's distortions, the lesson we take away from Gallipoli is that you can't decry your country's wars at the same time that you're echoing your country's official war propaganda.

Sources and Further Reading

Bush, Eric Wheeler. *Gallipoli*. New York: St. Martin's Press, 1975.

James, Robert Rhodes. *Gallipoli*. London: B. T. Batsford Ltd., 1965.

Kilts, Culottes, and Corsets

Braveheart (1995)

Directed by Mel Gibson

Written by Randall Wallace

Starring Mel Gibson and Patrick McGoohan

Mel Gibson as Sir William Wallace.
Photo by Andrew Cooper, © Paramount Pictures

Prior to directing the Stations of the Cross, Mel Gibson had always been more of an Old Testament–style action hero. Mad Mel's onscreen alter egos were usually too busy smiting in the name of vengeance seven times over to turn the other cheek. The eye-for-an-eye genre had always suited the actor, who recognized early in his career that revenge is a dish best served with popcorn in a packed movie house. No one played the action martyr better than Mel Gibson.

It's a role that has, on more than one occasion, seeped into the actor's off-screen persona. When critics accused Gibson of promoting anti-Semitism in *The Passion of the Christ*, the Biblical opus he cowrote and directed, they felt The Fury of the Mel. Gibson characterized himself as the victim of "vehement anti-Christian sentiment." His membership in an ultraconservative splinter sect of Catholicism—a group obsessed with rolling back twentieth-century church reforms to reinstate an all-Latin mass and medieval doctrine that holds the Jews collectively responsible for Christ's death—did make him an easy target of secular and liberal commentators.

But Gibson's histrionic response to his critics was, you might say, way beyond Thunderdome. The millionaire movie star openly fretted that his life might be in danger. He had already voluntarily excised one scene from *The Passion* involving the Jewish high priest Caiaphas because, Gibson explained, "they'd be coming after me at my house; they'd come to kill me." Presumably just like "they" had come after Jesus in the reportedly anti-Semitic version of the Christ story Gibson had filmed. When *New York Times* columnist Frank Rich wrote a piece calling Gibson's father a "Holocaust denier," Gibson lashed back at the journalist in vivid terms: "I want to kill him," he vented in a *New Yorker* interview. "I want his intestines on a stick. . . . I want to kill his dog." Not exactly a *what-would-Jesus-do?* moment. If Gibson weren't so staunchly committed to Latin-inflected Biblical literalism, the director's cut of *The Passion* would likely have featured Jesus peeling Himself off the cross and drop-kicking those Roman bastards to kingdom come.

But to accuse Gibson of having recently developed a Christ complex wouldn't be entirely accurate. (Nor, perhaps, would it be in the best interests of our pets.) In fact, Gibson has been bearing a rather obvious artistic cross since at least 1995, when he released *Braveheart*, a film he directed and starred in. Three hours into that epic, when Gibson's kilt-kicking Scotsman assumes the cinematic crucifixion position (you know: arms dolefully outstretched) for the *second* time in as many hours, you almost wish you hadn't gotten the message so clearly the *first* time.

It's easy to see why Gibson gravitated to the *Braveheart* story. The film is based on the outsize legend of Sir William Wallace of Elerslie, the thirteenth-century action martyr who led a fierce rebellion to drive the English from his native Scotland. Though in the end Wallace failed to liberate his people—he was captured, tortured, and executed at the symbolically significant age of thirty-three—his legend expanded to iconic proportions after his death. All but deified by his countrymen, he became a potent national symbol of freedom and independence.

Clearly, the parallels between the Wallace legend and Christ story weren't lost on Gibson. In fact, Gibson and his *Braveheart* screenwriter, Randall Wallace (no relation), pumped up the Christian imagery considerably. As a result, *Braveheart* plays a lot like a practice run for the Jesus movie Gibson would eventually get around to making (although the "prequel" would feature much more kilted shite-kicking). Unfortunately, in the course of beatifying Wallace for Christendom, Gibson and company wound up making a complete hash of history.

After centuries of mythologizing, the actual William Wallace has become thoroughly obscured by his own legend. The scant biographical details ascribed to Wallace's early life derive from a fifteenth-century poem written by Henry the Minstrel, also known as Blind Harry, neither moniker inspiring confidence in historical precision. According to historian Andrew Fisher, Blind Harry's observational authority is "unreliable for any serious student of history." So, we'll cut Gibson plenty of slack in the character and backstory departments. (For instance, as to whether or not the real Wallace sported a medieval mullet, like Gibson does in the film, we just don't know. So, we'll give him the achy-breaky hairdo, no questions asked.)

According to Blind Harry's melodious reportage, the actual William Wallace was a towering figure, six feet, seven inches in height and buffed like all get out. In other words, he wouldn't have been out of place in a medieval comic book—or, more accurately, in an "illuminated action palimpsest." Although Gibson reportedly measures a mere five feet, nine inches in his stocking feet, the Billy Ray Cyrus wig undoubtedly helped narrow the historical gap.

Blind Harry also trilled at length about Wallace studying for the priesthood, and thereby mastering not only French and Italian, but also Latin. Although some scholars make superior guttural noises whenever this assertion is uttered, there's reason to believe that young Wallace did indeed receive a faith-based education. As the second son of a minor Scottish nobleman, he would have been expected to enter the clergy, being ineligible for the cushy first-born-inherits-the-whole-estate entitlement that was customary in those days. If you're willing to put any stock in the claims of vision-impaired biographers who prance around in tights, Wallace was schooled by a priest-slash-uncle, who instilled in his young nephew a reverence for the values of freedom and liberty, thereby giving rise to Wallace's famous war whoop, "Pro Libertate!"

Like many of his countrymen, young Wallace developed an intense loathing for the land-usurping English, who were then squatting in much of Scotland. The English King Edward I, also known as "Edward the Longshanks" (a nod to his above-average chain-mail inseams), had brilliantly set the various factions of feudal Scotland against one another in a passive-aggressive strategy designed to result in the annexation of the country for himself.

Wallace's enmity for the English, coupled with an all-too-stereotypical Scottish tendency toward hotheaded outbursts, led him astray of his religious studies and directly into a string of bloody altercations with English authorities. The temperamental ex-seminary student quickly discovered that he had a knack for separating foes from their heads, limbs, and other appendages. By his twentieth birthday he was a notorious outlaw. By his mid-twenties, he was a guerrilla-style rebel, launching assaults on English soldiers from his redoubt in the forests of Selkirk. And by his late twenties, he was a national hero, a knighted general, and an official "Guardian of Scotland," bellowing his posh Latin catchphrase as he led the Scots to battle against the English.

Braveheart more or less follows Blind Harry's trail of historical breadcrumbs—especially the priestly details. But Gibson is loath to leave any of Wallace's rough edges showing. Blind Harry's Wallace slaughtered Englishmen rather indiscriminately, often for relatively petty reasons. For instance, when English soldiers confiscated a fish he had caught, Wallace decapitated one blighter, hacked another bloke to the collarbone, and lopped off the arm of a third, Monty Python–style. Another multivictim slaughter was provoked by little more than a rude remark about Wallace's bright green clothes. "Thou Scot, abide;" snickered an English swell on the street, "what devil clothed thee in so gay a garment?" Without so much as a "Prithee, good sir, I demand satisfaction," Wallace ran his dirk through the heckler's heart. Several such episodes forced Wallace take it on the lam, and made him a much-wanted outlaw.

William Wallace (portrait painted circa
1661).
Courtesy of Stirling Smith Art Gallery and Museum

Gibson's kilted hero, on the other hand, is a peace-loving lad, slow to anger, wishing only to marry his fair maiden and quietly till the soil. There's no mention here of Wallace's five years as an outlaw in the woods. Gibson's Wallace takes up the sword only to avenge the murder of his lady at the hands of vile, rapacious English constables. (In Hollywood, this is called "making it personal.")

Of course, every sympathetic movie biography burnishes its hero's character to one degree or another. But Gibson isn't content merely to modulate Blind Harry's theatrical excesses. Nor is he willing to settle for a minor character polish—instead, Gibson aims to shellac William Wallace into gleaming sainthood and Christlike martyrdom. As the film's title telegraphs, there are no downsides to Gibson's Wallace. He is virtuous in the extreme, completely incorruptible, always correct, more brilliant than thou, beloved by the good-hearted, blessed with the strength of ten men, etc., etc.

Gibson also commits the minor Hollywood sin of demoting his hero to commoner status in order to enhance audience identification. In reality, Sir William Wallace's father was a knight and a land baron. His grandfather was an important nobleman and official. In the film, Gibson's father is depicted as one of those salt-of-the earth farmers whose face is always smudged with the bonny sod.

In repurposing the Wallace legend into a more efficient Christ allegory, Gibson was assisted immeasurably by his writer, the aforementioned Randall Wallace. A former divinity student who at one point considered entering the seminary, Wallace specializes in screenplays that glorify the noble warrior, often at the expense of historical or political context (see *Pearl Harbor*, page 273, and *We Were Soldiers*, page 286). A devout Christian who draws inspiration from the Bible, Wallace has described *Braveheart* as "a pure sermon that I could preach from any pulpit, but more people would get the message if it were a film."

Hence *Braveheart*'s rather incongruous opening narration, in which King Edward the Longshanks is referred to as a "pagan," which he most certainly was not. In addition to "Romanizing" the English, screenwriter Wallace's three-hour sermon necessitated the invention of several Judas-style betrayals that never really happened. For instance, the movie depicts Robert the Bruce not just selling out our hero to Longshanks, but also jousting with Mel on the battlefield. Neither event happened. During the Battle of Falkirk, Bruce was miles away in a separate skirmish, fighting for Scotland (the good guys), not England (the evil empire).

Likewise, to suit their allegorical agenda, the filmmakers lash Gibson to a cruciform post, arms outstretched in glorious messianic martyrdom, as he's hauled in a cart to the place of execution. In reality, the English wisely steered clear of such blatant Christian symbolism. Opting for a less grandiose mode of transport, they dragged Wallace behind horses through the streets of London. At Smithfield, the rebel Scotsman was hanged, disemboweled, and beheaded. For good measure, the English burned his entrails and then quartered his body. Unconcerned about overkill, they subsequently planted his head on a spike on London Bridge and distributed the remaindered bits to uppity Scottish towns as an object lesson in English diligence.

Mel Gibson's liturgical approach to Scottish history didn't seem to bother modern Scots. The response from the homeland was remarkably supportive, particularly when the respondents were tourism officials happy to superimpose Mel's famous mug onto their historical brochures. Average Scots were also enthusiastic, thrilled to see their national hero glorified in a major Hollywood production. The movie made political waves as well, giving rise to a renewed movement for Scottish independence from Britain; its constituents called themselves "Bravehearts."

Historians—particularly those with Scottish accents—tended to be far less charitable to Mel. As one local Wallace expert put it: "Gibson has butchered our history as brutally as the English butchered Wallace." Ouch.

Among other aggressive historical revisions, Gibson and Randall Wallace:

- dismember actual time lines and invent pivotal events that never even happened, much less pivoted. In the opening sequences, for instance, a narrator announces that the year is 1280; the King of Scotland has died heirless; Longshanks has claimed the Scottish throne for himself; and that same "cruel pagan" has lured Scottish nobles into an ambush. Well, *not*. And not even *close*: King Alexander III didn't die until 1286; war didn't break out until 1296; and there were never any nobles ambushed and then hung dramatically in a mud hut. So why concoct such fictional nonsense? In order to have impressionable young Willie Wallace happen upon the carnage and forever be motivated to seek Hollywood-style revenge.
- paint the English, and especially Longshanks (played by Patrick "*The Prisoner*" McGoohan), as either completely evil bastards of the mustache-twirling variety or dithering gay blades. To drive these points home, director Gibson has the ailing Longshanks hurl his flamingly "daft" son's boy toy out of a convenient castle window in a scene so over-the-top, you'll want to rewind it and watch it again just to convince yourself you just saw what you think you just saw. Gibson also treats us to a dramatic snippet that has Longshanks imposing the dread policy of *Prima Nocte*, which basically grants English nobles the authority to rape Scottish brides on their wedding day. In reality, there is no evidence that the custom of *Prima Nocte* was ever in effect during the feudal period. But it sure makes the bloody limeys look even worse, and, boy, does it get Mel's blood boiling!
- invent a completely spurious and laughable plot twist that has Longshanks's daughter-in-law, the French-born Isabella, Princess of Wales, falling in love with Mel's badger-coiffed messiah. Not only that, but one thing leads to another, and she winds up pregnant with Baby Braveheart, who, we are led to believe, will become the future King Edward III! In reality, at the time

of Wallace's execution in 1305, Isabella was nine years old, living in France, and still two years away from becoming Mrs. Edward II. Furthermore, her son, Edward III, would not be born for another seven years. Talk about a drawn-out labor!

We could go on and on, epically. But we'll give the last word to J. C.—er, that is, to "Braveheart" himself. According to the *Village Voice*, shortly before the release of his Scotch-flavored passion play, Gibson commented, "I just know I'm going to get crucified."

Sources and Further Reading

Baronage Press. "Braveheart." http://www.baronage.co.uk/bphtm-01/wallace1.html.

Highlander Web Magazine. "William Wallace: The Truth Behind the Man." http://www.highlanderweb.co.uk/wallace.

Innes, Ewen. "Braveheart: Fact or Fiction?" Scottishhistory.com. http://www.scottishhistory.com/articles/independence/braveheart.htm.

Mackay, James. *William Wallace: Brave Heart.* Edinburgh: Mainstream Publishing, 1996.

Merony, John. Interview with Randall Wallace. *The American Enterprise,* May–June 1998.

Winter, Jessica. "Mel Gibson's Jesus Christ Pose." *Village Voice,* November 5–11, 2003.

Excalibur (1981)

Directed by John Boorman
Written by Rospo Pallenberg and John Boorman
Starring Nigel Terry and Nicol Williamson

Helen Mirren as Morgana, King Arthur's half sister, and
Robert Addie as their naughtily conceived son, Mordred.
© Orion Pictures Company

Of the thirty or so movies about King Arthur, John Boorman's 1981 film is the
most faithful to the legend. Certainly it's got to be more accurate than *Monty
Python and the Holy Grail*, or *A Connecticut Yankee in King Arthur's Court*. But
legends are not history. How close is *Excalibur* to the facts about the real, living, breathing King Arthur?

The answer: not at all—because in all likelihood, King Arthur did not exist.

As one might imagine with a story dating back over fifteen hundred years,
there are as many views on the historical Arthur as there are historians. In Boorman's film, as in its source material *Le Morte d'Arthur* by fifteenth-century
romanticist Thomas Malory, Arthur is the child of a union between the would-
be king Uther Pendragon and Ygraine, the wife of Uther's archenemy, the Duke
of Cornwall. Arthur becomes king when he pulls the super-sword Excalibur
from the stone into which Uther had driven it years earlier. Excalibur was given

to Uther by the Lady of the Lake, some kind of water nymph who apparently hands out swords to passing men.

Needless to say, that tale lacks a certain verisimilitude. But does the fantastical story of King Arthur have any basis in fact at all? The most charitable, yet still plausible, view is that Arthur is a historical composite, possibly inspired by an early Roman-British general or two, with a liberal helping of mythology and fanciful folklore thrown in for good measure.

The historical candidate most frequently cited is Lucius Artorius Castus, a Romanized Briton warlord of the second century, three hundred years before the legendary Arthur is supposed to have reigned from his Camelot. The obvious link is the name—the English form of the Roman "Artorius" is "Arthur," or something close enough to it. Artorius is alleged to have fought twelve great battles defending Britain from foreign hordes. Problem is, there's quite a bit of folklore and fog surrounding Artorius himself, and we can't be sure that any of those twelve battles actually took place. Researchers who have attempted to establish their veracity have had a great deal of trouble figuring out where these battles may have occurred. The battlefield sites have been placed anywhere from southeast England all the way up to Scotland.

Another Roman warlord, Ambrosius Aurelianus, is identified as Arthur on the basis of the *Historia Brittonum*, a ninth-century text attributed to Nennius, who's probably yet another made-up character. In any case, chapter fifty-six of the *Historia* details the adventures of Arthur, culminating in the Battle of Mount Badon, in which the great warrior king held off the invading Saxons. In other texts, this battle is said to have been fought by Ambrosius, leading to the conclusion that he and Arthur were one and the same.

Was there ever a Battle of Mount Badon, much less a historical Arthur? No one has been able to track down this British mountain with any certainty. Nennius's text doesn't give a hint of the location, but it does state that 960 of the invading enemy's men were struck down that day—all by Arthur himself! Wow.

Once again, we're back to a point where Arthur looks more like a superhero than an actual person. In ancient Celtic tradition, it was not uncommon to ascribe a historical reality to mythological figures, and that's apparently what happened to the mythical King Arthur. To its credit, John Boorman's film makes no claims to historical authenticity. Even the shining armor worn by Arthur and his knights is based on designs from the middle ages. Nothing so spiffy would have been donned by warriors in the second (or even the fifth) century A.D., supposedly the time of Arthur.

As little evidence as there is of a real King Arthur, there's even less for the other characters in the Arthurian legends dramatized by Boorman. Lancelot, Guinevere, Percival, Merlin the magician—all appear to be nothing more than figments of our collective imagination made real by repeated telling over centuries and millennia. The theme of Boorman's *Excalibur* is our need to believe in something greater than ourselves. In the Arthurian romance brought to the screen by Boorman, the people need their king; without him they starve, both literally and spiritually. Even the king needs something to believe in—the Holy Grail.

The need to believe is, in all likelihood, what transformed Arthur from a made-up hero of ancient Celtic tales into a "real" personage who we can gaze upon with wonder through the mists of ancient history.

Sources and Further Reading

Day, David. *The Search for King Arthur*. New York: Facts on File, Inc., 1995.
Green, Thomas. "The Historicity and Historicisation of Arthur." Arthurian Resources. http://www.arthuriana.co.uk/historicity/arthur.htm.
Nennius. *History of the Britons*. http://emedia.netlibrary.com/reader/reader.asp?product_id=2009566.

The Affair of the Necklace (2001)

Directed by Charles Shyer

Written by John Sweet

Starring Hilary Swank and Jonathan Price

Joely Richardson as Marie Antoinette. *Photo by Murray Close,* © *Warner Bros.*

The real Marie Antoinette.

It's unfortunate to see a perfectly fine historical scoundrel go bad by getting good on Hollywood's dime. *The Affair of the Necklace* manages to transform a fascinating lowlife and "adventuress" into that blandest of movie stereotypes, the misguided victim driven to criminal enterprise in order to right a wrong.

Based on an intriguing particle of eighteenth-century French history, the story concerns a beautiful swindler who called herself the Comptess de La Motte. In 1784 she masterminded a brazen scam that begat a notorious royal scandal, which in turn helped precipitate the French Revolution.

The film follows the basic outline of the tale accurately enough. What it gets completely wrong is the nature of the lady's character, and her motives.

Née Jeanne de Saint-Remy, the "Comptess" was most likely a con artiste par excellence who, by the age of twenty-five, had elevated herself by her own culotte straps out of poverty and into courtly society, by claiming a dubious noble lineage (the conveniently extinct Valois dynasty).

The larger flimflam for which Jeanne became famous centered on a garish 2,800-carat, 647-diamond necklace allegedly purchased on behalf of the Queen, Marie Antoinette. The patsy in the scheme was a lubricious roué in cleric's vestments, Cardinal de Rohan, the grand almoner. (Among other extra-clerical accomplishments, the Cardinal had set up "a private brothel . . . ran up gigantic debts, led the heir to the throne astray . . . and had the temerity to smuggle.")

Ambitious as he was criminally enterprising, Rohan hoped to follow in the outsize footsteps of Cardinal Richelieu, the Catholic cleric who had also steered the ship of state as France's prime minister. Unfortunately for Rohan, his own designs on the prime ministership had hit a queen-size snag—as a matter of fact, it was the queen herself. Marie Antoinette made no secret of her abject hatred of the dissolute, Austrian-baiting Cardinal.

Jeanne (who may or may not have been one of Rohan's mistresses; accounts vary on that point) knew a prime sucker when she saw one. Claiming to have access to the queen, Jeanne offered to act as a go-between facilitating back-channel correspondence between Marie Antoinette and the cardinal. Through a series of forged letters and royal impersonations, Jeanne subsequently manipulated the gullible Rohan into believing that Marie Antoinette craved not only rapprochement, but also bed privileges with the randy clergyman.

The "hook"—that moment in a con when a sucker is inexorably snared in the web of deception as a made gull—was a "secret" tryst between the queen and her ever-so-flattered pen pal in a secluded Versailles garden. Appearing from behind a topiary hedge at the appointed hour, the queen offered Rohan a rose, murmuring, "You know what this means." Bedazzled, flattered, and utterly smitten, Rohan failed to notice that his garden "queen" was actually a prostitute hired by Jeanne and dolled up to look like Marie Antoinette, her face conveniently obscured under a dark veil.

Convinced that his future paramour was ready to hand him the prime ministership, Rohan eagerly bit at Jeanne's bigger bait: the aforementioned necklace. Jeanne told Rohan that Marie Antoinette, famous for her love of diamonds, coveted a particularly ostentatious, bejeweled necklace worth 1,600,000 livres. In reality, Marie Antoinette had twice rejected the desperate entreaties of court jewelers to purchase the piece. Uncharacteristically, perhaps, she thought the necklace vulgar, and reminiscent of a slave collar. Originally commissioned by her late father-in-law, Henri XV, for one of his mistresses, the piece carried, in addition to its over-the-topness, the unsavory taint of old affairs.

Jeanne easily persuaded Rohan and the court jewelers—frantic to make a sale—that Marie Antoinette expected Rohan to acquire the necklace discreetly on her behalf, so as not to rouse the ire of the peasants. Rohan would serve as guarantor to the sale, against the unlikely possibility that the queen decided to stiff the jewelers of their just compensation. You can guess what happened next: Rohan delivered the necklace to Jeanne, who dispatched her lowlife husband to London to fence the 647 flawless diamonds.

Alas, the elaborate scam collapsed when the jewelers delivered their bill of sale to Versailles. Rather than handle the matter with discretion, the queen flipped her powdered pompadour and vociferously *j'accuse*'d her archenemy, Rohan, of forgery and fraud. Rohan, in turn, denounced and rightly blamed Jeanne de Saint-Remy, also known as the Comptess de La Motte, also known as the last of the Valois dynasty. The counterfeit comptess fingered Count Cagliostro, the notorious sham alchemist and continental con man. In all likelihood, Cagliostro had no involvement in this particular scandal (other than having an acquaintance with Rohan), but apparently an eighteenth-century scandal just wasn't a scandal without Cagliostro in the house.

In the sensational trial that ensued, none of the principles emerged unscathed. Both Cagliostro and Rohan were eventually acquitted of all charges, but only after extended stays in the Bastille. The vengeful Marie Antoinette saw to it that Rohan was stripped of his court title ("Grand Almoner"—to modern ears, no big loss) and banished from France. Jeanne de Saint-Remy was convicted, publicly flogged, branded, and imprisoned. (She'd later escape to England, where she'd pen her highly imaginative "memoirs.") Marie Antoinette was probably the biggest loser of them all. Already wildly unpopular with the public, the trial only excited further contempt for the queen. Many believed (wrongly) that Marie Antoinette herself had masterminded the necklace plot, in a spiteful effort to frame Rohan. Ultimately, Marie Antoinette's zeal for revenge fanned the popular discontent that would eventually deliver her to the guillotine.

As true stories go, this one doesn't skimp on dramatic—and comic—potential. Not surprisingly, the "diamond necklace affair" has through the years been the subject of numerous dramatizations, most notably Dumas's *The Queen's Necklace* and Carlyle's *Diamond Necklace*. Given such foolproof source material, it's hard to envision a movie version going as wrong as 2002's *The Affair of the Necklace*.

A film that begs for treacherous characters, poison bons mots, and crafty plot turns (in Hollywood terms: *Dangerous Liaisons* meets David Mamet) delivers instead blunt-edged earnestness (*After-School Special* meets hoopskirts and bustles). And where history offers up ambiguous motives and convoluted politics, Hollywood sorts things out with market-tested pop-psychology clichés.

The film's biggest failure is its wrongheaded characterization of Jeanne de Saint-Remy. History offers conflicting opinions of the woman behind the scandal, sometimes painting her as greedy con artist and other times (less plausibly) as a political provocateur intent on toppling the royal dynasty. Unfortunately, the film completely reinvents the character out of ninety-nine-cent whole cloth, asking us to believe that Jeanne really was a noblewoman unfairly deprived of her birthright. (Power-playing the sympathy card, the filmmakers tell us that her parents were murdered because they supported the common man against the will of the royals. Yeah, right.) In short, in a conscious effort to make the character "good" and "likeable," the filmmakers bought into Jeanne's own con.

Consequently, instead of a subtle and brilliant schemer, we get Hilary Swank and all of the farm-girl sincerity that entails (authentic eighteenth-century courtesans would have eaten the poor thing alive). All she wants is to get back the stuff that is rightfully her stuff—the Valois home and hearth. True, she resorts to perfidy and deceit, but it's OK because her intentions are righteous and pure and all-American: give me back my stuff!

Ultimately, Hilary Swank's comptess learns a valuable lesson: stuff is important—especially my stuff—but it's not as important as love. Seriously. Watching the film, you can't help hoping for Glenn Close to suddenly appear out of nowhere, T. rex–style, and swallow Jeanne de Saint-Remy-La Motte-Valois and her 647 diamonds whole.

Elsewhere, the film takes lesser historical liberties. And to be fair, these are mostly palatable inaccuracies, because they represent reasonable dramatic choices. For instance, in the film Cagliostro is portrayed as a willing coconspirator in the diamond necklace scam. Sure, it's pure fiction, but when you cast Christopher Walken, you've got to use him. It's the law.

OK, one final nitpick: in *The Affair of the Necklace*, Walken wields the most ridiculous Europa-on-the-Hudson accent since Harvey Keitel spouted French-fried Brooklynese in *The Duellists*.

Sources and Further Reading

Erickson, Carolly. *To the Scaffold*. New York: William Morrow and
Company, Inc., 1991.

McCalman, Iain. *Count Cagliostro: Master of Magic in the Age of Reason*. New
York: HarperCollins, 2003.

MacKay, Charles. *Extraordinary Popular Delusions and the Madness of Crowds*.
Litrix Reading Room. http://www.litrix.com/madraven/madne001.htm.

Elizabeth (1998)

Directed by Shekhar Kapur

Written by Michael Hirst

Starring Cate Blanchett, Joseph Fiennes, and Geoffrey Rush

Cate Blanchett as Queen Elizabeth I.
Photo by Alex Bailey, © Gramercy Pictures

Queen Elizabeth I.

All hail England's Goode Queene Elizabeth the First, naive in the worldly ways of leadership—until one Francis Walsingham, fearless private secretary and cunning advisor, takes her by her porcelain hand and pulls her up to indisputable glory. That, at any rate, is the refurbished history offered in *Elizabeth*, a costume biopic that boldly sacrifices historical fidelity so that cinema romance might bloom.

If the genuine article had been anything like Cate Blanchett's girlish Elizabeth, she wouldn't have lasted longer than a fortnight (or whichever ye olde calendar notation ye prefer) in the treacherous political currents of sixteenth-century England. Unlike Blanchett's bewildered gamine, who is hopelessly seduced by boyfriend Robert Dudley moments after her fabulous coronation, only to learn later that the cad is already married—the real Elizabeth was a cunning little sylph quite skillful at looking out for number one.

She had to be. Surrounded by a surplus of ill-wishers—including, but not limited to, the Hapsburg Empire, France and Spain, an inimical Pope, various random assassins, a ballsy Scottish claimant to her throne, a paranoid older sister who might have executed her at the drop of a ruff, and a panoply of hostile dukes—only the shrewdest of young royals could have avoided the chopping block. Considering how the real Elizabeth not only survived such trying times, but positively *thrived* in them (and for decades), Blanchett's milquetoasty waif begins to look less like an homage and more like an insult.

In reality, most of the events depicted in *Elizabeth* occurred over the course of many years. The film compresses the same into a more manageable time span of several months. The real Elizabeth I was born in 1533 to the infamous Anne Boleyn, second wife of Henry VIII. By the time Liz was three, Henry had already sent Boleyn to the chopping block, dissatisfied with her inability to produce a son and convinced, in the inimitable fashion of the day, that a wench as seductive as she just had to be a witch. What ensued for Elizabeth was a childhood brimming with perfidy and intrigue. Loyalists to Henry's Catholic first wife (Catherine of Aragon) saw Elizabeth as an illegitimate heir with a genetic predisposition toward her mother's sluttish antics. Meanwhile, passionate Protestants, who sympathized with the late Boleyn, saw Elizabeth as the country's best hope against an ambitious Hapsburg Empire and a disapproving Vatican. Many fans encouraged young Liz to seize power and edge out her older half sister, the Catholic Mary, who herself took the throne in 1553.

Formative years like those tend to take their toll on maidenly innocence and naiveté. For decades the real Elizabeth managed to placate her Protestant supporters while assuaging her crazy, jealous Catholic big sister, thereby avoiding the chopping block. Even after Mary imprisoned Liz on suspicion of treason, the savvy girl knew enough to leave no empty spaces in her appeal letters, gaps into which her enemies might otherwise drop forged addenda implicating her in a fake plot. Elizabeth was also sensible enough to invent a saintly image for herself early on; she took to wearing sober black dresses and little to no makeup, an affectation cunningly calculated to bolster the image of a demure, (Catholic) God-fearing little sister who posed no threat to her elder sibling.

Quick sotto voce aside: Liz had jaundice during her sister's reign. If director Shekhar Kapur had wanted to make Blanchett look truly authentic in the film's early scenes, he would have made her yellow.

That was the Liz who finally inherited the throne in 1558: a slightly amber, whip-smart valedictorian in the ruthless school of sixteenth-century politics. Unlike the ill-informed Elizabeth portrayed by Blanchett, the real queen knew very well that her lover Dudley (Joseph Fiennes) was married. All of Europe knew that. The continental hoi polloi also knew of Liz's tryst with philanderer Dudley. The whole drama was such common knowledge that some kings refused to send their sons to Elizabeth's court, worried that the queen's cooings with a married man might reflect poorly on their own upright empires.

Some scholars have even suggested that the unfavorable gossip born of the affair might account for the mysterious death of Dudley's wife, Amy. In the autumn of 1560 Amy was found at the bottom of a flight of stairs, broken necked and quite dead. At the time of the ostensible accident, her house had been suspiciously empty of servants. Ambassadors to young Queen Elizabeth's court noted that when Her Majesty was apprised of the situation, she appeared to be somewhat less than shocked—and more than a trifle pleased at the "news." It was only after Dudley married *again*, in 1579, without the queen's say-so, that Liz got royally pissed. At that particular point in history, the queen ordered that Dudley be seized and sealed, as hermetically as possible, deep inside a Greenwich tower.

Delicate Queen Blanchett, on the other hand, often seems outmatched by the burdens of absolute power. When informed that the French are making *le mincemeat* of her soldiers in Scotland, rather than throwing down some sort of jewel-encrusted gauntlet, she appears to come down with a case of the vapors. True, the real Queen Liz was criticized in some quarters for failing to flatten the Gauls in short order, but there's no evidence that she quivered like a lily, either.

As for the chalk-faced Gloriana image that young Blanchett sports at the end of the film, biographies indicate that Elizabeth didn't turn to heavy cosmetics until much later, in her middle age.

And what of Walsingham (Geoffrey Rush), the mysterious power behind the young throne? As it turns out, Walsingham couldn't possibly have had anything to do with Elizabeth's early decisions, since he didn't become her principle secretary until more than a decade later.

And last, there's the sex question. Director Kapur stages a highly apocryphal deflowering scene in the queen's chambers, complete with blowing canopies and tittering maids peeking in through windows. Scholars have unearthed no solid evidence that England's "Virgin Queen" ever lost her maidenhead to Dudley or anybody else, though rumors of illicit lovemaking dogged her. For her part, lifelong bachelorette Elizabeth always claimed virgin status.

Sources and Further Reading

Art, Suzanne Strauss. *The Story of the Renaissance*. Lincoln, MA: Pemblewick Press, 1997.

Erickson, Carolly. *The First Elizabeth*. Summit Books, 1983.

This chapter was written by Leslie Gornstein.

Shakespeare in Love (1998)

Directed by John Madden
Written by Marc Norman and Tom Stoppard
Starring Joseph Fiennes and Gwyneth Paltrow

"We are such stuff as dreams are made on," quoth the immortal Bard, probably unaware that a faraway realm called Hollywood would one day proceed to dream up such stuff about *him* as to gross $289 million worldwide (not including the DVD and VHS aftermarket). *Shakespeare in Love*, the movie, did to Shakespeare, the actual guy, what Shakespeare, the greatest of all dead white authors, had already done to historical figures ranging from the various numbered Henrys to Julius Caesar: that is, it filled in the gaps (and "slow parts") of history with all manner of dramatic whatnot.

But unlike Shakespeare, who often had to work his poetic magic around the stubborn facts of well-documented history, the authors of *Shakespeare in Love* had the creative luxury of sheer ignorance. Quoth John Madden (the English director, not the Ace Hardware spokesman): "The point about Shakespeare's life is that nobody knows anything." Addeth screenwriter Marc Norman (the bard of *Breakout*, starring Charles Bronson, and *Cutthroat Island*): "The great thing about writing about Shakespeare is that everyone in the world knows him and there are about five facts."

From those five or so facts, Madden, Norman, and script-puncher-upper Tom Stoppard wove a tangled web of informed speculation and outright fiction, which ultimately became 1998's cleverest (and Oscar-hoggingest) film. *Shakespeare in Love* takes place in the year 1593, at the end of the playwright's so-called "lost years," the mysterious decade between his departure from Stratford-on-Avon and reappearance in London. Scholars have long puzzled over the dramatist's rather spectacular transformation during that period from "the gifted hack of *Two Gentlemen of Verona* into the towering poet of *Romeo and Juliet*," in the words of Shakespeare expert Stephen Greenblatt. (In fact, it was Greenblatt who steered Norman to the "lost years" when the screenwriter asked him "what in Shakespeare's life might make a good plot.")

Shakespeare in Love posits an ingenious fictional explanation for that transformation: struggling London dramatist Will Shakespeare (Joseph Fiennes) finds his muse in a beautiful young noblewoman of light-through-yonder-window radiance, Viola De Lesseps (Gwyneth Paltrow). Inspired by their passionate, but ultimately doomed romance (he being a common entertainer from the wrong side of the Thames), Will channels his exquisite pain into his work, resulting in the great Shakespearean love sonnets and the beautiful tragedy of *Romeo and Juliet*.

Of course, it's pure fiction. Viola is an invention of the screenwriters, as is her jealous fiancé, Lord Wessex (Colin Firth). Another fabrication is the notion that *Romeo and Juliet* might have been inspired by an actual romantic entanglement between its author and a fair-haired lady, replete with balcony scenes and a tragic ending. In fact, the real Shakespeare—regardless of whom he was sleeping with at the time—stole the plot for *Romeo and Juliet* from earlier works about a doomed couple named "Romeo" and "Juliet" that had first been published in Italy a century earlier.

Still, like Shakespeare's own plays, *Shakespeare in Love* is an ingenious contrivance that blends historical and fictional elements in a plausible fashion. For instance, many of the supporting characters do have real-life counterparts. Philip Henslowe (Geoffrey Rush) did in fact own and operate the economically troubled Rose Theatre, which produced some of Shakespeare's early works. Henslowe's theatrical rivals—the Burbage family—operated the Curtain Theater, which vied with the Rose for the works of Shakespeare and Christopher Marlowe, just as depicted in the movie. London thespians Richard Burbage (Martin Clunes) and Ned Alleyn (Ben Affleck) are based on actual Elizabethan stage hams. The aforementioned Marlowe (Rupert Everett) was a contemporary and acquaintance of Shakespeare who died in 1593 in a pub brawl. (Some scholars argue that Marlowe wrote some the plays attributed to Shakespeare.) The morbid kid who announces that his favorite part of *Romeo and Juliet* is the death scene is a reference to the London playwright John Webster who, in Shakespeare's later years, would author plays in the "Tragedy of Blood" horror genre. And of course, Queen Elizabeth (Judi Dench) was indeed a theater aficionado (although she never would have attended one of the common playhouses such as the Rose or the Curtain).

Shakespeare in Love is brimming with accurate references to the Elizabethan theatrical scene and to Shakespeare's works. Women actors were indeed forbidden from participating in theatrical productions, which resulted in the man-in-drag stagecraft depicted in the film. And the theaters of the era were indeed often closed because of the plague, forcing many companies to tour the provinces.

Other references in the film are satirical, including the running gag that has Shakespeare cribbing lines for his plays from real life. It's a wry nod to his penchant for borrowing plots from previous works of literature (a habit not limited to the Bard; in fact, refashioning oft-told tales was the custom of the day). In one scene, a street preacher delivers a jeremiad against the "ungodly" Rose and Curtain theaters. "A plague on both your houses!" he shrieks as young Will Shakespeare dashes by, making a mental note of the line that will later famously find its way into *Romeo and Juliet*. In another scene, when Shakespeare complains of writer's block, Christopher Marlowe suggests key plot elements for Will's work in progress, *Romeo and Ethel, the Pirate's Daughter*. Will gratefully takes his friend's sound advice to change Ethel to Juliet. It's a subtle literary joke—a reference to the contentious theory that Marlowe is the true author of some of Shakespeare's works. Those literary lagniappes were probably the contribution of Stoppard, a playwright and screenwriter whose knowledge of Shakespearean arcana was previously on display in *Rosencrantz and Guildenstern Are Dead*, his play and 1990 feature film.

Also sprinkled throughout *Shakespeare in Love* are a number of comical anachronisms satirizing modern show-biz conventions, including gags about Shakespeare seeing a medieval shrink (a strict Freudian, he times the session with an hourglass), crooked loan sharks becoming producers, merchandizing tie-ins (a souvenir mug on Will's desk is inscribed "A Present From Stratford-Upon-Avon"), and the lowly status of the writer in show business (when someone asks who Shakespeare is, producer Henslowe snaps, "Nobody—that's the author").

But hands down, the most entertaining factual revision in *Shakespeare in Love* has to be its willful misinterpretation of the Bard's famous Sonnet Number Eighteen ("Shall I compare thee to a Summer's day?"). In the film, lovestruck young Will composes the poem in honor of his fair-haired lady Viola. Yet according to Stephen Greenblatt, writing in the *New York Times*: "The trouble is that one of the few things that scholars know about Shakespeare, apart from real estate transactions, minor lawsuits, and the bequeathing of his second-best bed to his wife, is that this poem (No. 18 in the 1609 edition) is one of a group of 126 sonnets apparently written to a fair-haired, wealthy young man." In other words, there's a pretty good chance that Shakespeare would rather have aimed his poetic eye at the straight guy, Ben Affleck, before wasting his best verse on a breeder like Gwyneth.

Sources and Further Reading

Burnett, Mark Thornton and Ramona Wray, eds. *Shakespeare, Film, Fin de Siecle*. New York: St. Martin's Press, 2000.

Greenblatt, Stephen. "About That Romantic Sonnet . . . " *New York Times*, February 6, 1999.

Lyall, Sarah. "The Muse of Shakespeare Imagined as a Blonde." *New York Times*, December 13, 1998.

Sterngold, James. "Just Like Real Life? Well, Maybe a Little More Exciting; Scholars Get Cameo Roles as Film Consultants." *New York Times*, December 26, 1998.

Girl with a Pearl Earring (2003)

Directed by Peter Webber

Written by Olivia Hetreed

Starring Scarlett Johansson, Colin Firth, and Tom Wilkinson

Vermeer's *Girl With a Pearl Earring*.

There have been movies based on books, TV shows, video games, songs, and, as this book is evidence, true stories. But not many have been based on paintings. *Girl with a Pearl Earring* is, to be honest, based on a novel—but both the book and the film are inspired by a masterwork often referred to as "The Mona Lisa of the North." ("North" because the artist was seventeenth-century Dutch master Johannes Vermeer. "Mona Lisa" because this ethereally beautiful portrait of an enigmatic young woman is itself enigmatic, almost 350 years after its creation.)

Vermeer's a bit of a mystery, too. The Registry of Probate details of his life are known. Born in 1632, he died suddenly at the age of forty-three. His wife's postmortem declaration that "owing to the very great burden of his children,

331

having no means of his own, he had lapsed into such decay and decadence, which he had so taken to heart that, as if he had fallen into a frenzy, in a day or day and a half he had gone from being healthy to being dead," suggests that the financial pressures of supporting a family of fourteen, count 'em, fourteen, stressed him out to the point of total breakdown. In those days in the Netherlands, painting was more a commercial trade than a lofty artistic pursuit. As trades go, painting was a rough one, especially in economically depressed Holland of the mid-seventeenth century.

The fictional film gets that detail right—Vermeer is shown cranking out paintings for money, taking little personal interest in his subjects. In his lifetime, Vermeer was not famous. After his death, he dropped into obscurity for many years. He left behind no self-portrait, at least nothing identified as one, so today we don't even know what Vermeer looked like. The wild mane and stubbly goatee sported by Colin Firth, who plays Vermeer in the film, appears to be drawn from a character in Vermeer's painting *The Procuress*. Art historians guess that a bushy-haired gentleman off to the side in the image may be Vermeer.

The rest of the story is pure fabrication, created by author Tracy Chevalier one night while staring at a poster of the famous *Girl* painting in her bedroom. In her book and in the film (the screenplay of which was written by Olivia Hetreed), a young peasant girl named Griet (Scarlett Johansson) goes to work as a maid in Vermeer's teeming household. The mercurial painter takes a shine to her when she displays an instinctive understanding of light and color. She has an artist's eye. She's also a seventeenth-century hottie, which attracts the attention of Vermeer's wealthy patron, a dirty old sod named Pieter Van Ruijven (Tom Wilkinson). He attempts at one point to have his way with the yet-unspoiled Griet, but settles instead for a solo portrait of her, to be displayed only in his—*koff, koff!*— "private gallery." But when Vermeer's high-strung wife finds out that Vermeer has borrowed her beloved pearl earrings, which he lets his peasant model wear for the painting, Mrs. Vermeer blows a gasket.

Director Peter Webber and cinematographer Eduardo Serra have done an uncanny job of fashioning each frame as a "Vermeer" of its own, paying close attention to each detail of furniture or costume, its hue, and the play of light over it. The realism of the film lies exclusively in its visuals. Given how little is known about Vermeer, there is no reason not to fabricate a story about his most famous work. The true identity of the girl in the picture is anyone's guess. Vermeer never wrote down names of any of his models. The most popular theories are that the girl is Vermeer's own eldest daughter, Maria. But if the scholars who date the painting to 1665-ish are right, Maria would have been only about ten or eleven—too young for the girl in the painting, whose slightly parted lips give her a subtle erotic charge.

Others believe the model may have been Van Ruijven's daughter, but that's doubtful, too. In those days it was unlikely that a young woman of society would allow herself to be painted in the girl's highly informal outfit, much less with a Muslim-looking turban on her head. (However, if it was Magdalena Van Ruijven, that would certainly give a whole new twist to the movie's implication that Van Ruijven plans to use the painting as a masturbation vehicle.)

The historical Van Ruijven was the heir to a brewery fortune. Some scholars question if he ever purchased a painting directly from Vermeer (who painted only thirty-five in his career), much less served as his sole patron, as he does in the fictional screenplay. John Michael Montias, who has studied Vermeer since 1975 and authored the definitive book on the Dutch painter, is convinced that he did. Van Ruijven, says the author, bought Vermeer's paintings "year after year." That and a generous mother-in-law are all that kept Vermeer's head above the financial waterline. When Van Ruijven passed on to the great gallery in the sky, in the same year that the younger Vermeer dropped dead, he left a hefty art collection to his son-in-law. Among the inventory: twenty-one Vermeers. *Girl With a Pearl Earring* may or may not have been one of them. The paintings were auctioned off in 1696, and the rather vague descriptions of each are the only record of which paintings were included. The title *Girl With a Pearl Earring* was not affixed to the painting until sometime in the twentieth century. No one knows if Vermeer managed to sell the painting while he was alive.

The pearl earring that serves as the source of so much conflict in the film was, likely, a faux number that Vermeer kept in his studio. He used the same earring in eight other paintings, but none as renowned as the one haunting the canvas that, 340 years later, inspired a major motion picture.

Sources and Further Reading

Chevalier, Tracy. *Girl With a Pearl Earring*. New York: Plume Books, 2001.
Janson, Jonathan. The Essential Vermeer Web Site.
    http://essentialvermeer.20m.com.
Montias, John Michael. *Vermeer and His Milieu*. Princeton, NJ: Princeton
    University Press, 1989.

The Return of Martin Guerre (1982)

Directed by Daniel Vigne
Written by Jean Claude Carrière
Starring Gérard Depardieu and Nathalie Baye

Gérard Depardieu as Martin Guerre, apparently transported into the future, when leather bomber jackets will briefly be considered "cool."
© European International Distribution, Ltd.

Most sixteenth-century French peasants could barely read or write, so they didn't leave behind many records of their daily lives, or even of their extraordinary adventures. The literate aristocracy had little interest in recording the activities of the peasant population, either. Something really weird had to happen for peasants to get their historical due. And that's exactly why the 1982 French film *The Return of Martin Guerre* was able to depict events that transpired four hundred years earlier.

The really weird case of Martin Guerre was set into print by Jean de Coras, a well-known jurist who presided over the really weird trial that forms the basis of the story's plot. The strange case seems inconceivable today. A man walks out on his wife and disappears for eight years. He comes back and resumes his life with her for another three years—until he's exposed as an imposter.

Even after a split of eight years, it's hard to imagine that a wife who was married to a guy for a whole decade could mistake another man for her husband.

The film never explains how this could have happened, but it does make the strong suggestion that the woman, Bertrande de Rols, willfully fooled herself into believing that a total stranger was the man she married, Martin Guerre. Why? Because the original Martin was a cold, scolding, sexually impotent husband who stole from his own father, then abandoned his family. The new "Martin" was good-natured, loving, hardworking, and attentive.

Put yourself back in 1557 and you can see how someone could pull off an impersonation, given at least a passing resemblance between imposter and impostee. There were no photographs. Peasants had neither the time nor the money to sit for a portrait. Even mirrors were a luxury afforded only to the elite. Your average peasant didn't even know what his or her own face looked like. Eight years went a long way toward erasing memories when there was nothing to which those memories could be compared.

The ersatz Martin scammed an entire village, including his own wife, despite the fact that he was actually a roguish gambler, drinker, and womanizer named Arnaud du Tilh. Arnaud was also known as Pansette, "the Belly," in honor of his ample appetites for food, booze, and women. According to the storyline of Daniel Vigne's film, Arnaud and Martin met during war and Arnaud gleaned enough information from Martin to later engage in medieval identity theft. The fake Martin, played by France's top movie star of the 1980s, Gérard Depardieu, possesses an uncanny knowledge of Martin Guerre's personal life, down to its most intimate, and we do mean intimate, details.

The historical Arnaud, when he finally confessed, denied that he ever met Martin. According to historian Natalie Zemon-Davis, Arnaud stumbled across two men from Atrigan (Martin Guerre's hometown) while returning from the army. The men mistook him for their long-lost neighbor. Those two fed Arnaud many details of Martin's life (and may have later collaborated in his con). Arnaud augmented his knowledge with inquiries of his own. It took him three years to prepare for his arrival in Atrigan, where he would walk straight into the life formerly occupied by Martin Guerre.

The Return of Martin Guerre takes a few liberties with the facts of this unusual matter. In the film, Arnaud, as Martin, walks into town one day as if dropped from heaven. The real imposter stayed at a nearby inn under the name

Martin Guerre and let word of his presence filter back to Atrigan over a period of days. The trial of the phony Martin actually stretched over months, whereas in the film it takes only days, and both Bertrande and Martin's uncle Pierre—the imposter's chief accuser—were imprisoned during the trial. The movie also has Pierre Guerre and his sons ambushing "Martin" with farm implements. Pierre is poised to kill the suspected imposter with a sickle when Bertrande throws her body on top of her husband's, saving his life.

The real story is that Pierre Guerre did attempt to place a contract on the life of his bogus nephew, but there was no assault, and no last-second rescue by the devoted, if bamboozled, wife. The film also omits Bertrande's Protestant beliefs, which would have been a subject of major controversy in the mid-sixteenth century, and the real Martin's Basque origins. Arnaud exhibited none of Martin's Basque-born personality traits, and that was one cause for suspicion.

Those details aside, *The Return of Martin Guerre* follows Corass's account of the Martin Guerre case faithfully. Zemon-Davis acted as historical consultant to the film, which offers one of the cinema's most realistic reconstructions of everyday life in medieval Europe.

Sources and Further Reading

Zemon-Davis, Natalie. *The Return of Martin Guerre*. Cambridge: Harvard University Press, 1983.

Mutiny on the Bounty (1935)

Directed by Frank Lloyd
Written by Talbot Jennings, Jules Furthman, and Carey Wilson
Starring Charles Laughton and Clark Gable

Blame Charles Laughton for the second major black mark that hangs over the long and notable career of British naval officer William Bligh. The first smudge on the good captain's legacy was, of course, the infamous mutiny against him by eleven of his crewmen on the HMS *Bounty*. As a result of that notorious insurrection, an otherwise obscure eighteenth-century cargo ship sailed into history, and ultimately into half a dozen motion pictures involving peg legs and incomprehensible nautical jargon. Laughton's blustery performance in the 1935 version, *Mutiny on the Bounty*, set the standard for all future portrayals of Bligh. (A standard that has yet to be met: do you remember Trevor Howard's Bligh, or Anthony Hopkins's Bligh? No? And yet you probably do recall Bugs Bunny's impression of Laughton's Bligh, even if you've never seen the movie.) But Laughton's performance also gave the real Bligh a PR black eye he just doesn't deserve.

The MGM movie "explains" the mutiny as a response to Bligh's violence and corruption. In it, Laughton orders just about every salty punishment you've ever heard of in a seafaring movie, and then a few you haven't, from keel haulings and ritual lashings to more arcane tortures involving gunwales and ship's rigging. As if that weren't bad enough, he starves his men in order to steal from the ship's stores. At wit's end, Clark Gable's master's mate—Fletcher Christian—momentarily drops his "tennis, anyone?" cheer and turns against Bligh in a "that's all I can stands, I can't stands no more" movie moment. (This being a movie made in the United States, Gable's American accent underscores the justness of his actions against this sadistic, British-inflected tyrant.) Gable and his fellow mutineers wrest control of the *Bounty* and set Bligh and a handful of his loyal crewmen adrift in a longboat. (In reality, eighteen crewmen were banished to the boat with their ship's master, who, cinematic promotions to the contrary, then held the naval rank of lieutenant, not captain.)

Historians generally concur that, although Bligh was a strict disciplinarian who ran a tight ship, he was far from the vicious, physically violent despot portrayed by Laughton. In fact, statistically speaking, Bligh was *less* violent than his contemporaries in the British naval officer corps. Yes, someone has run the numbers: according to historical ship's records, Bligh flogged roughly 11 percent of the *Bounty* crew. Compare that to the itchy cat o' nine tails wielded by both Captains Cook and Vancouver, who dealt floggings to 26 percent and 53 percent of their crewmen, respectively. In light of Bligh's relative passivism, historians have always been a bit baffled about what motivated the *Bounty*'s mutineers.

Theories have been propounded. The standard explanation is the one that Bligh submitted to the naval authorities after his incredible four-thousand-mile voyage back to civilization: "Spoiled" by the exotic pleasures of Tahiti, his crew rebelled at the resumption of strict ship discipline. Or so goes the theory. A more recent hypothesis proposes that it was violence of another sort that turned the *Bounty* crew against its master: his acerbic tongue-lashings. In *Mr. Bligh's Bad Language*, author Greg Dening argues that Bligh's constant verbal abuse and his ability to get under the skin of his men turned the crew against him.

New Yorker magazine contributor Caroline Alexander amplified that thesis in her 2003 book *The Bounty*, casting Bligh as the hapless victim of three centuries of unfair PR spin. Yet in attempting to rehabilitate Bligh, Alexander probably overshot her landing—exaggerating the master's virtues and dumping the bulk of blame on Fletcher Christian, whom she depicts as a mentally unbalanced scoundrel. Alexander glosses over the ample evidence of Bligh's anger-management problems ("violent tornados of temper," in the words an officer under his command on a later voyage) and the fact that he made a career of fending off mutinies against himself: after the incident on the HMS *Bounty*, Bligh nearly incited a second mutiny during the open-boat voyage from Tofua to Timor; on his journey back to Tahiti to hunt down the *Bounty* mutineers, Bligh's officers accused him of acting despotically; in 1797 he endured yet another mutiny as captain of the HMS *Director*; and later in life, when he was governor of New South Wales, his managerial charms persuaded local settlers to oust him from office and imprison him for two years.

Nautically speaking, the good captain seemed to have a talent for hoisting himself by his own petard.

Sources and Further Reading

Alexander, Caroline. *The* Bounty: *The True Story of the Mutiny on the* Bounty. New York: Viking, 2003.

Barrow, John, Sir. *The Mutiny of the* Bounty. Boston: D. R. Godine, 1980.

Dening, Greg. *Mr. Bligh's Bad Language.* Cambridge: Cambridge University Press, 1994.

Scheller, William G. "Desperate Voyage." *National Geographic World,* August 1998.

Amistad (1997)

Directed by Steven Spielberg
Written by David Franzoni
Starring Morgan Freeman and Matthew McConaughey

Matthew McConaughey as lawyer Roger Baldwin.
Photo by Andrew Cooper, © DreamWorks LLC

Moviemakers take a lot of creative license with history. We get it. Movies have certain storytelling requirements that real life can't meet. Even a movie about a rather grave matter such as the practice of human slavery in the United States is going to tinker with the facts to make a better movie. Or at least a movie that people will pay nine bucks to see. Hollywood has a right to take a few liberties. They pay enough money to buy the rights to these stories, after all.

They have a right—until they send out thousands of "study guides" to schools around the country, pushing their movie as a teaching tool for kids. Usually when Hollywood gets slammed for fashioning fantasy out of fact, the response is, "Hey, lighten up! It's just a movie. You get your history lessons in school, not at the Galleria multiplex." But when you promote your movie not as light entertainment, but as primary source material, you change the rules.

Dreamworks studio mass-mailed just such a "study guide" for Spielberg's "true" slavery melodrama, *Amistad*.

The "Amistad incident" is certainly true and remarkable. If there had been such a place as Hollywood in 1839, this story was made for it. A group of fifty-three slaves being transported from one end of Cuba to the other on a small schooner broke free and took over the ship, killing their captors. They left just two Cubans alive—the two slave owners—to steer the ship back to Africa. They floated for two months, then landed (due to some sly navigation by the two Cubans) on Long Island.

At first, the forty-four remaining West Africans (several had died on the boat), most of them of the Mende tribe, were set to be tried for murder. The case quickly shifted to a question of property when the Spanish crown and the Cuban slave owners decided they wanted their valuable slaves back alive. After the "Amistad Africans" won emancipation in a lower court, the federal government, under President Martin Van Buren, appealed to the Supreme Court. There, after eloquent arguments on their behalf—not only by the prominent Connecticut attorney Roger Baldwin, but none other than former president John Quincy Adams, as well—and despite a court packed with justices from Dixie, the Supremes ruled once again in the Africans' favor.

It was not, however, a blow against slavery. The court ruled only that because these Africans were not born as slaves, they were nobody's property.

Spielberg got the bare bones of the story, as outlined above, correct. Along the way, however, he threw in a couple of oddly chosen fictional characters, twisted the personalities of a few real people, and, in the biggest head-scratcher of all, made a movie about abolishing slavery with barely a mention of abolitionists.

Abolitionism was a religious movement; specifically, an evangelical Christian movement. There's no question that the leading abolitionists were humanitarians, but at the same time, abolishing slavery was seen as a golden opportunity to create more Christians. In this parallel eighteenth-century universe-according-to-Spielberg, one leading historical abolitionist is shown as a secret bigot, another is not shown as an abolitionist at all, and a third, a Christian minister, is left out of the movie altogether, replaced by a secular character who has very few lines. There is almost no mention of the religious side of abolitionism in the movie, and Spielberg goes out of his way to discredit abolitionists as radical chic dilettantes, or worse.

The abolitionist movement is represented in *Amistad* by two characters: Lewis Tappan, a real person played by Swedish actor Stellan Skarsgård, and

Theodore Joadson, a made-up person played by African American actor Morgan Freeman. (It is significant to mention Freeman's race in this context, because there were actual black abolitionists who were involved in the *Amistad* case.)

Notable among them was Reverend James W. C. Pennington, an escaped slave turned evangelical minister and internationally prominent abolitionist. It should be noted that Pennington did not become involved in the *Amistad* case until after the Supreme Court ruling, when he helped organize the *"Amistad* Africans'" return home—but as long as we're fictionalizing, it would have been nice for Spielberg to call some attention to this noteworthy figure in African American history.

Instead, Spielberg ignored Pennington and subbed in his own fictional character. To add further insult to this, the Dreamworks-produced "study guide" suggests that teachers hold the character Joadson—a figment of the filmmaker's imagination—up as an example of black abolitionism. That would be absurd on its own, but it becomes even more bizarre when you watch the movie and see that Freeman's character has nothing to do except act disgusted about slavery and fascinated by real Africans. There's nothing there to study.

Why opt for a phony black abolitionist when there were real ones at the ready? Author Barbara Chase-Riboud thought she knew the answer. Screenwriter David Franzoni had, prior to writing the screenplay of *Amistad*, worked on an adaptation of her *Amistad*-based novel, *Echo of Lions*. Her book featured a fictional black abolitionist. She sued Dreamworks for plagiarism, seeking to block the release of the film. That petition was denied, obviously.

The film's other purely invented character is a youthful judge, who is supposed to be a secret Catholic, named Coglin. President Van Buren fires the first judge, Andrew Judson, and brings in Coglin, in an attempt to rig the case and thus preserve the Southern vote in upcoming elections. This is another senseless alteration by Spielberg et al. Judson was, in real life, very much against abolishing slavery. But he stuck with the trial to the end and ruled that the "Amistad Africans" were not legally slaves.

The Africans' lawyer, Baldwin, is portrayed as the nineteenth-century equivalent of an ambulance chaser (the Africans call him a "dung scraper") just out of law school. The real Baldwin was forty-six years old when he took the case, was a lawyer and abolitionist of considerable standing, and three years after the case, ran for governor of Connecticut and won. Baldwin's ideological commitment to abolishing slavery goes unmentioned. Instead, Spielberg has Matthew McConaughey play Baldwin as the clichéd cocky-kid-who-learns-a-lesson.

The abolitionist who first takes up the *Amistad* cause, Lewis Tappan, is shown contemplating a strategy that would allow the Africans to be executed, because they would be more valuable to the cause as "martyrs." Joadson immediately accuses Tappan, with what the audience is to take as the ring of truth, of secretly hating blacks.

That's a strange and disconcerting libel on the memory of a man who was not only a leading abolitionist, but also a powerful advocate for improved race relations. In that era, he was almost alone in his public approval of interracial marriage. There's no indication that Tappan was a secret bigot, even by the standards of the day.

When the "Amistad Africans" finally sailed back to their homeland, a contingent of evangelical missionaries went with them. It's not that abolitionists had a cynical ulterior motive—as far as their movement (a large segment of it, anyway) was concerned, freeing the slaves and converting them to Christianity were basically the same thing, and were all part of the same humanitarian mission. You couldn't have one without the other.

You'd never glean that little wrinkle from *Amistad*. But while the film dismisses Christianity, it treats exotic African religious traditions with reverence. In itself, that's a wonderful thing—except that it's just not history. Far from revering the Africans for the purity of their culture, the abolitionists did everything they could to "civilize"—that is, Christianize—them. In the film, ex-president Adams meets with the "Amistad Africans'" leader, Cinque, at Adams's Massachusetts home. The two apparently did meet, but not at Adams's home. It is highly doubtful that as a result of the meeting, Adams developed sympathy for the Mende belief in ancestral worship, as he does in the screenplay, incorporating the concept into his final summation at the Supreme Court.

Spielberg's thematic choice may be a supplication to some form of political correctness—or he may have felt that a story whose heroes are devout Christian evangelicals would come off as too square. The hip multicultural vibe of native African spirituality seems undeniably cooler. Either way, *Amistad* is a powerfully made film that purports to tell a true story of slavery, but in the end, it's just another whitewash.

Sources and Further Reading

Exploring *Amistad*. http://www.sun.ac.za/forlang/bergman/real/amistad/history/msp/main_wel.htm.

Paquette, Robert L. "From History to Hollywood: The Voyage of 'La Amistad.'" *New Criterion*, March 1998.

Rosen, Gary. "*Amistad* and the Abuse of History." *Commentary*, February 1998.

The Patriot (2000)

Directed by Roland Emmerich
Screenplay by Robert Rodat
Starring Mel Gibson, Heath Ledger, and Joely Richardson

Francis Marion, the "Swamp Fox."

Cinematically speaking, the problem with the American Revolution is that the British Redcoats make for rather milquetoasty villains. All that crisp adherence to battlefield etiquette and tediously mannered "rules of war." And not a death camp in sight. For modern filmgoers familiar with the ghoulish territory of real twentieth-century war atrocities, the bloody Redcoats seem about as sinister as a marching band with bayonets.

In *The Patriot*, a film that is loosely based on historical events involving powdered wigs and muskets, the solution to the tepid villain problem proved simple enough: fabricate! The filmmakers supersized the "taxation without representation" nasties with heinous acts that the real Brits never perpetrated. Acts like, oh, torching helpless civilians locked inside a church.

Of course, director Roland Emmerich may have been under pressure to top the villains of his previous blockbusters—the skyscraper-smashing *Godzilla* and the White House–thrashing aliens of *Independence Day*. So where's the harm in inventing a little prayer-house holocaust? And so what if that bogus blaze bears an uncanny resemblance to a notorious atrocity committed not by British soldiers in 1780, but by Nazi storm troopers in 1944? That was when the Waffen SS massacred almost 650 residents of a French village, Oradour sur Glane, gunning down men and boys, then burning alive 205 women and children in a locked church.

While most American filmgoers seemed to buy into the reinvention of imperial Redcoats—personified in the film by blue-eyed Colonel William Tavington—as the eighteenth-century equivalent of Nazis, latter-day Brits tended to take exception to this depiction. The film raised a few hackles in the English newspapers—to put it mildly. They ripped it as "racist," and British historian Andrew Roberts wrote, "With their own record of killing twelve million American Indians and supporting slavery for four decades after the British abolished it, Americans wish to project their historical guilt onto someone else."

But the movie—in spite of its debatable historical underpinnings—is essentially a vengeance actioner customized for Mel Gibson, who at the turn of the millennium seemed to have cornered the market on vengeance actioners. In *The Patriot*, Gibson's "haunted man with a past who has been wronged and reluctantly returns to the warpath" is Benjamin Martin, a character reportedly based on a number of historical figures. In the movie, Martin raises a ragtag militia of guerrilla fighters to battle the bloody British after the posh-accented Tavington kills his son in cold blood. As they say in Hollywood pitch meetings, "Now it's personal."

The chief inspiration for Gibson's Benjamin Martin character was Francis Marion, a revolutionary fighter who launched raids on British troops from his base of operations on Snow's Island, in the thick of the South Carolina swamps. Marion proved elusive to the British soldiers sent to end his operations, earning himself notoriety as the "Swamp Fox." In *The Patriot*, Benjamin Martin also sets up a base in the midst of the South Carolina swamps, and comes to be known as "the Ghost." In early versions of the story, screenwriter Robert Rodat (who also wrote *Saving Private Ryan*) had Francis Marion himself as the protagonist. Unfortunately, the real Marion had a few skeletons in his closet, including a reputation for not merely owning slaves, but treating them to beatings and rape, which proved unappealing to enlightened Hollywood storytellers, who wisely opted instead for a fictional hero who, we learn early on, has already freed his slaves.

But Francis Marion's actual life served as loose inspiration for another aspect of Gibson's character. In the film, Benjamin Martin is tormented by an atrocity from his past: a revenge massacre he led against Indians and Frenchmen during the French and Indian War. Real historical figure Francis Marion did in fact fight Indians during that war, and on one occasion led a thirty-man scouting party into a known Indian ambush. A violent melee ensued and only ten men survived, Marion being one of them. But the skirmish was no massacre, and there's no evidence that Marion was haunted by the incident later in life.

The film draws on a number of other historical figures for other aspects of the Benjamin Martin character, including Thomas Sumter, a rogue fighter who refused to coordinate with the Continental Army, and Daniel Morgan, a Continental officer. Morgan devised the clever idea of using the militia as a decoy at the Battle of Cowpens to lure the British forces into what appeared to be an easy rout. After firing two rounds, the militiamen were instructed to retreat behind the line of Continental regulars, a trick that prompted the British regulars to break rank in anticipation of a quick victory. The film has the Continental Army hidden behind a rise, and the militia's retreat is not part of the plan. But this gives Mel Gibson's character an opportunity to pick up a fallen flag and run toward the camera, all guts and glory, which, naturally, rallies his men, who then win the battle.

This being a Hollywood interpretation of an actual battle, Benjamin Martin vanquishes the chief British baddie, the aforementioned Colonel Tavington, thereby avenging the death of his sons (Tavington manages to up Gibson's vengeance motivation by killing yet another of Martin's sons in the second act). In real life, the historical figure on whom Tavington was based—Lt. Colonel Banastre Tarleton, a soldier known for his brutal battlefield tactics and aggressive zeal (although he never burned a church filled with people)—survived the Battle of Cowpens and eventually returned to England.

Alas, in real life villains rarely get their just desserts in a way that wins a war, founds a nation, frees slaves, banishes personal demons, and restores a nuclear family to its rightful happiness. God bless Hollywood!

Sources and Further Reading

The Patriot Resource. http://www.patriotresource.com.

Foreman, Jonathan. "The Nazis, er, the Redcoats are Coming!" *Salon*, July 3, 2000.

Gordon, Daphne. "Distortion of History 101," *Toronto Star*, June 30, 2000.

REEL NINE
Out of the Past

Titanic (1997)

Directed and written by James Cameron

Starring Leonardo DiCaprio and Kate Winslet

Leonardo DiCaprio and Kate Winslet as two completely fake passengers on the *Titanic.* © *Universal City Studios Inc.*

James Cameron turned the most famous disaster of all time into the most successful movie of all time—financially, if not artistically—with a take that topped a billion dollars. *Titanic* also netted director/producer Cameron Academy Awards for Best Director and Best Picture, which he celebrated with a notably narcissistic acceptance speech. When he bellowed, "I'm king of the world!" he moved straight into Sally Field territory for high-cringe Oscar moments.

We can't be too hard on Cameron, though. He worked on *Titanic* for two years, and with a staggering (even by 2005's standards) budget of two hundred million dollars, Cameron put pretty much all of his Hollywood cred on the line for this motion picture. It could have—and many expected it would—turn into his very own *Apocalypse Now*, except without even a very good movie to show for it.

Judged on the basics of film storytelling, *Titanic* comes across as rather run-of-the-mill. Cameron, who also scripted, followed the lead of a 1953 film also called *Titanic* and placed a fictional and frankly trite "wrong side of the tracks" love story into the Titanic tragedy. There was never a Jack Dawson (Leonardo DiCaprio) nor a Rose DeWitt Bukater (Kate Winslet). Rose's dastardly fiancé, played with all the subtlety of a silent movie mustache twirler by Billy Zane, is another figment of Cameron's fertile, if highly conventional, imagination.

These literary inventions, however, interact with a cast of historical figures who range from the *Titanic*'s architect, Thomas Andrews, to the millionaire socialite John Astor to the "Unsinkable" Molly Brown whose take-charge antics in the lifeboat made her an instant legend.

Cameron's research into *Titanic* history was voluminous, and it shows. The director did not confine his studies to the library, either. He made a dozen dives to the floor of the North Atlantic and filmed the wreckage of the great ship. Some of that footage turns up in the film's opening sequence, in which a present-day salvage team goes treasure hunting in the wreck, though some wreckage shots were simulated on a Mexican soundstage.

Its authentic period details pushes *Titanic* from cornball melodrama to memorable cinematic spectacle. Despite a few minor inaccuracies, the film is the closest any of us will ever come to the experience of sailing on the *Titanic* herself. Even some of the details Cameron assigns to his fictional characters did happen to real people. According to lore, the wealthy Astor was crushed to death in the water when one of the *Titanic*'s colossal smokestacks broke off and toppled on him. In the movie, Jack's Italian immigrant friend is the one who gets crushed. Same cause of death, opposite economic class. (It should be noted that there is some doubt as to whether the Astor-crushing anecdote is true.) Another example: one survivor was rescued while floating on a slab of wood panel, as is the movie's Rose.

The real, non—computer-generated *Titanic*.

There are two major incidents in the film that sparked historical controversy, where Cameron may have taken a few too many liberties. One involves the character known as William Murdoch, the ship's first officer. Murdoch was in command of the *Titanic* during the night of April 15, 1912, when the ship scraped an iceberg.

Cameron's reenactment of the accident follows an account pieced together from survivors' testimony (the British Board of Trade and the U.S. Congress both held hearings on the disaster), which is generally (though not universally) accepted by *Titanic*ophiles. In the film, Cameron shows Murdoch issuing his urgent and, in *Titanic* lore, legendary "hard a-starboard" command, trying to swing the ship around the iceberg to the left (in that era, a ship's helm spun starboard, or right, to make the ship turn port, i.e., left).

As with the Kennedy assassination, or any other "where were you when you heard the news?" piece of history, the exact sequence of events that brought down the *Titanic* has been analyzed and debated in minute detail. The discovery of *Titanic*'s wreckage in 1985 helped form a somewhat sharper picture. Cameron's blockbuster was the first *Titanic* movie (and there have been more than a dozen of them, both theatrical and made-for-TV, as well as a Broadway musical) to show the ship snapping in two as it sank, a long-held suspicion confirmed by the finding of two halves of the ship on the ocean floor, a half-mile apart.

Needless to say, however, not even the wreckage can yield secrets of what took place on the *Titanic's* deck that night. Some "revisionist" historians argue that Murdoch never issued the famous "hard a-starboard" order at all—or that, if he did, he followed it with a "port around" (a turn to the right) in an attempt to snake around the iceberg, and that's when the impact happened. Cameron adopts the conventional scenario, the same one seen in every other *Titanic* movie: that the ship scraped the iceberg on its right side while turning left.

According to historian David Brown, in his book *The Last Log of the Titanic*, "Not only did this not happen, but it could not have happened under any circumstances. A starboard bow sideswipe 'collision' while turning left was impossible for a conventional ship in 1912. (Nor can it be done today.) The manner in which rudder-steered ships pivot in the water does not allow the actual damage received by *Titanic's* bow to have occurred during a left turn. Iceberg damage to the starboard bow while turning to the left absolutely would have necessitated bumping and grinding of the ice along the ship's starboard side all the way to its stern."

Murdoch's orders, if in fact he gave them, amounted to a colossal blunder. A different strategy, they say, might have easily avoided the sideswiping collision, or at least lessened its impact so that fewer than five of the ship's compartments would have been flooded. The ship was called "unsinkable" (though that hyperbolic term came from the newspapers, not from the ship's makers) because it could stay afloat with four compartments flooded. No one envisioned a scenario where the flooding would spread beyond four. Or if they did, they tricked themselves into believing it was impossible.

Captain Edward John Smith must have been in a state of denial himself. He knew that *Titanic* was headed for a treacherous ice field; he'd been getting warnings all day. It wasn't as if the crew was blissfully unaware of the bumps ahead in the road. Ice was a major subject of conversation that evening, according to testimony at the *Titanic* hearings. They were on the lookout for icebergs. Unlike in the movie, when the deck is brightly lit in order to give us a good look at Leo and Kate smooching, Murdoch ordered everything in front of the bridge darkened so there wouldn't be any light pollution (as we'd call it today). Also at odds with the movie, in which the iceberg is plainly visible against a starry sky, is the fact that the North Atlantic night of April 15 was moonless and pitch-black. The ocean was calm, described as almost pond-like.

The killer berg was basically invisible.

Despite all of these hazardous circumstances, before Captain Smith hit the sack, he ordered that the ship keep barreling along at twenty-two knots, a rather brisk pace.

The ship was only about five hundred yards away from the iceberg when the lookouts rang the emergency bell. It would have helped if they'd had binoculars. Cameron got that detail right.

Cameron doesn't assign much blame to Smith in the movie. It's Murdoch who gets the raw deal—so raw, in fact, that representatives from Murdoch's hometown in Scotland demanded and received an apology. Murdoch, in his hometown and pretty much everywhere else, was thought of as a hero who (though he may have made mistakes in trying to miss the berg) performed admirably in directing passengers into lifeboats, saving dozens of lives while giving up his own.

Quite contrary to the prevailing view, Cameron chooses to show Murdoch utterly losing his marbles as the ship goes down. The onscreen Murdoch shoots two men trying to push their way into a lifeboat—then he blows his own brains out.

Cameron's historical consultant Don Lynch said there was no evidence that Murdoch concluded his evening with a murder-suicide nightcap, and he has said that he urged Cameron not to use the scene, although he has noted that Cameron "didn't intend it to reflect badly on the Murdoch family." An official studio apology followed, along with an eight-thousand-dollar donation to a Murdoch memorial fund in the maligned first officer's hometown. Cameron defended his version of the Murdoch scene later, saying, "He's accepting full responsibility for the chaos around him. Murdoch was an honorable man who felt the burden of responsibility for the deaths which were to come." Did Cameron, perhaps thinking he was not only king of the world, but God as well, blithely invent the suicide scene to make a point?

A CBS TV movie broadcast a year earlier had Murdoch killing himself, and a passenger, too. A number of witnesses said they saw an officer commit suicide as the *Titanic* neared its final moments above water. Some identified the officer as Murdoch; others weren't sure. Other survivors said they'd heard shots, but didn't see what had happened. There were also reports of an officer who fired on passengers who tried to storm lifeboats. At the time when the suicide would have occurred—if it did—there were only two officers whose locations remain uncertain. One is Chief Officer Henry Wilde. The other is Murdoch.

If one of them did indeed commit suicide, the consensus leans toward it having been Murdoch, largely because he had the supposed motive—guilt over his hard a-starboard screwup. Whatever the truth, Murdoch's body was never found (only 378 bodies out of about 1,500 were). So we'll never know if he shot himself—and we will certainly never know what went on in his mind and his conscience.

The other questionable Cameron interpolation concerns the third-class passengers. As their cabin floods with water, the ship's crew locks the low-paying passengers behind steel gates, sealing them in steerage and sealing their fates.

Again, Cameron did not just make this up, though a certain kind of class struggle does seem to be one of his preoccupations in the film. The rich, first-class passengers are shown to be stuffy at best, and outright evil at worst—except for Rose, who gives an "up yours" to the upper class by falling for the broke, vagabond artist Jack and befriending his salt-of-the-earth pals in steerage, who dance and drink with gusto because they live for the moment, or something like that.

As with the alleged officer suicide, there were witness reports, albeit of uncertain veracity, that the steerage passengers were imprisoned below decks when the crisis hit. Was Cameron trying to make a political point by going with that grim version of events? Maybe, but the locked gates also made for a perfect plot device. As the ship fills with water, our made-up hero and heroine are, you guessed it, trapped in steerage! They're locked in, with the rest of the rabble. Will they escape in time? The suspense!

The facts are that a greater percentage of third-class passengers lost their lives than those of any other class—and a smaller percentage of their bodies were recovered, suggesting that more of them were inside the ship when it went down. Maybe they were locked in there. Or maybe they just had a harder time getting up to the deck. They had a longer way to go.

The gates on the *Titanic* were real, as they were on all commercial passenger ships of the era. Immigrants were the cash cow of shipping lines at the turn of the century. Even super-luxurious ships like the *Titanic* and its predecessor, the *Olympic*, made most of their money not off the snooty rich, but off the people who scraped together just enough for a ticket that bore their dreams for the New World. Problem was, immigrants carried lots of diseases, or so it was believed. The locked cages served as quarantines.

So *what* if Cameron "Hollywood-ized" the story of the *Titanic*, anyway? Nothing could be more "Hollywood" than the first *Titanic* movie ever made. Incredibly, the silent one-reeler *Saved from the* Titanic was shot and released less than *one month* after the *Titanic* sank. The leading lady was Dorothy Gibson, herself a survivor of the *Titanic*, who wasted no time cashing in on the tragedy.

Sources and Further Reading

Bill Wormstedt's *Titanic*. http://home.att.net/~wormstedt/titanic/.

Brown, David. *The Last Log of the* Titanic. Camden, ME: *International Marine*, 2001.

Encyclopedia Titanica. http://www.encyclopedia-titanica.org.

"Murdoch: The Man, the Mystery." http://www.geocities.com/murdochmystery/.

Gangs of New York (2002)

Directed by Martin Scorsese
Written by Jay Cocks, Steven Zaillian, and
Kenneth Lonergan
Starring Leonardo DiCaprio and Daniel Day-Lewis

Daniel Day-Lewis as William "Bill the Butcher" Cutting. © *Miramax Films*

The murder of Bill "the Butcher" Poole in 1855.

When the first edition of Herbert Asbury's *The Gangs of New York* rolled off the presses in 1927, the feisty criminal demimonde it chronicled had long since passed into the realm of what you might call "heightened memory." The high-stepping thugs who had rumbled and ransacked half a century earlier in the immigrant slums of lower Manhattan's Five Points district (the original bad New York neighborhood) had already gone the way of the plug hat and bare-knuckled pugilism. But they lived on, somewhat larger and rowdier than actual size, through the literary graces of newspapermen such as Asbury, who cheerfully dispensed that all-American brand of pulp journalism that had previously engorged the myth of the Wild West.

Asbury made no bones about it: the "genteel thugs" of his own era couldn't hold a candle to the brawling "old-timers" of Five Points, in large part because the original gangsters had been "touched by the magic finger of legend." That proviso dutifully dispensed, Asbury was off without further apology on a picaresque tramp through the impossibly crooked alleys of wicked old New York to catalog the teeming criminal fauna.

There were swaggering gangs by the dozens, including the colorfully named Dead Rabbits, the Roach Guards, the Gophers, the Swamp Angels, the Forty Thieves, the Daybreak Boys, the Shirttails, and the Plug Uglies. They battled in stovepipe hats and frock coats, armed to the teeth with knives, cudgels, pistols, and—more quaintly—slingshots and brickbats. The individual personalities were almost elemental: Hellcat Maggie, who filed her teeth to points and wore brass fingernails, the better to gouge eyeballs in street brawls; Kit Burns, who was only too happy to bite the head off a live rat; and the legendary Mose, the Bowery Boy chieftain who stood "at least eight feet tall" and clobbered foes with "the strength of ten men," we're told.

Down through the years, readers lucky enough to stumble upon a dog-eared copy of Asbury's book were treated to a slice of lurid Americana, a literary genre wedged somewhere between urban history and tall tale.

One of those readers was Martin Scorsese, who happened upon the book in 1970. *The Gangs of New York* struck a chord with the future director of *Mean Streets*, *Taxi Driver*, and *Goodfellas*, for obvious reasons. No film director has bettered Scorsese when it comes to capturing New York's gritty underside and the blind-alley shock of its sudden, unpredictable violence. In many ways Asbury's book seemed tailor-made for the Scorsese treatment—not least in its expressionistic sweep of its mayhem and carnage.

It would take Scorsese more than three decades to translate Asbury's catalog of nineteenth-century urban vice into a sprawling cinematic epic. In addition to the considerable challenge of extracting a narrative from Asbury's anecdotal reporting, there were other well-publicized obstacles, including battles with producer/art-house pugilist Harvey Weinstein over budget and running time. When *Gangs of New York*—the movie—finally premiered in 2002, its production costs had exceeded $110 million (Scorsese had ponied up $6 million of his own salary to cover budget overruns) and its running time weighed in at an epic two hours and forty-nine minutes.

Critics were quick to quibble with the film's historical details and, of course, Scorsese's reliance on Asbury's "unreliable" reporting. But as Scorsese himself pointed out, "The film is not historical documentary. The film is an opera." Indeed, like many artists before him, Scorsese had reinterpreted his source material, deploying it as a backdrop for Big Themes of his own—in this case, the birth of a dynamic American city in a crucible of violence and struggle, punctuated by "acts of fearsome spectacle." (In contrast, Asbury's stated purpose was relatively modest: "To chronicle the more spectacular exploits of the refractory citizen who was a dangerous nuisance in New York for almost a hundred years.") The actual narrative that Scorsese and screenwriter Jay Cocks built atop Asbury's historical foundation is a fairly conventional Hollywood tale of revenge. The film opens as the Irish immigrant members of the Dead Rabbits gang, led by Liam Neeson's Priest Vallon, prepare to battle their archrivals, an anti-immigrant gang called the Native Americans. The battle is soon underway in the streets of Five Points, as the gangs engage in a surreal, tribal, almost balletic bloodletting driven less by explicit gore than by trick camera work and a polyrhythmic Peter Gabriel on the soundtrack.

Thus, the film's premise is set when the ruthless leader of the Natives, William "Bill the Butcher" Cutting (played by a bat-shit-crazy Daniel Day-Lewis), slays Vallon and takes control of Five Points. Cutting spares Vallon's young son, who in this scene is portrayed by a child actor, but who grows up, in a thankless lap dissolve to become a vengeance-seeking, but nonetheless charming, Leo DiCaprio. The plot thickens as DiCaprio returns to Five Points, bluffing, scrapping, and—yes—charming his way into the Natives gang, where he becomes a surrogate son to the Man He Must Kill.

For history buffs keeping a scorecard, Scorsese plays fast and loose with certain historical details. Although the Dead Rabbits and the Native Americans were dominant gangs in lower Manhattan during the mid-nineteenth century, they never battled over the Five Points turf, which belonged to the Irish immigrants who packed its filthy tenements (the district was built atop a fetid swamp). The Natives were based in the Bowery; an immigrant-hater like Day-Lewis's Cutting wouldn't have lasted a night in Five Points.

The Neeson and DiCaprio characters are pure fiction, but Cutting is based on two actual persons. The first was a Native gang leader named Bill "the Butcher" Poole, described by Asbury as a "champion brawler and eye-gouger." Like many a gangster of the day, Poole threw his lot in with a political party—in this case, the immigrant-bashing Know Nothings—who used the gangs as enforcers, especially to intimidate voters and fix ballots on election day. Poole was murdered (eight years before the film's composite character Cutting bites the dust) by associates of a political operative and thug who had fought with Poole earlier in the evening. Though he was shot in the gut, he lived on for another week, long enough to offer his famous, possibly apocryphal, parting words, "Good-bye boys: I die a true American." In the film, Day-Lewis offers this death-scene epitaph to DiCaprio, but here it's loaded with symbolic import that goes beyond the obvious reference to the name of his gang. Namely, it underscores Scorsese's central theme that violence and corruption are integral to, and inseparable from, the American urban experience. Earlier in the movie, Cutting literally wraps himself in the American flag to lecture DiCaprio's Amsterdam Vallon on the role of violence and intimidation on the streets and in the American political system: "Fear," he says. "That's what preserves the order of things."

The other historical figure that inspired the Cutting character was a roguish politician named Captain Isaiah Rynders. A former pistol-and-knife fighter, Rynders went on to marshal Five Points gangsters to the bidding of Tamanny Hall. However, unlike the Irish-despising Cutting, Rynders was a regular "Eierphile," which enabled him to exert control over the gangs of Five Points. (In the film, Cutting wrests control of Five Points by slaying the leader of the Dead Rabbits.)

Scorsese's major departure from historical accuracy arrives at the film's climax, in his depiction of the Draft Riots of 1863, the most violent civil uprising in American history. The Draft Riots ignited after President Lincoln ordered the implementation of a military draft to fortify Union troops in the midst of the Civil War. The well-to-do could avoid military service by paying a three-hundred-dollar fee, which enraged New York's lower classes—mostly Irish immigrants, who began the six-day uprising with an attack on a local army draft office. That much, the movie depicts accurately. But Scorsese downplays the other major factor that drove the working classes to the streets: racism against blacks, along with empathy for the policies and slave economy of the Confederate South. To his credit, Scorsese depicts some of the mob lynchings of African Americans, but in reality the atrocities were far more numerous and brutal, and they were central to the uprising. (At one low point in the week of violence, the mob burned an orphanage for black children to the ground.)

The Draft Riots lasted nearly a full week, and were quashed only after the Union Army began firing on New Yorkers. The movie gets that right, but adds the dramatic embellishment of navy ships firing on the haywire landlubbers (that never happened).

What Scorsese gets right is the look and feel of the Five Points slums and its underground economies of vice. Here, his historical detailing is spot-on, and his cost overruns clearly paid off: the alleys are perfectly crooked, the subterranean basements properly hellish, the ramshackle tenements ready to collapse, the archaic weaponry ready to fly, Hellcat Maggie poised to gouge eyeballs. The devil—not to mention the fun—is in the details.

Sources and Further Reading

Anbinder, Tyler. *Five Points: The 19th-Century New York City Neighborhood That Invented Tap Dance, Stole Elections, and Became the World's Most Notorious Slum.* New York: Free Press, 2001.

Asbury, Herbert. *The Gangs of New York: An Informal History of the Underworld.* New York: Thunder's Mouth Press, 1927.

Sante, Luc. *Low Life: Lures and Snares of Old New York.* New York: Farrar Straus Giroux, 1991.

Jeremiah Johnson (1972)

Directed by Sidney Pollack
Written by John Milius and Edward Anhalt
Starring Robert Redford

Robert Redford as Jeremiah Johnson. © *Warner Bros. Inc.*

When Hollywood adapts a true story for the big screen, the result is usually—
and necessarily—larger than life. *Jeremiah Johnson* is an odd exception. In the
sensitive hands of star Robert Redford and director Sidney Pollack, the true
story of "Liver-Eatin' Johnson," an Indian-slaying cannibal who cut (and ate)
a bloody swath through the Rocky Mountains, has been drained of its san-
guinary gusto. Not only is the film version devoid of liver-eatin', there's no cannibalism to speak of, and nary a bloody scalping to be had in its brief, but
leisurely, 108-minute run time.

That's not to say that the movie doesn't succeed on its own terms. An epic
fable of man and nature, filmed on location in the spectacular mountains of
Utah, the film resonates with a quiet majesty. But *Jeremiah Johnson* is more a
product of Hollywood circa 1972—when ecology and antiwar pacifism topped
the liberal agenda—than of its chief literary source material—a lively little book
called *Crow Killer: The Saga of Liver-Eating Johnson*, by Raymond W. Thorp and

Robert Bunker. (The film also credits *Mountain Man*, a Vardis Fisher novel loosely based on Johnson's exploits.)

In *Crow Killer*, Thorp and Bunker compiled the oral legend of John Johnson, a real nineteenth-century figure regarded as the fiercest and, in many ways, strangest of the mountain men who trapped in the Rockies. Early last century, Old West historian Thorp interviewed many of Johnson's contemporaries; Western author Bunker later compiled those accounts in narrative form. As with any yarn, the tale grew with each telling, and by the time Thorp had it down on paper, its foundations were already firmly planted in that historical nether region where fact and mythology blur together. With good reason, the epic story has been called "America's Beowulf."

The opening lines of *Crow Killer* leave no doubt as to the kind of tale it is: "One May morning in 1847, Crow Indians killed and scalped John Johnson's pregnant wife; for many years thereafter, he killed and scalped Crow Indians. Then he ate their livers, raw."

In the course of his decades-long "death trail," Johnson would kill three hundred Crow braves, taking as many scalps and eating as many livers.

As an archetypical tale of vengeance, the saga of Liver-Eatin' Johnson would seem tailor-made for a high-spirited Hollywood treatment. Indeed, had it been made ten years later, after the *Rambo* films brought "revenge cinema" into high vogue, the film might well have borne a closer resemblance to its inspiration. As it is, though, Redford et al opted to "noble up" the source material, in part by de-emphasizing the central revenge theme, eliminating the unpleasant gore (and flesh eating), and even giving the protagonist a more august-sounding first name.

The movie and book both follow the same basic outline: Johnson—the strong, brooding type—sets out to avenge his Indian bride's death by tracking down the Crow braves who killed her. The film version gives the Crow warriors a semi-justifiable motivation for the initial atrocity: they murder Johnson's squaw after he trespasses on their sacred burial land. In reality, the slaughter of the girl—the daughter of a local tribal subchief—had no motive behind it other than the self-glorification of a band of young Crow braves. According to the account set down in *Crow Killer*, Johnson's beautiful wife ("The Swan") was pregnant with the mountain man's child at the time of her death. Upon returning to his isolated cabin after a long winter of trapping, Johnson found buzzards picking at the skulls of both his wife and his unborn baby.

The real John "Liver-Eatin'" Johnson,
circa 1880. *Courtesy of Dorman Nelson*

The real Johnson apparently took to his bloody mission with some relish—you don't slaughter and eat the livers of three hundred Indian braves without enjoying your work on some level. Of course, in the cinematic version the peaceable Redford succumbs only to an initial rampage. Sating his taste for vengeance after slaughtering the Crows responsible for Swan's murder, it's left to the Crows to initiate the subsequent ambushes.

As word of the real Johnson's vendetta—and taste for liver—spread throughout the Rockies, the Crow Indians west of the Continental Divide did in fact set about retaliating. Their chief, Big Robert, ordered twenty of his best braves to track down and kill Johnson, whom Native Americans were by then calling *Dapiek Absaroka*: "Killer of Crows." (The more prosaic mountain men of the area gave him his other epithet, "Liver-Eatin' Johnson.") Because tribal honor forbade sending more than one brave at a time after a single enemy, Big

Robert ordered the twenty assassins to take separate trails, and not return until one of them finished the job. None of them ever did.

To be fair to Redford and company, the outsize legend of John Johnson might very well be too large for literal translation to the big screen. The man, as he was later described by those who knew him, would not be out of place in a modern superhero comic. Red-bearded, standing six-foot-two "in his stocking feet" and weighing 250 pounds, Johnson was a bare-knuckled killer who could choke a grown man with one massive hand, and (as he did more frequently) dispatch a foe with a lethal kick to the head. That was his preferred technique for sending Crows to their maker. Then, as always, "he snapped off the scalp, he carved under the ribs, he ate the dripping liver."

Why the historical Johnson insisted on this gruesome ritual remains a mystery; not even the trappers who knew him as well as one can be expected to know a walking cipher ever offered an explanation for that. But the ghastly practice certainly augmented his legend and put a shiver through the spines (and probably the internal organs) of his Crow enemies.

Of course, the film version steers as wide a berth around such messy details as the space that strangers must have given the real Johnson on his infrequent visits into local towns to sell scalps and buy supplies.

Not surprisingly, Hollywood's liver-abstaining version of the Johnson tale excised another grisly episode that has at least some basis in truth. In the winter of 1861, Johnson embarked on a five-hundred-mile trek to sell whiskey to the Flatheads. Two hundred miles into his journey, the Crow Killer was captured by Blackfoot Indians, who intended to sell him to his Crow enemies for a handsome bounty.

Of course, you can't keep a good Liver Eater down. In the middle of the night, the story goes, Johnson snapped free of his bonds, drop-kicked his whiskey-lubricated guard, and scalped the unconscious brave. Then, using his Bowie knife to expert effect, he carved the Indian's leg off at the hip and draped the bloody limb over his shoulder. Escaping into the night wearing only his buckskin pants (the Indians took his shirt), he then loped, on foot, two hundred miles through a furious blizzard, gnawing on the Indian's leg for sustenance. Wait—it gets better. Hiding out in a cave one night, Johnson lit a campfire to thaw himself and warm his frozen take-out meal. When a mountain lion entered the cave uninvited for a snack of roast Indian leg, Johnson used the disputed vittles (thankfully, still mostly frozen) to beat the big cat into submission. That commotion apparently roused a sleeping bear in the back of the cave, and Johnson once again shook a leg, dispatching the outmatched bear whimpering back to its lair.

The sight of Redford wildly swinging a human leg would probably have been too much for audiences to take, even those who made it all the way through *The Way We Were*. So the filmmakers were probably wise to omit this scene from their version of the Crow Killer saga. (However, that scene might work extremely well in a remake starring The Rock.)

Though the purportedly true story of Liver Eatin' Johnson only vaguely resembles the Hollywood version, in a weird way, the real Johnson and his cinematic stand-in each wound up where the other one started. Redford long ago fled Tinseltown for the wild, open spaces of Utah. And the bones of John Johnson, the mighty mountain man who ate three hundred Crow livers, now reside in a California grave several miles west of Hollywood.

Sources and Further Reading

Askenasy, Hans. *Cannibalism: From Sacrifice to Survival.* Amherst, NY: Prometheus Books, 1994.

McLoughlin, Denis. *Wild and Woolly.* Garden City, NY: Doubleday & Co., 1975.

Thorp, Raymond W. and Robert Bunker. *Crow Killer: The Saga of Liver-Eating Johnson.* Bloomington, IN: Indiana University Press, 1983.

The Last Emperor (1987)

Directed by Bernardo Bertolucci
Written by Mark Peploe and Bernardo Bertolucci
Starring John Lone and Joan Chen

John Lone (first row, center) as puppet emperor Pu Yi.
© Columbia Pictures Industries, Inc.

The sorry saga of Henry Aisin-Gioro Pu Yi, the last emperor of China, isn't exactly what you'd call a natural fit for the epic film format. Known as the "puppet emperor" and "imperial weakling," Pu Yi acceded to the throne at age three, only to be deposed before he hit puberty. Raised as a pampered prisoner behind the walls of Beijing's Forbidden City, Pu Yi spent the rest of his life serving as the willing tool of whichever government happened to be lording over China at the moment. When the Japanese invaded Manchuria and rechristened it Manchukuo, Pu Yi eagerly signed on to be its quisling emperor. After World War II, he became the hapless pawn of Maoist propagandists aiming to "rehabilitate" (i.e., brainwash) the former boy emperor into a shining example of a humbled communist worker. Passive, inert, and malleable, Pu Yi bears a closer kinship to Woody Allen's Zelig or Peter Sellers's Chance the Gardener than to Lawrence of Arabia, Spartacus, or any other epic hero of Cinemascope proportions.

Translating Pu Yi's story to the big screen as anything other than a tragicomedy about an "impotentate" who rises to his level of incompetence poses obvious problems. In *The Last Emperor*, director Bernardo Bertolucci opted not to deal with those problems. Instead, he frames a traditional movie epic around a decidedly un-epic personality, essentially filming *around* the paradox at the heart of his film. As if to compensate for the void at the center of the story, each frame of the movie is filled with rich sensory details—from the lavish costumes to the lush musical score to the striking vistas of the actual Forbidden City, where the Chinese government gave Bertolucci unprecedented permission to film. As a result, the movie often feels more like a wide-screen travelogue than a poignant tragedy writ large. (That was enough to satisfy Hollywood; *The Last Emperor* earned a record nine Oscars, including awards for Best Picture and Best Director.)

Bertolucci's cooperation with the Chinese government may have limited his thematic options. Pu Yi's final useful role had been as a public symbol of neutered imperialism. That was the point of his alleged "autobiography," *From Emperor to Citizen*, which was in fact written by a committee of communist party propagandists. Not only is *The Last Emperor* based on that book, but the shooting script was officially sanctioned by the Chinese government, as well. That may explain the movie's most controversial feature: its generally positive depiction of the Manchurian prison camp where Pu Yi was "remolded" into a productive communist worker. In the film, the camp is a clean-yet-austere facility governed by guards and interrogators of the firm-but-fair school. During their free time prisoners quietly study or achieve relaxation through tai chi. Pu Yi is encouraged to write a truthful "confession," suggesting, as one critic later noted, that Maoist "reeducation was a kind of psychotherapy."

In fact, those who actually visited the northern prison camps during the mid-twentieth century described a vastly different picture—one of brutal living conditions, hard labor, starvation, torture, summary executions, and brainwashing (hence the famous term, "Manchurian candidate"). One survivor of the camps (few were ever released, despite their supposed successful "reeducation") wrote that he lived "often in abject misery, sometimes literally starving and always haunted by hunger."

Although it's possible that Pu Yi received better treatment than the majority of inmates (after all, he was being groomed to become a useful public symbol), the outcome of his incarceration was no less shattering. According to Lucien Bodard, a French novelist and former journalist who interviewed Pu Yi during his stay at the Manchurian prison camp, the ex-emperor had been reduced to a "crushed convert," who was "pale-faced and sweating," "quaking with fear." Writing in *Encounter* magazine shortly after the release of *The Last Emperor*, Bodard recalled that Pu Yi, "his brain well and truly washed," had given the interview "wallowing in humiliation, just as his 'reeducators' (who were looking on) wished him to do." Reciting a "catalogue of misdeeds," Pu Yi offered that "he would be equally happy, whether the masses called for his death or whether they pardoned him."

That image is a far cry from the hale and hardy Pu Yi in the film, who leaves the prison (thanks to a rare pardon by Chairman Mao himself) in perfect emotional condition, happy to restart his life as a lowly gardener.

Some critics pointed to Bertolucci's own political leanings—he is a long-time Marxist—in an effort to account for the director's glossing over of the harsh realities of the prison camps. Much ado was made of Bertolucci's coproduction agreement with the Chinese government, which he signed as "Bernardo Bertolucci, member of the Italian Communist Party." Of course, a smart communist doesn't need a degree from the London School of Economics to realize that sucking up can be good for business.

Bertolucci's other major departure from historicity might also be related to politics. Nowhere in Pu Yi's official "autobiography" is mention made of what historians politely call the emperor's "ambiguous sexuality." Yet according to several biographers, the ex-emperor was either bisexual or homosexual. Pu Yi's sister-in-law once claimed that "the Emperor had an unnatural love for a pageboy. He was referred to as the male concubine." A 2001 tell-all biography that became a bestseller in China added a few details: the paramour was a boy eunuch with "red lips and white teeth" with whom Pu Yi had "out-of-the-ordinary relations." (And, as if "white teeth" weren't already scandalous enough, the biography added that Pu Yi had taken hormone shots to cure impotence.)

Bertolucci steers a wide berth around the commonly known factoid that Pu Yi probably did more than his share of lording over his retinue of eunuchs. Bertolucci portrays Pu Yi as a ladies' man who beds his two wives at the same time. When asked backstage at the Oscars why he left out the gay angle, Bertolucci reportedly snapped, "It would have opened up a whole new can of worms." Many critics assumed that Bertolucci had ix-nayed the royal gayness so as not to offend his Chinese hosts. Of course, there may be a more commerce-friendly explanation: after a string of box-office flops, Bertolucci needed a big hit. It's just as likely that the director was concerned about placating the homophobic Cineplex-going mandarins of middle America.

Sources and Further Reading

Behr, Edward. *The Last Emperor*. New York: Bantam Books, 1987.

Bernstein, Richard. "Is *The Last Emperor* Truth or Propaganda?" *New York Times*, May 8, 1988.

Brackman, Arnold C. *The Prisoner of Peking*. New York: Van Nostrand Reinhold, 1980.

Chu, Henry. "The Last Emperor Is Raked Over the Coals Again." *Los Angeles Times*, May 9, 2001.

Pu Yi, Henry. *From Emperor to Citizen: The Autobiography of Aisin-Gioro Pu Yi*. New York: Oxford University Press, 1987.

Sanello, Frank. *Reel v. Real: How Hollywood Turns Fact Into Fiction*. New York: Taylor Trade Publishing, 2003.

Lawrence of Arabia (1962)

Directed by David Lean
Screenplay by Robert Bolt and Michael Wilson
Starring Peter O'Toole and Omar Sharif

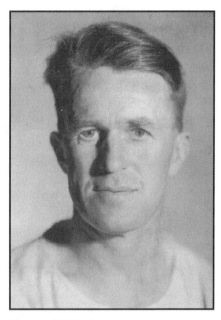

Peter O'Toole as T. E. Lawrence.
© Columbia Pictures

The real T. E. Lawrence.

The first problem with attempting to sort reality from cinematic embellishment in *Lawrence of Arabia* is that the epic's real-life subject, T. E. Lawrence, was a wild fabulist himself. "I prefer lies to truth," Lawrence once remarked, "particularly where they concern me."

David Lean's multi-Oscar-winning epic stands as a landmark in movie evolution. In the 1950s and early 1960s, when *Lawrence* was released, historical costume epics were to the industry what special-effects-packed action movies are today. And, as with today's blockbusters, many historical epics were spectacular flameouts. The Richard Burton–Liz Taylor disaster *Cleopatra* almost collapsed its studio, 20th Century Fox. Others, such as the Charlton Heston Biblical vehicle *The Ten Commandments*, stand today as monuments of kitsch. But *Lawrence of Arabia* stood above them all, and even today holds up as a classic not only of the "epic" genre specifically, but of moviemaking in general. Eschewing, for the most part, large-scale re-creations of famous battles and cast-of-thousands crowd scenes, Lean concentrated on the character of Lawrence himself, who, as portrayed by then-newcomer Peter O'Toole, came across as an ambiguously homosexual megalomaniac with a perverse, quasi-sexual attraction to pain—his own most of all.

T. E. Lawrence was a British intelligence officer stationed in the Middle East during World War I. The British were not only trying to beat the Germans there by vanquishing their surrogates, the Turkish Ottoman Empire, but were also playing their own "Great Game" against the Russians and the French for ultimate control over the region. The days of the sun setting on the British Empire were far enough in the future to appear unimaginable to Britain's ruling class. The British wanted what the Turks possessed, and the British plan was to incite an "Arab revolt" against the Ottoman rulers in order to get it. Lawrence was the instrument they deployed to guide the supposed revolt to suit British ambitions.

Having crossed the desert on foot as a student several years earlier, as well as having labored to unearth Mesopotamian ruins for the British Museum, Lawrence was a hard-core Arabist who knew the language, the geography, and, most important, the social mores of the Middle East with great intimacy. He was the perfect man for the mission.

No one believed that more than Lawrence himself, whose memoir of his Arabian adventures, *The Seven Pillars of Wisdom*, is considered as much a literary classic as Lean's film is a cinematic one, and it is just as filled with crazed exaggerations and shameless lies. Arguably the most outrageous fabrication perpetrated by Lawrence was the fiction that he and a band of gallant Arab guerillas commanded by Prince Feisal liberated Damascus from the Turks. The truth of the matter was that Anzac troops (which consisted of a combined Australian and New Zealander force) captured the city three days before Feisal's ragtag "camel corps" arrived. Lawrence wasn't even with the Arabs. At the time he was under an Australian commander.

Lawrence's whopper was so blatant that Lean simply sidestepped it in the storytelling of his film. We never see Lawrence or Feisal's Arabs entering the city. Instead, we see the British arrive, only to be told that Lawrence and Feisal were already there. Which was true enough, but hardly the entire story. Nonetheless, Lawrence's bullshit served a tremendous propaganda purpose for the British.

They needed the world to believe that their million soldiers in the Middle East accomplished virtually nothing compared to a spontaneous outbreak of nationalist fervor by fewer than four thousand Arabs under the leadership of mercenary Bedouin sheiks. The tall tale legitimized British hegemony and laid the pavement for the strife that still tears the Middle East apart today, almost a century later.

Lawrence's most curious fabrications, however, although only hinted at by Lean, comprise an integral thread in the fabric of his epic character study, even in their compromised form. Those were Lawrence's celebrations of his own apparent sadomasochism. *Seven Pillars of Wisdom* includes numerous descriptions of cruelty, torture, and murder perpetrated by Lawrence's Arab charges with (according to Lawrence) his enthusiastic approval.

Given the climate of the era and the pre–Ratings Code self-censorship of Hollywood moviemakers, there was only so much Lean could do to show this rather dark aspect of Lawrence's enigmatic persona. Lean includes the characters of Faraj and Da'ud, Lawrence's two teenage valets, with whom he enjoys what appears to be a somewhat more than avuncular relationship. In the book, the fictional teenage manservants are made to endure any manner of exotic beatings, supposedly as disciplinary action for their many merry pranks. None of these are shown in the movie, though in the film Lawrence eventually kills both boys, one by allowing him to die in quicksand, the other as an act of mercy to prevent the Turks from capturing the lad, who was wounded in an accident, and having their way with him. Despite the unavoidable nature of the two killings, Lawrence in the film confesses with considerable self-loathing, "I enjoyed it."

In his literary opus, Lawrence also details various inventive methods of torture and execution allegedly witnessed and sanctioned by himself. But according to his recent biographer Michael Asher, none of the macabre techniques Lawrence describes were part of any local Arab culture; indeed, in that culture, personal honor was considered so important that killing a man was preferable to causing him loss of face. All of which leads to the conclusion that the torture rites detailed by Lawrence were figments of his own perverse imagination—some type of wish fulfillment, perhaps.

O'Toole (who is, incidentally, a foot taller than the actual Lawrence was) played Lawrence with a swishiness that was unmistakable even in the relatively innocent times of 1962. It may also be significant that Lean allows not a single speaking role to a woman in his entire 228-minute epic. Lawrence was widely believed to be gay, though if he was, there is no record of anyone claiming to have had a relationship or sexual encounter with him. No one—of either gender. Yet Lean couldn't have been far off. Lawrence's own writings certainly reveal some kind of homosexual yearning in addition to a particular craving for pain. The incident that forms the centerpiece of Lean's character study and of Lawrence's own self-study is his capture by Turks, who beat and sodomize him (though Lean tastefully omits any allusion to anal rape). But there's no evidence other than Lawrence's own writing that such an incident ever occurred.

It also appears that while Lawrence reveled in his self-portrait as a ruthless sadist, even those incidents of sadism described in his book appear to be nothing but fantasy projections of his own masochism. The most famous, or infamous, of these is the "no prisoners" massacre at Tafas. Lean includes the episode much as Lawrence recounted it. After coming across a village wiped out by retreating Turks, Lawrence's men catch up to the perpetrators of the atrocity, at which point Lawrence issues the fatal command, "No prisoners." In Lean's film, O'Toole gives Lawrence a bug-eyed, psychotic visage throughout the scene. Once the battle ends, his white Arab robes are drenched in blood.

That account coincides more or less with Lawrence's own. Other eyewitnesses to the Tafas massacre gave a different picture, of Lawrence attempting to protect Turkish prisoners rather than giving orders for them to be murdered. While in the deeper recesses of his psyche Lawrence may have fancied himself a thrill-killer and dungeon master, his true personality was far more benign.

Can Lean be held accountable for repeating Lawrence's own exaggerations and lies? Why not? His memorable portrayal of T. E. Lawrence has given history its most powerful image of a man whose legacy in the Middle East is still palpable today, and certainly was in 1962. Perhaps he should have looked beneath the flowing robes of the self-admitted liar to find a character considerably more complex and twisted than even Peter O'Toole could embody.

Sources and Further Reading

Asher, Michael. *Lawrence: The Uncrowned King of Arabia*. New York: Overlook Press, 1998.

Fromkin, David. "The Importance of T. E. Lawrence." *New Criterion*, September 1991.

Lawrence, T. E. *The Seven Pillars of Wisdom: A Triumph*. Reissue Edition. New York: Anchor Books, 1991.

Rabbit-Proof Fence (2002)

Directed by Phillip Noyce
Written by Christine Olsen
Starring Everlyn Sampi and Kenneth Branagh

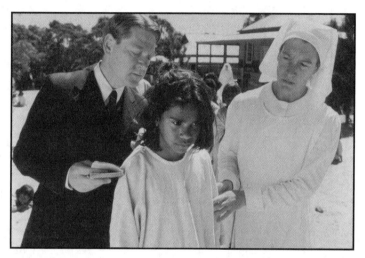

Kenneth Branagh as A. O. Neville and Everlyn Sampi (center)
as Molly Craig. *Photo by Penny Tweedie, © Miramax Films*

In 1931 three young aboriginal girls were forcibly taken from their families in Western Australia and relocated to a camp fifteen hundred miles to the south. As victims of an official government policy that aimed to reeducate and assimilate mixed-race aboriginal children into the white population, fourteen-year-old Molly Craig and her cousins Gracie Fields, age eleven, and Daisy Kadibil, age eight, weren't all that remarkable.

Over the course of six decades, thousands of "half-caste" aboriginal children were snatched from their homes and shipped to distant camps, where they were force-fed Christian values, purged of their native customs, and reformed into dutiful domestic servants. But cultural conversion was only part of the master plan. Under the tutelage of ambitious administrators such as A. O. Neville, the "chief protector of the aborigines" in Western Australia from 1915 through 1940, the white government sought to interbreed mulatto aborigines with whites to eradicate the "blackness" from their race. Neville and his successors hoped "to merge the blacks into our white community" so that "we could eventually forget that there ever were any aborigines in Australia."

As an experiment in eugenics with an aim toward genocide, the policy was an abject failure. Aborigines did not go gently into that good night on a comfortable "pillow for a dying race," as patronizing whites such as Neville had envisioned. Today, Australia's aboriginal population numbers just under four hundred thousand—a fraction of the country's 19.7 million people, but up from the estimated three hundred thousand that existed when the first Europeans arrived more than two hundred years ago. Not only did the government policy fail on its own dubious terms, but it also left a legacy of cultural disruption that continues to haunt aboriginal families to this day. By the time the policy was officially abandoned in 1970, thousands of families had been torn asunder, many never to be reunited. The children who had been removed from their families and tribes are today known as "the stolen generations."

Molly, Gracie, and Daisy were luckier. They fought back and spectacularly thwarted the government's plans for them. Two days after their forced relocation to the grimy Moore River Native Settlement, a reservation and reeducation camp for light-skinned aborigines, the girls escaped and traveled—on foot—more than a thousand miles back to their home in the southwestern Australian settlement of Jigalong. They navigated by following Australia's wire-mesh "rabbit-proof fence," a barrier that bisected the continent from north to south, built to keep marauding western rabbits out of fertile eastern farmlands. During their nine-week trek, the girls outsmarted and evaded mounted police, native trackers, and search aircraft, while surviving some of Australia's most inhospitable desert terrain.

Their story might never have been told outside the tribal confines of Jigalong had Molly's daughter, Doris Pilkington, not heard the tale from her aunt, Daisy. Like her mother, Pilkington had also been a victim of the government's efforts to "assimilate" the mixed-race aborigines. Taken from Molly when she was only three, Pilkington had grown up as a ward of the Moore River Native Settlement and, later, at a Christian mission. It wasn't until she was an adult of twenty-five that she managed to locate and reunite with her mother, who was still living in Jigalong. When she heard the oral retelling of her mother's great escape, she decided to put it down in writing.

The resulting book, *Follow the Rabbit-Proof Fence*, published in 1996 by University of Queensland Press, augmented Molly and Daisy's recollections of their 1931 trek with Pilkington's own historical research. Screenwriter Christine Olsen subsequently optioned the book, wrote a screenplay incorporating still more new research, and convinced director Phillip Noyce to downshift from creating Hollywood epics (Noyce's work includes *Patriot Games* and *The Bone Collector*) to lens a smaller film in his native Australia.

Like the book, *Rabbit-Proof Fence* tells the story of Molly, Gracie, and Daisy in stark and unsentimental terms. In less able hands, the story of three young girls returning to their "mummy" might have quickly bogged itself down in treacle. Thanks to Noyce's pitch-perfect casting of three first-time actors (Everlyn Sampi, Laura Monaghan, and Tianna Sansbury) in the lead roles, the film exudes a quiet, unpretentious intensity.

The film's dramatic distortions are minimal and understandable, given the special requirements of storytelling on the big screen. In Pilkington's book (and presumably in reality), Molly and Gracie don't resist when the local constable takes them away. Their families greet the traumatic event with fatalistic surrender, mournful wailing, and self-inflicted wounds. Clearly, the aborigines were so intimidated by agents of the white government that resistance wasn't even considered. In the movie version of the abduction, Noyce ups the drama quotient by staging a chase scene and a violent struggle as the girls and their mothers fight tooth and nail to stay together.

Noyce also tinkers with reality by having Chief Protector of the Aborigines A. O. Neville (Kenneth Branagh) visit the Moore River Native Settlement while Molly, Gracie, and Daisy are (briefly) inmates there. In fact, Neville wasn't at the camp at the same time as the girls, and they never personally encountered him elsewhere, although they certainly tormented him for weeks by cleverly thwarting his best efforts to "recover" them. Of course, it's perfectly understandable why Noyce invokes dramatic license in this instance: film protagonists must have face time with their antagonist.

Some critics of the film (chiefly, conservative white Australians opposed to having the government compensate members of the stolen generation) have quibbled with another of Noyce's dramatic alterations. There's a key scene in which Neville (the girl inmates call him "Mr. Devil") selects lighter-skinned girls at the camp for transfer to a better mission. In the scene, Neville inspects Molly but finds her too dark for the honor. In reality, the transfer of lighter-skinned girls out of Moore River camp on the basis of skin tone didn't begin until 1933, two years later.

Less forgivable is Noyce's invocation of that standby Hollywood cliché, the Magical Native. In one unwarranted scene that does not appear in the book, Molly's mother and grandmother chant in that mystical aboriginal trill that always delivers imperiled movie characters to safer harbors. In *The Right Stuff*, aboriginal magic kept John Glenn's space capsule aloft, and here it delivers a spirit-guide hawk to show Molly the way home. (Thankfully, Peter Gabriel, who composed the film's musical score, resisted the urge to cue a bumptious didgeridoo here.)

But apart from that quibble, the distortions are relatively minor. In the main, *Rabbit-Proof Fence* quite accurately portrays not only the girls' canny self-sufficiency and courage, but also the misguided paternalism of white administrators like Neville, whose crackpot racist theories sustained a national tragedy for more than six decades.

Sources and Further Reading

Australian Broadcasting Corporation. "Doris Pilkington: Reunion." The Space: ABC Online Arts Gateway. February 21, 2002, http://www.abc.net.au/arts/books/stories/s424264.htm.

Darling, Cary. "New Films Shine Spotlight on the Humanity of Aborigines." Knight-Ridder Newspapers, December 19, 2002.

Horsburgh, Susan. "Home Truths: Molly and Daisy Craig's Childhood Trek in Australia's Outback Inspires the New Film *Rabbit-Proof Fence*." *People*, December 9, 2002.

Pilkington, Doris. *Rabbit-Proof Fence*. New York: Miramax Books, 2002.

Salhani, Claude. "Rabbit-Proof Fence: The Aborigines' Plight." United Press International, November 15, 2002.

Gandhi (1982)

Directed by Richard Attenborough
Written by John Briley
Starring Ben Kingsley, Candice Bergen, and Martin Sheen

Ben Kingsley as Gandhi. © *Columbia*
Pictures Industries Inc.

The real Gandhi.

There's a certain mantra that most any director of a biopic or history flick repeats ad nauseam. It goes something like, "Well, we wanted to get to the essence of the thing, even if not everything in the movie is literally true." Check out promotional interviews for biopics and you'll hear it again and again. But to our knowledge, Richard Attenborough's *Gandhi* is the only film that comes out and says it right at the beginning of the movie, albeit phrased rather more eloquently.

"No man's life can be encompassed in one telling," reads the film's epigraph. "There is no way to give each year its allotted weight, to include each event, each person who helped to shape a lifetime. What can be done is to be faithful in spirit to the record and to find one's way to the heart of the man."

It's curious that, of all the historical movies ever made, including a few directed by Attenborough himself, this one bears the disclaimer on its own celluloid. Attenborough's three-plus-hour epic is indeed faithful to the historical record of Mohandas K. Gandhi's achievements and his revolutionary (in several senses) adherence to nonviolence, which he saw as both a moral imperative and a powerful political weapon.

At the same time, Attenborough almost scrupulously *avoids* the heart of the man, choosing to beatify Gandhi instead. It is not an indefensible choice. Released almost thirty-five years after Gandhi's death by an assassin's bullets and four decades after his world-shaking nonviolent revolt against British colonial rule over India, Attenborough's *Gandhi* came at a time when the great man had become little more than an impersonal name on a page in high school history textbooks, the relevance and moral force of his life a pale shadow of their realities. Attenborough, who'd struggled to make a Gandhi biopic for twenty years, sought to resurrect the man for a modern generation. The resulting film won nine Oscars, including Best Picture, Best Director, and Best Actor (for Ben Kingsley's uncanny performance as Gandhi).

There was nothing to be gained, perhaps, by drawing Gandhi in anything but the best possible light. In this movie he is the Mahatma—the "Great Soul"—but he is more a caricature than a character.

Omitted, thusly, are any mentions of the Mahatma's amusing and occasionally annoying idiosyncrasies. His forty-year refusal to have sex with his wife (or anyone else) is briefly touched on, but his interesting habit of sleeping with young women, chastely, to prove that he had "conquered desire" goes unmentioned. As does his practice of employing the lavatory as kind of a conference room—while he was using it. (Then again, it was a simple matter for anyone to avoid taking a meeting with Gandhi while he was, shall we say, otherwise occupied. The Father of India scheduled his daily bowel movements by his watch. He was also fond of enemas, as well as various dietary fads.)

Given that they had no marital relations from the time Gandhi and his wife were thirty-six years old on, one would imagine that their relationship was a tad strained. You'd never get that impression from the movie. Attenborough shows us just one moment of conflict, for which Gandhi quickly apologizes. Otherwise, Kasturbai, Gandhi's wife since the age of thirteen, follows her husband adoringly, even slavishly.

It is true that Kasturbai devoted herself to her husband's cause of Indian independence through nonviolence. At the age of seventy-four, she died in a British-run prison. The film gives the cause of her death as "a massive thrombosis." That little fabrication provides a convenient excuse for avoiding a touchy issue that would have surely undermined Gandhi's credibility with a contemporary audience. In fact, Kasturbai suffered from a bronchial infection that could have been wiped out with penicillin, but her husband wouldn't allow her to get an injection. He opposed all medicine administered by needle through skin. Having neglected her in life, he allowed her to die because he refused to be so much as mildly flexible in his beliefs.

Gandhi's backward attitude toward sex would have alienated him, for sure, from a 1982 audience—or a 2002 audience. Or a 1972 audience. The countercultural kids of the '60s who staged their own nonviolent (at least in theory) movement could not have been too comfortable to learn that their ideological idol condemned sex as, basically, a really bad thing.

Gandhi's celibacy wasn't some kind of Siddhartha-style path to enlightenment. The puritanical Gandhi was convinced that men and women should never make whoopee except for the express purpose of whoopeeing up some offspring. (He was not terribly well disposed toward homosexual behavior, either.) Sex for fun was a sin in his universe. In Gandhi's view, women were incapable of experiencing sexual pleasure and therefore had no desire for sex; it was therefore the duty of men to resist temptation and remain celibate.

Gandhi once met the pioneering American birth control crusader Margaret Sanger, and he got into an argument with her. Gandhi was vehemently opposed to birth control—because, as far as he was concerned, sex without the chance of conception was nothing but lust, and lust met with Gandhi's utmost disapproval.

None of that material is in the movie, and to be fair, none of it is germane to the theme of Attenborough's film. Even at three hours and ten minutes, there's no way (as the disclaimer notes) to include every aspect of a man's life or his character. Especially a character as complex as Gandhi.

There aren't many points where this film can be faulted for historical inaccuracy. Attenborough condenses portions of Gandhi's career. His South African period, during which Gandhi fought the government's legalized discrimination against Indian immigrants, lasted a total of twenty-one years, divided into three segments. He left South Africa and returned twice between 1893 and

1914, living in India in the interim. The movie gives the impression that Gandhi returned to India as a stranger in his own land, and he hardly ages at all during his South African period.

The movie's first strong "civil disobedience" scene shows a South African policeman beating Gandhi mercilessly as Gandhi tries to burn the identity card that all Indians in the country had to carry. Gandhi did burn the card, but he was never beaten as we see in the film.

The movie also skips over Gandhi's alliance with the British in the Boer and Zulu wars. In both instances, he organized Indian ambulance corps to support the British colonial war efforts—the exact colonial force he later became world famous for opposing. Clearly, Gandhi underwent considerable spiritual growth over the years. Attenborough elects not to confuse his audience by documenting Gandhi's evolution. He's interested only in the heroic, saintly Gandhi. The Gandhi we meet at the beginning of the film in South Africa is essentially the same Gandhi who dies at the end—just in different clothes (although, toward the end there, he wore hardly any clothes at all).

The great failure of Gandhi's life—his inability to keep Indian Hindus and Muslims from killing each other or to hold the newly independent India together as one nation—that's one negative Attenborough couldn't ignore. It was the reason why an extremist Hindu newspaper editor gunned down the Mahatma on January 30, 1948. Attenborough, however, minimizes the animosity between Gandhi, the Father of India, and Mohammed Ali Jinnah, the Father of Pakistan. In one scene, we see Gandhi making his bizarre and untenable proposal to name the Muslim separatist Jinnah prime minister of India, but we never get a feel for the deep animosity between the two men. Jinnah resigned from India's Congress party as soon as Gandhi made his final return to India from South Africa. For his part, Gandhi referred to Jinnah as "evil" and "a maniac."

Attenborough shows us Gandhi the Great, but never Gandhi the Man. But he *was* a man, not a deity. That was painfully plain to Gandhi's own country-folk during his lifetime. Attenborough gives only a fleeting indication of the ill will toward Gandhi that existed in a huge segment of India's Hindu majority. In the film, his assassination seems to come out of the blue—because we aren't told that there was a bombing attempt on his life just a few weeks earlier. The sad reality is that Gandhi was not the godlike figure among his own people that the film displays. His religious openness wasn't anything that most Hindus or Muslims were interested in sharing. Nor was his devotion to the cause of India's "untouchables," Hindus born outside of the religion's caste system and treated worse than animals. Gandhi spent almost as much of his career campaigning for their rights as he did waging his nonviolent war of independence against Britain. But "untouchability" is part of the Hindu religion that goes back thousands of years. Today, there are still 160 million untouchables in India, almost all of whom live in poverty.

Gandhi became a hero to the people of India not because of his elevated spirituality or his enlightened pacifism. They loved him because he took no crap from the British, and they bought into his nonviolence program because it worked. When it came to their own religious hatred, however, Indians were just fine with violence, and plenty of it. The same day that Britain granted India independence, the country was split in two. Jinnah's dream of a Muslim state, Pakistan, was fulfilled. The two countries have been at war ever since, and today, both have nuclear weapons. Gandhi's ideals may be worshipped, but in his own country and throughout the world, they are rarely followed. Attenborough's well-intentioned but one-dimensional tribute to the Mahatma had no chance of changing that sorry fact.

Sources and Further Reading

Feuerlicht, Roberta Strauss. "Biography of M. K. Gandhi." The Progress Report. http://progress.org/gandhi/gandhi01.htm.

Furbee, Mary and Mike. *The Importance of Mohandas Gandhi*. San Diego, CA: Lucent Books, 2000.

McGeary, Johanna. "Person of the Century: Mohandas Gandhi." *Time*, January 3, 2000.

Nanda, B. R. Gandhi. "A Pictorial Biography." http://www.mkgandhi.org/biography/index.htm.

Severance, John B. *Gandhi: Great Soul*. New York: Clarion Books, 1997.

Malcolm X (1992)

Directed by Spike Lee
Written by Arnold Perl and Spike Lee
Starring Denzel Washington and Angela Bassett

Angela Bassett and Denzel Washington as Betty Shabazz and Malcolm X. *Photo by David Lee, © Warner Bros.*

A biopic of Malcolm X, the now-iconic "black nationalist" leader, had been in the works for more than twenty-five years when director Spike Lee forced his way into the picture. Malcolm X was slain by rival Muslims on February 21, 1965. According to his daughter, Attallah Shabazz, it was "shortly after" the assassination that film producer Marvin Worth approached Malcolm's widow, Betty, and author Alex Haley about making a film of Malcolm's life based on Haley's newly published book, *The Autobiography of Malcolm X*.

It didn't take long for Haley's book to be recognized as not only a classic in African American literature, but one of the great books of the twentieth century, as well. Yet development of the film project dragged. By 1991, when the final deal was cut, Haley was dead, as were original screenwriters James Baldwin and Arnold Perl (Perl nonetheless received credit, with Lee, on the finished film). The director tapped to helm the project was Norman Jewison. Jewison's 1967 (wholly fictional) film *In the Heat of the Night* was in its time the most searing indictment of American racism that Hollywood had dared to produce. To Lee, however, the selection of a white director—regardless of his credentials both professional and ideological—was "a crime." Lee insisted that an African American director be put in charge of the project and furthermore, that the African American director be Spike Lee.

Lee may have had a point about the film's credibility. It's arguable, but it probably did require a black director. Lee's finished product, on the other hand, raises the question of whether his concern was to protect the integrity of Malcolm X's legacy, or to advance the Hollywood career of Spike Lee. Despite his well-documented struggles to complete the film (he reportedly had to seek extra financing from wealthy African Americans such as his old Nike ad straight man, Michael Jordan), Lee's Malcolm X was a Hollywood creation, made palatable to the broadest possible audience. He made a film that, while committing no egregious historical errors (unlike Jewison's later "true" racial-justice drama *The Hurricane*), succeeded mainly in modulating the real Malcolm X to the point that he fit the politically correct Hollywood cliché of a black man who is noble and dignified, yet, upon closer examination, is revealed as unthreatening and ineffectual.

The real Malcolm X made a strict point of behaving in a noble and dignified fashion. But he was, to the mainstream American society of the early 1960s, extremely threatening—in fact, terrifying. And it took an assassin's shotgun to render him ineffectual.

Denzel Washington was cast as Malcolm X before Lee came onboard. Somehow, Washington's understated acting style seems all wrong for the forceful presence of Malcolm X. While Malcolm's advocacy of armed resistance for black people is alluded to, we never see Washington deliver Malcolm's historic "Ballot or the Bullet" speech. Nor do we hear him declare that black people need to stockpile weapons and form a "black nationalist army."

Lee shows Malcolm's progression from the separatism advocated by the Nation of Islam to a more inclusive form of traditional Islam in which all races can participate. In reality, the journey took Malcolm much further. Lee never lets Malcolm mouth the nutty, near-psychotic eugenic theories of Nation of Islam founder Elijah Muhammad. But Muhammad taught, and Malcolm unquestioningly accepted, that white people were created in a prehistoric genetic experiment carried out by a devil named Yacub, who grafted demonic genes onto the pure black seed line. Lee also leaves out Muhammad's, and therefore Malcolm's, belief that the white man would be demolished in a coming apocalyptic race war, a belief that, perhaps coincidentally, was later echoed by cult leader and white supremacist Charles Manson.

As much as Malcolm inveighed against white supremacy, he once met with Ku Klux Klan leaders to discuss the prospect of acquiring land for a separate black state. He was aware that his views on racial separatism were not too different from those of the cracker racists he despised. That incident is not mentioned in Lee's film, nor is the connection between the two extreme ideologies made clear.

Malcolm X's life contained two great triumphs. The second of these was his victory over his own racism, which Lee's film documents—but, by watering down Malcolm's bizarre racial theories, Lee sucks much of the power out of Malcolm X's spiritual progression. Not incidentally, Lee gives his audience nothing but the most superficial representation of Malcolm's thinking even in his later, post–Nation of Islam period.

Malcolm X is generally idolized because he took no crap from the white man—because he represented "black manhood," a point made explicit in Lee's documentary-montage epilogue to the film. Lee buys into this oversimplified version of Malcolm X uncritically. The true Malcolm X was not simply a tough-talking orator who took every opportunity to blast "racists" and "blue-eyed devils"; he was a sophisticated critic of capitalism and western colonialism who declared his affinity for Lenin and Stalin, and who once said that he believed that freedom for black people would come with the aid of the Soviet army.

Well, on second thought, that part of his thinking may not have been too sophisticated—but at any rate, Lee includes none of it in his portrait of Malcolm X. Instead he reduces Malcolm's mission to, as bell hooks phrased it, "a masculinist phallocentric power struggle between white and black men." hooks cites the film's most stirring scene, in which Malcolm commands a rigidly regimented battalion of "Fruit of Islam" (Nation of Islam men) to face down a white police captain (played by Peter Boyle, whose casting must have seemed significant to a student of film history like Lee—Boyle launched himself to movie stardom with his role as a redneck, bigoted construction worker in the 1970 film *Joe*). To Lee, the racial struggle isn't one involving complex historical and ideological forces; it's a big dick competition. But it was not that way for Malcolm X, who struggled to understand how the currents of history had resulted in the subjugation of black people by whites.

Malcolm's first personal triumph was his reformation, through the Nation of Islam, after a criminal youth that had landed him in prison. Inspired by the teachings of his newfound demigod, Elijah Muhammad, the former Malcolm Little went from abusing drugs and hustling on the streets to a level of self-discipline so fanatical that the term "puritanical" hardly does it justice. In depicting this transformation, however, Lee makes a curious and inexplicable choice. He drops Malcolm's family from the story.

Lee invents a fictional prison inmate named Baines (played by Albert Hall, who would later portray Elijah Muhammad in Michael Mann's *Ali*) who introduced Malcolm to the Nation of Islam. It was, in truth, Malcolm's brother Reginald and other siblings who introduced him to the teachings of "The Honorable Elijah Muhammad." The only mention of any siblings at all in the film comes in a flashback, which depicts Malcolm's boyhood home being attacked by Klansmen and his father apparently being murdered. We see his brothers and sisters then, but never again in the movie, even though they were perhaps the most important influences in his conversion to Elijah Muhammad–style Islam—and his steadiest source of emotional support.

In the end, what is missing most from Lee's *Malcolm X* is not any single fact or character. It's an intangible—the sense of the tremendous terror and loathing that Malcolm X inspired in mainstream America. And mainstream America included more than whites. The black middle class also had no use for Malcolm X and regarded him and his teachings with revulsion. In our era, hip-hop culture has turned the image of the angry black man and even the "Afrocentric" racial philosophies of Elijah Muhammad (who was eventually renounced by Malcolm X) into marketable commodities. Malcolm X himself became a popular emblem displayed on T-shirts and baseball caps even before Lee's film came out, thanks largely to rap performers such as Public Enemy.

In the early 1960s, however, that same image of the "angry black man" was profoundly shocking to a huge segment of the American public. Malcolm X was the living embodiment of that image—as was Muhammad Ali, whose friendship and later split with Malcolm X goes unmentioned in Lee's movie. Thanks to Lee's film, a generation's lasting impression of Malcolm X is that of a handsome, appealing, Oscar-winning movie star. Someone we'd all be proud to take home. Malcolm X wouldn't recognize himself.

Sources and Further Reading

hooks, bell. "Consumed By Images." *Artforum*, February 1993.

Malcolm X: A Research Site. www.brothermalcolm.net.

X, Malcolm. *The Autobiography of Malcolm X.* As told to Alex Haley. New York: Ballantine Books, 1999.

The Right Stuff (1983)

Directed by Philip Kaufman
Written by Philip Kaufman
Starring Sam Shepard, Ed Harris, Dennis Quaid,
Scott Glenn, and Fred Ward

Sam Shepard and the real Chuck Yeager.
© the Ladd Company

When *The Right Stuff* touched down in theaters during the fall of 1983, audiences greeted it with the pointed indifference usually reserved for a space shuttle launch (or worse, PBS coverage of a space shuttle launch). Based on Tom Wolfe's 1979 nonfiction bestseller about the origins of America's manned space program, *The Right Stuff* seemed to have all the ingredients of a sure-thing blockbuster: here was an epic, true story celebrating American ingenuity and audacity in the face of what movie press kit writers prefer to call "impossible odds." Writer/director Philip Kaufman had piloted what may be the best film of his career—a towering historical adventure on a human scale, brimming with can-do heroism, nostalgia, humor, and a powerful sense of place and time. Yet the typical audience response gauged somewhere between "so what?" and "hey, where's the stuff about the moon?" (Adding insult to injury, *The Right Stuff* just barely edged out twin Stephen King crapfests *Cujo* and *Christine* for the not-so-coveted number-thirty-three box-office position.)

The Right Stuff's three-hour running time and its ensemble cast of then-unknown actors probably conspired to keep audiences at bay. Bad timing sealed the deal. If ever there were a case of a movie delivering the right stuff at the wrong time, this was it. At the height of the Reagan Revolution, the film's unusual blend of earnest hero worship and errant political satire didn't sit well with audiences looking for simpler escapist fare, such as the year's box-office champion, *Return of the Jedi*, a straight-ahead fairy tale of soldiering teddy bears and a wicked daddy redeemed.

But *The Right Stuff*'s complicated attitudes toward its subject matter were firmly anchored in Tom Wolfe's book. Although fully realized as a visual creation, Kaufman's movie remained extraordinarily faithful to Wolfe's themes, which simultaneously mythologized and deflated aspects of the early space program.

Scrupulously observed and reported, Wolfe's book nonetheless drew a romanticized portrait of its protagonists, test pilots of the 1950s who had "the right stuff"—that is, the willingness to risk death on a daily basis while "pushing the outside of the envelope." These men included Chuck Yeager, the U.S. Air Force pilot who broke the sound barrier, and the seven pilots and aviators who would become the Project Mercury astronauts. Wolfe saw them as latter-day cowboys—plainspoken, sometimes unruly broncobusters in flight suits "hanging their hides out over the edge." Wolfe offered the drawling, reserved Yeager as the ideal specimen in this elite group. (Yeager would later define the essence of "the right stuff"—and the pilot who's got it—with characteristic modesty: "There's no emotionalism involved. He's got a job, he's got to do it, and if you get killed, that's the way it goes.") Of course, the irony was that Yeager, the best of the bunch, never made it into space because he lacked the college degree that NASA required of its Mercury recruits.

Part of Wolfe's purpose in idealizing the unsung Yeager was to bring the other, more famous flyboys down to earth, thereby deflating the media hype that inaccurately cast them as choirboys with crew cuts. With his usual sharp eye for detail, Wolfe brought the Mercury jocks to life on a recognizably human scale, complete with occupational tics and vanities also hanging out over the edge. Standard specs included the "pilot ego," which expected "a little adulation on the order of the Pope's"; the fraternal devotion to the "holy coordinates" of "Flying & Drinking and Drinking & Driving"; the extreme competitiveness; and the frequent marital infidelity.

Wolfe's book also offered a running satirical commentary on the hysteria that erupted after the Soviets successfully launched Sputnik I, the world's first artificial satellite, into low earth orbit in 1957. Wolfe chronicled NASA's desperate attempts to score a countercoup in the space race, to the extent of treating its newly minted astronaut corps like test monkeys, as Yeager noted. The book scorned the efforts of politicians, the press, "and other technological illiterates with influence" to exploit the guys with the right stuff as public relations pawns in the Cold War.

Kaufman fought to maintain Wolfe's premise and themes. When the director came to the project, he had inherited a more conventional Hollywood script, written by the ubiquitous William Goldman (*The Princess Bride, Butch Cassidy and the Sundance Kid*). Goldman had simplified the story by ignoring the first half of Wolfe's book, which focused on Yeager and the other 1940s test pilots at Edwards Air Force Base who blazed a trail for the future astronauts. Kaufman decided that Goldman's script "left out quite a very important factor here—something called 'the Right Stuff'!" As Kaufman recalled in a 2003 interview in *Airpower* magazine, "It really starts at Edwards and it starts with Yeager, and that's what we [had] to show—how that thing is at the heart of it all. The astronauts were the ones who later carried that spirit—that kind of magical, unmentionable thing—up into outer space." Kaufman jettisoned Goldman's script and started over, beginning with Yeager's historic supersonic flight of 1947.

Thus Kaufman restored Wolfe's central theme, a rumination on a distinctly American form of quiet heroism. Kaufman set out to explore how that "elusive quality survive(s) in the midst of the American circus, the chaos, public commotion, the panic, that all threaten to stamp it out."

Though true to its source material, *The Right Stuff* exaggerated aspects of Tom Wolfe's prose for big-screen comic effect. Whereas Wolfe had taken caustic pleasure in deflating the "technological illiterates" who hyped the space race for political gain, Kaufman pushed the outside of the comedy envelope, occasionally into the realm of semicaricature. Thus, Lyndon B. Johnson (Donald Moffat) sputters and sulks like a spoiled twelve-year-old; President Eisenhower comes across as a clueless boob; and NASA's technicians and engineers are either feckless yes-men or arrogant martinets (with German accents) contemptuous of the astronauts. It's all quite entertaining, and as far as the politicians go, the cartooniness is hardly objectionable. But Kaufman's skewering of the NASA geeks seems a little unfair.

In fact, according to the real Wally Schirra, one of the original Mercury 7 team (portrayed in the film by Lance Henriksen), the astronauts and NASA's technical team got along famously—and necessarily. "We worked very closely with the engineers," Schirra said in a documentary bundled with *The Right Stuff* Special Edition DVD. "They were buddies; they still are. That kind of loyalty was unbelievable. . . . Test pilots were trained to work with those engineers and become team players. They called us immediately if they saw something they didn't like." Contrast that comment to the film's exaggerated depiction of the NASA engineers haughtily dismissing the astronaut's demands for the most basic pilot necessities, including a control stick and a window in the tiny Mercury space capsule.

In another dramatic distortion, the movie has the astronauts butting heads with a German scientist over the design of the capsule. Although the character is never named, the obvious inference is that he is Werner von Braun, NASA's famous rocket scientist. Of course, in reality von Braun, being a propulsion specialist, had nothing whatsoever to do with the engineering of the capsule.

The surviving members of the Mercury 7 also took exception to the film's suggestion that Gus Grissom (Fred Ward) prematurely "blew the hatch" on the Liberty Bell 7 capsule after its splashdown, causing the spacecraft to sink to the bottom of the Atlantic. "I really dislike the movie portraying Gus as having screwed up that way," said Schirra. "He did not." To be fair to Kaufman, the scene in the film is left deliberately ambiguous; we never see Grissom detonating the explosive bolts on the hatch ("screwing the pooch," in flyboy argot). But the real Grissom did come under considerable pressure after the incident, and this, the film quite accurately recounts.

Kaufman also invokes dramatic license in the scene that depicts John Glenn's (Ed Harris) historic first orbit of the earth. As Glenn's capsule passes over Australia, a tribe of aborigines performs a ritual around a bonfire, sending sparks lofting into the night sky to protect the capsule. Kaufman then cuts to the space capsule, now enveloped by the mysterious glowing "fireflies" that the real Glenn encountered in space. It's a lovely visual metaphor suggesting that the divide separating primitive magic and the fragile technology that puts a man into orbit isn't quite so vast as we might wish. Of course, the reality of Glenn's fireflies wasn't nearly as poetic: the glowing specs were radiation particles, burning through the unshielded capsule and frying the retina of Glenn's eye.

If the film took certain liberties with the NASA side of the story, its re-creation of Yeager's test-piloting days at Edwards Air Force Base was somewhat more factual. To quote the real Yeager: "Me as a technical advisor, I made sure it was." Still, the film has Yeager stationed at Edwards from the late 1940s through the early 1960s; in reality, Yeager left the base in 1954.

Kaufman pulls several chronological fast ones in the film's penultimate scene. As the Mercury astronauts watch Sally Rand perform her famous fan dance in a tribute to them in Houston, Yeager attempts to break the air altitude record over the Mojave Desert. In fact, the two events took place seventeen months apart. What's more, Yeager's flight—in an F-104 jet that had been mod-ified with a rocket booster—was an extremely well-planned event, not the spur-of-the-moment, seat-of-his-pants affair shown in the film. What's more, his friend and ground technician Jack Ridley, depicted in the scene offering him a stick of gum before the flight, had in reality died nine years earlier. Finally, the jet glimpsed in the movie is a standard F-104 without the booster rocket that made Yeager's 104,000-foot climb possible.

One last point on the subject of verisimilitude: in *The Right Stuff*, Kaufman wisely steered clear of *Star Wars*–style optical effects, choosing instead to re-create the classic space flights using a combination of stock footage and physical mod-els shot against real backdrops. Consequently, the spacecraft in *The Right Stuff* often seem even more convincing than those in films such as *Apollo 13* (see page 392). That film was produced a decade later with the aid of advanced computer-generated special effects, which, as always, wind up looking exactly like computer-generated special effects.

Sources and Further Reading

Accurso, Anthony. "Director's Cut: An Interview with *Right Stuff* Director Philip Kaufman," *Airpower*, November 2003.
"The Real Men with the Right Stuff." *The Right Stuff*, special ed. DVD. Warner Home Video, 2003.
Wolfe, Tom. *The Right Stuff*. New York: Farrar, 1979.
Yeager, Chuck and Leo Janos. *Yeager: An Autobiography*. New York: Bantam Books, 1985.

Apollo 13 (1995)

Directed by Ron Howard
Written by William Broyles Jr. and Al Reinert
Starring Tom Hanks, Gary Sinise, and Ed Harris

Bill Paxton, Kevin Bacon, and Tom Hanks as the crew of
Apollo 13. *Photo by Ron Batzdorff, © Universal City Studios Inc.*

Apart from the obvious triumph of putting men on the moon, NASA's Apollo
space program gave us a bonanza of unexpected windfalls—the microchip, GPS
satellites, Teflon, and Velcro among them. Unfortunately, along with the boons,
the space agency also unloaded a few bombs, most gratingly the catchphrase,
"Houston, we have a problem." If we hear one more idiot in a bar use that line
in reference to anything other than a main bus B undervolt in the command/serv-
ice module of an Apollo spacecraft, we may very well start withholding our childlike sense of wonder at the majesty of manned space flight. We mean it.

To be fair to NASA, the real culprit behind the popularization of "Houston, we have a problem" is Tom Hanks (who is also not easily forgiven for foist-
ing "Life is a box of chocolates" on a parrot-like segment of the American
population). In *Apollo 13*, an otherwise commendable movie, Hanks, portraying real-life astronaut Jim Lovell, delivers the line that launched a thousand
clichéd repetitions by idiots in bars. The 1995 movie is based on NASA's greatest victory-from-the-jaws-of-defeat moment, the Apollo 13 mission of 1970,

The actual Apollo 13 crew from left to right: commander James A. Lovell Jr., command module pilot John L. Swigert Jr., and lunar module pilot Fred W. Haise Jr. © NASA

which would have put the fifth and sixth men on the moon. Instead, disaster struck the Apollo 13 crew fifty-six hours into the journey, two hundred thousand miles from the earth. The lunar mission was quickly scrapped as thousands of NASA technicians, scientists, and astronauts mounted a heroic rescue effort.

The actual quote, first uttered by Jack Swigert then repeated by Lovell, the mission's commander, was "Houston, we've *had* a problem." Moments earlier, the astronauts had been startled by what they described as a "pretty large bang." Flashing warning lights on their instrument panel indicated that pressure in one of two oxygen tanks on the service module, which was located just underneath the cabin, had dropped to zero in eight seconds. Lovell, Fred Haise, and Swigert didn't know it at the time, but the oxygen tank had exploded, ripping a gaping hole in the side of the command module. The oxygen tanks fed the spacecraft's fuel cells—the power system that generated electricity, breathing oxygen, and water. With the life support systems seriously damaged and the main propulsion engines out of order, Swigert and Lovell's famous line turned out to be quite an understatement.

All gripes about catchphrases aside, *Apollo 13*, the movie, is a remarkably accurate representation of what really happened on that white-knuckled mission, both in space and back on earth at mission control. Credit on that count goes to director Ron Howard, who recognized the inherent dramatic value of the real story and resisted the standard Hollywood urge to punch up the melodrama.

It helped that Howard had a lot to work with when it came to source material. The film is based on Lovell's book (coauthored with journalist Jeffrey Kluger) *Lost Moon*, an authoritative take on the subject, for obvious reasons. As the book demonstrates, the real Apollo 13 rescue mission succeeded precisely because it was a masterful collaborative effort that combined the skills, talents, and improvisations of hundreds of knowledgeable contributors. It had to happen that way, because manned space flight is one of the most complex endeavors imaginable, requiring a mind-boggling array of people and precision parts working in perfect unison. And when things go off-plan, you can imagine the degree of complexity and coordination it takes to get them back on track.

The film captures that extraordinary complexity almost perfectly. Howard zooms in on the nitty-gritty details—the efforts to save the spacecraft's dying batteries by flipping switches in just the right order; the seat-of-their pants slide-rule calculations that determine whether the astronauts will angle gently into earth's atmosphere or skip off it like a stone; the carbon-dioxide filter jury-rigged from random junk onboard the spacecraft (the movie prop looks exactly like the real thing documented on NASA's Web site).

Howard's previous work with ensemble casts paid off in spades here. Wisely, he avoided the temptation to repurpose a story about heroic collaboration to fit Hollywood's standard "one-man-must-save-the-universe" formula. That doesn't diminish the achievement or heroism of Lovell and his crew by any means; instead, by focusing on the big picture rather than injecting a lot of silly Buck Rodgers heroics, Howard never cheapens their story. His cast is certainly up to the challenge. There are no histrionic star turns here. Hanks, Gary Sinise (as astronaut Ken Mattingly), Bill Paxton (as Haise), and Kevin Bacon (as Swigert) are all admirably restrained, and they deliver their lines in a low-key, twangy "astronaut-ese" that feels authentic. Ed Harris also turns in a mostly understated performance as Gene Kranz, the Houston flight controller (although at one point Harris manages to blurt out another of those annoying movie catch phrases: "Failure is not an option!").

Apollo 13 is not entirely devoid of cinematic distortion, but the embroidery is minor and readily forgivable. Digital effects shots showing the Apollo 13 spacecraft corkscrewing out of control through space were greatly exaggerated for dramatic effect. In reality, the ship's post-explosion wobble was much more subtle; if it had been as bad as depicted in the film, the story would likely not have had a happy ending.

Another embellishment: the tension between astronauts Swigert and Haise. Swigert joined the crew as a last-minute replacement for Mattingly, who had been grounded on account of his possible exposure to measles. In the film, Haise enrages Swigert by implying that the newbie crewmember caused the explosion. Looks are exchanged, tension is built. But according to the real Fred Haise, that never happened. Nor did the PG-13 dialog. "Most of the off-color or vulgar lines were not ours," Haise explained in live chat on Space.com. "And the crew conflict was something Hollywood added to make us seem more human." What about the line in the movie where Haise confides to Lovell, "I think ol' Swigert gave me the clap pissing in my relief tube"? The real Haise didn't directly address this issue in his online chat. He did, however, note that he returned to Earth with a urinary tract infection.

Apollo 13 has several "movie moments" that seem too good to be true, including the string of bad omens that occur before the disaster. At one point, Lovell's wife, Marilyn (Kathleen Quinlan), is in the shower when her wedding ring falls off her finger and into the drain. It's one of the few unbelievable moments in the film. Yet, in their commentary on the DVD edition of *Apollo 13*, the real Jim and Marilyn Lovell swear that it really did happen.

Sources and Further Reading

"Apollo 13: 'Houston, We've Got a Problem.'" EP-26. Produced by NASA Office of Public Affairs. Washington, D.C.: U.S. Government Printing Office, 1970. http://www.jsc.nasa.gov/er/seh/13index.htm.

Chaikin, Andrew. "Lights, Camera, Liftoff: Apollo 13 Goes Hollywood." Space.com. April 12, 2000. http://www.space.com/news/spacehistory/apollo13_film_reality_000412.html.

Lovell, Jim and Jeffrey Kluger. *Lost Moon: The Perilous Voyage of Apollo 13.* Boston, MA: Houghton Mifflin, 1994.

"Transcript of a Live Chat With Fred Haise." Space.com, April 11, 2000. http://www.space.com/peopleinterviews/fred_haise_chat.html.

All the President's Men (1976)

Directed by Alan J. Pakula
Written by William Goldman
Starring Robert Redford and Dustin Hoffman

The real Bob Woodward. © *2002 Lisa Berg*

Normally, Hollywood waits for the ink to dry on history's first draft before issuing the inevitable script notes. Sometimes, however, early intervention by a savvy producer can help steer unruly reality into more movie-appropriate channels. If not for Robert Redford's rapid response during the early days of the Watergate scandal, history might have settled for a somewhat less memorable account of how journalists Bob Woodward and Carl Bernstein exposed the chicanery of the Nixon White House and helped topple a president. That's not to suggest that Woodward and Bernstein distorted facts or invented details in their bestselling book, *All the President's Men*. But Redford's early involvement with the two journalists clearly had an influence on the dramatic structure of their famous 1974 book, which star and producer Redford later adapted into the even more famous 1976 movie.

As early as 1972, Robert Redford had wanted to make a film about Woodward and Bernstein, two obscure *Washington Post* reporters assigned to the then-lonely Watergate beat. Woodward and Bernstein ("Woodstein," as they were collectively known) had been far ahead of the journalistic pack in reporting on a scandal that began with a botched break-in at the Watergate office complex in Washington, D.C. The two reporters had quickly linked the burglars—who had been arrested with cameras, bugging devices, and lock picks—to the Nixon White House. Doggedly pursuing the story at a time when their journalistic peers were asleep at the switch, "Woodstein" began exposing a trail of corruption that led directly to the White House.

Redford first approached Woodward and Bernstein shortly after Nixon's reelection in 1972, but the reporters were too involved in their investigation to meet with the actor. Several months later, Redford returned to Washington and cornered the pair long enough to make his pitch. By then, Woodward and Bernstein had landed a book contract with Simon & Schuster. Redford bought the film rights to the unfinished book for $450,000. Redford, who planned to play Woodward in the movie version, then proceeded to advise the reporters on *how* to write the book.

Woodward himself acknowledged as much two years after *All the President's Men* hit the bestseller lists. "Redford was a factor in getting us to write the kind of book we wrote," he said in an interview. Years later, Woodward would downplay Redford's influence over his and Bernstein's decision to frame the book as a (more movie-friendly) personal narrative. But Woodward and Bernstein's literary agent at the time, David Obst, has suggested that Redford's input was in fact quite influential. Obst said in an interview on Fox News, "The boys kind of got stuck on how to write it. In fact, they turned in a draft, and the publisher kind of hinted that they'd like their money back. And they were really kind of stuck. And then [Woodward] had dinner one evening with Robert Redford and William Goldman, a screenwriter, and shortly thereafter, [Woodward and Bernstein] came up with this brilliant idea of doing the book as [their] own personal story."

Obviously thinking about the special needs of a successful movie, Redford had advised Woodward and Bernstein to insert themselves as characters in the book. According to the reporting team, Redford suggested that they write about not just what they discovered during their investigations, but how they discovered it. In other words, Redford's early involvement actually helped shape the direction—or at least the narrative style—of history in the making.

The extent of that influence is debatable. Some observers have suggested that "Woodstein's" most dramatic character in the book—the mysterious government source identified only as Deep Throat—was an invention inspired by Hollywood's courting of the reporters. In their reporting for the *Washington Post*, Woodward and Bernstein had not referred to any of their unnamed sources as Deep Throat. That colorful epithet appeared in print for the first time in the book. Many years after the fact, Obst shared his own theory with TV newsreader Brit Hume. After Redford convinced the duo to frame the book as a "personal story":

Obst: "Suddenly this character of 'Deep Throat' showed up, and . . . "
Hume: "Had you ever heard of this 'Deep Throat' figure before that time?"
Obst: "No. There was no 'Deep Throat' character."

But as journalist Timothy Noah persuasively countered in a *Slate* magazine article, "Obst deduces that there was no Deep Throat from the fact that he, David Obst, never heard of Deep Throat until he read *All the President's Men*. The main problem with Obst's theory is that there's no shortage of other people who had heard of Deep Throat." That list includes Barry Sussman, Woodward and Bernstein's editor at the *Washington Post*; *Post* executive editor Ben Bradlee; and Howard Simons, the *Post* managing editor who is credited in *All the President's Men* with nicknaming the secret source. (Simons is deceased, but according to Noah, Sussman says that Simons had "discussed Deep Throat with him back in 1972 and 1973"—at least two years before the publication of the book.)

Although Woodward and Bernstein refuse to identify their famously pseudonymous source, they have consistently maintained that Deep Throat was neither a dramatic invention nor a composite of several different sources. Still, Deep Throat's theatrical utility is obvious—in the book, Woodward furtively meets with his chain-smoking source in a darkened underground garage. It's like something out of a spy novel. Although Woodward's descriptions of those meetings are probably accurate, there's little doubt that he took to heart Redford's advice to dramatize. Consequently, history probably romanticizes the Woodward-and-Bernstein story more so than it might otherwise have.

But it wasn't all give with Redford. His time spent with the reporters had a reverse osmosis effect, as well. The movie version of *All the President's Men* perfectly captures the look, feel, technique, and culture of print journalism circa 1972. Redford and costar Dustin Hoffman, who signed on to play Bernstein, spent weeks with reporters in the *Washington Post* offices and on their reporting beats. Director Alan J. Pakula and screenwriter William Goldman also sat in on editorial sessions, in a largely successful effort to absorb the details of a major newspaper operation for re-creation on the big screen. Technicians and set design-ers took photos of the *Post*'s editorial offices and borrowed actual blueprints so that they could re-create the building down to the last detail on a Burbank soundstage. (The film's set decorators had actual waste paper shipped from the *Post* offices to California and scattered it about the set.) With an eye for detail that was either reportorial or obsessive-compulsive, the filmmakers re-created the Watergate burglary in the real Watergate building; the actors playing the burglars used the same model walkie-talkies as the real burglars had; and the actor playing the security guard who discovers the break-in was in fact the actual security guard who had discovered the break-in. By shooting the film in a low-key documentary style, Pakula further bolstered the sense of realism running through the film.

So how accurate was the actual story told on screen? Every movie narrative based on a true story necessarily pares down the complexity of real life. While *All the President's Men* is no exception to that rule, the film is remarkably faith-ful to the reporting in the book. Credit must go to screenwriter Goldman and director Pakula for compressing a vastly complex story into a lucid plot that works both as drama and historical précis.

Critics correctly noted that *All the President's Men* gives the inaccurate impression that the work of two industrious reporters brought down a president. In fact, although "Woodstein" deserves the credit for doggedly pursuing the story when no one else much cared about it, and for putting the Watergate scandal on the map, an array of other players contributed to the exposure of White House crimes and misdemeanors, including journalists at other papers, congressional investigators, and judges, among others. If their names are some-what less recognizable than Woodward and Bernstein's, blame Redford for not offering *them* early script notes.

Sources and Further Reading

Bernstein, Carl and Bob Woodward. *All the President's Men*. New York: Simon & Schuster, 1987.

Noah, Timothy. "Yes, Virginia, There Is a Deep Throat." *Slate*, May 8, 2002. http://slate.msn.com/id/2065560.

Rosenberg, Scott. "Unmasking Deep Throat." *Salon*, May 7, 2002.

Toplin, Robert Brent. *History by Hollywood*. Chicago: University of Illinois Press, 1996.

The Falcon and the Snowman (1985)

Directed by John Schlesinger

Written by Steven Zaillian

Starring Timothy Hutton and Sean Penn

Sean Penn (left) as Daulton Lee and Timothy Hutton as
Christopher Boyce.
Photo by Dave Friedman, © Orion Pictures Corporation

The espionage escapades of Christopher Boyce and Daulton Lee drained the
CIA of some of its most important secrets from 1975 and 1977. Yet somehow,
Boyce and Lee's two-year adventure in dealing highly classified documents to
the Soviet Union made for a singularly undramatic Hollywood film.

That was puzzling. You'd think that a true tale of drug dealers, spy satellites,
KGB agents, and stolen CIA documents would add up to a rather engaging
thriller.

In 1974, after dropping out of Harbor Junior College, Loyola University,
and California Polytechnic, in that order, twenty-one-year-old Boyce got a job,
through his father's connections, at TRW (called RTX in the film), a major
defense contractor in Southern California. TRW handled some of the CIA's
most sensitive, classified work orders, developing spy satellites. The CIA was in
constant contact with TRW, corresponding via encrypted messages daily. Sometimes the CIA misrouted transmissions to TRW that were meant to go some-

where else. But no one worried about it, because everyone at TRW who could see the messages had high security clearance.

Somehow, through no doing of his own, Boyce skyrocketed up the security clearance ladder. He found himself working in TRW's "Black Vault," the repository for top-secret CIA documents and cipher keys. One of Boyce's responsibilities was monitoring classified CIA message traffic.

What his bosses and even his parents did not know was that, even as he became one of TRW's most trusted, Christopher Boyce was undergoing a crisis of faith. He had developed grave and growing doubts about the government of his own country. The Vietnam War and Watergate rocked the confidence he'd held during his conservative upbringing. In that respect, Boyce was no different than millions of young Americans. The difference between Boyce and those other millions was that Boyce was privy to information about clandestine operations of his government that were never supposed to become public knowledge. Boyce was appalled to learn that the CIA systematically violated treaty agreements with one of its closest allies, Australia, by withholding vital intelligence data. The CIA also meddled—secretly, of course—in Australian domestic politics, infiltrating Aussie labor unions and engaging in other hanky-panky.

Boyce resolved to strike back at the U.S. government. His idea: give as many of those classified top secrets as he could get his hands on to America's archenemy, the Soviet Union. Christopher Boyce would become a spy. He recruited his childhood altar-boy buddy Andrew Daulton Lee—by then a prosperous cocaine trafficker (hence the nickname "the Snowman")—to act as his partner and courier.

Sounds like a thriller, but *The Falcon and the Snowman* could just as easily have been a penetrating character study. Why *does* a well-to-do, conservative son of an FBI agent—as Boyce was—wake up one day and decide to become a Communist spy? Seems like a good question. But John Schlesinger's film offers nothing but pat answers.

The problem, as best as we can diagnose it, appears to be that Schlesinger and screenwriter Steven Zaillian aspired to docudrama verisimilitude, but couldn't shake off the orthodoxies of mainstream Hollywood storytelling. It is conventional in Hollywood films that a character's every action must be "motivated" in the most simple, mechanical way possible. So why did Boyce betray his country? According to the film, the answer is obvious: he was angry with his father!

Boyce, played by Timothy Hutton, clashes with his father from the first moments of the film—despite the fact that Robert Lindsey's book (of the same title) clearly states that even with their developing philosophical estrangement, "theirs was never a stormy relationship." Nevertheless, the movie gives us the clear impression that Boyce turned traitor in order to rebel against a domineering, close-minded dad.

Boyce's true motives were far murkier. His alienation from his family was part of it. "What has transpired never would have happened" had he not been raised in a staunchly conservative home, Boyce said in a 1982 interview. In the same interview, granted to a reporter for Australia's version of *60 Minutes*, Boyce described his "primary purpose" as "personal, personal grudge," though he never specified against whom he held this grudge. He also said that he knew he would be caught, and that becoming a martyr "was a unique way to express myself."

Zaillian's script lifts some of Boyce's lines directly from that interview and places them in Hutton's mouth during a scene in which Boyce is under FBI interrogation, shortly after having been arrested. When Boyce describes security at TRW as "Keystone Kops," that's from the *60 Minutes* piece. When he responds to the FBI agent's asking whether he worries that he has endangered the lives of American citizens, his quip, "They're already in jeopardy" comes straight from the interview as well.

Daulton Lee was a full-time drug dealer whose motivation in the film for turning spy is even simpler than Boyce's. This time, the moviemakers didn't need to dumb it down, because Lee himself was dumb enough. He turned traitor for money. Nothing subtle about that. His secondary motive, portrayed in the film and taken straight from Robert Lindsey's book, was that he faced a drug charge, and he chose to go on the lam rather than turn snitch for the cops.

Neither the film nor the book makes a big deal of it, but one of the more perverse ironies of the case is that, given what amounted to a choice between betraying his country and betraying other drug dealers, Lee betrayed his country. That tells you the type of person Daulton Lee was. But Schlesinger (who had already won an Oscar for *Midnight Cowboy*) and Zaillian (who would go on to win an Oscar for *Schindler's List*) insert moral qualms into the heart of Daulton Lee—moral qualms about becoming a spy that simply never existed.

"It's wrong," Sean Penn, playing Lee, declares. He then proclaims himself a patriot "and proud of it." He flatly refuses Boyce's offer.

In Lindsey's book, Lee laughs at Boyce's "business proposition" and tells him, "Man, you're crazy." But his rejection of the deal is described as merely "tentative," and shortly thereafter, looking for a way out of his own legal and financial mess, Lee counts himself in.

Lee was the consummate amoral cynic. Why play that down? When *Falcon* came out, it would still be seven years before Quentin Tarantino emerged on the scene and showed the moviegoing public that amoral cynicism could be pretty cool. Hollywood formula demands that audiences "identify" with lead characters, and it demands that each major character follow an "arc." Lee, like many of us in life, had no "arc." He was simply a crook. To him, selling secrets was the same as selling drugs—a quick way to make a ton of money without doing much work.

It seems to us that the moviemakers calculated that audiences would be turned off by the real, unfiltered Daulton Lee, so they transformed his sleazy, unrepentant criminality into something of a fall from grace.

The movie continues to mute the real Lee's sociopathic narcissism by omitting his defense after his arrest for espionage—that defense being to stab Boyce in the back. Lee went so far as to claim that Boyce actually worked for the CIA as part of some bizarre "disinformation" plot. Lee betrayed his country, his best friend, and even his Soviet contacts, to whom he lied repeatedly. The only people Lee refused to betray were other dope dealers. That's where he drew the line.

Lee's conspiracy theory was designed for no other purpose than to save his own ass. Lindsey's book, however, recounts some of the mysteries of the case that could, possibly, point to a deeper CIA plot in which both Boyce and Lee were pawns. Why, exactly, was a twenty-one-year-old college dropout granted a high-level security clearance after less than one year in a menial job at TRW? Why, Lindsey wonders, was the fugitive Lee able to pass back and forth across the Mexican border at legal checkpoints over and over? And, most intriguing, when Lee visited the Soviet embassy in Mexico City, why wasn't he photographed? He must have been. The CIA kept that embassy under constant surveillance. Why wasn't the agency alerted to Lee's antics much sooner?

Or were they?

Curiously, the movie asserts at least one element of the CIA theory as hard fact. The folder containing records of the CIA's ultrasecret, but obsolete,

"Pyramider" satellite project was "mistakenly" left in the open—easy pickings for Boyce. In the movie, as he reflects on that incident, Hutton's Boyce declares the Pyramider folder "bait."

Bait? Are Schlesinger and Zaillian suggesting that the CIA was on to Boyce all along—and even that they used the two for some nefarious purpose? If that is what the director and writer believe, they never elaborate on their theory in the film.

There are numerous minor examples of Hollywood-izing in the movie. In one scene, Lee gets into a car chase with a local cop. His younger brother David is in the car. Lee tells him to jump out, showing admirable concern for his brother's welfare. In the real incident, the passenger was one of Lee's stoner friends. The car belonged to Lee's brother, which actually cast him under suspicion.

Nor does the movie mention, even in its final text scroll, that Boyce (who was sentenced to forty years) escaped from prison in 1979 and proceeded to rob seventeen banks. He was caught, again, nineteen months later.

Boyce was an avid falconer (hence his nickname, "the Falcon"). In the film his arrest occurs moments after he has freed his final bird. That's not what happened—he had a friend free the bird when he was in jail—but it makes for a nicely cinematic, if ham-handed metaphor.

In fact, that scene sums up what's wrong with the film version of *The Falcon and the Snowman.* Though they accurately followed the broad factual outlines of the story, the moviemakers added a layer of Hollywood cliché over the truth wherever they could. They would have been better off throwing out the facts of the case and starting their screenplay from scratch, fictionalizing the whole film. Then they could have tailored it to fit the parameters of mainstream movies. Adding gratuitous touches of high melodrama to the fascinating facts of the case made *The Falcon and the Snowman* feel more phony than fiction.

Sources and Further Reading

"A Spy's Story." *60 Minutes (Australia)*, May 23, 1982.

Lindsey, Robert. *The Falcon and the Snowman: A True Story of Friendship and Espionage.* Guilford, CT: The Lyons Press, 1979.

McCollum, Sean. "Secrets for Sale." *New York Times Upfront*, April 2, 2001.

Summer of Sam (1999)

Directed by Spike Lee
Written by Victor Colicchio, Michael Imperioli, and Spike Lee
Starring John Leguizamo, Mira Sorvino, and Michael Badalucco

John Leguizamo and Adrien Brody as two characters who never really existed, and, therefore, didn't lose sleep during New York's Son of Sam murders.
Photo by David Lee. © Touchstone Pictures. All Rights Reserved.

When word got out in 1998 that Spike Lee was filming a fictional account of the 1976–1977 "Son of Sam" murder spree, families of the victims picketed several shooting locations. Several gave outraged interviews, decrying Lee's alleged exploitation of their grief for financial gain. Lee took a beating in the press.

Apparently, the movie's PR tag line, "It was a time they'd never forget," was spot-on. More than two decades later, memories of the terror remained raw. Even convicted Son of Sam killer David Berkowitz, who had become a born-again Christian, gave a tearful interview in which he expressed regret that the movie would resurrect "the madness, the ugliness of the past." Lee's movie was a nostalgia trip for the demented.

Lee, for his part, protested that his rights as an artist came first, and he asserted that the film would not "glorify David Berkowitz." He was right. It didn't. Berkowitz is not much of a character in the movie, depicted as a deranged slob who scribbles graffiti all over his own apartment and shoots his neighbor's dog when he's not shooting people. All of Berkowitz's seven attacks, which killed six young people, are depicted in the film. You can see why the families of the victims would be disturbed.

All of the attacks were reenacted on film as accurately as possible, considering that the best witnesses—the victims themselves—tended to be dead. Accurately, that is, except for the possibility that Berkowitz did not commit all of the attacks.

In 1987 freelance investigative reporter Maury Terry published a book called *The Ultimate Evil*, making a case that the Son of Sam murders were committed by a Satanic cult based in Yonkers' Untermeyer Park. Berkowitz, Terry said, committed only two of the murders and acted as a lookout during the others. There were five different shooters, Terry reported, one of them a woman. Ten years after Terry's book came out, but a year before Lee filmed his movie, Berkowitz granted Terry an interview and "confirmed" the basic thrust of Terry's book. He said that he was, in fact, part of the Untermeyer cult. The killing spree was part of a Satanic plot to "cause chaos." He shot some of the people he was convicted of shooting, but not all of them.

None of the cult allegations made it into Lee's film. Terry wasn't involved in the movie at all. Lee stuck to the public story, in which Berkowitz was ordered to kill by a talking dog. We even get to see the dog trot into Berkowitz's grubby apartment and qualify for the SAG daily rate by delivering a few lines.

Instead, the movie is like the bleak, depressing flip side of *American Graffiti*. George Lucas's period masterpiece gazed back across eleven years at the dying moments of Kennedy-era optimism. *Summer of Sam* captured the darkest days of Carter-era malaise, from a vantage point of twenty-two years after the fact.

As dreary as things were in the Good Ol' USA on the whole circa 1977, they were worse in New York City. Two years earlier, the city had come close to declaring bankruptcy. The economic outlook was not much prettier in 1977. The Sam-inspired wave of terror came along with a record heat wave and, on July 13 (seventeen days after Son of Sam's fifth attack, and eighteen days before his final one), a power blackout plunged the whole suffering city into darkness—with no air conditioning.

Lee depicts all of these events in *Summer of Sam*, casting himself as a deadpan (fictional) TV news reporter whose narration fills in the expository gaps.

The blackout uncorked the anger that had simmered all summer long in New York. The citizens of the great city decided to help themselves to whatever merchandise they could get their paws on, inflicting hundreds of millions of dollars in looting and vandalism damage in twenty-five hours.

With the killer on the loose, discos emptied and women with shoulder-length brown hair (the physical type allegedly preferred by the mad gunman) hacked off their locks and donned blonde wigs, all of which is shown in Lee's film (from a script cowritten by Michael Imperioli, best known as Christopher on *The Sopranos*).

One thing Spike Lee evidently is not and never was, however, is a punk rocker. While 1977 was the pinnacle of New York punk, and Lee takes the film on a field trip to CBGB's along with his Bronx-based mooks, he gets almost every detail wrong. Memo to Spike: dog collars and foot-high Mohawks were an eighties thing. In 1977 ripped jeans and safety pins were still the vogue—and safety pins were mostly an English affectation.

As it turns out, punk rockers may not be the only group who suffered at the hands of Lee's tendencies toward stereotype: Italian American groups accused Lee of stereotyping young Italian men, as well. *Summer of Sam* is a largely faithful portrayal of a depressing, vaguely insane era. Unless you're a punk or a goombah.

Sources and Further Reading

Geller, Andy. "Summer of Insanity as Killer Terrorized City." *New York Post*, June 27, 1999.

Newton, Michael. *Raising Hell: An Encyclopedia of Devil Worship and Satanic Crime*. New York: Avon Books, 1993.

Terry, Maury. *The Ultimate Evil: An Investigation Into America's Most Dangerous Satanic Cult*. Garden City, NY: Dolphin Books, 1987.

Scandal (1989)

Directed by Michael Caton-Jones
Written by Michael Thomas
Starring John Hurt, Ian McKellen, and Joanne Whalley-Kilmer

Bridget Fonda as Mandy Rice-Davies and Joanne Whalley-Kilmer as Christine Keeler. © *British Screen Productions*

Judged by the jaded standards of the post-Clinton era, the extramarital sex habits of a conservative British war minister in 1961 seem like rather tame fare. But back in those days, when postwar England was just starting to swing, the episode that came to be known as "the Profumo Affair" toppled a government, ended the career of a rising political star, and, not incidentally, cost the life of an innocent man.

It took twenty-eight years for the Profumo Affair to come to the screen. Although, on paper, its brew of sex and espionage seems to make it an ideal film subject, it's understandable why American filmmakers didn't seem to be all that interested in it. While the scandal made headlines Stateside, there was no strong U.S. angle to hook domestic audiences. Britain's another story. Former War Secretary John Profumo, once headed for the prime ministership, quit politics after the scandal and devoted the rest of his life to quiet charity work. Decades after the incident, there remained great sensitivity in England to the idea of bringing the scandal back into the public eye.

Besides, the true villain in the scandal was long dead. He killed himself to escape disgrace while still on trial for pandering back in 1963. His name was Stephen Ward, and he was an osteopath by trade, and by all accounts a skillful one. His clients included celebrities and numerous members of the British aristocracy. Ward also had a fondness for young, pretty women. Several could usually be found hanging around his London flat, and a couple of showgirls named Christine Keeler and Mandy Rice-Davies lived with him for a while. Ward often encouraged his two social worlds to intersect. One of the results of his social experiment was that Profumo (who was married to a well-known actress) conducted a brief affair with Keeler.

While that transgression was bad enough, and made far worse when Profumo lied about it on the floor of Parliament, it turned out that Keeler was simultaneously carrying on with a Soviet diplomat named Ivanov who, it turned out, was a spy. The security risks of Profumo's behavior were obvious.

When the scandal broke, the government sought a scapegoat, someone to blame for the whole sordid thing. Ward fit the bill. He was investigated and eventually arrested, charged with pimping for Keeler and other girls. His friends deserted him. His clients no longer came by for their regular spinal adjustments. He went on trial, where prosecutors vilified him as a pervert and a communist, the embodiment of evil. Lonely, broke, and facing the prospect of a prison sentence he could not tolerate, Ward committed suicide with a massive dose of sleeping tablets. And so was Ward's place in history etched—until the mid-1980s, when new research debunked the prosecution's characterization of Ward and revealed that he was working for the British intelligence service MI5. When scandal struck, his handlers in the spy agency left him out to dry, and die.

Clearing Ward's name was apt justification to revisit the scandal, regardless of Profumo's feelings. Michael Caton-Jones's film is Ward's story, and it presents an accurate picture of his life from the point when he met Keeler until his death. If anything, the film suffers from its attention to the facts, cramming in incident after incident without much attention to a coherent narrative. As a result, the details of the somewhat complex scandal are murky in the movie.

Keeler's character in the film comes off considerably better, and better clothed, than the real Christine. Ward discovered her when she was dancing topless in a

London club. Actually, *posing* topless would be a better way of putting it, because city ordinance at the time allowed women to appear bare-breasted onstage only if they did not move around. So Christine stood stock-still in a line of seminude girls at the back of the stage. The film makes her the star of the show, and a fully costumed one, at that. For that matter, even though the real Christine's place in British history is assured only by acts performed while nude, the actress portraying Miss Keeler is filmed with the utmost discretion, even in her one unavoidable nude scene: Christine met Profumo while emerging nude from a swimming pool at one of Ward's parties.

Nude scenes (or lack thereof) aside, Caton-Jones's version of Christine is far more attached to Ward than the narcissistic teenager with whom Ward lived, but never slept, could ever have been. Her weepy remorse at the trouble she's caused Ward never existed. It's as if Caton-Jones is trying to turn the sad and rather pathetic story of Stephen Ward into a romantic tearjerker, which is difficult because Keeler and Ward never had a romance and, though Keeler had no compunctions about climbing into the sack with any two-legged male she could find, she and Ward never had sex.

One of the most famous anecdotes to come out of the scandal involves the "man in the mask." This stemmed from a party, attended by Ward and numerous members of London's upper class and high society. Allegedly, at this soiree, the partygoers lounged nude, except for one man who wore only a maid's apron and a mask, "because he was so well known." According to the story, the man was flogged by the other dinner guests, and quite enjoyed himself in the process. The masked man was said to be of very high social standing—a friend of the queen's, in fact.

Caton-Jones plays that scene for all it's worth, and who can blame him? In reality, the incident was far more mundane than the rumors (which were first reported by *Washington Star* columnist Dorothy Kilgallen) and the movie would have it. The "man in the mask" was no one important; he was a Yorkshire businessman, he wore a pair of striped shorts, not an apron, and no one beat him at this otherwise normal dinner party, which was given by one Mariella Novotny. The businessman greeted guests in this bizarre fashion as a gag, when the Novotny butler called in sick.

But the movie's version of the event does make for the most amusing scene in the film.

Sources and Further Reading

Irving, Clive et. al. *Anatomy of a Scandal: A Study of the Profumo Affair.* New York: William Morrow and Co., 1963.

Knightley, Philip and Caroline Kennedy. *An Affair of State: The Profumo Case and the Framing of Stephen Ward.* New York: Athaneum, 1987.

Quiz Show (1994)

Directed by Robert Redford

Written by Paul Attanasio

Starring Ralph Fiennes, John Turturro, and Rob Morrow

Ralph Fiennes (center) as Columbia University professor
Charles Van Doren.

Maybe we really do live in cynical times, but if any of the current "reality" TV game shows—*Survivor* and so forth—were exposed as phonies, the winners fixed in advance, would anyone be truly shocked? Sure, there would be a scandal, but after more than a half-century of TV-dominated culture, we've become a nation of jaded media sophisticates. There's a tacit understanding that even "reality" television is not much more "real" than its scripted counterpart, and both are pretty far removed from real life.

Five decades ago, when television was a thrilling novelty, there was no reason to believe that what was offered as truth on TV was anything but. "Reality TV" was a far bigger phenomenon in those days than now, in the form of quiz shows. They offered the weekly drama of ordinary Joes competing for then-fabulous sums of money by answering arcane trivia questions. As many as fifty million Americans made it a point to tune in to the best-rated quiz shows, enthralled by the sheer human drama of it all. When a congressional committee revealed that the quiz shows were no less scripted than *The Colgate Comedy Hour*, America's cherished national naivete suffered a serious setback—before finally shattering under the weight of the subsequent two decades.

As the *Washington Post* editorialized at the time, the quiz show scam "robbed people of a kind of faith that it is dangerous to destroy in a democracy."

Quiz show champions became the American idols of the era for their ability to answer the most obscure questions from the most esoteric regions of history and culture. The most famous of them, Columbia University prof Charles Van Doren, made the cover of *Time* magazine and earned a regular spot on NBC's *Today Show* after his apparently incredible run on the network's quiz show centerpiece, *Twenty-One*.

Robert Redford's chronicle of the quiz show scandal purported to explore the ethics of public lying and its effect on both the public and the liars. Strangely, he and scripter Paul Attanasio undermined their own message by producing a film filled with its own distortions, so much so that one of the major investigators of the affair dismissed Redford's movie as "a farce."

That investigator, assistant district attorney Joseph Stone (a retired judge by the time the film came out) had good reason to feel perturbed. He had convened the first grand jury investigation into the scandal, the records of which were inexplicably sealed, and did more than any other legal or political official to bring the fix to light. Yet somehow, Stone was AWOL from Redford's film entirely. As if he didn't even exist.

The protagonist of *Quiz Show* is Dick Goodwin, a cocky young congressional aide who, in the film, conducts his own gumshoe investigation after a New York judge sneers at his request to unseal the grand jury files. The ersatz Goodwin blows the story wide open single-handed.

Who was Richard Goodwin and how did he become a cinematic sleuth? Goodwin was, indeed, a congressional aide in 1958, when the scandal broke. He later became a noted political speechwriter (for John F. Kennedy among others), author, and husband of equally noted historian Doris Kearns Goodwin. His role in exposing the quiz show scandal consisted primarily of taking a train from Washington, D.C., to New York, meeting with Stone, and persuading a judge to release the sealed documents—the exact opposite of what occurs in the movie.

It didn't take much persuading, or shoe leather. Both Stone and Goodwin knew that no judge (especially no judge who aspired to the federal bench) would refuse the United States Congress, of which Goodwin was then the unlikely embodiment.

More to the point for purposes of the film, Goodwin is the author of *Remembering America: A Voice From the Sixties*, the literary property that Redford acquired as the intended basis for his motion picture. Goodwin himself was hired as a consultant to the production.

But Goodwin's book—more specifically, the single chapter from the book that discusses quiz shows—is rather sketchy in its details. Redford and Attanasio filled in the gaps with invented scenes and fabricated dialogue. One actual participant in the scandal, network executive Albert Freedman, reported that "everything they have me saying is fantasy." Freedman, played by Hank Azaria, comes off in the flick as a pointedly amoral worm.

The engaging, handsome, and genuinely intelligent Van Doren became a central figure in the downfall of the quiz shows. The movie correctly shows him clinging, until the bitter end, to the lie that he never received the quiz answers in advance, only to break down and confess in front of congressional investigators. His three-year ordeal is scrunched into several months in movie time. The whole scandal unfolds with lightning quickness in the film. Van Doren's cordial-but-tense relationship with Goodwin forms the emotional nucleus of the film.

The high point is an exchange in which Goodwin tells Van Doren, "I know you're lying, Charlie. We can prove it." Van Doren, in defiance of his sealed fate, blithely replies, "I'm sorry you feel that way, Dick." The moment is taken verbatim from Goodwin's account. Except that the conversation transpired in Washington, in a rental car. Redford places the scene in a kayak as the pair paddle across an idyllic Connecticut pond. The interaction between the two men throughout the film is considerably more complex than it actually was.

Goodwin simply did not do much of what he is shown doing in the film. Much of that fell to Stone and the whistle-blowing contestants. On the other hand, many contestants refused to blow the whistle, even when under oath. This amazed Stone, who said he had never seen perjury committed on such a huge scale. What was truly amazing was that rigging a TV game show was not, at that time, illegal. Dozens of otherwise ordinary, respectable people were willing to commit a crime to cover up something that was legal.

In the aftermath of the scandal, fixing a TV game show became a federal offense. What is not a crime, nor should it be, is misrepresenting the historical record for the purposes of entertainment—though it was in the name of "entertainment" that the network execs behind the quiz show fix rationalized their own actions. But straying from the facts as far as Redford does in a film that purports to confront the ethical conflict between truth and profit at least presents a head-scratching moral dilemma for Hollywood storytellers who take their material from fact.

Sources and Further Reading

Goodwin, Richard N. *Remembering America: A Voice From the Sixties.* Boston: Little Brown, 1988.

The American Experience. "The Quiz Show Scandal." http://www.pbs.org/wgbh/amex/quizshow/filmmore/index.html.

Venanzi, Katie. "An Examination of the Quiz Show Scandals of the 1950s." http://www.inform.umd.edu/EdRes/Colleges/HONR/HONR269J/.WWW/projects/venanzi.html.

Thirteen Days (2001)

Directed by Roger Donaldson
Written by David Self
Starring Kevin Costner and Bruce Greenwood

(Left to right) Steven Culp as Robert F. Kennedy, Bruce Greenwood as John F. Kennedy, and Kevin Costner as Kenny O'Donnell. *Photo by Ben Glass, © New Line Cinema*

Want to give an aging political pundit a stroke? Who doesn't? Here's how. The easiest way to induce windbag apoplexy is to make a movie about President John F. Kennedy.

Oliver Stone learned this the hard way when he created *JFK* (see page 428). In that film, he presumed to question the orthodox, if publicly unpopular, view that President Kennedy was assassinated by a lone gunman. A decade later, another Kennedy flick threatened to again tweak the forces of academic dogma by purporting to portray an inside account of Kennedy's most crucial incident in office, the Cuban Missile Crisis.

Thirteen Days is also unique in its portrayal of Kennedy as neither a relentless womanizer nor the victim of an assassination. He is, as played by proficient Canadian actor Bruce Greenwood, simply the president of the United States. How novel. More than that, he is the president facing the most perilous predica-

The real Robert F. Kennedy and John F. Kennedy.

ment any president ever faced. A poor decision on his part would have ignited a nuclear war and incinerated eighty million Americans.

As with any historical incident, particularly one involving President Kennedy, how you understand the events of those eponymous "thirteen days" in October 1962 depends on your personal prejudices. Was the missile crisis Kennedy's finest hour, when he proved himself a leader of men and decision-maker to be reckoned with? Or was it the near-disastrous result of his own reck-lessness, from which he, and the world, barely escaped? Even the length of the crisis depends on your point of view. Was it the period from October 16 to October 28, 1962? That was the span from the day that Kennedy first saw CIA photos of Soviet missile bases in Cuba to the day they were removed.

Or did it really begin as early as August 22, when U.S. intelligence learned of a Soviet military buildup on the island? The Soviet ambassador dismissed the weaponry there as "defensive," and Kennedy took his word for it.

Leading up to *Thirteen Days'* premiere in January 2001, professional his-torians and political columnists whose careers dated back to the JFK era were gripped with panic. It was revealed that the film's biggest (and only) star, Kevin Costner, would be acting the part of the historically insignificant Kenneth O'Donnell. O'Donnell was a special assistant to the president. His duties con-sisted largely of filling out the presidential schedule. He was kind of a glorified booking agent. He was also a Harvard buddy of the president's brother and closest advisor, Attorney General Robert Kennedy.

O'Donnell didn't figure much in policy decisions. To call his role in the missile crisis "minor" would be generous. In tapes of the high-level missile meetings (recorded surreptitiously by Kennedy and not released until 1996) O'Donnell pipes up only twice.

Costner, it was believed, would never accept a role as such an inconsequential character. The actor's career track consisted of star vehicle after star vehicle in which he'd cast himself as a messianic superhero: *Dances with Wolves, Robin Hood, Waterworld*. With Costner serving as executive producer, there was justifiable apprehension that *Thirteen Days* would become *Kenny O'Donnell Saves the World*: a patently ridiculous scenario. These fears were heightened when it was reported that Kevin O'Donnell, Kenneth's son, way rich in his own right (he made a fortune cofounding the internet company Earthlink), poured millions of his own cash into the film.

Now, *someone* had to finance this film. Reportedly, three studios and no fewer than eight directors were at one time involved with the project, only to drop it. It's not difficult to understand why. This is a movie with no car chases, no romance, no space aliens, no meteorites hurling toward Earth, no Marvel Comics superheroes, no beautiful women, and no especially handsome men (face it: Costner's a bit past his prime, and Greenwood's a fine looking fellow, but he's no Jack Kennedy). There is no sex and almost no violence.

In the only violent sequence, we witness the shoot down of Major Rudolf Anderson, a U-2 pilot who was the only fatality of the Cuban Missile Crisis. The filmmakers re-create Major Anderson's crash as accurately as they can, given that there's no way to know exactly what Anderson did in the moments before he was hit.

That's the highlight of the movie as far as "action" goes. It's no surprise, then, that some of the money required to finance the film had to come from someone with a personal interest in the project. So did Costner and the younger O'Donnell turn the president's schedule-maker into the Man Who Saved Civilization?

Not really. There's no question that the film inflates O'Donnell's activities—to the point of melodrama. Certainly O'Donnell never phoned a pilot and ordered him to fib to his superiors about getting shot at over Cuba. One historian, Graham T. Allison, found that scene stunningly "unreal." Others complain that the film presents O'Donnell as a "third Kennedy brother." However, according to Harvard University historian Ernest R. May, who transcribed many of the secret Kennedy tapes, "only once or twice in *Thirteen Days* does O'Donnell do or say anything that he might not actually have done or said."

May notes that O'Donnell was "an important figure in the White House." The fact that he was admitted at all to the exclusive meetings of "ExComm" (the special "Executive Committee" assembled by the Kennedys to manage the crisis) proves that he was a valued member of Kennedy's inner circle. At one point in the tapes, O'Donnell is heard in what May called "a tart exchange" with Defense Secretary Robert McNamara—so it's safe to say he was not deferential when it came to expressing his views.

O'Donnell comes off in the film as more of a player than he actually was, but it seems fair to conclude that he at least might have been more involved, in an off-the-record way, with the Kennedys' decision-making process than the official records show. *Thirteen Days* is inaccurate about O'Donnell, but it isn't unrealistic.

(Oddball aside: The character of Kenny O'Donnell makes one brief appearance in Stone's *JFK*. He's only in the "Director's Cut," and you'd have to watch the credits to know it's supposed to be him. But in his brief moment onscreen, he is seen illegally ordering the president's slain body out of the Dallas hospital before an autopsy can be performed—implying that O'Donnell was part of the conspiracy against President Kennedy, a most unlikely prospect.)

Another commentator, none other than Watergate figure John Dean, took the movie to task for ignoring revelations about the Kennedys in Seymour Hersh's tabloidy exposé, *The Dark Side of Camelot*. Per Hersh, O'Donnell was not only the president's schedule maker, he was JFK's pimp. It was part of O'Donnell's job, says Hersh, to keep the libidinous president supplied with willing young women.

What that has to do with the Cuban Missile Crisis is difficult to say, but Hersh raises the more salient point that Kennedy's covert attempts to have the CIA assassinate Cuban leader Fidel Castro may have been a factor in the crisis. Castro may never have accepted Soviet troops and weapons on his soil had not Kennedy angered him.

By ignoring that inconvenient piece of history, the film perpetuates the "myth" rather than the reality of the crisis, says Dean. He makes a valid point.

On the other hand, the film deserves credit for making clear something that Kennedy understood, but historians generally have not: the Cuban Missile

Crisis was not about Cuba—it was about Berlin. The Berlin Wall was just a year old, and the Soviet client state of East Germany badly wanted to annex West Berlin, a "free" city in the heart of the communist country.

"The one and only safeguard for West Berliners was the U.S. threat to use nuclear weapons against the Soviet Union," writes May. "Anything that weakened the credibility of this threat could have forced the U.S. president to surrender West Berlin or else initiate what could have turned into a global nuclear war."

By placing missiles capable of delivering nuclear weapons in Cuba, Soviet Premier Nikita Kruschev was trying to wrench Berlin away from Kennedy. The movie lifts dialogue directly from the transcribed secret tapes to hammer home the point that Berlin was Kennedy's main concern. In that respect, the film is more accurate than many accounts by journalists and historians.

The movie has also been criticized, by conservative pundits mostly, for showing the joint chiefs of staff—the country's top military leaders—pushing Kennedy to start a war. In the film, they suggest launching a sneak attack on the missile bases, followed by a full-scale invasion of Cuba. Right-wing columnist Charles Krauthammer condemned this depiction as a "lie," albeit an "ideological" one. The movie, Krauthammer griped, shows the American military brass, as represented by Generals Curtis LeMay and Maxwell Taylor, as "unredeemed warmongers."

Never mind that LeMay is infamous for his "bomb them back into the Stone Age" quote in the early days of the Vietnam War. LeMay and Taylor did lobby the president forcefully for military action against Cuba—action that would surely have resulted in exactly the scenario Kennedy feared: the Soviets would attack Berlin, and all-out nuclear war would follow close behind. The generals were convinced that force was the only option, and they had little patience for Kennedy's insistence on considering alternatives. A tense exchange in the film between LeMay and Kennedy, in which LeMay appears to taunt the president, declaring smugly, "You're in quite a fix," was quoted straight from tape transcripts.

In the end, Kennedy proved the generals wrong. A naval blockade of Cuba worked, and Kruschev backed down and pulled his missiles off the island. The film also correctly includes a backroom deal, negotiated by Robert Kennedy, that had the United States pulling its own missiles out of Turkey. But those missiles, as the film also notes, were obsolete and set to be junked anyway. The secret deal was nothing but a sop to the Soviets that let them feel they were saving face. The missile crisis was solved without force, without an invasion of Cuba, and, except for Major Anderson, without casualties.

Whether the generals were "unredeemed warmongers" is another matter of interpretation—both of history and of the film *Thirteen Days*. Decades later, Kennedy's defense secretary McNamara preferred to characterize the generals' approach as "a mistake," one that he believes would not be repeated if a similar crisis arose today. (Memo to McNamara: George W. Bush says hi.)

"In a crisis I think the experience of the Cuban Missile Crisis would cause both military and civilian security advisers to apprise it, to be much, much more cautious, much, much more careful than many were during the thirteen-day period of the Cuban Missile Crisis," said McNamara, in an interview with PBS. "That would be my expectation. It's both my hope and my belief."

Sources and Further Reading

Beschloss, Michael R. *The Crisis Years: Kennedy and Kruschev, 1960–1963.* New York: Edward Burlingame Books, 1991.

Brubaker, Paul. *The Cuban Missile Crisis in American History.* Berkeley Heights, NJ: Enslow Publishers, 2001.

Chang, Laurence and Peter Kornbluth, eds. *The Cuban Missile Crisis, 1962.* New York: The New Press, 1992.

Dean, John W. "Does *Thirteen Days* Get it Right?" Salon, January 19, 2001.

Krauthammer, Charles. "Costner, Cuba, and the Kennedys: Hollywood Takes a Stab at the Cuban Missile Crisis and Almost Gets It Right." *Weekly Standard.* January 1, 2001.

May, Ernest R. "Thirteen Days in 145 Minutes." *American Prospect.* January 1, 2001.

Schindler's List (1993)

Directed by Steven Spielberg
Written by Steven Zaillian
Starring Liam Neeson and Ben Kingsley

Ben Kingsley (left) as Itzhak Stern and Liam Neeson as Oskar Schindler.
Photo by David James, © Universal City Studios Inc.

For almost two decades after World War II, stories of non-Jews who saved Jews from death in the Holocaust remained obscure. Few people, outside the eleven hundred Jews he rescued and their families, had ever heard the name Oskar Schindler. The curious tale of Schindler, a swastika-sporting Nazi war profiteer who practiced bribery, confidence games, and roguish charm to keep the hands of Hitler's butchers off his Jewish slave-laborers, received no publicity until the early 1960s.

In 1968 MGM put cash on the table for the motion picture rights to Schindler's life story, but the project rotted, as so many Hollywood ideas do, in that place today's biz insiders call "development hell." MGM never produced a Schindler movie, but in 1982 Australian author Thomas Kennealy did publish a novel about Schindler. At the time, director Steven Spielberg was building his rep with cute little movies about cuddly creatures from other planets.

After another twelve years, Spielberg had the clout (and then some) to turn Kennealy's "historical fiction" about Schindler into a "serious" film. By that time, Oskar Schindler was twenty years dead—and he was an overnight sensation. With Spielberg as the teller, the Schindler incident immediately became the best-known story of the Holocaust.

Until *Schindler's List* was made, the Nazi extermination of six million Jews was never considered palatable fodder for Hollywood's "dream factory." For a mogul of Spielberg's standing to make a Holocaust movie was unprecedented. America treated the release of *Schindler's List*, whose three-hour run-time suited its gravitas, as a major cultural milestone. The president of the United States attended the premiere in 1994.

The film is laden with lump-in-the-throat moments straight out of the Spielberg Manual of Style, including what must qualify as one of the most crassly manipulative scenes ever filmed: a large group of women are herded into the "showers" at Auschwitz and forced to stand naked under the spouts for agonizing moments of uncertainty as they, and the viewers, brace for the inevitable flow of poison gas—only to have shower heads finally spray forth plain water after all.

Spielberg collected the plaudits he no doubt expected for his courage, vision, and all that. Whether he expected it or not, he got ripped too: he was accused of pasteurizing the horrors of the Holocaust for popular consumption and of rendering history's greatest horror as heartstring-plucking entertainment. It's not necessarily our place to render that type of moral-aesthetic judgment. We have to pat Spielberg on the back, however, for his admirable restraint when it comes to the Hollywood practice of embellishing the historical record. Even when his Academy Award–winning film hits its most contrived emotional notes, *Schindler's List* doesn't devolve into fantasy. Not too far, anyway.

Nearly every significant moment in the film is supported by eyewitness or participant recollection, even the "girl in red" scene. Watching in horror from a hilltop as Nazis massacre Jews in the ghetto below, Schindler spies a little girl in a red coat, toddling through the chaos. The film is otherwise shown in black-and-white, and that red coat is the only splash of color that appears until the epilogue. A typical Spielberg unsubtlety? Sure—but the red coat moment comes from Schindler's own journals.

The seemingly incredible "shower scene" derives from personal accounts, too. A group of women, designated by Schindler's now famous "list" for relocation to his own factory, were mistakenly misdirected to Auschwitz, where they were herded into "showers," which turned out to be real showers.

The "list" was Schindler's inventory of Jews employed in his own, privately run concentration camp, where he insured that living conditions were essentially humane and where the inmates were under Schindler's very illegal protection from Nazi extermination. For most of the war, Schindler shielded "his" Jews from the worst of the atrocities (albeit making a fortune off their unpaid labor in his factory at the same time). The "list" became a necessity toward the end of the war. Until then Hitler had allowed "essential" Jews—those whose forced labor, mostly in munitions plants, was deemed necessary for the war effort— to live. When he knew that he was going to lose the war, however, Hitler ordered all Jews, "essential" or not, to the death camps. Up to that point, Schindler had conned his Nazi friends into believing that his workers were of the "essential" variety, but when the order came down to "liquidate" Plaszow labor camp (where Schindler's factory was based), Schindler drew up a list of names and handed it to the camp's psychopathic commandant, Amon Goeth.

In addition to being a degenerate murderer, this particular Nazi was (like many of his colleagues) deeply corrupt. Schindler bribed Goeth into placing the listed Jews in Schindler's personal custody instead of wiping them out.

The three hundred women who mistakenly ended up at Auschwitz were on his list. Schindler did the impossible and extracted them from the death camp— his most astonishing accomplishment. How he managed to rescue the women, no one knows to this day. Spielberg's script follows the theory that, with German defeat imminent, even the hardest hard-core Nazis were on the make for any means to finance their postwar escape. He shows Schindler (Liam Neeson) visiting Auschwitz in person, where he plies a death camp commander with diamonds.

That is a plausible theory, though it would have been a monumental personal risk for Schindler to show up at Auschwitz and offer a face-to-face bribe to an important Nazi. He took many great risks in his effort to save Jewish lives, but none quite that brazen.

In her memoir, Schindler's widow gives a different account of the rescue. According to Emilie Schindler, her husband called upon a female childhood friend identified only as Hilde, the free-spirited daughter of a German industrialist. Mrs. Schindler described Hilde as "strikingly beautiful, slender, and graceful," and reported that Schindler dispatched her to Auschwitz to "personally take care of the release of the women." Hilde got the job done. Emilie Schindler never learned how, and Hilde never told her.

"But I suspect," wrote the widow Schindler, "that her great beauty played a decisive part."

Spielberg largely downplays the contributions of Schindler's long-suffering wife. She gamely weathered his extramarital affairs, which numbered in the hundreds, even thousands, while playing an essential role in aiding the Jewish workers under Schindler's care. Schindler is credited with smuggling in extra food rations and other amenities for his charges. Emilie asserted that it was she, not her husband, who coordinated that dangerous exercise in humanitarianism.

The movie rightly paints Schindler as a morally ambiguous character who unreservedly reveled in his prodigious wealth accrued from the toil of his Jewish slaves, but who simultaneously put his own life on the line by shielding them from Nazi executioners. How he evolved from shameless war profiteer to selfless savior, on the other hand, is not explained. In fairness to Spielberg, there apparently was no evolution.

Schindler is generally described as "an enigma," "a complex man," and a "contradictory personality." All of those descriptors are accurate, and Spielberg struggles with the lack of "character arc," demanded by the "rules" of screenwriting. If anyone's allowed to rewrite those rules, it should be Spielberg, but he nonetheless appears torn between his reverence for the true persona of Schindler and the need for his onscreen Schindler to undergo Hollywood-mandated "change."

Almost as soon as he came to Krakow, Poland, following the tracks of conquering Nazi tanks, Schindler began helping local Jews. He warned them of *Aktions*, sudden crackdowns by the SS in which Krakow's Jews were attacked and murdered en masse. We never see him doing that in the film. If we saw the good side of the early Schindler, it would dampen the drama of his later decision to rescue more than a thousand Jews. Schindler wouldn't comfortably fit the "rogue savior" stereotype that Hollywood adores. Under the usual formula, the lovable scoundrel must experience some startling, character-changing revelation, thus giving the audience a satisfying moment to feel the emotions of his transformation into a hero. Schindler, the real one, never experienced any such moment. He was always a savior. And always a rogue.

The way Schindler behaved after the war, right up to his death in 1974, proved that the man never changed. He moved to Argentina for a while alongside his wife and the families of a few "Schindler Jews." A few years later, he inexplicably abandoned them there while he relocated to Germany. Emilie never saw him again.

His wartime good deeds finally gained public recognition in 1961. In Germany, a country that had supposedly renounced its Nazi past, the publicity earned him nothing but scorn and abuse. He was a "traitor," a "Jew kisser." (Schindler was once imprisoned by the Nazis for planting an avuncular smack on a little Jewish girl who gave him a birthday present. Actually, Schindler was jailed three times, two more than Spielberg shows.) Schindler found friends among the Jews he had rescued two decades earlier. They financed annual trips to Israel for him, where he slept in every morning, consorted with various mistresses, and lounged away each afternoon in cafés. He subsisted mainly on the financial goodwill of the "Schindler Jews," who gratefully gifted him with cash, making no judgments on how he spent it. Usually, he spent it on booze and women. Then he would come back asking for more money. In 1968 MGM paid him the then-impressive sum of fifty thousand dollars for the option on his story. He blew that dough in a hurry, too.

Schindler in life was the sort of character Hollywood directors don't know how to handle, particularly directors as quintessentially "Hollywood" as Spielberg: the character who stays the same. He never "grows," never "learns a lesson." His "motivation?" That's pretty murky, even to himself. Later in life, whenever he was asked why he did what he did, Schindler gave generic, pat answers.

"There was no choice."

Or, "When you know people you have to behave toward them like human beings."

In the movie, Spielberg re-creates a true incident in which a grateful survivor, in the hours after Schindler announces that the war is over and his workers are free, allows his fellow workers to yank out his teeth with pliers, for the gold fillings. They melt the gold to manufacture a one-of-a-kind ring, inscribed with the Talmudic motto, "He who saves one life saved the entire world." It was the best they could do as a token of appreciation.

It's a very moving scene in Spielberg's film. What the movie doesn't show is that years later, one of the Schindler Jews noticed that Schindler wasn't wearing the ring. Didn't the ring have enormous sentimental value? The man asked Schindler what became of it. Schindler told him he'd sold the gold ring—and used the money to buy schnapps.

Sources and Further Reading

Robinson, Plater. *Schindler's List Teaching Guide*. New Orleans, LA: Southern Institute for Education and Research, 1995.

Roberts, Jeremy. *Oskar Schindler: Righteous Gentile*. New York: The Rosen Publishing Group, 2000.

Schindler, Emilie. *Where Light and Shadow Meet*. New York: W. W. Norton and Co., 1996.

"Schindler: The Man Behind the List." *A&E Biography*. VHS 1998.

JFK (1991)

Directed by Oliver Stone
Written by Oliver Stone and Zachary Sklar
Starring Kevin Costner, Tommy Lee Jones, and Gary Oldman

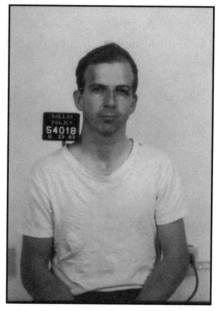

Gary Oldman as Lee Harvey Oswald.
© *Warner Bros. Inc.*

The real Lee Harvey Oswald.

JFK, it could be said, is the movie that gave birth to this book. There have been a lot of films based on actual events, and more often than not, journalists and academics greet these releases with knives sharpened and fangs bared. Justifiably, in many cases. Nothing unusual about that—but there's never been a movie as viciously and unrelentingly flayed as Oliver Stone's *JFK*. That sorry episode is what got the debate about history and Hollywood rolling for real.

Regardless of how you felt about Oliver Stone or the Kennedy assassination itself, the torrent of media bile directed at this movie had to be a little unsettling. And puzzling. There had been films about the assassination of President John F. Kennedy before. In 1973 the Dalton Trumbo–written *Executive Action* had a cabal of right-wing industrialists and oilmen, alarmed by Kennedy's dangerously progressive policies, contracting a hit ("executive action") on the president, carried out by mercenaries who station three different riflemen in Dealey Plaza and set up Lee Harvey Oswald as an innocent patsy.

The *Executive Action* conspiracy is not far removed from the plotline of Stone's three-hour epic, released eighteen years later. Yet *Executive Action*, despite its release only a decade after the actual event, when the memory was still raw, generated no controversy worth mentioning.

The blitzkrieg on *JFK* commenced long before the Warner Brothers–backed movie was ever threaded through a projector. Before, for that matter, the movie had finished filming. The media got hold of an early draft of Stone's script and began exenterating it while Stone was still reenacting the Kennedy assassination in Dallas, with Dealey Plaza dressed up as a movie set. The rancor toward the movie—indeed, as former Kennedy aide Frank Mankiewicz pointed out, the very *idea* that such a movie could exist—was savage and merciless.

The *New York Times* in particular dedicated almost thirty articles (including letters and op-ed pieces) to shredding the film. The *Washington Post* published an article by its longtime intelligence correspondent, George Lardner Jr., that skewered Stone's movie for its many "errors and absurdities, large and small" a full *seven months* (almost to the day) before the film's release. Around the same premature period, a writer for Tribune–owned *Dallas Morning News* (hometown paper of the place of the Kennedy assassination) decried Stone's then-unmade film as "morally repugnant." In fact, the same article also branded as "morally repugnant" the Time-Warner corporation and, indeed, "anyone who pays American money to see the film." (Presumably, foreigners who spent their own currency to see it were fine.) The week of *JFK*'s release, *Newsweek* (owned by the *Washington Post*) put the controversy on its cover, announcing, unambiguously, that "Oliver Stone's New Movie Can't Be Trusted."

The *Times'* longtime Hollywood reporter, Bernard Weinraub, filed a "story" (more of an opinion piece, actually) denouncing Warner Brothers for releasing the film at all, espousing the viewpoint that movie studios have a "responsibility" to suppress politically controversial subject matter. The paper's distinguished liberal columnist, Tom Wicker, produced a particularly vehement hit piece as well.

Says Mankiewicz, "The *New York Times* and its allies in the major commercial media set out—and nearly succeeded—not just to discredit Oliver Stone and his film, but to destroy it."

The media assault was bizarre and unprecedented—except perhaps (as Stone himself pointed out) by the Hearst newspapers' attack on *Citizen Kane* fifty years earlier. In that case, the media's motive was plain. *Kane* was an unflattering character study of Hearst himself. With *JFK*, the question is the same as the question asked by Stone's hypothetical "Mr. X" character about the assassination itself.

Why?

What was it about this movie that posed a clear and present danger (in the minds of the major media, at least)?

The assailants' motives are many and varied. As Mankiewicz notes, the most adamant attackers, including Wicker and Lardner, were "directly involved in reporting the events of November 22, 1963," but in the ensuing three decades "hardly gave the event a backward glance." The movie indicts not only the overly credulous reporting of those journalists at the time, but the course of their entire careers, and, more than that, their whole view of American politics—a view that holds that the assassination, while certainly a personal tragedy and a "loss of innocence" for the American public, was insignificant in political terms. Absurd as it seems, in their view the murder of the president was a pop culture event, not a political one.

There's also the jealousy factor. A Hollywood movie reaches far more people than a piece in the *New York Times* could ever hope to.

Another brand of jealousy: some of the film's opponents had written conspiracy books of their own. Journalist Anthony Summers and early Warren Report critic Harold Weisberg were among that group. It was Weisberg who obtained the purloined first-draft script that served as the basis for the way-early articles that tore into Stone's project.

Whatever the psychology or hidden agendas of the pilers-on, on a superficial level they all attacked *JFK* for the same alleged crime: Stone "twisted history." This is the only legitimate criticism of the film (other than aesthetic criticisms, of course). The motion picture in question, sayeth the sages, distorts historical facts to make a political point.

Does it? It would take a book of its own to address the facts in the film. There's no way to confirm this, but *JFK* must be the most fact-heavy film in Hollywood history. The screenplay is a triumph of expository dialogue. There's hardly any dialogue in there that doesn't explicate one point of fact or another. Heck. We'd write that book, if it hadn't already been written. One year after *JFK* came out, Stone and his collaborator, Zachary Sklar, published *JFK: The Documented Screenplay*. They included 340 notes, citing the source of every major or controversial assertion of fact in the script. In the months before and after his movie came out, Stone spent plenty of time rebutting his critics, but the book was the ultimate comeback. Every time he's accused of inventing, warping, or spinning facts to suit his own ends, he can always point to research in the book. The sources can then be judged on their own merits.

The real problem is that people still bicker over the sources. For every fact cited as gospel by a conspiracy "buff," there's a Lone Assassin Loyalist who'll bust a blood vessel screaming that it's not true. And it works the other way, too. Which does not mean that the entire history of the assassination is a Rorschach blot. It means only that establishing veracity in this case has already been the subject of hundreds of books on both sides of the issue, with hundreds more to come, undoubtedly. When someone says that Stone warped the historical record, that person is really saying that his facts that don't fit his or her own particular theory.

The most glaring example is Stone's choice of a hero. He needed some central character to tie together the multifarious threads of assassination conspiracy research into something resembling a narrative—and he sure wasn't going to use Earl Warren. That left only one choice: the only law enforcement official to ever prosecute a trial in the assassination case, New Orleans District Attorney Jim Garrison.

From 1966 until 1969, Garrison chased a New Orleans connection to the Kennedy assassination. Garrison's investigation culminated in the arrest and trial of a prominent New Orleans businessman, Clay Shaw, whom Garrison believed was somehow involved in planning the assassination.

Of all the JFK assassination "conspiracy theorists," the only one who's received worse public pillorying than Stone is Earling Carothers "Jim" Garrison. He's been vilified as a charlatan, a political opportunist, a mafia stooge, and a lunatic. The Most Trusted Man in America himself, Walter Cronkite, denounced Garrison as "evil" for his persecution of the "innocent man," Shaw.

By the time Stone's movie reached screens, Garrison was terminally ill. In one of his final interviews, for a documentary entitled *Beyond JFK*, he is shown flat on his back in a hospital bed. He died in 1992. But his frailty and impending death did not temper the renewed verbal assault directed at him then by, well, many of the same commentators who assaulted him the first time around.

They found it especially galling that Stone cast Kevin Costner in the role of Garrison. Costner was still polishing his Oscars he'd won for *Dances with Wolves* just a year earlier. In 1991 he was the biggest movie star in the business. Not only did Costner bear no physical or temperamental resemblance to the jocular-yet-bellicose, six-foot-six Garrison, worst of all as far as the anti-*JFK*ers were concerned, Costner came with an onscreen persona best described as "heroic everyman." Kind of an updated Jimmy Stewart. The Costner likeability was at direct odds with their picture of Garrison as a reckless, ruthless, grandiloquent self-aggrandizer.

Stone's perception of Garrison couldn't have been more different. To him, Garrison was a Capraesque figure, which was exactly the reason he cast Costner.

"I've never found Garrison to be the 'kook' pictured by a hostile press," Stone wrote in *Premiere* magazine. Instead, says Stone, Garrison is a literate, eloquent, and patriotic military veteran, former FBI agent, and appellate judge. As to Garrison's much-publicized personality flaws ("arrogance and paranoia among them," wrote Stone), the director chose to omit them from his portrayal because, "Either you had to make Garrison the issue or make Kennedy the issue. I chose Kennedy."

As was made quite clear from the voluminous op-ed critiques of his film (though not from reviewers, who generally admired *JFK*), the film's detractors would have preferred that he had chosen Garrison.

Stone acknowledged (in the same *Premiere* article) that he used Garrison as a vessel, through which he channeled four decades of assassination research. Other researchers, before Garrison and after, formulated many of the ideas that issue from Costner/Garrison's lips.

"It is typically Capraesque that private citizens have done the work while government bodies stagnated," remarked Stone. Stone also invented the aforementioned "Mr. X," supposedly an ex-military "black ops" man who meets secretly with Garrison in Washington and spells out the reasons why Kennedy was killed—on a purely anonymous basis. No such person existed, much less acted as a "Deep Throat" for Garrison. The character is based largely on Colonel L. Fletcher Prouty, who was indeed an ex-military man once involved in covert operations. Many of the assertions in Mr. X's lengthy soliloquy are Prouty's. Far from anonymous, Prouty has expressed his views in two published books and countless on-the-record interviews.

Nonetheless, in its broad outline anyway, *JFK* followed the course of Garrison's investigation. It begins in 1963, shortly after the assassination, when Garrison learns that Oswald (played by Gary Oldman) lived in New Orleans through the spring and summer of that year. Garrison arrests David Ferrie, a strange-looking man (and a possible acquaintance of Oswald's) who, for reasons unknown, had driven to Texas through a torrential rainstorm the night of the assassination. But the FBI sets Ferrie free without charges.

Garrison picks up the investigation again in 1966, after a conversation with Louisiana Senator Russell Long. Long surprises Garrison with his cynical view of the Warren Commission Report: "That dog don't hunt!" Garrison zeroes in on Ferrie once again, only to have Ferrie die suddenly as soon as his name surfaces in the press as a suspect. (Oddly enough—and this Stone does not include—the last known person to see Ferrie alive was journalist George Lardner Jr., the same Lardner who wrote the aforementioned *Washington Post* attack piece in 1991.) At that point, Garrison decides to arrest Clay Shaw. After a month-long trial in which Garrison and his assistants went to great lengths to show that there was a conspiracy, Shaw is acquitted. (Jurors later said that Garrison had persuaded them that Kennedy was killed in a conspiracy, but not that Clay Shaw was part of that conspiracy.)

That is the basic outline of *JFK*'s plot, and of the real-life Garrison investigation. In his movie, Stone took many of the boilerplate dramatic liberties common to historical films. He used composite characters. The convict Willie O'Keefe (Kevin Bacon) is an amalgam of Garrison's star witness, Perry Russo, and several other lesser figures. Stone also melodramatizes the mundane roles of real characters. For example, Garrison's assistant DA, Lou Ivon, did not quit his job, as does his character in the film. Stone even invents a female member of Garrison's investigative team, presumably to make the cast more palatable to a '90s audience. In reality, Garrison had no distaff staffers.

Naturally, Stone and his fellow screenwriter invented most of the dialogue. But not all of it. Warren Commission testimony is quoted verbatim, as is testimony from Garrison's trial of Clay Shaw. One speech that was only partially invented was Garrison's lengthy closing argument, in which he exhorts jurors to "ask not what your country can do for you, ask what you can do for your country," and calls for the opening of sealed assassination files that were mandated closed until 2039.

Curiously, some of the film's attackers scoffed that Garrison never made a closing argument, leaving the chore to his assistants instead. On the contrary, he manifestly did make the statement, and his wording was very similar to the speech delivered by Costner in the film—including the Kennedy quote and the call to open secret files.

The merits of taking such dramatic license are debatable, but there are films discussed in other chapters of this book that take far greater liberties than Stone took with *JFK*. So why is this the most vilified historical film of all time? There are probably as many reasons as there are vilifiers, but they all can be boiled down to one thing: they hated what Stone had to say. This wasn't a matter of prettying up some celebrity's messy life for a biopic, or adding a few car crashes to ratchet up the action quotient. To its critics, *JFK* was a film that offended their deeply held view of the world. Stone questioned their religion.

Most Hollywood movies aim for quite the opposite—to comfort and reassure their audience. *JFK* doesn't ask its viewers to leave feeling good. It asks them to think. To question. Apparently, judging by the assault on the film, that is the last thing some in the media want you to do.

Sources and Further Reading

Garrison, Jim. *On the Trail of the Assassins*. New York: Sheridan Square Press, 1988.

James, Rosemary and Jack Wardlaw. *Plot or Politics?* New Orleans, LA: Pelican Publishing House, 1967.

Stone, Oliver and Zachary Sklar. *JFK: The Documented Screenplay*. New York: Applause Books, 1992.

INDEX

Numbers in italics denote illustrations.